Egyptology: The Missing Millennium

UCL PRESS

Egyptology: The Missing Millennium

Ancient Egypt in Medieval Arabic Writings

Okasha El Daly

UCL
PRESS

First published in Great Britain 2005 by UCL Press
An imprint of Cavendish Publishing Limited, The Glass House,
Wharton Street, London WC1X 9PX, United Kingdom
Telephone: + 44 (0)20 7278 8000 Facsimile: + 44 (0)20 7278 8080
Email: info@cavendishpublishing.com
Website: www.cavendishpublishing.com

Published in the United States by Cavendish Publishing
c/o International Specialized Book Services,
5824 NE Hassalo Street, Portland,
Oregon 97213-3644, USA

Published in Australia by Cavendish Publishing (Australia) Pty Ltd
45 Beach Street, Coogee, NSW 2034, Australia
Telephone: + 61 (2)9664 0909 Facsimile: +61 (2)9664 5420
Email: info@cavendishpublishing.com.au
Website: www.cavendishpublishing.com.au

British Library Cataloguing in Publication Data
Daly, Okasha El
Egyptology: The Missing Millennium.
Ancient Egypt in Medieval Arabic Writings
1 Egyptology – Islamic Empire 2 Egypt – History – to 640 AD –
Historiography – Sources
3 Islamic Empire – Intellectual life
I Title
932'.0072'0174927

Library of Congress Cataloguing in Publication Data
Data available

ISBN 1-84472-063-2 (Hardback)
ISBN 1-84472-062-4 (Paperback)

3 5 7 9 10 8 6 4 2

Printed and bound in Great Britain

بسم الله الرحمن الرحيم

وجعل الله حاجتنا الى معرفة أخبار من كان قبلنا، كحاجة من كان قبلنا الى أخبار من كان قبلهم، وحاجة من يكون بعدنا الى أخبارنا.

God made inherent in us the need for knowledge of the history of our predecessors, just as was the need of our predecessors for history of their predecessors, and just as will be the need of those who shall come after us for our history.

Al-Jaḥiẓ (d 771 CE) *Al-Ḥaywan* 1: 42

Preface

> In the late eighteenth century almost nothing was known about the ancient civilization of Egypt and the Near East except what had been recorded in the Bible and by the ancient Greeks and Romans. (Trigger 1989: 39)

This is but one of many quotations that express a particular attitude to the discovery of Ancient Egypt. It is such attitudes that caused me to embark on a study of medieval Arabic texts which describe and discuss the culture and civilisation of Ancient Egypt. This book sheds some light on a neglected period of a thousand years in the history of Egyptology, from the Moslem annexation of Egypt in the 7th century CE until the Ottoman conquest in the 16th century. Part of the impetus came from my own training in Egyptology, during which almost no mention was ever made of any medieval Arab contribution. But my upbringing as an Egyptian had made me aware of some of the sources that could fill the gap between the classical sources and those of the late European Renaissance.

My objectives in this book are threefold: first, to demonstrate that medieval Arabs were interested in, had knowledge of and attempted to interpret the culture of Ancient Egypt. Secondly, to show the relevance of these materials to the study of Ancient Egypt by bridging the gap between the works of the classical writers and those of later Europeans. Thirdly, to encourage further study of the medieval Arabic material available, some of which could help archaeologists with descriptions and with the excavation and interpretation of sites, and perhaps even to reconstruct monuments which have long since disappeared.

My method of study has been to collect as many Arabic sources as possible, mainly from the 7th to 16th centuries. Some of these sources have already been published, but many are manuscripts from various Arabic collections around the world. I have searched library catalogues to identify manuscripts that seemed most relevant, and obtained copies of many of these. It is a serious obstacle to research that Arabic manuscripts are scattered around the world, many of them difficult to access, time-consuming to find, and expensive to copy. Worse still is what Khalidi (1994: xi) calls 'the daunting obstacle of the size of the historiographic corpus . . . which amounts to several hundred thousand volumes' for the period under study.

In these Arabic sources I have searched for references to Ancient Egypt to establish the interest of the writer in issues relating to Ancient Egypt, and the level of understanding of these issues. This corpus on Ancient Egypt was then analysed for evidence of a reliable understanding of ancient Egyptian themes and materials in the light of our current knowledge in Egyptology. From these I have identified and sometimes attempted to reconstruct medieval Arabic concepts of pre-Islamic Egypt.

A different problem facing research in this area lies in the Arabic sources themselves. Of those which have been published, few have been translated, edited or commented on in any meaningful way. Medieval Arabic manuscripts on natural sciences, for example medicine, chemistry and mechanics, have been better acknowledged by scholars, but the medieval treatment of the chronicles and antiquities of ancient nations have, on the whole, been deemed fantastic and exotic stories devoid of historical value (Saleh 1980: 39–46; James 1997: 30).

In selecting source material and deciding on its relevance to my objectives I have been guided by my training in Egyptology. I am conscious that my views as a native on what is relevant may often differ from those of an outsider. This problem has been expressed much more ably and fully both by Abdul Latif Tibawi (1979) and by Edward Said (1995) in their analyses of *Orientalism*. I have generally selected writers who are recognised scholars in their fields, and who show a profound interest in Ancient Egypt. I have also used some reliable narratives of epics and stories which reveal perceptions of Egypt's past.

Medieval Arabic can be difficult to translate because of the variety of meanings derived from the same root, and I have come across many serious errors in previous English translations, which have been widely used without awareness of their pitfalls. The task of translating such Arabic texts into English, for someone whose mother tongue is not English, is even more daunting; this was commented upon long ago by no less an authority than Edward Sachau, the translator of Al-Biruni, who called this task 'an act of temerity' (Sachau 1888 1: xlviii). With all this in mind, I have relied on my own translations of the Arabic sources unless otherwise stated. The sources used were all written in Arabic, with a few exceptions of material written in Persian and translated into Arabic (eg Naṣir-e Khisraw *Sefernama*).

I concentrate on Moslem writers, again with a few exceptions, regardless of their ethnic background, as it is usually Islam that incurs blame for cutting Egyptians off from their ancient heritage and pharaonic past. With the spread of Islam, Arabic became for some centuries the *lingua franca* of science and knowledge, used by Moslems and non-Moslems and Arabs and non-Arabs alike. These sources may be classified as:

- accounts of travellers and geographers;
- historical and hagiographic writings;
- books on deciphering ancient scripts;
- accounts and manuals of treasure hunters;
- books on alchemy.

Chapter 1 is an introduction discussing the circumstances that led to the neglect of these Arabic sources in Egyptology and the importance of studying this missing link. Chapter 2 presents some of the sources available to medieval Arabs for their knowledge of Ancient Egypt, and explains the various elements that contributed to the making of an *interpretatio Arabica* of Ancient Egypt. Chapter 3 is devoted to treasure hunters. Egyptian monuments have always been perceived as places of concealment of great treasures. The chapter describes treasure hunters, their manuals, state regulation, and the economics of the profession. Examples are given of these manuals and their relevance to current archaeological work. Chapter 4 demonstrates how medieval Arab archaeological methods, and descriptions of ancient sites and objects, are in many ways as clear and scientific as those of present day archaeologists. Chapter 5 shows that the interest in ancient Egyptian scripts continued beyond classical writers, and describes attempts by some medieval Arab scholars, mainly alchemists, to decipher the hieroglyphic script, having realised that it has an alphabet. I give examples of Egyptian signs correctly deciphered. Chapter 6 shows the great interest of ancient Egyptian religion for medieval Arabs and illustrates their understanding of its multi-faceted nature and their interpretation of the many intact temples. It discusses the role of magic, the nature of royal cults, animal cults and holy sites as seen through their eyes. Chapter 7 is devoted to discussing Egyptian *mummia*, mummification and burial practices of both humans and animals as well as the medicinal use of *mummia* in Arabic medicine. Chapter 8 relates how Egypt was thought of by medieval Arabs as the land of science *par excellence* and gives examples of different scientific *mirabilia* attributed to scientists of pre-Islamic Egypt. Chapter 9 discusses the Arab concept of Egyptian kingship and state administration, and shows the survival of some ancient Egyptian institutions such as *H̱rdw n k3p* – 'Children of the Room' – into the medieval period. I include a case study of Queen Cleopatra to show how the Arabic romance of this queen differs significantly from its Western counterparts. In my conclusions I make recommendations for further work that I hope others may be inspired to pursue.

As many of the medieval Arabic writers may not be known to readers, I include an appendix of biographies of those whose works have formed the basis of my study.

This book straddles two seemingly different disciplines – Egyptology and medieval Arabic studies. However, it is addressed mainly to an audience with *Egyptological* interests and, though most of the sources used here belong to the field of medieval Arabic studies, I do not follow all the conventions of scholars working in that discipline. I have adapted as much as I could of the conventions of Arabic studies in order to create links between these two artificially separated disciplines, which have for too long been surrounded with insurmountable barriers meant to keep outsiders away. These barriers need no longer remain an obstacle now that researchers can draw on the resources for the benefit of both Egyptology and Arabic studies.

Okasha El Daly
January 2005

Acknowledgments

My grateful thanks to Fekri Hassan, David Jeffreys, Peter Ucko, John Tait and Stephen Quirke, who have constantly and generously offered help and advice. I owe special thanks to my friend Terence DuQuesne for his insightful remarks and constant help and for making his extensive library freely available. I also thank Margaret Drower, TGH James, Robert Morkot, George Hart, Paul Frandsen, Alessandra Nibbi and Ruth Massey for their help and advice. I owe an immense debt to Kenneth Kitchen and Charles Burnett for their generous remarks and encouragement.

I thank my former teachers at Cairo University – Fayza Haikal, Gaballa A Gaballa and Abdel Halim Nureldin – for their encouragement. Thanks are also due to my friends Mohammad Abdel Raziq and Louay Saied, who inspired me during our many discussions of the relevance of Arabic sources to Egyptology. I found their enthusiasm most encouraging.

I am grateful to Stephen Shennan, Kevin MacDonald, Ruth Whitehouse, Anna Lethbridge, Sally MacDonald, Mervat Nasser, Luigi Caparrotta, Mary Horbury, Jane Jakeman, Lucia Gahlin and Magdy El-Alfy for their help and encouragement. I thank Zeynep Inankur, Kathy Judelson, Nadia and Kamal Bayoumi, Mahmoud Khodier, Ehab Farag and Marius Kociejowski for help in obtaining copies of some manuscripts and books. I also thank Geoffrey Tassie, Ivor Pridden, Roy McKeown and Hugh Kilmister for assistance with the figures. My thanks also go to Robert Kirby and his always helpful staff at the library of the Institute of Archaeology, UCL. I thank Doris Nicholson at the Bodleian Library for her generosity. My grateful thanks too to the staff of the libraries at Al-Furqan Islamic Heritage Foundation, the British Library, the Wellcome Trust, SOAS, the Chester Beatty Library, Dublin, Ataturk Library, Istanbul, and the Bibliothèque Nationale, Paris. My family in Egypt has been most supportive and I thank them wholeheartedly for waiting patiently all these years, particularly my uncle Mohammad Ibrahim Ewais, to whom I owe most special thanks. Words cannot express the debt I owe to my wife Diana, who has been my mainstay throughout this research. Suffice it to say that if it were not for her support, this book would not be in your hands now.

The inspiration behind this research was ignited by a brief meeting with the eminent scholar and historian of Islamic sciences, Fuat Sezgin, at his office in Frankfurt in the summer of 1979. He and his wife Ursula Sezgin are behind the current Renaissance in the field of studies of Islamic Sciences: to them I humbly dedicate this contribution.

My inspiration was sustained by Edward Said's unwavering struggle against the onslaught of cultural imperialism and distorted interpretation of the *other*. From its inception I felt his spirit hovering above my research. May his luminous soul be pleased with this work.

Contents

List of Figures

Figure 1 ***(colour)*** A watercolour by Petrie of a medieval Moslem tomb at Bab Al-Wazir, Mamluk cemetery, Cairo. © Petrie Museum of Egyptian Archaeology, University College London. W 13.8 cm, H 22.7 cm.

Figure 2 Map of Egypt in Ibn Ḥawqal (*Ṣurat*: facing page 128).

Figure 3 A drawing of the Lahun pyramid area to the left of the text. MS Arabe 2764 fol 71a. Courtesy Bibliothèque Nationale, Paris.

Figure 4 A New Kingdom stela showing the Sphinx with the small royal figure below his head. After Hassan 1951: fig 39.

Figure 5 ***(colour)*** A medieval astrologer offering incense at the Temple of Akhmim (*Kitab Al-Bulhan* MS Bodleian Or 133 fol 29a). After Carboni 1988: pl 18 and pp 71f.

Figure 6 The Lighthouse of Alexandria in Al-Gharnaṭi, early 12th century. After Ferrand 1925: pl II.

Figure 7 From the Scala Magna of Ibn Kabr. A list of vegetables in Coptic-Arabic (MS Or 1325 fol 117a British Library). After Budge 1928: 81.

Figure 8 ***(colour)*** An example of Arabic texts on Fatimid textiles emulating Egyptian hieroglyphs. Two Arabic words that are repeated (*Al-Yomn wa Al-Iqbal*) mean 'Prosperity and Good Fortune'. Cairo, Museum of Islamic Art No 596. Courtesy of the Museum of Islamic Art, Cairo. My thanks to Mohamed Abbas Selim (cf Stillman 1997: 49 fig 15).

Figure 9 A statue of Darius I (522–486 BC) from Susa. After *Cahiers de la délégation archéologique Française en Iran* 4: 204 fig 20 (cf Myśliwiec 2000: 147 fig 41).

Figure 10 Egyptian inscriptions on the base of the statue of Darius I. After *Cahiers de la délégation archéologique Française en Iran* 4: 205 fig 21 (cf Roaf 1974; Myśliwiec 2000: 150–51 figs 44–45).

Figure 11 Detail of the same statue of Darius I showing the titles and names of Darius I in Egyptian hieroglyphs. After *Cahiers de la délégation archéologique Française en Iran* 4: 208 fig 24 (cf Myśliwiec 2000: 149 fig 43).

Figure 12 ***(colour)*** Egyptian hieroglyphs/symbols inspired tool designs in medieval Arabic alchemy. Abu Al-Qasim Al-^{c}Iraqi (*Kitab Al-Aqalim Al-Sab^{c}ah* MS Add 25724 fol 11a British Library).

Figure 13 An automated waiter designed by Al-Jazari (12th/13th century). Some Egyptian symbols were used by the designer. *The Book of Knowledge of Ingenious Mechanical Devices*: fol 224; cf MS 3472 Topqapu Serai Library, Istanbul, fol 216.

Figure 14 Use of hieroglyphs for *Nb, M3^{c}t, R^{c}* (and perhaps *T3wy*) in Islamic Art for Mamluk emblems. These denote Lord of Justice, The Sun, of the Two Lands. After Mayer 1933: 30. By permission of Oxford University Press.

Figure 15 The Coptic alphabet with its phonetic values and order correctly identified. Dhu Al-Nun Al-Miṣri (*?all*, MS Muallim Cevdet K 290 fol 12a, top and 12b below).

Figure 16 Egyptian alphabet according to Ibn Waḥshiyah (*Shauq*, MS Arabe 6805 fol 92b on the right and 93a on the left). Courtesy Bibliothèque Nationale, Paris.

Figure 17 Ibn Waḥshiyah *Shauq*: fol 93b to the right and 94a to the left.

Figure 18 Ibn Waḥshiyah *Shauq*: fol 94b to the right.

Figure 19 Ibn Waḥshiyah *Shauq*: fol 56a to the left.

Figure 20 Ibn Waḥshiyah *Shauq*: fol 56b to the right.

Figure 21 ***(colour)*** Hieroglyphic signs with their phonetic values below in a different colour in Abu Al-Qasim Al-^{c}Iraqi (*Al-Aqalim* MS Add 25724 British Library), fol 21b.

Figure 22 ***(colour)*** Abu Al-Qasim Al-^{c}Iraqi *Al-Aqalim*: fol 22a.

Figure 23 Egyptian alphabet deciphered in Abu Al-Qasim Al-^{c}Iraqi MS Arabe 2676 fol 18a. Courtesy Bibliothèque Nationale, Paris.

Figure 24 ***(colour)*** A stela of King Amenemhat II (ca 1928–1895 BCE) of the Twelfth Dynasty, as copied in Abu Al-Qasim Al-^{c}Iraqi (*Al-Aqalim* MS Add 25724 British Library), fol 50a.

Figure 25 A script named after the Ṣufi/alchemist Jabir Ibn Ḥayan in Dhu Al-Nun (*Ḥall* fol 36b top). Many letters resemble Egyptian Demotic.

Figure 26 The Egyptian god Horus copied in a medieval Arabic book of magic, *Kitab Al-Mala?is* (MS Bodleian Arabe d 221 fol 49a to the left and 51a to the right). Courtesy Bodleian Library (cf Beeston 1962: pl II).

Figure 27 The primordial god Nu emerges from chaos, lifting up the Sun's Barge. From the Book of Gates on the alabaster sarcophagus of King Seti I presently at Sir John Soane Museum, London. After Budge 1908: 25 (cf Hornung 1992: 108).

Figure 28 The Ouroboros serpent protects the sun god. Papyrus of ?r Wbn, Egyptian Museum, Cairo (Piankoff and Rambova 1957: 2, pl 1; cf Hornung 1990a: 107).

Figure 29 ***(colour)*** The Egyptian Ouroboros copied with hieroglyphs in the alchemical book of Abu Al-Qasim Al-^{c}Iraqi (*Kitab Al-Aqalim Al-Sab^{c}ah* MS Add 25724 fol 4a British Library).

Figure 30 *Mummia* listed as medicine written in Egyptian script according to Ibn Waḥshiyah (*Shauq* MS Arabe 6805 fol 77a to the left). The word for *mummia* is written on third line from the top, with a human head.

Figure 31 The 'Obelisk of Pharaoh' from Heliopolis, as copied and used in a book on alchemy by Abu Al-Qasim Al-^{c}Iraqi (*Kitab Al-Aqalim Al-Sab^{c}ah* MS Add 25724 fol 15a British Library).

Figure 32 An Egyptian obelisk in Abu Al-Qasim Al-^{c}Iraqi (*Kitab Al-Aqalim Al-Sab^{c}ah* MS Add 25724 fol 2a British Library). Here the body of the obelisk is standing on a step base, displaying alchemical elements.

Figure 33 Names of the archangels Michael and Gabriel correctly written in Coptic in Abu Al-Qasim Al-^{c}Iraqi (*Kitab Al-Aqalim Al-Sab^{c}ah* MS Add 25724 fol 21b British Library).

Abbreviations and Notes

d	died
db	died before
da	died after
d ca	died circa
EI^2	*Encyclopaedia of Islam*, 2nd edn, 1960, Leiden: Brill
PM	B Porter and R Moss, *Topographical Bibliography of Ancient Egyptian Hieroglyphic Texts, Reliefs, and Paintings*, 1st edn 1927–51, 7 vols, Oxford; 2nd edn 1960, ed J Malek, Oxford: Griffith Institute
WB	A Erman and H Grapow, *Wörterbuch der ägyptischen Sprache*, 1926–63, 7 vols, Berlin: Akademie (reprint 1971)

Notes

1 Primary Arabic sources are referred to as follows: the surname of the author is followed by the first word of the title of the book inside brackets, eg Al-Baghdadi (*Al-Ifadah*: 26). Titles of many Arabic books start with the word *Kitab*, meaning 'Book', so this is disregarded. In cases where a book is widely known under a word other than the first word in its title, I use the generally accepted title: for example, Al-Maqrizi's book *Al-Mawa^c^iẓ wa Al-I^c^tibar* is cited here as *Khiṭaṭ* as it is most commonly known.

2 In citing manuscripts, the folio number is followed by the letter *a* for recto and *b* for verso.

3 All dates for Arabic materials are given as CE (Common Era). Occasionally I have included the Moslem Hegira dates, in which case they are followed by AH.

Conventions of Transliteration

ء	″
أ	a
ا	a
ب	b
ت	t
ث	th
ج	j, g
ح	ḥ
خ	kh
د	d
ذ	dh
ر	r
ز	z
س	s
ش	sh
ص	ṣ
ض	ḍ
ط	ṭ
ظ	ẓ
ع	^{c}
غ	gh
ف	f
ق	q
ك	k
ل	l
م	m
ن	n
ه	h
و	o,u,w
ى	i, e, ee, iy
ة	ah, t

NB: For Ancient Egyptian letter *alef* = *3* is used.

CHAPTER 1

INTRODUCTION

THE MISSING LINK IN EGYPTOLOGY

The discipline we call Egyptology, the study of Egyptian archaeology, is held to be a product of modern Western scholarship. It is also claimed that it was only when Jean-François Champollion and his European successors succeeded in deciphering Egyptian hieroglyphs and reading texts that Egyptology was born. Those concerned with the sources for the study of Ancient Egypt usually list them in this order:

1 ancient Egyptian sources, basically the remains of the material culture;

2 contemporary Near Eastern sources and later classical sources;

3 Renaissance sources from the 15th century onwards;

4 modern Egyptology, excavation and studies.

Standard studies of sources normally include accounts of European travellers to Egypt, but nowhere do we find any kind of reference to the medieval Egyptian/Arab scholarly contribution to these studies (see for example Baines and Malek 1980: 22–29). Even when one single reference is made in all these studies to one medieval Arabic traveller to Egypt, Al-Baghdadi, it comes after the author has already reached the conclusion that there was 'little interest in Egypt's ancient past' (David 2000: 51–61). So we have a gap in our sources of more than a thousand years, between those of the Classical period and those of the European Enlightenment. This book attempts to narrow that gap and show the value of the contributions during this millennium, in particular those of medieval Egyptian writers.

The book is also an inquiry into the image and interpretation of the culture of Ancient Egypt in medieval Arab sources, from the Moslem annexation of Egypt in the 7th century CE until the Ottoman conquest in the 16th century.

THE CURRENT VIEW

Until the late 18th century, little was known in the West about Ancient Egypt, as is illustrated by quotations such as the following:

> The long period of ignorance, during which scholars floundered in a morass of esoteric theories, came to an end with the discovery of the Rosetta Stone. (James 1997: 30)

It has also been asserted that continuity from Ancient Egypt to the present was totally absent:

> Si la confrontation entre l'Egypte traditionnelle et les cultures grecque et romaine qui s'y sont développées est à la fois un tournant dans l'histoire de l'Egypte et l'occasion d'un renouveau culturel authentique, l'ère chrétienne et, plus tard, l'ère islamique éloignent irrémédiablement l'Egypte de son passé pharaonique. (Valbelle 1994: 38)

In spite of this assertion of discontinuity, Dominique Valbelle follows this alleged fact immediately by recognising that many ancient Egyptian popular practices are still alive today, apparently without seeing any contradiction.

The same can be said of a similar assertion made by Ulrich Haarmann:

> Any continuity from ancient to Islamic Egypt was irretrievably and doubly cut off, first by the adoption of Christianity in Egypt in the 4th century and then, three centuries later, by the Islamic conquest. Memories of the world of the pharaohs had long since been forgotten by Egyptians who had been incorporated into the Greek, the Roman, the Byzantine, and, by the 7th century CE, the expanding Islamic world. (Haarmann 2001: 191)

These recent views echo an earlier one by no less an authority than Idris Bell:

> With good reason did Mommsen call Islam 'der Henker des Hellenismus' 'the executioner of Hellenism'. In this new world of dogmatism and religious bigotry, Christian or Mahommedan, there was no room left for the clear-eyed sanity of Hellas. Egypt had become once more a part of that Oriental world from which the fiery genius of Alexander had separated her for a thousand years. (Bell 1922: 155; cf his later version: Bell 1948: 134)

These quotations reflect views that were widely held by scholars involved in Egyptology, namely that there was no knowledge of Ancient Egypt, outside the context of European literature, from the Classical to the Enlightenment periods. The quotation from Haarmann is particularly surprising from a scholar of medieval Islamic/Arabic studies. It illustrates a general Eurocentric view that sees the culture of Ancient Egypt through a Western prism. However, such views are not limited to scholars in the West. Even among modern Egyptian scholars we encounter a similar view: for example, El-Shayyal concluded that before the writings on the history of Ancient Egypt by the 19th century Egyptian scholar Rifa^{c}a Al-Ṭahṭawi:

> Ancient Egyptian history was never given its due appreciation by Muslim historians. First because they knew very little about it, and secondly because that period represented, in their opinion, a period of idolatry which stood in direct contradiction to the monotheism of Islam. (El-Shayyal 1962: 32)

Another eminent Egyptologist, ^{c}Abd Al-^{c}Aziz Saleh (1980: 39–46), made no mention of any medieval Arab contribution in his massive work on the history of Egypt and Iraq. While citing his sources for the study of Ancient Egypt, he referred to classical sources and then passed directly to the French Expedition at the end of the 18th century. In an earlier book, Saleh (1962: 244) dismissed medieval Arab writers in one single phrase, referring to post-classical writers on

Egyptian civilisation as being 'only associated with myths, magic and fantasies of which they had a greater share than their predecessors'.

This was echoed by Crone and Cook (1977: 114) and Cook (1983), who suggested that medieval Egyptians were not as interested in their ancient heritage as were their counterparts in Iran. It is true that medieval Egyptians do not seem to have displayed a chauvinist nationalism, but they seem no less proud of their past, as can be seen from the list of Egyptian historians who wrote almost exclusively on the history of Egypt from as early as the first century of Islam (Enan 1969, 1991; Donner 1998: 225). They wrote national histories without chauvinist nationalism. This attitude was deeply rooted in the Egyptian mind, which has, as Donald Redford (1986: xvii) put it, 'a strong sense of its own past'. This can be seen, for example, in a relief from the east wall of the second court of the Ramesseum, West Thebes, where attendants at the annual festival of the god Min are shown carrying statues of kings Menes, Nebhepetre Mentuhotep, Ahmose, Amenhotep I and Thutmose I (Murnane 1995: 694). This Egyptian consciousness of national longevity was displayed to Herodotus by the priests of the temple of Ptah at Memphis, who read a long king-list to their visitor from a papyrus, which listed pharaohs from the first human king Menes onwards (Herodotus II: 100; Moyer 2002: 70). This list was perhaps similar to the famous King-List of Abydos. This interest in the past continued into medieval Egypt.

While Haarmann (1980) suggested that medieval Egyptians had indeed some interest in Ancient Egypt, he summarised their general attitude towards Egyptian antiquities as destroyers, treasure hunters and curious tourists (Haarmann 1996: 622). This is not the case with all medieval Egyptians, as many displayed great pride in the country and its antiquities. This can be seen, for example, in the writings of Ibn Al-Kindi (*Faḍail*), Al-Idrisi (*Anwar*), and Al-Qalqashandi (*Ṣubḥ* 3: 304ff and especially 310).

In medieval Arab sources for the history of Egypt it was the norm to start with a chapter on the virtues and excellences of Egypt, as indeed was the case with their treatment of other countries (Gottheil 1907: 258). Indeed, books were dedicated entirely to these virtues of Egypt, as reflected in their titles (eg Al-Kindi *Faḍail*; Ibn Zulaq *Faḍail*).

This same attitude of pride in Egypt and its past can even be seen in accounts of the most religiously pious Arab writers. One example is that of the 10th century geographer/traveller, Al-Muqadasi, who starts his account of Egypt with this sentence:

> This is the region of which the pharaoh took pride above all humankind and at the hand of Joseph, maintained the entire world . . . It is one of the [two] wings of the world and its glories are countless. (Al-Muqadasi *Aḥsan*: 193)

This was not a romantic conception of Egypt, since on the same page, and also later, Al-Muqadasi is aware of the country's shortcomings:

> When this region is fortunate, then you need not ask about its richness and low prices; but when it [suffers] drought, then Allah is the [only] refuge from its famine, which lasts seven years, so that they (the people) eat dogs and are afflicted with most terrible epidemics. (Al-Muqadasi *Aḥsan*: 202)

This is a more accurate reflection of the attitude among medieval Arab writers with regard to the past and present glories of Egypt, as well as to its disadvantages.

OBSTACLES THAT FACED THE DEVELOPMENT OF INDIGENOUS EGYPTOLOGY

It is perhaps as a result of the views quoted above that the study of Egyptology, which since Napoleonic times has been led by European and American scholars and institutions, has almost totally ignored the vast number of medieval Arabic sources and other contributions in Arabic written between the 7th and 16th centuries. In 1942 the eminent British Egyptologist HW Fairman wrote that, although Egyptology was an international science, the Egyptian contribution to it was 'Nil' (Reid 1985: 244).

It is quite clear that the study by medieval Egyptians and Arabs of Ancient Egypt, its language, religion, monuments and general history, flourished long before the earliest European Renaissance contact. Contrary to the prevailing view that Moslems/Arabs/Egyptians had no interest in Ancient Egypt, the sources show not only a keen interest, but also serious scholarship that seeks to understand and benefit from the study of Ancient Egypt.

However, this process of study was discontinued and obstacles were placed in the way of the development of a later indigenous school of Egyptology, for reasons which have been discussed by Mokhtar (1965), Reid (1985, 1990, 2002) and Wood (1998). The main reason was the desire of early Western Egyptologists and others to keep Egyptians out of Egyptology by discouraging them from participation and study, thus leading to their marginalisation and to inevitable Western dominance of the subject. Yet Reid (2002) was able to show in his painstakingly researched recent work that many modern Egyptians are proud of their pharaonic as well as their post-pharaonic heritage.

It must be recognised that there was a trend among some Westerners to object to the teaching or promotion of native Egyptians, and this was not limited to Egyptology, as sciences such as medicine suffered a similar fate (Sonbol 2000: 58). Even today, Arab scholars complain bitterly about the lack of indigenous schools dedicated to writing history from a native viewpoint rather than merely reproducing Western texts (Saidan 1988: 184ff). The same complaint is made by young Egyptian scholars, who complain bitterly about the Western dominance of Egyptology (Saied 1999).

The situation was made worse by the colonial educational authorities, who excluded Egyptian history from the curriculum. For example, in 1905, secondary school history courses almost exclusively concerned European history, with textbooks bearing the following titles (Salamah 1966: 288):

- *Outlines of General History* by Renouf.
- *Landmarks of European History* by MacDougal.
- *General Sketch of European History* by Freeman.

Unfortunately, the effect of this focus on European history lasted long after the end of colonialism, as noted by the Egyptian scholar of the history of science ᶜAbd Al-Ḥalim Muntaṣer, who could not recall ever hearing the name of any Arab scholar in any science during his primary, secondary or university education, but only the names of European scholars (Muntaṣer 1973: 80). Sadly, this has also been my own experience whilst studying Egyptology. The eminent Egyptian scientist Rushdi Said complained in his recently published memoirs that his history lessons on the pharaonic period were very few and did not include 'any ties between us and these ancient [Egyptians]' (Said 2003: 16). One of the serious implications for Egyptology courses in Egypt is that our ancient history is taught from a Eurocentric viewpoint. Thus, for example, the Persian kings who conquered Egypt in the 5th century BCE are portrayed as being full of hatred towards the Egyptians and their religion, exactly what their contemporary Greek/*European* enemies wanted to believe (Tuplin 1991: 259f). In fact there is no evidence in our archaeological record of any Persian atrocities (cf Vasunia 2001: 21 n 34). It is true that Egyptians did rebel against Persian rule, but they did this with equal vigour against all foreign rulers and occasionally also against some of their own monarchs.

An additional problem during the British Mandate was that teaching took place mainly in English under the instruction of a leading missionary, Mr Dunlop, who was in charge of Egyptian education, and who excluded native Arabic-speaking teachers (Marlowe 1970: 290–92). Indeed, Arabic was treated as a dead language and was taught in the same way that Latin was taught in the West. In addition to all this, the British High Commissioner, Lord Cromer, insisted that Egyptians would have to be christianised if they were to have any hope of being civilised (Cromer 1908 2: 535ff). Under Lord Cromer and his colleagues, the sole aim of education policy was to produce Egyptians who would be suitable only for the lower echelons of government bureaucracy (Lloyd 1933 1: 162).

Another reason for the exclusion of Egyptians may have been the desire to claim ancient Egyptians as proto-Europeans (Fletcher and Montserrat 1998: 402) by showing that only Europeans were interested in the study of their history (cf Dittmann 1936). Such a view was not limited to Europeans. Ismael Pasha, the ruler of Egypt between 1863 and 1879, aspired to make Egypt '*European*', styling himself as a '*European ruler*', at least in appearance (Vatikiotis 1980: 73; Reid 2002: 96). Prominent native Egyptian scholars such as Ṭaha Ḥusayn and Ahmad Lutfy Al-Sayyid voiced similar views, and attempted to set out the foundations for closer cultural and historical links with Europe by teaching Egyptian history with an emphasis on the Greco-Roman period at the expense of its pharaonic past (Reid 2002: 211). Indeed, in 1938, Ḥusayn wrote a still widely respected book entitled *The Future of Culture in Egypt* in which he said it was 'utter nonsense to consider Egypt as part of the East' (Ḥusayn 1938: 24), though he was in fact referring to the Far East (China, Japan and India), which he suggested had nothing in common with Egypt. This may have been a result of his French education with its Hellenistic influence (Barbulesco 2002: 297). But Ḥusayn was wrong. Take the example of India. Sir Flinders Petrie excavated evidence of an Indian presence in Egypt in what he called the 'Foreign Quarter' in the southern part of Memphis (Petrie 1909a: 3 (7); 1909b: 13; Harle 1992). Some fascinating insights into cultural exchanges between Egypt and India have already been published which suggest that such contact may date as far back as Egypt's New Kingdom period – 15th–10th centuries BCE (DuQuesne 1995; Stricker 1997) – and that it flourished from the Greco-Roman period onwards (O'Leary 1957: 96–130; Fynes 1993; Salomon 1991).

It was in this atmosphere that Ahmad Kamal, one of the first native Egyptians in modern Egyptology (Sallam 1998; Saied 2002), explored the historical and linguistic links between Egypt and Arabia, as a contribution to the pan-Arabism/ nationalist movement and to the debate about Egypt's identity (Reid 2002: 212). His massive unpublished work, *Dictionary of Ancient Egyptian Language*, in 22 volumes, aimed to establish linguistic links between Egyptian and Arabic (Al-Ma^{c}luf 1923: 306). But Kamal's attempts to publish this dictionary were frustrated by the French and British Egyptologists who were in charge of Egyptian Antiquities and of university education at that time (Mokhtar 1965; Reid 1985). After his death, promises to publish, by the Ministry of Education and Al-Muqtaṭaf Journal, were never realised (Al-Ma^{c}luf 1923: 301), though recently the first volume, covering the letter aleph (A), has been published in Cairo (Kamal 2002).

Kamal tried in many of his works to show that the links between Egypt and Arabia were not just linguistic but also cultural and religious. For example, he discussed (eg Kamal 1902) the worship and origin of the same deities in Egypt and Arabia.

The question of the nature of the links between Egypt and its Arabic neighbours are part of a wider debate about Egypt's cultural identity. The literati often present the argument as a dichotomy, sharpening the contrast between Egypt's pharaonic heritage and its contemporary Islamic one. In resolving such conflicts, the obvious solution is to appeal to a common origin that transcends divisive issues of creed or political loyalties, as was successfully achieved until the Ottoman invasion of Egypt in the early 16th century. This debate continued to dominate Egypt during the 19th and 20th centuries (Gershoni and Jankowski 1998; Haarmann 1991) and is relevant even today (Hassan 1999).

PREVIOUS RELEVANT WORKS

Although no systematic research seems to have been carried out on the medieval Arabic sources in order to inform the study of Egyptology, there have been a few attempts by scholars who have taken an interest in some aspects of the Arab contribution to our knowledge of Ancient Egypt. They are mainly but not exclusively 'orientalists' who, with few exceptions, have a limited knowledge of Egyptology. The interest seems to have started with some of the early European pioneers of modern Egyptology. For example, the Jesuit priest Athanasius Kircher in the mid-17th century, using Arabic sources brought to Europe by others, produced several works on ancient Egyptian themes and was known particularly for his work on the Coptic language (on his life and works see Godwin 1979). The English astronomer Greaves visited the Giza Pyramids, and in 1646 published a thorough study, relying both on his own observation and on medieval Arabic sources (Baines and Malek 1980: 24). Blochet produced a series of articles (1907–15) in which he showed the medieval Arab interest in Egyptian hieroglyphs, and how Moslem artists drew on some hieroglyphs as motifs in Islamic art. Reitemeyer (1903) studied some descriptions of medieval Egyptians by Arab geographers. Graefe (1911) studied and translated into German the section on the pyramids in Al-Maqrizi's book *Khiṭaṭ*. Toussoun (1922–23; 1936) used a number of Arabic sources in his study of the branches of the Nile and of the Lighthouse of Alexandria. Prince Yousouf Kamal (1926–51) edited a large selection of Arabic descriptions of Egyptian monuments and early Arabic maps of Egypt. Nemoy (1939) studied and translated into English Al-Suyuṭi's treatise on the pyramids which appeared in the latter's book *Ḥusn*. Wiet studied and edited several medieval Arabic works and translated a number into French. His particular interest in Arabic descriptions of Egyptian antiquities can be seen in his introduction to Fr Vattier's French translation (1666) of a now lost major Arabic work on Ancient Egypt by an Arab writer named Murtaḍi (Wiet 1953). This book is of particular interest as it was translated during the 17th century, perhaps as part of an attempt to encourage the French king Louis XIV to adopt Leibniz's project to conquer Egypt by showing the king and his public how rich, yet how easy to occupy, Egypt was (for this project see Youssef 1998: 35ff and its appendix).

Gawad (1947) drew attention to the value to archaeologists of the work on the pyramids by Al-Idrisi, *Anwar*, a theme echoed by Sezgin (1988) in her introduction to the facsimile edition of this book. Al-Manawi (1966) produced an excellent survey of the Nile and its economic and social impact, in medieval Arabic sources which reveal names and locations of various branches, most of which had later disappeared.

Fodor (1970) studied the Arabic legend of King Surid, builder of the Great Pyramid at Giza, and also (1992) traced Egyptian elements in some Arabic love spells. Fr Vantini (1975) made available in English most known references to Nubia in Arabic sources. Haarmann (1978–) dedicated several papers to the study of the medieval Moslem response to certain pharaonic monuments, in particular the Sphinx and the pyramids. Until his recent sudden death, he, more than anyone, had emphasised the importance of studying medieval Arab sources and their attitudes to the pharaonic past. Roemer (1985) commented on the Moslem attitude to the pharaonic heritage, and Meincke-Berge (1985) commented on the medieval reuse of ancient antiquities in Cairo. Abbas (1992) has studied accounts by some medieval Arab travellers of their visits to the Egyptian tourist attractions and found them on the whole reliable sources of information. Jakeman (1993) has given a detailed survey of ancient Egyptian monuments reused in medieval buildings in Cairo, commenting on the response of some Moslem sources to the hieroglyphic inscriptions. Recently a brief survey of some of the well known medieval Arab travellers who described the pyramids has been published (Bakr 2001).

Other attempts have been made by Egyptologists who, with a few exceptions, have had limited knowledge of the medieval Arabic sources (eg Kamal 1896, 1902, 1903; Maspero 1899; Stricker 1939, 1942; Habachi 1940; Sauneron 1952; Giorgini 1965; De Meulenaere and Mackay 1976; Wildung 1977b; and more recently

Kuhlmann 1983; Jeffreys 1985, 1999; Hassan 1993; El-Kholi 2003). Gaston Maspero in particular was appreciative of some medieval Arabic works relevant to the study of Ancient Egypt, such as the book *Akhbar Al-Zaman*, believing that some of the ideas contained therein had been shown by modern archaeological work to be reliable. On the whole, these studies addressed certain specific issues, such as the use of medieval Arabic descriptions of a particular pharaonic monument, or the use of data from Arabic sources to enlighten the study of an individual issue. But there has been no comprehensive study attempting a synoptic treatment of Ancient Egypt in the Arabic sources.

CHAPTER 2

THE MAKING OF AN *INTERPRETATIO ARABICA* OF ANCIENT EGYPT

INTRODUCTION

The approach of medieval Arab writers to Ancient Egypt was different from that of their later Western colleagues. Importantly, it differed from the initial Western approach in that it was not seeking to validate the Scriptures, or indeed the Qur'an, but was part of a genuine general interest in the history of humanity, the study of which was seen by the adherents of Islam both as a need and as a duty. The long and varied contacts between Egypt and the lands of Arabia served as a foundation for the understanding of Egyptian culture. For Moslems a new impetus did indeed come from the Qur'an and the Ḥadith (the basis of Islamic canon law), but these did not in themselves serve as historical or archaeological records that needed validation. The Moslem annexation of Egypt lifted the yoke of the Byzantines and brought the Arabs within the physical reality of the country's pharaonic past, and into direct contact with its monuments and the ancient dominant culture of the Nile Valley, where they were eventually absorbed into the culture. The opportunity was there for Arab scholars to learn about the ancient culture through direct contact with learned Copts, and through observing its monuments and artefacts. This created in some Arab writers a need to explore extant classical sources, both written and oral, to satisfy their growing appetite for greater knowledge. The same process can be seen in the exegeses of the Qur'an which had to draw on Jewish sources in order to furnish their works with detail. This all contributed to a very rich corpus of Arabic material on Egyptian culture that to this day remains largely unexplored by modern Egyptologists.

THE ARAB APPROACH TO THE STUDY OF ANCIENT EGYPT

The study of ancient nations occupies a prominent place in the extant Arabic historiographies and was embedded in pre-Islamic poetry that glorified the past deeds of tribes and groups and gave a detailed genealogy of each one (Khalidi 1994: 1–5). Much of this poetry is now lost to us, as it basically depended on oral tradition, and probably only a small fraction of it has survived (Khalidi 1994: 6). A sense of common origin may have been behind early attempts during the first two centuries of Islam to collect historical materials on pre-Islamic Arab kings, as seen in the works of Wahb Ibn Munabbih (d 732) and Al-Aṣmaᶜi (d 828) (Khalidi 1994: 6–7). From within this rich tradition of Arabia, Islam emerged with its own vision of history as displayed in the Qur'an, one which treats historical narrative as eternally present (Khalidi 1994: 8), thereby forming the foundation which distinguishes Arabic historiography – its universality, a genre which is to be understood within the concept of the oneness of humanity as well as within the valued diversity of its ways. Some early Arab scholars regarded the study of history as a human necessity:

> God made inherent in us the need for knowledge of the history of our predecessors, just as was the need of our predecessors for the history of their predecessors, and just as will be the need of those who shall come after us for our history. (Al-Jaḥiẓ (d 771 CE) *Al-Ḥaywan* 1: 42)

It is often assumed that Moslems were bent on destroying *pagan* monuments of pre-Islamic cultures, but the reality was different, and such destruction was exceptional. Al-Baghdadi in the 12th century (*Al-Ifadah*: 110) was well aware of the value of these monuments for studying the past and expressed his admiration for Moslem kings for having looked after and protected their monuments, on the grounds that this had a number of benefits:

- monuments are useful historical evidence for chronologies;
- they furnish evidence for Holy Scriptures, since the Qur'an mentions them and their people;
- they are reminders of human endurance and fate;
- they show, to a degree, the politics and history of ancestors, the richness of their sciences, and the genius of their thought.

On a more mundane level, many Moslems were aware of the economic value of some of these monuments, and even during military action would save items for sale as war spoils, including idols. We know this from the record of a shipload of figurines sent by the Caliph Muᶜawiyah Ibn Abi Sufyan to be sold in India (Al-Baladhuri *Ansab* 4:1: 130; Yasin 1950: 230).

The history of pre-Islamic Egypt, like all other histories, was divided into two main periods: pre-Flood and post-Flood. The Flood is calculated to have taken place, according to Abu Maᶜshar (9th century) in his book on *Historical Astrology* (*Al-Milal* 1: 22–23), 3,671 years before Islam, or approximately 3100 BCE. This date is interesting as it coincides with the founding of the First Dynasty in Egypt, with minor variations (eg Kitchen 1982: 238 has it ca 3200 BCE and Grimal 1992: 49 has it 3150 BCE).

For an Arab writer the post-Flood period extended to his own time. A good example is Al-Maqrizi's *Khiṭaṭ*, which covered Egyptian history from pre-Flood until his own time, and which dedicated long sections to Jewish as well as Christian materials. In fact these two sections were weighty enough to warrant a separate, well-edited publication (Diab 1997, 1998; cf Wüstenfeld 1979).

This may help to explain the widely differing interests in Ancient Egypt to be found among medieval Arab writers. Some were eager to understand Egyptian religious thought and practices, seeing in them one origin of Islamic teachings and even a source of inspiration (see Chapter 6 below), in contrast to most contemporary Egyptologists who still treat Egyptian religion as 'almost exclusively keyed to the state beyond death and [with] precious little this-worldly relevance', a misconception commented on by Terence DuQuesne (2002b: 40). The main interest among early Western Egyptologists focused on philological studies and on the collection of as many Egyptian antiquities as possible to form the basis of a detailed art-historical study. But the medieval Arab sources were more interested in discovering ancient Egyptian sciences, particularly alchemical knowledge.

Though the ancient Egyptians were, to judge from some in 18th century Europe, 'marginal to sacred history and thus worth little more than the Confucians' (Gerbi 1973: 153), most early Western travellers and Egyptologists had their conceptions of Ancient Egypt formed by biblical texts. This was also true of learned societies such as the Egypt Exploration Fund (later Society). The first archaeologist it funded to work in Egypt, Édouard Naville, was specially chosen for his religious conservatism, perhaps because the Society received funds specifically to excavate biblical sites (Wortham 1971: 110). The Society published the results of his work in 1888 under the evocative title *The Store-City of Pithom and the Route of the Exodus*, and new members of the Society were promised, for an annual subscription of £1, a free copy of the excavator's report and a 'genuine Hebrew-made mud brick' from Pithom (Hobson 1987: 40). This is perhaps not surprising in view of the fact that the list of distinguished sponsors included the Archbishop of Canterbury, several bishops and the Chief Rabbi (Drower 1982: 9). This biblical inspiration was, more than any other consideration, behind the Society's first choice of sites to excavate in the Delta (Spencer 1982: 37).

Even today the articles governing the Society's work include among the objects for which it was established (3:B): 'elucidating or illustrating the Old Testament narrative, or any part thereof, insofar as the same is in any way connected with Egypt, or any country adjacent or near thereto' (see the Memorandum and Articles of Association of the Egypt Exploration Society, The Companies Acts 1948 to 1981: 1). However, the next archaeologist to be employed by the Fund to work in Egypt, Flinders Petrie, accompanied by his wife Hilda (Drower 1985), adopted a more scientific method in archaeology. But Petrie was still conscious of the need to retain the financial support of religious groups, as can be seen for example in the titles used for his reports (eg Petrie 1906, 1911, 1934; cf Bierbrier 1995: 331) and in those of Hilda, who dedicated her book to 'the donors who valiantly support our digging' (nd but after 1933: Introduction). At the end of the book by Hilda Petrie, as well as in those by Petrie himself (eg 1934), donations are requested to further the work, to be sent to Lady Petrie either at University College London or to her 'Biblical Research Account' in Jerusalem. Some demands made by Petrie's employers were unreasonable, such as the request from Miss Amelia Edwards 'to bring back a thousand bricks from Tell el Maskhuta, for distribution to subscribers', who, she felt sure, would treasure a genuine brick, made, as the Book of Exodus relates, 'without straw, by an Israelite in bondage' (Drower 1985: 99–100). It is perhaps less widely known that Petrie took a close interest in Islamic monuments, to judge from the number of his paintings of them, particularly those in Cairo's medieval cemeteries; these were executed in such detail that they could be used to reconstruct any that may have been demolished since then. A representative example of these paintings can be seen in **Figure 1** (for more of Petrie's paintings of Islamic monuments see Drower 2004). Petrie also collected thousands of Islamic art objects and Arabic papyri now housed at the Petrie Museum, University College London, which are beginning to receive scholarly attention. He published many of these Islamic/Arabic materials in his study of glass stamps and weights (Petrie 1926). In addition Petrie, deservedly called the Father of Modern Egyptology, took an interest in other parts of the Arab world in order to establish early contact routes with Egypt, and he arranged for his colleague Ernest Mackay (Mackay *et al* 1929) to excavate in Bahrain in 1925 (Drower 1985: 320–21). It is to be lamented that this did not start a trend for Egyptologists generally to take an interest in working in other Arab countries (particularly Yemen), though there are a few exceptions (eg Caton-Thompson 1944 (cf de Maigret 1996: 117; Bierbrier 1995: 87); Fakhry 1952; Saleh 1980, 1992; Kitchen 1994, 2000).

The Scripture-based view may help to explain why Egyptology, for many, is still concerned solely with 'Egypt of the Pharaohs' and, as Fayza Haikal has noted (1993: 1), it was 'considered that Ancient Egypt was dead after the New Kingdom'. This complaint is echoed by Jan Assmann (2002: 282) when he notes that 'many accounts of ancient Egypt do end with the demise of the New Kingdom, as if that were the end of Egyptian civilization altogether'. Even when their interests go beyond the *pharaonic*, such scholars will still not include the archaeology of *Islamic Egypt*. This is well illustrated by the title of a recent proposal to establish a 'Pre-Islamic Egyptian Archaeological Database' (Weeks 1996). This arises from an obvious failure to perceive the intrinsic relationship between pharaonic material cultural remains and those of Islamic Egypt, as can be seen, to cite but one example, by the amount of reused material from the former in the building of the latter. Also, evidence gathered from Islamic archaeology presents a brilliant opportunity, according to the eminent American Egyptologist John A Wilson, who, more than 50 years ago, warned Western scholars against neglecting Islamic archaeology (Wilson 1954: 5). But the prejudice may run deeper, judging from the continued treatment of Egyptian culture as a 'dead culture' by scholars of Egyptology (see the critique of van Walsem (1997) in his groundbreaking paper that has not received the attention it deserves).

To return to the question of Scripture-based archaeology, I do not comment on this approach to Egyptian archaeology; it was by no means limited to early Western Egyptologists, since it can also be seen in many of the Arab sources. Yet, in spite of various references made to the Qur'an or the Ḥadith in the works of Arab writers, it is apparent that neither the Qur'an nor the Ḥadith stopped them from forming their own understanding of the past. This point is best illustrated by quoting from Al-Idrisi (d 1251), an Egyptian historian who answered the criticism made by Al-Baghdadi (d 1231) that the pyramids were not mentioned in the Qur'an, as follows:

> The Revealed Books were revealed to show the intellect and remind the forgetful, and to make clear the path of righteousness and prevent people from falling into the flames, and to impress with evidences those who are stubborn, and demonstrate all the interests in the living world as well as the hereafter. They are not to tell about what will happen in the future or happened in the past which is what people often want to know of the epics of kings and marvels of land and sea. Where these are

> mentioned, it is generally only with enough detail to give examples to those with insight. (If these Revealed Books mention historical places) it is only an addition to the main story, not for their own significance. The reference to ᶜAin Shams (Heliopolis), called in the Old Testament R'misis, occurred only as a consequence of the mention of the Israelites when the Pharaoh summoned them to corvée to repair what had been damaged and had fallen. [The Pharaoh] evacuated to it from Memphis. ᶜAin Shams at that time was the Shrine of the Sun where the Egyptian Ṣabaeans perform their religious duties and traditions. It is one of the Seven Holy Temples of the world. With this (story), God reminded the Israelites so that they remember his beautiful favours in rescuing them from the servitude of the Pharaoh, and thank Him. (Al-Idrisi *Anwar*: 79–80)

This statement is not an isolated illustration of a *rationalist* historian, but belongs to a well established Islamic tradition which dates from the formative period of Islam and forms an integral part of its teachings, based on elements in the Qur'an (Hourani 1971: 147; Huff 1993: 111 and nn 81–82).

Finally, it is important to note that most medieval Arab writers took a more comprehensive approach to Egypt as they studied its past and present, its monuments and inhabitants, and its landscape, including its flora, fauna and geology. In one case the writer Ibn Basam (ca 12/13th century) gives us, in addition to the historical and archaeological description of Tinnis (Tinnis Island, to the north-east of Al-Manzalah Lake and west of Port Said), a detailed name-list of more than 100 of its birds and 63 of its fish, as well as names for the different types of local fishing boats (Ibn Basam *Anis*: 186f (editor's introduction on p 177)). Al-Bakwi (15th century) described the same place and referred to the presence of over 130 different birds and over 78 fishes, probably based on the account of Ibn Basam (Al-Bakwi *Talkhis*: fol 20a; for recent archaeological work on this island see Gascoigne 2003).

These issues were not always treated consistently even by the same writer, but the general attitude among the medieval Arab writers was that Egypt was not just a place where antiquities decorated the landscape; it was a living culture which had produced the antiquities, among other products. Moreover, they stated that the material remains of this culture were the result of the hard work of highly talented people who lived under the threat of natural calamities and famine, as is described by Al-Muqadasi (*Aḥsan*: 193, 202), Al-Baghdadi (*Al-Ifadah*: 132ff) and Al-Maqrizi (*Ighathat*).

EARLY CONTACTS BETWEEN EGYPT AND ARABIA

The Egyptian presence in and trade relationships with neighbouring countries dates back to the predynastic period, and perhaps earlier, and has mutual influences (Wilkinson 1999: 150ff; Zarins 1989). Foreigners appear in almost every type of Egyptian document, showing the rich and mixed racial fabric of society (Bresciani 1990; Johnson 1999) as seen in the population of a city such as Memphis (Thompson 1988; Smith 1992). To the Arabs, Egypt was not a strange or distant place. They had long been trading with and working in Egypt (Muhammad 1979). They appear in ancient Egyptian Demotic records under the name *ALBY* or *ARBY*, which cite events that took place during the Twelfth Dynasty when kings named 'Amenemhat' and 'Sesostris' conquered the Arab Land *p3 t3 3lby* (Zauzich 1991: 6). Arabs appear in Egyptian sources possibly much earlier (Hitti 1970: 32ff; Ahmad 1987; Al-Ghonimi 1993). Some contacts are of a military nature, as we can see from another Demotic papyrus which mentions an Arab prince writing to a hostile Egyptian pharaoh who was threatening to invade his land (Collombert 2002). But the extant military texts and campaigns of the various states in the ancient Near East should not blind us to the long periods of peace and cordiality between Egypt and its neighbours.

Arab names, attested in Arabic as well as other Semitic languages, are frequent in Egyptian records. The names of the Hyksos rulers are clearly Arabic (ᶜAbd Allah 1979: 89), and Badawi (1948: 60f) noticed that both the Hyksos and the Arabs had the same appreciation for the donkey. Arab names are attested during the Middle Kingdom (Posener 1957), throughout the New Kingdom (Saleh 1972, 1978; Schneider 1992, 1993; Hess 1993; Ward 1994; Hoch 1994: 567) and up to and including the Greco-Roman period (Altheim and Stiehl 1964: 386–91; Pestman *et al* 1981: 136ff; 306ff; Abd El-Ghany 1989; Hanson 1992; La'da 2002: 21ff). Peoples who appear in Egyptian documents under the names *Sh3sw* and *ᶜ3mw*, usually translated as Bedouins or Asiatics, are most likely Arabs from Arabia (Giveon 1971: 165, 172). In Demotic and Greek tax records, Arabs appear to have received favourable treatment (La'da 1993: 189). A Greek papyrus from the 2nd century BCE mentions Αραβων κωμη, *'kom Arab'*, an Arab village or town in the area of Lycopolis, Asiut, in Upper Egypt (Petrie 1907: 30). Other Arab communities in Upper Egypt are also attested (McGing 2002: 47). The presence of such villages or towns may be a result of migrations or of the resettlement of Arabs who may have been brought to Egypt at the end of victorious military campaigns of the pharaohs. One single Asiatic campaign by Amenhotep II (ca 1425–1401 BCE) brought back to Egypt 89,600 captives from a very wide range of social and ethnic origins (Janssen 1963: 142). More Asiatics were brought and settled in the Fayum area during the Ramesside period (Sauneron and Yoyotte 1950: 70). In addition, the designation *p3 t3 n n3 hk*[*r*], The Land of the Arabs, appears in Egyptian texts (Osing 1998: 254). It also appears as *Hgr,* as found on the statue of Darius I (**Figure 10**) as a designation for north-western Arabians (Roaf 1974: 135f). It appears as *Hkrw* in the Temple of Edfu as a designation for Arabs (Giveon 1971: 166; O'Connor and Quirke 2003: 12). Even today Arabs are known as *Abna' Hagir*, Children of Hagir. This name in its feminine form *Hgrt* is attested in Ancient Egypt (Ranke 1935: 231 no 11) as well as in its masculine form *Hgr/Hkr,* which name was adopted by a Late Period pharaoh, Hakoris, of the Twenty-ninth Dynasty, who acceded to the throne ca 393 BCE (Ray 1986: 150).

Long before the arrival of Islam, South Arabian tribes migrated to Egypt, in particular the tribe of Luata, some of whom travelled further along the coast of North Africa (Rizkana 1971: 92). Later, when the Moslem campaign headed towards Al-Bahnasa (Oxyrhynchus, located on the Bahr Yusuf, some 190 km south of Cairo) in Middle Egypt, they were fought not only by the *Roms* but also by Arabs said to be from the tribes of, among others, Lakham and Judham (Al-Waqidi *Futuḥ*: 72). Al-Waqidi (*ibid*: 68) gives an interesting account of an earlier battle, also in Middle Egypt, and quotes a Moslem fighter who observed that after the battle:

> We found the ground covered with the dead of the *Roms*, Sudanese and Begga, and many others, and mixed with them a group of dead Moslems who could not be distinguished; they (the enemy) had crosses on their hands, while Moslems did not, so we separated them and collected palm-leaf stalks and canes and placed over every dead man a stalk or cane on the battle-ground.

Thus it was impossible to distinguish these different groups on racial grounds, including skin colour, as they all belonged to the same ethnic group.

This pattern of Arabian tribal migration into Egypt and North Africa as well as Palestine continued after the advent of Islam (Al-Maqrizi *Al-Bayan*), as illustrated in the famous Arabian epic of Banu Hilal (Lyons 1995 1: 13f).

Another interesting aspect is that of names that are considered to be typically pharaonic, such as Ahmos, which is also found in early Arab histories as a name of an ancient Yemeni warrior, Aḥmos (احمس) Ibn Iuf Ibn Anmar (Al-Aṣmaᶜi *Tarikh*: 70). Conversely the famous old Arabic name Khensa' (خنساء) is also the name of the wife or sister of the Twenty-fifth Dynasty Egyptian/Nubian king Piye (Kitchen 1986: table 11; Morkot 2000: 174). The same is true of place names, as in the example of the Island of Masira, off the coast of Oman in the Arabian Sea, which was named Sarapis, after the Egyptian god, in the 1st century work *Periplus of the Erythraean Sea*, and whose inhabitants were said already to 'use the Arabian Language' (Schoff 2001: §33 pp 35, 146).

Arabs established their own cult centres in Egypt and also participated in the worship of Egyptian deities (Rabinowitz 1956; Grelot 1972: 338ff; Vittman 2003: 181). Some entered the Egyptian temple service; for example, a trader from South Arabia (Yemen) named Zaydil (Zaidullah) Ibn Zayd seems to have worked as a *wᶜb* priest for a temple in Memphis, where he died around 263 BCE during the reign of Ptolemy II (Saleh 1992: 94; Kitchen 1994: 47; Swiggers 1995; Vittmann 1998: 1241ff). His wooden sarcophagus, now in the Egyptian Museum in Cairo, is inscribed in South Arabian script. It tells us that he imported from his native land various products for use in the temple service. In the text he prays to Arabian deities and to the Egyptian god Osir-Hapy. The latter name is written in an Arabised form, *Athir Ḥp*, rather than the more common Hellenised form Serapis. This is surely a sign of his assimilation into Egyptian native tradition, as noted by Yihya (1979: 154). The suggestion that Zaydil was allowed to work in the Egyptian priesthood only because of the declining standards of Egyptian practice (Rhodokanakis 1924: 116; ᶜAli 1969: 36) is perpetuating a myth, since the reality is that many people with Arabic names, attested from the New Kingdom, served in the Egyptian temples. One example was an Arab called Khalid, the father of a *wᶜb* priest under Ramesses XI (Schneider 1992: 177 no 376).

These South Arabians working in Egypt were in a long-established tradition of Egyptian acceptance of foreigners in various high offices of government and society (Kitchen 1982: 70; Murnane 2000: 109). South Arabian traders were familiar participants in Alexandrian festivals well into the Hellenistic period (Saleh 1992: 84).

That there was two-way traffic can be seen from the examples of ancient South Arabian sculptures (ca 3rd century BCE) which show obvious Egyptian influence (Tarn 1929: 18f; Deblauwe 1991: 135). Another example is the reported presence of an Egyptian-style obelisk in the Oasis of Tayma (Taima), Saudi Arabia, dedicated by a local priest whose name was derived from Osiris (Yousef 2002: 77). The Egyptian presence along the Arabian coast was undoubtedly strengthened by a reconnoitring expedition sent by King Ptolemy II about 269 BCE (Hölbl 2001: 65).

This two-way traffic is also illustrated by the many names of Egyptians in Mi'naean records (Müller and Vittmann 1993), by the many references to Egypt in South Arabian records (Robin 1994), and from what Fakhry (1952 1: 136) calls a 'rather astonishing' number of Egyptian antiquities found in Yemen. In general, trade formed an important part of the long-established relations between Egypt and Arabia (cf Meeks 2002; 2003).

These early contacts might also help to explain the strong similarities between many of the stories in Arab folk literature in its formative pre-Islamic period, for example the 'Arabian Nights', and ancient Egyptian stories (Golénischeff 1906; Horovitz 1927; Kákosy 1982: 75). The stories of the Arabian Nights and other Arabian epics, with their rich descriptions of monuments and old towns, are yet to be exploited by archaeologists and surely are worthy of study.

Contacts between Egypt and various parts of the Levant certainly date back to the formative period of Egyptian culture (Wilkinson 1999: index). One textual illustration of later contacts with Syria and Palestine comes from the well known story of Sinuhe, an Egyptian official at the beginning of the Twelfth Dynasty who fled there from Egypt upon hearing news of the assassination of the dynasty's founder, King Amenemhat I (ca 1962 BCE). Sinuhe speaks of being recognised by a local chief who had once been to Egypt, and of how well he was treated by the Syrians during his travels (Parkinson 1997: 29). Even if some of the detail of this story is not accurate, the perceptions of the storyteller remain relevant.

In addition to the documented links between Egypt and Mesopotamia, there are episodes which are not apparent from the archaeological record but whose historicity may be supported by medieval Arab sources. For example, it was suggested that a Babylonian king, Nebuchadnezzar, conquered Egypt and killed her lame pharaoh (*fir^{c}un al-a^{c}raj*) (Al-Mas^{c}udi *Muruj* 1: 61), then took back with him thousands of Egyptians who settled in Babylon. If this is true, then currently, archaeological data regarding this event is still lacking as this 'Babylonian incursion left no mark on Egyptian tradition' (Kitchen 1986: 407 n 969). We have only the Arabic tradition to help explain what was regarded as a natural phenomenon in Arab sources, namely the many place names common to both Egypt and Babylon/Iraq such as Waset, the name of a city in central Iraq, as well as the native name for Thebes, capital city of New Kingdom Egypt, and Nile, a river and place name in Iraq, as well as the river of Egypt (for more such names see Yaqut *Al-Moshtarik*). The same is also true of some royal names, such as that of Queen Nitocris, an Egyptian queen at the end of the Sixth Dynasty (Manetho Fr 20), and also a daughter of the Twenty-sixth Dynasty king Psammetichus I (664–610 BCE), which was either a name or an epithet of a Babylonian queen (Herodotus I: 185; II: 100). Incidentally, the name Thebes (which could in Egyptian be *T3 ipt*, and in Arabic طيبة *Ṭaiba*) is also the name of 'Al-Medina Al-Munawarah' (the Luminous City) where the Prophet Muhammad is buried. His mosque there is regarded by Moslems as the second most holy, after the one at Mecca.

The well-established relationship between South Arabia and Ancient Egypt was maintained and even developed after the advent of Islam, as a number of Yemenite tribes migrated to Egypt, seeing common bonds between the two countries as centres of ancient civilisations, and regarding themselves, as did Egyptians, as heirs of these civilisations (Fodor and Fóti 1976: 160 and n 13).

INFLUENCE OF THE QUR'AN AND THE ḤADITH

The impetus for Arab study of the sciences, including history, originated in religious beliefs and in the Qur'an in particular (Nasr 1968: 65, 94). The same can be said of the Arabs' study of Ancient Egypt. Moslems start from the Qur'anic concepts of the unity and common origin of humanity combined with the natural diversity of human beings, which should act as an incentive for different peoples to seek out and get to know others:

> O human beings, We (God) created you of a male and a female
> (from a single pair) and made you into (different) nations and tribes
> that you may (seek to) know each other. (Q49: 13)

The study of universal history based on this principle views history as a source of knowledge and guidance (Al-Ahsan 1999: 71). Religious as well as ethnic differences were seen as part of the natural order of the world, and this attitude filtered down to the masses, as seen for example in the popular culture of medieval Cairo (Staffa 1974: 338). This is in contrast to the current Western view of the world as either a sphere of supremacy for one power or an arena for conflict between civilisations.

An Arabic view is clearly expressed by the scholar Ṣaᶜid Al-Andalusi (d 1168): he says that people in all corners of the universe have a common origin but differ in certain aspects: ethics, appearance, landscape and language (*Ṭabaqat*: 3). His writings, like most Arab sources, treat Egyptian history as part of the universal history of all humanity. These sources also link Egypt and Sudan to the history of the Arabs through a common ancestry (*Akhbar Al-Zaman*: 80).

Links were also claimed between Egypt and Islam through Hajar, the Egyptian wife of Abraham. The Prophet of Islam was himself married to an Egyptian named Maria who was sent to him from Egypt, accompanied by her sister and a servant, carrying with them various gifts. About a dozen of the Prophet's Ḥadith (sayings attributed to him) are reported as being in praise of Egypt itself, its produce and its people (Ibn Ẓahira *Maḥasin*: 74f). According to this tradition, the Copts had kinship (*ṣilat raḥim* صلة رحم) with the Arabs and hence enjoyed a close relationship with the new regime (Bashear 1997: 69). The Prophet's Ḥadith on the subject of Egypt and its inhabitants probably played an important role in forming the general Moslem view of the country and its people.

The number of Ḥadiths relating to Egypt and attributed to the Prophet varies from one authority to another. Ibn Ẓahira (*Maḥasin*: 75–77) narrated 10 Ḥadiths on the virtues of Egypt. An example of this is:

> You are going to enter Egypt a land where *qiraṭ* (money unit) is used. Be extremely good to them as they have with us close ties and marriage relationships (*dhimah wa raḥim* ذمة ورحما).

The Prophet is referring here to ties between Arabs and Egyptians that go back to the marriage of the Prophet Ibrahim (Abraham) to the Egyptian woman Hajar, the mother of Ismael. Ismael is regarded as Father of the Arabs, whilst Hajar is seen as their Mother. It was Ismael and his father who were credited with building the Kaᶜaba, the most holy place in Islam (Q2: 127) and Moslem sources refer to Egyptian craftsmen rebuilding it (Al-Kindi *Faḍail*: 12). The Prophet Muhammad is widely quoted in Moslem sources (eg Al-Kindi *Faḍail*: 14; cf Gottheil 1907) as having uttered these five Ḥadiths:

> When you enter Egypt after my death, recruit many soldiers from among the Egyptians because they are the best soldiers on earth, as they and their wives are permanently on duty until the Day of Resurrection.
>
> Be good to the Copts of Egypt; you shall take them over, but they shall be your instrument and help.
>
> Egypt has the best soil on earth and its people are the most generous of all people.
>
> Blessing (*al-baraka*) was divided into ten parts, nine for Egypt and one part for the other lands. This will be always manifest (*baraka* بركة) in Egypt more than in all other lands.
>
> Be Righteous to Allah about the Copts (*itaqu Allah fi al-qibṭ* اتقوا الله فى القبط).

The Arabs' respect for and appreciation of these ties with the Copts was not merely an emotional response to the Prophet's praise, but certainly this very early interest in Egypt on the part of no less an authority than the Prophet would have encouraged writers and travellers not only to observe its monuments, but also to study its history, and contemporary knowledge and practice. This is often explained by the writers themselves in the introduction to their works (eg Ibn ᶜAbd Al-Ḥakam *Futuḥ*; Al-Idrisi *Anwar*; Al-Suyuṭi *Ḥusn*).

In addition to these personal links with Egypt, another major spur to Arab interest in Ancient Egypt, and other ancient civilisations, is the advice in the Qur'an which urges Moslems to study and visit other lands, cultures and languages, and specifically to study ancient civilisations such as Egypt. A few examples from the Qur'an illustrate this:

> Do they not travel through the land, so that their hearts (minds) may thus learn wisdom and their ears may thus learn to hear? For it is not the eyes which are blind, but the heart in the breast. (Q22: 46)
>
> Say: Travel through the earth and see how creation started. (Q29: 20)
>
> Do they not travel through the earth and see what was the end of those before them (who) were more numerous and superior in strength and monuments in the land? (Q40: 82)

These Qur'anic verses do not form a body of historical knowledge in themselves, but they surely indicate the significance of historical consciousness for early Moslems, and by naming specific ancient civilisations the Qur'an encouraged its adherents to further their interest in historical knowledge of these civilisations. Egypt is named, or clearly alluded to, some 30 times in the Qur'an (eg Q2: 61; 10: 87; 12: 21, 99; 43: 51; for a complete list of all verses see Al-Suyuṭi *Ḥusn* 1: 10), and as a result, many medieval commentators on the Qur'an researched and interpreted these references, some of them in the context of the stories of Joseph, and of Moses and the Israelites (Youssef 1991: 27ff).

It should not be forgotten that whilst Egypt is referred to in the Qur'an some 30 times, it is mentioned in the Bible some 680 times (Youssef 1991: 6).

The Egyptian scholar Abu Ja^c^far Al-Idrisi (d 1251 CE) dedicated the first chapter of his book (*Anwar*: 5–11) to citing Qur'anic verses that would motivate Moslems to study monuments and histories of ancient peoples. He also tells the story of the Moroccan man who went on pilgrimage to Mecca and, on his return home, hastened to attend the lessons of his master, the Sage Shaikh Abu Zakaria Al-Biyasi, who taught medicine and other sciences. His teacher welcomed him back warmly, then said:

> Tell me about what you have seen of the pyramids of Egypt, but not what you were told.

The student replied:

> O teacher, I have nothing of direct sightseeing to tell you.

To this the teacher responded angrily:

> Despicable is the student of knowledge and wisdom whose endeavour does not arouse his determination to see the like [of the pyramids], nor stirs his eagerness and passion to see whatever can be seen of marvels. There was nothing to prevent you from informing [us] about them and from [speaking] as a witness here of what you saw, but a swift ride, or a push of a boat. The sluggish one does not deserve to be adorned with the essences of wisdom.

The student immediately departed back to Egypt for no other reason than to see the pyramids (Al-Idrisi *Anwar*: 15).

This is a good example of genuine interest in the heritage of Ancient Egypt following the guidance of the Prophet to seek knowledge wherever it may be found. The Prophet did not in any way qualify or specify where the search for wisdom and science should take place. The result of this may be seen in books on the 'quest for knowledge' such as that of Abu Hilal Al-^c^Askari (d 1009), in which he speaks of seeking knowledge without limiting it to religious knowledge. In fact, nowhere in his book do we find any reference to religious knowledge *per se*; his was a quest for all knowledge. The Prophet himself went even further, making it 'incumbent upon every Moslem man and Moslem woman to seek knowledge' (cf Soliman 1985: 3–4; Nasr 1968: 65), thus encouraging the search for and appreciation of wisdom for its own sake, and allowing Moslems to form their own understanding of the past.

There is also a view, still widely held, that Moslems regard anything before Islam as pagan, *jahliyah*, invalid and opposing Islam, and therefore of no interest to them (cf Djahiliyya in EI^2 2: 383–84). This is an oversimplification. The Qur'an does not treat all pre-Islamic people in the same way but distinguishes between those who believe in god and those who do not, and makes it clear that Moslems must believe in and treat equally all previous religions and their prophets without distinction (Q2: 285). It is also important to point out that the Moslem concept of *jahliyah* not only refers to the pre-Islamic period but can be and is used to describe certain manners and customs even of our own time (Hassan 1984: 19). The Prophet also made it clear that his role was to complete the task started by the many prophets before him, saying:

> My position and that of the prophets before me is like that of a man who built a home with great care and beauty but a brick in a corner was missing. So people walk around it, admiring it, but saying: there is a gap, there is a brick missing. So I am this brick and I am the last of the prophets. (Al-Bukhari *Ṣaḥiḥ*: *kitab al-manaqib*, no 3535)

This clearly indicates the position of Islam in the overall scheme of human history, seen from the Moslem viewpoint of the time: that Moslems were building on the existing foundations of their predecessors and filling in a gap, which must surely have given them a sense of the enduring continuity of tradition. Moreover, the theme of continuity from antiquity was also in keeping with the views of some Moslem schools of thought that past and present are both part of an overall divine scheme (Khalidi 1994: 66). In fact, the medieval Moslem higher education curriculum embraced the accumulated knowledge of the previous and contemporary Hellenistic world as well as those of the Orient, India and China (Stanton 1990: 53). True knowledge regardless of its source was deemed compatible with Islamic thought since 'nothing but good could result from the proper use of knowledge and reason' (Stanton 1990: 95).

THE MOSLEM ANNEXATION OF EGYPT

It may be useful to give a brief description of what is known of the advent of Islam to Egypt. The Arabic word usually used to refer to this event is *fatḥ* فتح which, like many Arabic words, has a very wide spectrum of meanings, the first of which indicates 'opening, introduction, and revelation', before the later meaning of 'conquest'. I therefore use the word 'annexation' as it is closer to the original Arabic, though it too is not entirely satisfactory. It is also important here to draw attention to a common confusion between the words 'Islamic' and 'Arabic', even amongst scholars who refer to the *Arab* conquest of Egypt and other countries, when they should refer to the Islamic conquest or annexation, since the Moslem forces were composed of different ethnic groups, not just Arabs.

The annexation of Egypt took place during the Caliphate of ᶜUmar (13 H/634 CE–23 H/644 CE), when an army of some 4,000 Moslems of different ethnic origin arrived at Babylon, the Roman fort (Old Cairo), and started a process which, after a number of battles, reinforcements and negotiations, mostly with the Byzantine garrisons, ended with the Moslems taking over Egypt in 20 H/641 CE (for details see Butler 1978; and for recent literature EI^2 7: 146–86). The Moslems had been dealing in the main with the Byzantines (*rom/rum*), at that time the masters of Egypt. Native Egyptians had not been as involved with the hostilities, and were therefore regarded by the Moslems as kin who welcomed Moslems rather than defeated enemies. The implications of this were vital for Moslem jurists, who had to decide whether Egypt had been taken over peacefully by treaty (*fatḥ sulḥ*), or by military force (*fatḥ ᶜunwah*). This was necessary in order to settle the issues of land ownership and taxation. The matter was not entirely straightforward, since parts of Egypt had been taken over in battle and other parts by treaty. Long debates ensued and the Caliph himself was asked for his legal opinion. Gradually a consensus emerged among most of the Moslem scholars and jurists that Egypt had been taken over by treaty. This meant that Egyptian land remained the property of Egyptians, who were then accorded the rights of *Ahl Al-Dhimah* (those under the protection of Moslems), in addition to being also of *Ahl Al-Kitab*, people who believe in a Revealed Holy Book, which includes Zoroastrians, Ṣabaeans, Jews and Christians, who, according to Islam, are entitled to the same rights under Moslem rule as their fellow Moslem citizens – *lahum ma lana wa ᶜaliyhim ma ᶜaliyna* – which means 'They [Peoples of the Book] have the same rights and obligations as us [Moslems]'. This was not the case in those countries taken over by force, where the land was divided up amongst the victorious Moslems as spoils of war. (For details see Al-Baladhuri *Futuḥ*: 214–25; Ibn ᶜAbd Al-Ḥakam *Futuḥ*: 84: 90; Murad 1996: 19–70.)

Moslem annexation did not seem to disrupt the daily life of the native Egyptians themselves, as contemporary documents suggest a continuity of normal activity in the country (Allam 1992: 2), as was indeed the case with other Moslem annexations, according to Cameron (1997: 14), who agrees with archaeologists currently working on this period that 'there was no sudden disruption in either urban or rural life at the time of the conquest'. Evidence from early Arabic papyri also shows an uninterrupted continuity of pre-Islamic styles of writing and administration long after the Moslem annexation (El Daly 1983: 34; Frantz-Murphy 1991: 11).

THE COPTS

Medieval Arab writers used the word قبط *qipṭ* or *gypṭ* (Copt) to denote both ancient and contemporary indigenous Egyptians, thereby reflecting their perception of the connection and the continuity between the past and the present. The word *gipti* or *giphti* was a Talmudic name for Egyptians, long before the Moslem annexation of Egypt (Krause 1980: 731; Fontinoy 1989: 91; for other variations of the word see Aufrère and Bosson 2000: 8). The Arabs continued to use it, often as a designation for all Egyptians, regardless of religious belief (Diab 1998: 14), well into the Mamluk period (1249–1517), as can be seen from biographies in which many Moslems are called Copts, though some may have been recorded thus because they were descendants of native Christians (Petry 1991: 618). Since then the word has been used mainly for Egyptian Christians.

Some Arab genealogists (eg Al-Masᶜudi *Muruj* 1: 357) speculated that Qift/Copt was the name of the eldest son of Miṣr, grandson of Noah, after whom the country was named. Miṣr divided the land between his four sons, Ṣa, Atrib, Ashmun and Qifṭim, after whom were named the towns of Sais, Athribis, Ashmunein and Qift. King Miṣr put Qifṭim in overall charge and gradually he and his descendants dominated the land of his brothers, thereby giving the name Qifti/Copts to all the inhabitants. There seems to be no knowledge among Arab writers of the association with *ḥwt-k3-ptḥ*, the name of the main temple of Ptah at Memphis, which is now widely held to be the origin of the word Αἴγυπτος/Aegiptus/Egypt (for a recent survey see Aufrère and Bosson 2000). But the origin of the latter was more plausibly thought to be in the Egyptian word *3gabt* used of both the Nile and the land (Naville 1917: 230; Saleh 1962: 11).

The native Egyptians seem to have carried on with their way of life unchanged under the new rulers. Arab travellers, such as Al-Muqadasi (*Aḥsan*: 193) visiting Egypt at the end of the 10th century after almost 400 years of Islam, noted that 'the customs of the Copts prevail' and that people were still conversing in Coptic (Al-Muqadasi *Aḥsan*: 203). The Coptic community may well have faced troubles at various periods at the hands of some Moslem rulers, but so did their fellow Moslem compatriots, to judge from the names of those who led rebellions against such rulers. Finneran (2002: 66) noted that 'the real threat to their [the Egyptian Copts'] survival came from fellow Christians' and from their rivals, the Chalcedonian Melkites and other devotees of Christian schisms (cf Winkler 1997: 91ff). When the Moslems arrived in Egypt, the Coptic Patriarch Benjamin was already in hiding after the sustained efforts of the Byzantine emperors to enforce their orthodoxy on the so-called nonconforming Copts (Butler 1978: 3, 176f). Benjamin was restored as the head of the 'weakened and almost lifeless' Coptic Church by the Moslem campaign leader ᶜAmr Ibn Al-ᶜAṣ (Butler 1978: 439ff). The a decline in the number of Egyptian Copts is nearly always interpreted as a result of either maltreatment by the Moslem rulers or the heavy burden of the *jiziyah* (poll tax). This suggestion is demeaning to those who converted to Islam for genuine reasons and even to those who may have done so to escape the inter-church theological complexities and conflicts that have bedevilled Christianity since long before the pre-Islamic period (Rufailah 1898: 28).

Studies on the relationship between Copts and their fellow Moslems tend to focus on the periods of trouble, when in fact the overall nature of this relationship over time has, according to the Copts themselves, been cordial (Legrain 1945: 78; Qiladah 1993; Ghali 1993). This is shown by the tolerance that allowed various religious creeds to flourish side by side, as evidenced by the vast amount of religious literature belonging to the Jewish, Gnostic, Manichaean, Hermetic and other traditions. Perhaps nothing demonstrates to me this harmony more clearly than the shared artistic tradition in which ancient Egyptian art motifs form the basis of much Coptic and Islamic art, for example the patterning commonly referred to as *Arabesque*, together with the known employment of Coptic artists in the decoration of both Christian and Moslem buildings and materials, drawing extensively on both pre-Islamic and Islamic art for the decoration of churches (Hunt 1985, 1998; Bolman 2002 especially chapters 7 and 8).

THE COUNTRY

For Arab geographers, the world was divided into seven zones, as illustrated by Al-Biruni (d 1048) (Nasr 1978: fig 8), and this map was copied later by Yaqut (d 1228) (*Mu*ᶜ*jam* 1: 24–32). The third zone, in the south-west, includes Egypt, the Levant, Sudan, Morocco and lands in between and adjacent to them. For Al-Maqrizi (*Khiṭaṭ* 1: 31) Upper Egypt is situated in the second zone while Lower Egypt is in the third zone.

The name used in the Arabic sources for Egypt is *Miṣr* مصر, which in Arabic means 'country, urban centre and border' and may be of ancient Egyptian derivation from the word *mḏr* with a wide range of meanings including 'protected border' and 'walled in' (Saleh 1962: 7ff; Faulkner 1962: 123). This name *Miṣr* is known also in other ancient languages of the Near East long before the advent of Islam (Altheim and Stiehl 1964 1: 74ff; Bosworth 1993: 146). Ibn Al-Faqih (d 902) in his book *Al-Buldan* (115), after citing the meaning of Egypt as above, added that 'Egypt was called *Maqdunia* [Macedonia] in Greek', which may be a confusion resulting from the name of the founder of Alexandria, Alexander of Macedon. We find the same name *Maqdunia* also used by Al-Masᶜudi (*Muruj* 1: 304) as a name for Egypt, including Alexandria, during the reign of Cleopatra and her consort Mark Antony.

There seems to be general agreement in the medieval Arabic sources that *Miṣr* is the name of the country, but Al-Maqrizi (*Khiṭaṭ* 1: 46ff) in his chapter entitled 'Derivations of Miṣr, its meaning and different names', said that its name in the 'First time (*Al-Dahr Al-Awal*) before the Flood' was 'Jizla' which may be from the ancient Egyptian word, *ḏsrt* (may also be pronounced *Jisra/Jizla*), meaning 'Holy [Land]'. It is also possible that this name is derived from the Egyptian *dšrt* with the meaning 'Red Land' which designated the uncultivated land (Otto 1975: 76) and also Egypt (WB 4: 494).

The measurements of the land of Egypt were calculated in keeping with the Greek tradition of giving distances in the number of days needed to travel them. Ibn Al-Faqih (*Al-Buldan*: 115) said that Egypt was 40 nights in length and the same in width. As for the borders of Egypt, according to Al-Iṣṭakhari (*Al-Masalik*: 39), Egypt stretched from the Sea of the Rom (the Mediterranean, which was also called by some medieval Arab writers the Green Sea, eg Al-Qazwini ᶜ*Ajaib*: 93) between Alexandria and Barqa, down to Nubia at Aswan, and then to the land of the Beja beyond Aswan, ending at the Sea of Al-Qulzum (ie Red Sea), then crossing it at Al-Qulzum (Clysma, Suez) and proceeding into Sinai until reaching the Mediterranean again beyond Al-ᶜArish and Rafah. These are standard descriptions of the Egyptian borders in the medieval Arabic sources (see for examples the maps from Al-Iṣṭakhari *Al-Masalik*: facing p 41; and Ibn Ḥawqal **Figure 2** here).

One of the questions that occupied the minds of some medieval Arab writers was how the land of Egypt originated, and we are given some hints of a vague knowledge of a concept of prehistory, knowledge of which was lost to Egyptians in the medieval period. Al-Masᶜudi, citing the opinions of 'the specialists', said:

> The land of Egypt was under the water of the Nile, which spread from Upper Egypt down to the Low Land, ... until some obstacles blocked the water, and the soil which the current moved from one place to another, then [the Nile] went to certain parts ... Water gradually receded enabling people to settle and build and they channelled the water, dug canals and put up dams but this [knowledge] was lost from its people, because the length of time took away [from them] knowledge of how [their ancestors] lived. (Al-Mas^cudi *Muruj* 1: 346)

Al-Mascudi's idea that Egypt was originally covered by sea water follows Herodotus (II: 12) but his suggestion that a very long time had passed since this formative period and that his contemporary Egyptians had lost all knowledge of such prehistoric events is of great significance. If we add to this what he wrote of the age of life on earth which he estimated, according to his Indian sources, to be hundreds of millions of years made up of cycles of 36,000 years each (Al-Mascudi *Muruj* 1: 77), we can appreciate that he had an awareness of the early period of human existence on earth which we call prehistory.

In spite of the common depiction of Egypt in Arab sources as a mirror of heaven on earth, lush and pleasant, some writers were well aware that some components of this actually came from outside the country. For example, Ibn Faḍl Allah said:

> Most merits (محاسن *maḥasin*) of Egypt are brought to her, so much so that someone even said that the four elements are brought to her: water, which is the Nile, is brought from the south, the soil is brought in the water otherwise it is only sand that does not grow plants, fire from wood which is imported into it and air/wind blows from one of the two seas, the Rumi and the Qulzum [Mediterranean and Red Sea]. (Ibn Faḍl Allah *Masalik*: 16)

Ibn Faḍl Allah is indeed correct in identifying the external source of Egyptian soil as being carried to the country by the Nile, which, as Rushdi Said (1990: 9) noted, 'has shaped not only the physical traits of the country but also its history and the nature of its human settlement'.

SOURCES AVAILABLE TO MEDIEVAL ARAB WRITERS

Arabs, who established themselves in Egypt and found the country and its people amicable, soon merged with the local population and sent for their families and tribes to join them. This brought to Egypt thousands of new Arabs from the new lands of Islam, including particularly Yemen and Iraq (Al-Maqrizi *Al-Bayan*). They were able to see for themselves the pharaonic antiquities, having already known of the wealth of its ancient pharaohs from the Qur'an and from earlier travellers. The reality of living and interacting with native Egyptians gave many Arabs an impetus to learn more about the country's past. Reasons for this interest were firstly, as explained above, for the sake of knowledge itself, and secondly from a realisation that the present state of Egypt had derived from its past. A clear example of this in one vital area was taxation, which continued to depend annually on the level of the Nile flood.

Moslems/Arabs acquired their knowledge of Egypt's past through several routes, which I summarise below.

Direct observation and native folktales

As Arab travellers flocked into the Nile Valley, and saw the spectacular monuments about which they probably knew little, they immediately started to collect the traditions and folktales circulating among the population (eg Ibn ᶜAbd Al-Ḥakam *Futuḥ*). From the 10th century onwards material was collected more critically, and was sifted and arranged, as can be seen in Al-Masᶜudi and Ibn Waṣif Shah (ᶜAbd Al-Ḥamid 1954: 98). It is important to remember that Egypt had a long tradition of oral transmission of historical knowledge, as can be seen in the ancient Egyptian phrase *r3 n r3* 'mouth to mouth', which was also an important teaching method (Morenz 1996: 28; Saleh 1966: 293f; Assmann 2002: 123). These folktales in their written forms were very popular in Demotic/Greek texts (Tait 1994) and continued in medieval Islam in the form of *Qiṣah/Sirah* and *Waᶜẓ* 'story/biography telling' and 'preaching for admonition' (Berkey 2001: 14), and their popularity has continued to the present day (Reynolds 1995).

Another important source was direct observation, made during travel, of the lives of the people, of the flora and fauna, and of a landscape scattered with the impressive remains of the past. Many of the Arab travellers were also keen observers of ethnographic material. One of these is Al-Muqadasi (*Aḥsan*), regarded by Fahim (1989: 52) as an excellent but not unique example of Arab ethnographers with a wide interest in local language, customs and economy as well as geography, history and archaeology. This material also includes oral transmission of folktales of native heroism and of a distant past evidenced by the presence of motifs, and even whole episodes from Demotic literature, which found their way into early Arabic epics. Such folklore is yet to receive adequate treatment by modern historians of Ancient Egypt (see the current debate in Redford 2003: 3).

Discourses with Egyptian savants

Another major source of information for Arab writers was the Coptic monasteries and their monks. Whilst travelling, Moslem visitors regularly stayed in monasteries and many befriended the monks. It was not just convenience that caused them to stay at monasteries during their desert travels (El Daly 2000: 29); many flocked to them, especially those by the Nile, to enjoy the natural beauty spots and the solitude as well as the hospitality of the monks, who were well known for their good wine (Diab 1998: 150ff). Even some of the rulers of Egypt, notably Ahmad Ibn Ṭulun (d 884), used to spend a few days at a time in contemplative retreat in the Monastery of Al-Quṣir (Al-Qusayr), on the Muqaṭam Mountain near Tura, south of Cairo (Al-Balawi *Sirat*: 118). Sadly, this famous monastery of Apa Arsenius is now inaccessible and almost totally unknown (Grossmann 2001: 173). During the first century of Islam, close ties were established between Moslems and Coptic monasteries (Abdel Tawab 1986), and by the 10th century CE Moslem writers had developed a keen interest in the monasteries, an interest described as 'a significant feature' of the century (Farag 1964: 43).

It was during such visits, and within their normal social intercourse, that debates took place as a way of learning more about the Copts and their festivals and traditions, including popular history. It is possible that Coptic monks had at their disposal written records which they were prepared to give to their Moslem guests, as we are told by Al-Dawadari (*Kanz* 3: 214f), who was given a Coptic book on history from the White Monastery at Suhaj in Upper Egypt. Al-Dawadari also said (*Kanz* 3: 219) that such a book was used by Al-Mas^cudi and that he himself had compared the texts of Al-Mas^cudi with the Coptic Book. It became important for writers to cite such ancient books among their sources (Radtke 1992: 178).

Such Coptic books were still in use in the time of Al-Maqrizi, who cited 'The Coptic Book, written in Ṣai^cdic dialect and translated into Arabic, on the taxation of Egypt' (*kitab qibiṭi bi'l-lughat al-ṣa^cidyah mima nuqila ila al-lughat al-^carabyah fi kharaj Miṣr*) (see this and other similar titles in Haridi 1984 2: 96). Some other Coptic sources were also available in Arabic and were among the first to be translated for the Umayyad Prince Khalid Ibn Yazid in the 7th century (Al-Nadim *Al-Fihrist*: 303). The Umayyad court was already a haven of Christian-Moslem cordial exchanges. There a Christian theologian, John of Damascus, was an almost permanent resident at the court (Louth 1996: 16).

It is often reported that whenever an ancient Egyptian text was found that needed to be read, a monk from a nearby monastery would be sought out to help. For example, a book written in *Al-Qibiṭiyah Al-Ula* (the first Egyptian language) was found at Giza near the pyramids and was sent to a monk at the monastery of Qalmun in Fayum to be read (Al-Idrisi *Anwar*: 100; the same story is repeated by Al-Bakwi *Talkhis*: fols 31b–32a). This seems to have been a natural part of the general Arab attitude that the Copts 'as inhabitants of Egypt, were knowledgeable about the temples and their inscriptions and the sciences contained in them' (Al-Magriṭi (attributed to) *Ghayat*: 310).

Classical sources

The other major sources used by Arab writers were the extant Greek and Latin sources on Ancient Egypt which were widely available in their original languages and also in translations in either Arabic or Syriac and perhaps also Aramaic and Persian.

A glance at the index of Al-Nadim (*Al-Fihrist*) shows that many classical sources were already known and quoted in Arabic writings in the 10th century and we have the Arabic versions of many of the classical sources, for example Josephus (Pines 1971), who was quoted extensively by Arab writers such as Al-Shahrastani.

Herodotus, Manetho, Plutarch, Plato and Plotinus among others were known and it was perhaps these sources which were being referred to by Al-Biruni (*Al-Athar*: 84) when he said that he acquired 'Books which had the periods of reigns of the kings of Ashur of Mosul, and the periods of the kings of the Copts who were in Egypt, and the Ptolemaic kings . . .'. One can add to these Eastern sources which are yet to receive detailed study, including Indian, Ḥarranian, and Syriac. Even Moslem mosque preachers were familiar with and interested in these sources, as can be seen from many examples such as the one cited by Rosenthal (1962) of a preacher in the mosque of Ḥarran lending the famous historian Ibn Al-ᶜAdim (13th century) a Ḥarranian book.

Jewish sources: 'Judaica, Al-Israeliyat'

The Qur'an and the Ḥadith refer to several past civilisations and historical events but with little detail. Moslem believers eager for detail had to search among the 'People of the Book', ie adherents of other religions with divinely revealed holy books – mainly, but not exclusively, Jews and Christians. Qur'anic references to pre-Islamic prophets encouraged Moslems to study the history of those earlier prophets, thereby creating a body of historical writings known in Islamic literature as *Qiṣaṣ/Tarikh Al-Anbiya'* 'Stories/History of the Prophets', some written by well-known commentators on the Qur'an such as Ibn Kathir and Al-Thaᶜalabi (Nagel 1986). The work of the latter, *Qiṣaṣ Al-Anbiya'*, was even more popular than his Qur'anic exegesis (Watendonk 1976: 343). Since knowledge of these histories is an essential part of the duties of the believer (Ferro 1984: 53), this led to the creation of universal histories in which Moslem historians treated pre-Islamic materials with respect, and made extensive use of them, for example in what is known in the field of Islamic studies as Judaica (*Al-Israeliyat*). These relate Jewish stories which circulated among Moslems as a result of contact with the Jews living among them, especially those who converted to Islam, such as Kaᶜb Al-Aḥbar (Schmitz 1978: 316–17). Moslem interpreters of the Qur'an, chroniclers and historians often relied on the Judaica for details of certain historical events, such as the creation of Adam and Eve, which are cited in the Qur'an with little detail. Arabic translations of various biblical and other religious texts were already circulating among the people of Arabia, which presented a rich and detailed source for Moslem writers (Rabiᶜ 2001: 49–54). The Judaica enriched the Qur'anic exegeses but also alarmed some Moslem scholars, who regarded them as myths and called for them to be re-edited and purged of the Judaica (Rabiᶜ 2001: 382). But this goes against the Islamic view which treats the history of humanity as one universal history in which each group or people has its place (Radtke 1992: 544). Moreover, the extensive medieval Arab use of Judaica to reconstruct the history of ancient Egypt must have been due in part to the hundreds of biblical references to Egypt. It was natural, therefore, to compare the Hebrew data with the Egyptian realities. Also of interest, but requiring a separate study, is just how many Jewish traditions betray their ancient Egyptian origin, such as the use of the Egyptian sun disc and the scarab in royal Judaean tradition (Taylor 1993: 261 and figs 2–7) which may also have been observed by Arabic writers.

Arabic sources

As interest in learning about Ancient Egypt expanded and demand for books on the subject increased, a corpus of texts was soon available in Arabic, written by

Arabs, and these became the basis for later studies. That the study of Ancient Egypt was popular among medieval Arab scholars can be seen from the list of books covering Ancient Egypt quoted by Al-Idrisi (d 1251) in his study of the pyramids (*Anwar*: 251ff), many written by native Egyptians. Just a few of their titles illustrate the point:

- 'Secrets of the temples and the ancient sciences of the Egyptian sages'
- 'Chronicles of Egypt, its treasures and pharaohs'
- 'The unique jewel on the chronicles of Ancient Egypt'
- 'Priestly talismans (statues)'
- 'The sciences of hidden treasures'.

(See the full list of Arabic books on Ancient Egypt used by Al-Idrisi in Appendix 2.)

The same can be said of Al-Maqrizi (d 1440), who cited dozens of previous works which he had used on the history of Egypt, many on its pharaonic past (Guest 1902; Haridi 1983–84). Extensive citations added to the authority of the writer and showed his vast knowledge of earlier sources.

This interest of native Egyptians in their own history continued during Ottoman rule and even under the French occupation, as can be seen from the books of a number of historians such as Ibn Zunbul, Al-Bakri, Al-Isḥaqi and Al-Sharqawi (Holt 1968; ᶜAbd Allah 1991: 83f, 175ff). Most of these books are on the history of Islamic Egypt but start with descriptions of its pharaonic past.

It was from this long tradition that the early modern Egyptian historians, Rifaᶜa Al-Ṭahṭawi and Ali Mubarak, drew their inspiration (on these 19th century Egyptian historians see El-Shayyal 1962; Crabbs 1984; Reid 2002: 93ff). They were among some 300 students sent by the ruler of Egypt, Muhammad Ali Pasha (originally from Kavalla, now in Greece) to Europe at the beginning of the 19th century, to acquire an up-to-date knowledge of Western sciences which would be useful in building a modern military force (cf Fahmy 1997). Rifaᶜa, a graduate of Al-Azhar, accompanied the Egyptian students to France as their Imam, to lead prayers and give religious counselling. Once back in Egypt he published a book on his impressions of Paris, but more importantly, over the following three decades, he wrote several historical and literary works. In 1868 he published a book on the history of Ancient Egypt that started with its pharaonic past and ended with the Moslem annexation under the title *Anwar Tawfiq Al-Jalil fi Akhbar Miṣr wa Tawthiq Bani Ismael* (El-Shayyal 1962: 32). This title may be translated as 'Glorious light on the chronicles of Egypt and documentation of the descendants of Ismael'. His book was well received by scholars from different backgrounds, including those of Al-Azhar, in spite of its glorification of pharaonic Egypt (Reid 2002: 109f). Rifaᶜa Al-Ṭahṭawi is regarded in modern Arabic literature as the pioneer who ushered in a new Arab Renaissance (Muṣṭafa 2002: 76–80; cf Sorman 2003).

Ali Mubarak was also greatly interested in the history of Ancient Egypt, and produced an encyclopaedia on the topography of the country, *Al-Khiṭaṭ Al-Tawfiqiya*, which systematically examined ancient sites (cf Dykstra 1999). His main sources were medieval Arabic works on topography, such as that of Al-Maqrizi, in addition to contemporary sources and his own studies (Baer 1968). He had the potential, with help from his fellow historian Rifaᶜa Al-Ṭahṭawi, based on their schooling in both native and French education, to develop a modern native Egyptology school that looked to medieval Egyptian scholars for inspiration. Unfortunately, this opportunity was lost, for reasons discussed above, and even today Egyptology is widely regarded as a European/Western study.

CHAPTER 3

TREASURE HUNTING

> In the land of Egypt, there are great treasures and it is said that most of its land is of buried gold; it is even said that there is no place [in Egypt] which is not full of treasures. (Ibn Al-Wardi *Kharidat*: 31–32)

INTRODUCTION

The search for hidden treasure to exploit is perhaps one of the oldest of pursuits. Much of it is carried out with the hope of personal gain, some perhaps for scholarship and reputation, some for personal enjoyment, and some to sell illegally for financial gain. The medieval Arab sources show great interest in finding ancient treasure, some for personal gain, but some for the benefit of the state and its people, and some for study purposes.

Egypt was, and still is, held as the land of hidden treasures, a perception encouraged in Arabic writings by the Qur'anic descriptions of the fabulous wealth of the Pharaoh, and of Qarun from the tribe of Moses. Ancient Egyptian pyramids, temples, tombs and their surroundings were perceived as depositories of vast wealth protected by magic. This is not a naïve perception, as modern archaeological work has shown that such precious materials were in fact deposited by ancient Egyptians, a prime example being the tomb of King Tutankhamun in the Valley of the Kings. Temples were also depositories of treasures (Hovestreydt 1997), for example the Temple of Hathor at Dendera (Cauville 1995: 16) and the Temple of Ṭod (Vandier 1937; Bisson de la Rouque *et al* 1953). In the case of Dendera, it must always have been a place famed for treasures, as reported by Al-Dimishqi (d 1328) (*Nukhbat*: 328) who said that a hoard of precious metals including gold was found by a stranger, digging illegally, who was caught and handed over to the authorities in Cairo together with a hundred sacks full of the treasure. This treasure hunter was imprisoned. There was indeed a goldsmith's workshop (probably for alchemy too) at Dendera (Derchain 1990).

For treasure hunters, it was often fatal to attempt to reach these treasures without the appropriate skills and tools, and thousands lost their lives and money in the quest. The common belief among medieval Arab writers, that ancient Egyptian tombs were protected by demons wielding knives to cut off the heads of intruders, may indeed be based on observation of ancient Egyptian seals used by the necropolis guards, such as those found on the entrance to the tomb of Tutankhamun (Goedicke 1993). These seals are usually decorated with figures of the jackal, or Anubis, the guardian of the dead, often showing enemies with their arms tied behind them and their heads cut off to render them harmless. Similarly, gatekeepers wielding knives are commonly depicted on tomb walls.

As the state came to depend on the financial yields of treasure, the profession of treasure hunter was organised by the state from the time of Ibn Ṭulun in the 9th century. From then on, permits to excavate ancient sites were required, in addition to the presence at all times of an official representing the ruler.

Materials collected from Egyptian sites, in particular those which did not at the time have monetary value, were sometimes kept by rulers as curios.

Ongoing attempts, from medieval times to the present day, to curb the illegal quest for treasure have always failed despite regulation and severe penalties, as can still be seen today from frequent newspaper reports.

TREASURE HUNTING IN ANCIENT EGYPT

In Ancient Egypt, with its vast treasure of great antiquity, treasure hunting became a full-time profession and at times was even under state patronage. The tradition of exploiting ancient treasure certainly goes back to pharaonic Egypt. This is seen in the 'Admonitions of Ipuwer' who lamented that even the royal treasury had been completely robbed during the First Intermediate Period (Parkinson 1997: 166ff).

Records of police investigations into tomb robbery in the New Kingdom show the spread of the practice (Breasted 1927 4: 246ff). At the end of the New Kingdom treasure hunting was officially instigated and sanctioned to help the ailing economy (Reeves and Wilkinson 1996: 204f). The same process was also recorded during the Ptolemaic period. According to Strabo (*Geography* 17.1.8–9), a Ptolemaic king stole the gold coffin from the tomb of Alexander the Great and replaced it with one made from alabaster or glass.

Treasure attracted hunters not only in Egypt but wherever ancient civilisations had flourished, as shown by Wahb (*Al-Tijan*: 87, 209f, 220f) who describes hidden treasures in South Arabia, and by the anonymous folktales *Al-Ḥikayat Al-ᶜAjiba* (57ff) describing those of Iraq and Persia. But even when the medieval Arab sources narrate tales of treasure hunting in countries other than Egypt, they often use recognisable pharaonic motifs, showing the influence of Egypt as the land of treasures par excellence. Al-Qalqashandi (*Ṣubḥ* 3: 310) quoted earlier Arabic sources stating that Egypt had countless treasures, saying that 'it is said that it has no place without a treasure'.

There is a wealth of material in Arab writings which not only describes excavations and finds, throwing light on the methodology and beliefs of the period, but also provides some continuity to the present day, when illegal searches for 'Pharaohs' Treasures' are a daily occurrence (ᶜAbd Al-Bar 2000: 70ff). As an indication of the growing illegal search for such treasure, current demand for the material known in Arabic as '*Z'ibaq aḥmar*', 'red mercury', has increased greatly because of the belief among today's treasure hunters that its use in the magic formula performed to open up the treasures makes the formula more effective (ᶜAbd Al-Bar 2000: 73)

The continuation of treasure hunting into modern Egypt was of great concern to early archaeologists. Gaston Maspero, who was familiar with the circulating Arabic manuals for treasure hunters, asked Ahmed Kamal to publish one such manual. His idea was that, by making widely available what is perceived to be secret knowledge at the disposal of only a small elite, such books would be discredited and would become less effective for instigating illegal excavations. So in 1907 Kamal published the text *Kitab Al-Dur Al-Maknuz wa Al-Sir Al-Ma*^{c}*zuz fi Al-Dalayal wa Al-Khabaya wa Al-Dafa'n wa Al-Kunuz*, 'Book of the Treasured Pearls and Hidden Secret on Indications, Cachets, Burials and Treasures'. It was published by the Egyptian Antiquity Service and printed at the French Press. Whether this initiative was as successful as Maspero hoped is debatable (Daressy 1917: 175). But the work also drew attention to its possible value for archaeologists interested in the topographical study of Egyptian place names and other geographical information (Daressy *ibid*). In spite of expressing doubts as to the value of such an endeavour, Daressy (*ibid*: 176ff) himself managed to extract some useful information on place names from it. It may be that the full potential of these manuals to archaeologists has not yet been realised.

The manuals I have studied give many names of sites unknown to present day archaeologists, particularly in the Delta where the sites have disappeared under recent urban development.

IMPETUS FOR ARAB TREASURE HUNTERS

Medieval Arab fascination with Egypt as the land of hidden treasure was reinforced by the Qur'an in the story of the Pharaoh and Moses. There are several references to the wealth and treasures of Pharaoh (Q10: 88; Q26: 57–58). Great treasures also belonged to Qarun, a member of Moses' tribe (Q28: 76–83) whose wealth was said to have been so vast that it required a team of strong men to carry even the keys to the vaults. The treasures of Qarun were sunk into the earth by God as a punishment, and were presumably hidden in the land of Egypt (cf the story of Korah and his group in the Old Testament, Numbers 16: 1–35). This was also the fate of the treasures of Pharaoh for disobeying God. His throne was said to have reappeared whenever the Nile level dropped very low, possibly at the island of Giza known as *Jazirat al-dhahab* (Island of Gold) (Al-Wahrani *Manamat*: 184–86).

For medieval treasure hunters, proof of ancient wealth was still evident in their own time from the vast wealth commanded by local Egyptians (Copts). Many wealthy Copts enjoyed showing off their riches and status to visiting rulers and caliphs, and gave them huge amounts of money as gifts, as recorded during the visits of ^{c}Abd Al-Malik Ibn Marwan in the year 709 CE, and Al-Ma'moun in the year 833 CE (Al-Qaddumi 1996: 119f and 128f). These stories of vast wealth in the hands of contemporary Copts, seen and described by Arab writers, were indications that the tales of their ancestors' vast hidden treasures must be true, adding more fuel to the passion for treasure hunting, if indeed such was needed.

It was also known that the ruling classes of Islamic Egypt had accumulated vast wealth, some of which was carefully hidden, particularly in times of political or economic trouble. According to Al-Suyuṭi (*Al-Kanz*: 54) a Mamluk named Saif Al-Din Ibn Salar, originally a Tartar slave, was arrested and his wealth confiscated by Sulṭan Qalaun (ruled 1280–90). Even after his arrest, a servant informed the authorities that they had missed gold treasures plastered behind two walls and underneath a fountain. Gossip about events such as this, even hundreds of years later, must have encouraged many others to seek out treasures, and this still continues.

ECONOMICS OF TREASURE HUNTING IN ISLAMIC EGYPT

Medieval Arabic sources (eg *Akhbar Al-Zaman*: 243) describe the ancient Egyptian exploitation of hidden treasure for the national economic benefit of the country, citing for example the deeds of a king called 'Zalma' who 'exploited some treasures and spent them on building towns and housing, and dug many canals'. This has an echo of a real ancient Egyptian practice by which pharaohs ordered the digging of irrigation canals and the building of new towns, as can be interpreted from early iconography showing the king of Egypt involved in water projects (Butzer 1976) and from the spread of the title *imy-r3 niwwt m3wt*, 'Overseer of the New Settlements' (for this title see Jones 2000 1: 150f).

In Islamic Egypt the economic benefits of finding treasure continued to play a significant role in maintaining interest in ancient Egyptian sites, as the State, at times, came to be largely dependent on exploiting gold from pharaonic tombs. During the 9th century, Ibn Ṭulun discovered huge amounts of pharaonic gold which he spent on building a hospital, his famous mosque and other state projects (Al-Balawi *Sirat*: 76). This gold was estimated to be more than 4,000 kilograms in weight (Al-Shurbagi 1994: 106).

STATE REGULATION OF TREASURE HUNTING

Having realised the economic potential for the state treasury, Ibn Ṭulun made the exploitation of these gold resources a state monopoly (Rabie 1972: 169) and decreed that nobody was to be allowed to dig anywhere without first seeking permission from the authorities and then being accompanied by a state official (Al-Balawi *Sirat*: 195). This is perhaps the oldest official attempt to organise the profession of 'Treasure Hunters', or '*Al-Maṭalibeen*' ('seekers'), under the supervision of a senior official close to the ruler.

The profession reached its zenith under the Fatimid Dynasty (10th–12th centuries), perhaps partly due to the Fatimids' interest in the ancient sciences of alchemy, magic and astrology which were all associated with Ancient Egypt and were also useful to treasure hunters. During the reign of Al-Mustanṣir (mid-11th century), some 18,000 books on these 'Ancient Sciences' were found in the palace library which held, according to some accounts, more that 600,000 books (Ibn Al-Ṭuwayr *Nuzhat*: 127; Al-Maqrizi *Itᶜaz* 2: 294; Halm 1997: 77). In addition to being a profession, treasure hunting was also an occult science (Irwin 1994: 187–88), and was treated as a serious topic by some of the most eminent early Arab scholars such as the 9th century Al-Kindi (Burnett *et al* 1997). Al-Mustanir appointed a senior confidant to head the profession, named 'Emir Al-Maṭalibeen' (Overseer of Treasure Hunters). As well as being in charge of the treasure hunters he collected the dues for the Caliph. So considerable was the wealth and importance of this Emir that the traveller Naṣir-e Khisraw, who visited Egypt in the mid-11th century, said of him:

> While I was in Egypt (in the year 1050), news arrived that the king of Aleppo, whose ancestors had been kings of Aleppo, had rebelled against the Sulṭan, his overlord (Caliph Al-Mustanṣir). The Sulṭan had a servant called 'ᶜOmdat Al-Dawla' who was the Emir of the Maṭalibeen and enormously rich and propertied. Maṭalibi is what they call the people who dig for buried treasure in the graves of Egypt. From the Maghreb (Morocco) and the lands of Egypt and Syria come people who endure many hardships and spend a lot of (their own) money in those graves and rock piles. Many a time buried treasure is discovered , although often much outlay is made without anything being found. They say that in those places the wealth of the pharaohs is buried. Whenever anyone does find something, one fifth is given to the Sulṭan and the rest belongs to the finder. At any rate the Sulṭan dispatched this 'ᶜOmdat al-Dawla' to that province with great pomp and circumstance, outfitting him with all the trappings of kings, such as canopies, pavilions, and so on. When he reached Aleppo he waged war and was killed. He had so much wealth that it took two months for it to be transferred from his treasury to the Sulṭan's. (Naṣir-e Khisraw *Sefernama*: 129, English trans 62)

This royal servant, named Rafq in Al-Maqrizi (*Itᶜaz* 2: 137 and 209ff), must have had a very high status with the title 'ᶜOmdat al-Dawla' which means 'Doyen' or 'Pillar of the State' (Al-Pasha 1989: 407ff). The tithe of one-fifth required by the Sulṭan is in keeping with contemporary interpretation of Islamic law, which allowed the finder to keep his find provided he gave one-fifth to the Sulṭan (ᶜAbd Al-Bar 2000: 89).

The supervision of treasure hunters which started under Ibn Ṭulun developed, under the Fatimids, into a guild with its head known as Naqeeb Al-Maṭalibeen 'Chairman of the Guild'. Al-Maqrizi (*Itᶜaz* 2: 88) regarded the death of one such chairman as an event important enough to be noted in his historical annals, in this case a man named Abu Al-Ḥassan ᶜAli Ibn Ibrahim Al-Nursi (d 1010 CE).

Treasure hunters from North Africa and Greater Syria, as well as from Egypt, were encouraged to search for hidden treasures at their own expense under the supervision of the government (Al-Shurbagi 1994: 107).

As well as being a career, treasure hunting was also a popular hobby. Ibn Qadi Shuhba, listing the death of Sheikh Muhammad Ibn Mubarak Al-Athari (The Antiquarian), Keeper of the Relics of the Prophet, among the events of the year 1403 CE, said of him that:

> He was obsessed with treasure hunting, spending all his earnings on the search, but never gained any. (Ibn Qadi Shuhba *Tarikh* 4: 391)

The hobby was likened to a plague by Al-Baghdadi (*Al-Ifadah*: 111), who noted that even poor people took up treasure hunting and would go to rich people to borrow the money needed, giving false assurances and claiming to have acquired esoteric knowledge that would guide the hunter to treasures. Remarkably, this same phenomenon of the quest for treasure beneath Egyptian monuments has continued since the medieval period (Najib 1895: 77; Bachatly 1931; Wainwright 1931; Isma'il 1934: 82–85) and it is still regularly reported in Egyptian newspapers that rich businessmen are being deceived by treasure hunters. These persons normally disappear with the large amounts of money extracted from their sponsors, who are usually too embarrassed to report the tricksters to the police as, of course, the whole endeavour is illegal (eg *Al-Ahram*, 6 September 2001, 10 December 2001).

MANUALS OF TREASURE HUNTERS

This new industry needed sources that people could utilise in their search for treasure; so practitioners from a variety of groups, such as alchemists, magicians and experienced treasure hunters, wrote many guide books which proved to be best sellers. These books, which usually have in their titles a reference to treasure hunting, became holy books for the hunters. Practitioners of magic produced a different type of material, as the treasures were supposed to be protected by ancient magical talismans which had to be neutralised using specific spells before one could enter and find the treasure. These were already popular in the 10th century when Al-Nadim (*Al-Fihrist*: 379) wrote of them. Most of the standard books on magic include a few such spells (eg Al-Buni *Shams*: 399f, 408f; Al-Maghrabi *Shumus*: 39ff). Al-Maghrabi gives one of the longest spells, entitled *Fi Fatḥ Al-Kunuz* 'On Opening the Treasures'. It required 21 days of contemplative solitude in a remote area. At the end of this period would appear:

> a tall dark servant with large head, riding a horse and [with] a huge lion. He will speak to you but do not answer him. After 35 days, a person will appear, with a dog's face and a human body. He will greet you, do not answer him and he will go away. On day 42, seventy men wearing green shall greet you and you shall answer their greeting. They will say that whatever you demand, they have. Then you will say: 'I ask from Allah and then from you that you gather me with (introduce me to) the Prince, your Sulṭan, the successor of Dimryat the hero, called Al-Ṭaous' (The Peacock). They will say yes and they will leave you. On day 47, a white city will appear to you. It has a great army of cavaliers occupying the valley and the mountain and their noise reaches the horizons. Then, tents will be set up at the gate of this city. The first tent is a dome of green silk with a red ruby on top, and inside it is a golden throne inlaid with pearls and rubies. There you will see an army dressed in white and among them is the *Imam* (Leader) called Al-Ṭaous dressed in a garment that blinds the eyes with its brilliance, and above his head are the Spirits and the Leader of the pious *jinnis* and the Ruler of the *ᶜifrits* and treasure guardians.
>
> After hearing welcoming words, you shall offer incense of *liban dhakar* (olibanum), red *sandal* (sandalwood) and *sant* (acacia). When the king burns this incense, you shall say: 'O King Al-Ṭaous, I request from you the secret of turning rocks and opening caves and homes and whatever more I want.' The king then will call the heads of his court and all will gather around the burning incense which is their food. When the smoke stops, he will order his vizier who in turn will order his jinnis and ᶜifrits to open whatever you want whenever you read the spell. They all answer yes

> and disappear immediately. Now you can continue your contemplation for a while longer and be grateful to Allah, as from now on you will be able to open anything you want by reciting the spell and burning the incense. (Al-Maghrabi *Shumus*: 39ff)

This is followed by the text of the spell which invokes all kinds of spirits and even prophets like Akhnukh, Soliman and Muhammad. As with most spells it is not intended to be easily understood.

Another spell by the same magician (Al-Maghrabi *Shumus*: 43f) is entitled 'On Lowering the Water' (*fi taghwir al-miyah*), and explains how many ancient treasures were protected by magic water. Then follows a spell in the form of a Table with 47 squares. Each square holds a word and a whole line forms a Qur'anic verse (Q67: 30) which says: 'Say. See ye! If your stream be some morning lost [in the ground], who then can supply you with clear flowing water?'

Treasure hunters were interested not only in gold. Throughout their manuals, references are made to looking out for medicines such as *koḥl*, which heals blindness, and medicine for leprosy (MS Arabe 1765 Bibliothèque Nationale, Paris: fol 38a). In addition, some were seeking ancient Egyptian books of wisdom and sciences, especially magic (Al-Idrisi *Anwar*: 100). In the Arabic epic of the pre-Islam Yemeni king Saif Ibn Dhi Yazan, he travelled through Egypt's pharaonic landscape searching for 'The Book of the Nile' (Lyons 1995 1: 11, 2: 241f). This followed much earlier traditions as told in the Demotic story of Setne searching in ancient tombs for the magic book of Thoth (Griffith 1900; Lichtheim 1980: 127). It was common for alchemists to claim to have found hidden books on alchemy, written by Hermes, in underground passages of Egyptian temples.

Some treasure hunters were also reliable sources of information for scholars of Egyptian history, as we read in Al-Idrisi (*Anwar*: 75f), who was told by Sheikh Abu Al-Futuḥ Al-Maṭalibi (the head of treasure hunters) of an expedition with a group of his colleagues in the area east of Ḥelwan. Al-Idrisi collated this account with that of another head of treasure hunters who brought to him a book on the subject that refers to about 70 pyramids on Muqaṭam Mountain:

> Walk east until you pass by the area with lots of black roots like wood (Petrified Forest) till you find a cave . . . and until you get to a high mountain leading to the tombs. Look down the valley and you will see a mound stretched in the valley of a mountain, and nearby seventy pyramids of black stones. Measure from the front of each pyramid seventy one feet and dig. Go down seventy steps cut out in the mountain; you will find closed houses to right and left. Open carefully; you will find money, gems and inlaid jewellery. (Al-Idrisi *Anwar*: 76)

At least some features of this landscape can be recognised, in particular his reference to the Petrified Forest which is in the vicinity of the area now called Qaṭamiyah in the desert east of Maᶜadi, Cairo (on this forest see Ibrahim 1943, 1953; Said 1990: 466 with other references therein). It has only recently been made a Nature Reserve Area, after much petrified wood had been carried off with the sand supplied as a building material for the people of Cairo. The rest of Al-Idrisi's account is yet to be investigated.

In the manuals, the way to treasure is often via churches or monasteries and, in fewer cases, mosques, which surely indicates a knowledge, or at least an expectation, among treasure hunters that they were built on top of ancient sites. This is not an unreasonable expectation, as many Christian and Moslem places of worship were indeed built within or on top of earlier pharaonic buildings (eg the Mosque of Abu Al-Ḥagag on top of Luxor Temple, the churches in the temples of Philae and El-Sebou[c], the Monastery of Jeremias in Saqqara and the monasteries that once topped the Hatshepsut Temple in Deir Al-Bahri, Luxor. For Coptic sites within pharaonic sites see Meinardus 1965, especially 313ff).

The treasure hunters were already attracting unwanted attention in the 13th century. Al-Jobri wrote a book exposing deceptions in various trades and professions, in which he dedicated a whole chapter to the tricks of the treasure hunters (*Al-Mukhtar*: 81f). He lamented that the temptations of treasure hunting cut across all classes of society from lowest to highest. But the purpose of writing manuals for treasure hunters was not always personal gain. The author of MS Arabe 2765 Bibliothèque Nationale, Paris (fol 64b) states that his motive in encouraging treasure hunting was to raise funds for charitable causes. This reason was not accepted by a leading Moslem Jurist, Ibn Al-Haj (d 1337). In his book (*Al-Madkhal* 3: 138–44) he judged treasure hunting to be incompatible with the teaching of Islam and called it an illness. It seems from his work (*ibid*: 142) that treasure hunting in his day had reached a dangerous level and was carried out not in secret but in daylight and in public, leading to the demolition of many public and private buildings. If one wanted to have someone's property destroyed, all one had to do was produce a false paper, making the forgery look ancient by passing it over incense, referring to an antique treasure under that property, and leaving it where treasure hunters would find it. Ibn Al-Haj also commented on the spread of treasure-hunting manuals, saying they too were forgeries to make money from the poor. Perhaps the most important legal judgment he handed down was that any treasure found in Egypt, a country which was 'annexed by peaceful agreement' (*ahl sulḥ*), belonged to its people and their descendants collectively (*Al-Madkhal* 3: 143).

EXAMPLES OF MANUALS

I have studied in depth three of these manuals in the Arabic collection of the Bibliothèque Nationale, Paris. These are MSS Arabe 2764, 2765 and 2767. They are unascribed and are likely to have been selections copied from a master manual of an older author, as most of the text is repeated between these three manuscripts. It is difficult to assign a date to them but MS 2765 was copied in the 17th century (De Slane 1883–95: 498). In MS Arabe 2764 folio 89a, the writer says he copied it from *Kitab Al-Umm Al-Akbar fi Kashf Ma[c]adin Miṣr Babylun min Tarikh Al-Mulk* (The Grand Original Book on Discovering the Minerals of Egypt, of Babylon, from the [beginning of its] History of Kingship). There are also repetitions within the same manuscript, which did not escape the eagle eye of a reader/owner who left a note with this observation on the margin of the page (MS Arabe 2764 Bibliothèque Nationale, Paris: fol 84a). Other similar books on the subject are sometimes attributed to Al-Buni (13th century) (eg MS Arabe 2763 in the same library; cf De Slane 1883–95: 498).

Throughout these manuscripts are pseudo-ancient Egyptian scripts, and some in Coptic, inserted here and there, probably to reassure the reader of the authenticity and credibility of the book.

The first manuscript (MS Arabe 2764) has a title page which is signed by several owners, and someone has added above the title 'Had this been named treasure of treasures, it would be more apt'. The actual title is *Ghayat Al-Ma'arib fi Al-Manaya wa Al-Khabaya wa Al-Maṭalib* which may be translated as 'The Ultimate Desires on Precious and Hidden Treasures'. There is no introduction in spite of two words at the top of folio 1b saying 'Introduction to the Book'. It starts immediately with instructions for finding treasure in Wadi Digla (Maadi, Cairo).

MS Arabe 2765 lacks its title page but starts with a statement that this is the book of 'Collection of Directions or Indicators' *'Majmu^c Al-Dalayal'*. MS Arabe 2767 lacks an opening but has a title, *'Dalayal Al-Kunuz'* 'Indicators of Treasures'.

In MS Arabe 2764 (fol 88a, b) and repeated in MS Arabe 2765 (fol 82a, b) is a description of the road to the oases from Esna to the west that eventually leads off to *Wadi Al-Muluk* (Valley of the Kings). This road was still known and used, as noted by the Egyptian archaeologist Najib (1895: 323) at the end of the 19th century.

In the same manuscript, MS Arabe 2764 folios 8b and 9a, there is a reference to hundreds of crocodiles and a turtle visible at Bahnasa. In folio 16b, the *Deir Abu Hermes* (Monastery of Jeremias in Saqqara) is mentioned and, close by, the *Ṭariq Al-^{c}Ijl* (Road of the Bull), which may be a reference to the *mit rhnt* (present day Mit Rahineh, Memphis), the ancient causeway on which the procession of the dead bull travelled for burial in the Serapeum at Saqqara. This *mit rhnt/rhneh* was one of the names used for Memphis (Saleh 1962: 38; Nureldin 1998: 242) and it is made up of the word *mit* which means 'way, road' (Badawi and Kees 1958: 95) and *rhni* meaning 'Rams', in particular the Sacred Rams of Amon (Badawi and Kees 1958: 141; WB 2: 441) which adorned the processional avenue. In folio 15a, the writer refers to a road in the area as *Mijar Al-^{c}Ijl* (Tug-way of the Bull), suggesting possible knowledge of the ancient Egyptian sacred way of the burial procession of the sacred Apis bulls, which were embalmed in the temple at Memphis and then carried for burial at Saqqara (Smith 1974: 13, 79–82; Dimick 1959).

In folio 49a, the author describes the *Magharit Al-Qiṭaṭ* (Cave of Cats) where thousands of cats are laid on shelves cut into the rock. Such grottoes, where other animals such as crocodiles had been stacked, are indeed known, one example being that at Maabda near Asiut (Effland 2003). In folio 58b, the author describes *Manaḥat Al-Qiṭaṭ* (Cat Burial/Funeral) at the Saqqara/Abu Sir necropolis. Cats were sacred in Ancient Egypt and, like humans, were identified after their death with the god Osiris, and likewise received dignified burials, which have been found at Saqqara as well as in many other parts of Egypt (Malek 1993: 124, 127f). In folio 63a Tel Basta (Bubastis) is mentioned. Interestingly, in folios 66a, b and 70b the author claims to decipher several scripts including Egyptian, Greek and Pahlavi (Old Persian), but none seems to have been correctly written or deciphered. The manuscript contains many naïve drawings of statues and images encountered inside ancient tombs and in several places the text is accompanied by drawings of the sites, where local landmarks are recorded. One very good example of these drawings is of the Lahun pyramid area in folio 71a (**Figure 3**).

Folio 85a describes Dahshur and its seven tombs of mud brick belonging to the Royal Harem. This pyramid is of Amenemhat II, where De Morgan in the years 1894–95 found on its western side the tombs of a queen and four princesses.

In folios 85b–86a we have descriptions of the Temple of Dendera and its underground parts. Folio 86a also describes the temple of Qift (Coptos) with its ceiling decorated with a picture covering its whole length and representing 'Miriam' (Mary). This is an interesting equation of the Egyptian star goddess Nut with Mary. As none of the ceiling stones of this temple has survived, this text represents what may be the only eye-witness account we have of it. Another important reference is in folio 86a, describing Naqada and its many lined burial pits on the surface of the ground.

In folios 86b and 87a, the writer refers to the Shama and Ṭama (the colossi of Memnon, Western Thebes), but while local legends have them as two lovers and the sounds they produce as whisperings of love (El-Hagagy 1997: 59), this author makes them a king, Shama, and his female cousin Ṭama. But what is clear from the medieval Arab writings is that the sounds the colossi were famous for in antiquity were still audible. Al-Ṭarif and its many basin-like tombs are described in folio 87a.

We encounter in some treasure hunter manuals (eg MS Arabe 2765 Bibliothèque Nationale, Paris: fol 81b) instructions for removing entire ancient buildings, in this case a mastaba near the Sphinx. This manuscript (fol 143b) repeats an instruction which is very common in the manuals – to look out for sherds as an indication that one has reached an ancient site. The manuals often warn their users against disturbing, or even touching, the dead unless it is absolutely unavoidable.

Al-Maqrizi is another important source on treasure hunting, to which he devotes a whole chapter entitled 'Hidden Treasures' (*Khiṭaṭ* 1: 106–09). He starts with a religious justification for digging up treasure by narrating an incident in which the Prophet Muhammad was reported to have passed by the tomb of Abu Righal near Al-Ta'if (Saudi Arabia). The Prophet told his companions the story of Abu Righal, a chief of the tribe of Thaqif, and said that buried with him was *ᶜamoud min dhahab* (a gold bar/sceptre). His companions excavated the tomb and did indeed find the gold object. This has been taken by Al-Maqrizi as proof that digging up pre-Islamic tombs for treasure was sanctioned. He then refers to massive treasures hoarded by the rulers of Egypt, especially the Romans, who were said to have hidden much treasure in Egypt before their departure, making detailed notes of the locations, and depositing these notes in the Grand Cathedral of Constantinople. This may be near the truth, as, for example, the treasure found at the temple of Philae, after it fell to the Christians, was taken to Constantinople in the 6th century CE (DuQuesne 2003: 11). Alternatively, he said that the Romans did not write these notes but collected books already written by the earlier Greeks, Chaldaeans and Egyptians. This may have been as a result of the story from the time of ᶜAmr Ibn Al-ᶜAṣ, the first Moslem ruler of Egypt, who decreed that Egyptians must turn over to him their hidden treasures, and he thereby acquired many tons of gold (Ibn ᶜAbd Al-Ḥakam *Futuḥ*: 87).

Stories of finding treasure moved between the world of reality where real objects were found and the world of myth where the ancient objects are endowed with magical powers. So Al-Idrisi (*Anwar*: 138–39) cited a story of two Egyptians from Cairo who became destitute and decided to travel to Upper Egypt in search of work. As soon as they started the journey, they found a scroll containing instructions to go to Giza and dig at a certain spot, where a glass box would be found which would enrich them. They followed the instructions, and found inside the box a jar of 'pharaonic glass' which contained one dinar which, in spite of their disappointment, they took to exchange in the market, only to realise as they did so that they had another dinar still in their hand, together with the money received for the first one. So they realised that this dinar was a magic one. As for the jar which contained it, this too turned out to be magical: it turned water into wine.

Belief in stories of finding treasure was not limited to commoners. Al-Maqrizi (*Khiṭaṭ* 1: 107) tells the story of ᶜAbd Al-ᶜAziz Ibn Marwan, Ruler of Egypt (685–705 CE), without giving his source, but which is in fact Al-Masᶜudi (*Muruj* 1: 366f). This ruler is said to have spent a huge amount of money on costly but unsuccessful attempts to recover ancient treasures, as a result of which a thousand men lost their lives.

The same source (Al-Masᶜudi *Muruj* I: 368) also gives a detailed account of searching for treasure in the time of Al-Ikhshid (ruled 935–46). In this case, an ancient book written in an ancient language was found by treasure hunters. The book described a place beside the pyramids, containing amazing treasures. When Al-Ikhshid was told of this, he allowed the treasure hunters to excavate it. They dug deep until they found tunnels and standing wooden coffins set in niches cut into the rock. The wooden coffins were covered in paint, most likely bitumen, that prevented their decay. The images were varied: old and young, men, women and children. Their eyes were inlaid with jewels and some had gold and silver masks. When some of the coffins were broken into by the treasure hunters, they found inside them dead bodies, and next to each were stone jars full of the same paint material used against decay. This paint was believed to be a medicine which was powdered and mixed with other odourless substances. When placed on fire, it produced wonderful scents, the like of which had never been known. Every wooden coffin was made in the image of its occupant, and next to each one was an inscribed alabaster statue. The exact date of this find as given by Al-Masᶜudi is the year 940.

This particular account became very popular and was quoted in its entirety by Al-Bakri (*Al-Maslik* 1: § 877), who in turn was quoted by Al-Idrisi (*Anwar*: 142f), who gives Al-Bakri as its source without referring to the original Al-Masᶜudi source.

According to Al-Maqrizi (*Khiṭaṭ* 1: 110), some of the finds during the governorship of ᶜAbd Al-ᶜAziz Ibn Marwan were sent to the Umayyad Caliph in Damascus. When ᶜUmar Ibn ᶜAbd Al-ᶜAziz became Caliph (ruled 717–20), he was delighted to display his Egyptian collection to his guests. This was a group of stone model figures of the type commonly found in Egyptian tombs (D'Auria *et al* 1988: 93f). It is interesting to note how the Caliph interpreted this material. He thought that these offerings were fossilised, or transformed into stone, as a punishment by God of the Pharaoh of Moses. But more interesting is that this is a rare account of ancient Egyptian objects being kept by a Moslem caliph, not in Egypt, and sometimes being put on display for his visitors. Al-Maqrizi also quotes (*Khiṭaṭ* 1: 110) a description by a visitor to Egypt named Al-Muḍarib, of what seem to be wooden workshop models, familiar to Egyptologists as funerary equipment from ancient tombs (D'Auria *et al* 1988: 102, 113ff).

EXPLOITATION AND DEMOLITION OF MONUMENTS

Damage to ancient Egyptian monuments increased as entire monuments were sometimes demolished and removed for their stones. Columns in particular were in great demand for building churches and mosques, as can still be seen today. Al-Baghdadi (*Al-Ifadah*: 102) saw in Alexandria more than 400 pillars similar to 'Pompey's Pillar', which came from the area around it, and which were broken up and piled on the beach to protect the coastline against the waves and to prevent enemy ships from landing. This destruction was said by Al-Baghdadi to have been committed by Qraga (Qaraqush?), the Governor of Alexandria during the reign of the Ayyubid Sulṭan Ṣalaḥ Al-Din Yousuf Ibn Ayub (Saladin) 1169–93. Al-Baghdadi found unacceptable the use of pillars to protect the shore as the reason for demolishing the archaeological material, calling this act 'a work of childish folly committed by those who do not distinguish between a beneficial act and a heinous one'. Al-Baghdadi (*Al-Ifadah*: 105) directed much of his anger at those who were busy in Memphis demolishing all sorts of ancient buildings in search, not so much for stones, but for the metal (copper) which he suggested was used by ancient Egyptians to 'bond the stones together'. The use of copper dovetail clamps to bond stones is indeed attested in ancient Egyptian masonry (Arnold 1991: 124).

Al-Idrisi (*Anwar*: 39) laments the demolition of several small pyramids in Giza and the removal of their stones for building Cairo's walls and bridges, by Qaraqush, the vizier of Saladin. In the time of Saladin, a man named Ibn Al-Shahrzuri, with a group of treasure hunters, worked his way into a cave known as *Magharat Al-Judhu*ᶜ 'Cave of the [date? tree] trunks' close to *Al-Haram Al-Muwazar* (the Pyramid of Khafraᶜ/Chephren) where he found 'very many unusual marvels'. This identification of the Al-Muwazar pyramid as that of Chephren is confirmed by Al-Idrisi himself (*Anwar*: 58). The exploitation of stones from the Giza pyramids was not a new phenomenon even then, as many such stones were reused by King Amenemhet I of the Twelfth Dynasty in building his own pyramid at Lisht (Goedicke 1971).

Al-Idrisi (*Anwar*: 33f), quoting among others Abu Al-Ṣalat Ummayya Al-Andalusi (d 1134) (*Al-Risalah*: 27), tells the story of the Caliph Al-Ma'moun (ruled 813–17) who came to Egypt in 816 to quell an uprising. He was enthusiastic about reading books on sciences and wisdom. During his visit to Egypt he searched in vain for someone to tell him about the pyramids, so he ordered an excavation. When the pyramid of Khufu was finally opened, after long struggles using fire and vinegar (Al-Idrisi *Anwar*: 128), they found behind the opening a green water jar full of gold, 1,000 dinars (ie the jar held about four kilos of gold), which turned out to be exactly the amount of gold spent on breaking into the pyramid. The jar was said to be made of *zabarjad* (chrysolite) and Al-Ma'moun took it home with him to Baghdad together with all the other things he had collected from Egypt (Al-Idrisi *Anwar*: 129). Once inside the pyramid they found ascending and descending corridors. At the top they found a cubic room, the length of each side being eight cubits. In the middle was a sealed marble container, and when its lid was broken open they found a decayed body. Al-Ma'moun, curiosity satisfied, prevented them from exploring further. This description is reasonably correct in spite of its confusion of burial chambers. The top room referred to here may be the second burial chamber known also as the Queen's Chamber as its measurements almost exactly correspond with this account (5.80 × 5.30 m, height 6 m) (for recent measurements see Lehner 1997: 112).

According to Al-Idrisi (*Anwar*: 36, 124f), the first time that the Moslems/Arabs were said to have been able to understand the nature and history of the pyramids was during the rule of Khumarawayh (ruled 884–96). It was he who searched for the original entrances to the pyramids, and his workers spent two years excavating before they found a standing marble stela which looked like a door (false door). When they removed it they found on the back writing in hieroglyphs, *qalam al-barabi*. This was read, translated, Arabised and turned into a poem:

Some of what exists reached my knowledge,
but I have no knowledge of the Unknown which Allah knows.
I excelled in the craftsmanship of whatever I wished to endure,
And I perfected it, but Allah is Stronger and Mightier.
Sixty months I spent travelling around,
Surrounded by a devastating army.
Until I passed by all humans and djinns,
And was stopped by waves of the great dark sea.
I became certain that there is no thoroughfare
Beyond my place and no further travel.
I returned to my kingdom and rested in Egypt,
For days bring miseries as well joys.
I am the owner of all the pyramids in Egypt,
And the first builder of its temples.
I left in them signs of my efficiency and wisdom
Which shall never decay or disappear.
They hold great treasures and wonders.
Time is sometimes kind and sometimes harsh.
My seals shall be opened and my wonders uncovered,
By a follower of a prophet coming at the end of Time,
In the House of Allah, who guides his affairs,
So he rises and is begged by those who glorify him.
Eight, nine, two, four and ninety,
This is known to astrologers.
Afterwards, seventy years will pass,
And then the temples shall be abused and destroyed.

Inside them are all my treasures,
But I see they shall be covered in blood.
I carved my speech in rocks that I cut,
Which shall remain long after I perish.

Al-Idrisi goes on to say that when this text was interpreted and read to Khumarawayh, he no longer desired to reach what was inside the pyramids. He was curious about the calculations of the period referred to, but nobody was able work this out.

Al-Idrisi (*Anwar*: 141f) also quotes Jabir Ibn Ḥayan's book *Al-Naqd* when he says that Egypt and its pyramids are the most precious treasures on earth. Jabir is quoted describing the unique nature of some of the hidden treasures of the pyramids. One pyramid held 30 pharaonic glass jars full of red elixir, each one containing a pound in weight. The other pyramid contained fine gems of different colours so old that they were no longer recognisable. Al-Idrisi (*Anwar*: 72–73) also tells about the treasure hunters who recently (ca early 13th century) opened a hole in the northern façade of the third pyramid (Menkaure). It took them six months and all they found inside was a dead man with inscribed gold leaf in an unknown script. An eyewitness who took part in this event relayed this account to Al-Idrisi.

Al-Idrisi (*Anwar*: 75) was told by Abu Al-Futuḥ Ibn Abi Al-Ḥassan Al-Maṭalibi, the chief of the treasure hunters, that he went out with a group to the 'Mountain of Al-Qena near Ḥelwan'. They crossed a lake surrounded with rushes and reeds and walked for about two miles to the east until they saw a mountain with five stone statues of horses. These were likely to be sphinxes which from a distance looked like horses. At the base of the eastern side of the mountain was a small pyramid, the height of two persons, built of white stone. He was told by another chief of treasure hunters that there were 70 pyramids in the area.

Al-Idrisi (*Anwar*: 141) also tells the story of a group of treasure hunters who entered a pyramid during the reign of Al-Afḍal (ruled 1186–96). They lost one of the group and as they despaired of finding him after three days, his head appeared out of a wall, and he was red, and was shouting a meaningless sentence in a loud voice which was not in Arabic: *'al-ṣabkh ṭabkh biriṣamah ṭulul* الصبخ طبخ برصامة طلل'. They fled and a search was started for someone who could interpret this *kalam kahini* (priestly speech, Hieratic). After a long search in all the monasteries, a monk was found who interpreted it as 'This is the fate of those who violate the sanctity of kings in their homes'. This is a further piece of evidence that Moslems/Arabs believed that they could have ancient Egyptian deciphered by monks in monasteries, though in this case the decipherment itself is doubtful.

CHAPTER 4

MEDIEVAL ARAB ARCHAEOLOGICAL METHODS AND DESCRIPTIONS

INTRODUCTION

Medieval Arab sources reflect a wide range of interests in ancient and contemporary cultures, as can be seen in Al-Biruni's works on India and in the extensive coverage of ancient Babylonia (see eg Streck 1900).

Egyptian monuments were visited regularly by Moslems and non-Moslems alike, to judge from the number of travel accounts and the amount and variety of graffiti (Vachala and Ondráš 2000: 76). Arab poets were much inspired by these monuments where they used to spend some of their leisure time (Badawi 1965).

Al-Mas^{c}udi, Al-Suyuṭi and Al-Maqrizi are examples of writers presenting comprehensive coverage of Egypt from 'before the Flood' to their own time. The writings show a broad interest in all the buildings and artefacts that they saw around them dating from ancient Egypt. Their descriptions of the Lighthouse of Alexandria, of which few are known to current archaeologists, are in fact closely matched by recent reconstructions. There is a large volume of works on temples, some of which give us a clear contemporary picture of buildings now totally or partially destroyed. Medieval Arab interest in history and archaeology was not limited to Egypt but also covered other ancient cultures, where much evidence can be verified.

MEDIEVAL METHODOLOGY

From observing the many archaeological sites around them, some Arab scholars developed a deep interest in archaeological exploration and described attending the opening of ancient tombs or the uncovering of other ancient sites.

An outstanding example of scholarship is Abu Al-Ḥassan Al-Hamadani of Yemen (d 945), a distinguished geographer who wrote one of the earliest and most complete sources on the geography of Arabia (Faris 1938: 1). He also wrote an encyclopaedic work on the archaeology and history of South Arabia entitled *Al-Iklil*. Unfortunately much of it is lost, but of the remaining volumes, number eight is dedicated to his own archaeological works or those carried out by people whom he knew in Yemen. His archaeological methodology can be summarised as follows:

- observing and describing the site;

- excavating and recording of finds with exact provenance, descriptions and measurements;
- using knowledge of ancient writings to read ancient Himyarite inscriptions;
- analysing the finds in light of religious and historical texts and oral history.

Al-Hamadani also set out to write a manual of palaeography, which may be the first such exercise ever attempted. Palaeography does not seem to have been known in the West before the 17th century, or perhaps early 18th century, when it was introduced by Bernard Montfaucon in 1708 in his seminal work *Palaeographia Graeca* (Coulmas 1999: 384). Al-Hamadani cited the reason for writing his palaeography as follows:

> Most of the disagreement among people with regard to Himyarite inscriptions centres on the variations in the forms of the character [of its alphabet]. A character or letter may have four or five forms, while the person who reads it is familiar with only one form. Since, as a result, mistakes have crept in, we have decided to record underneath each letter in the alphabet the various forms of its Himyarite equivalent. (English trans in Faris 1938: 72)

Another important work of archaeological methodology is that of Al-Idrisi (d 1251), an Egyptian historian whose extensive study of the pyramids can readily be accepted as a serious Egyptological and archaeological study. His methods and interests, as displayed in his book *Anwar*, include:

- reasons for the importance of the study of the pyramids;
- description of the route to the site;
- description of the pyramids and their inscriptions;
- measuring, and checking previous measurements;
- analysis of the form of the pyramid and reasons for building, with a critical review of literature (more than 22 authorities quoted) on the subject (Haarmann 1996: 608);
- study of sediments as an indication of the flood level (Haarmann 1996: 609);
- chemical analysis of clay in building material, by studying its mineral content in order to check place of origin (*Anwar*: 118);
- regular visits to the site to see it in different conditions, and to recheck measurements;
- noting stones reused at Jeremias Monastery, Saqqara as evidence of earlier dates (*Anwar*: 108), an observation confirmed by modern research (Martin 1994).

To these can be added the widespread practice of giving the exact pronunciation of names of places, people and things, particularly according to local tradition (eg Yaqut *Mu*ᶜ*jam*). This means that many ancient place names have been preserved in Arabic that might shed light on questions still open to debate, for example the name of Punt. The book on geography by Ibn Saᶜid Al-Maghrabi (d 1286) gives an account of the land on the Nile between Al-Kanim in the south and Nubia in the north, in which he refers to the country of Punta بلاد بونته (Ibn Saᶜid Al-Maghrabi *Kitab Al-Jughrafiyah*: 96; cf El Daly 2002).

The manuals of treasure hunters I have described above include some remarkable advice, as some of their authors developed personal skills in locating and identifying ancient tombs. One author (MS Arabe 2765 Bibliothèque Nationale, Paris: fol 143b) advised his readers to look out for areas where the earth is covered by broken pottery as an indication of ancient tombs. In another manual entitled *Ghayat Al-Ma'rib* (MS Arabe 2764 Bibliothèque Nationale, Paris: fol 54b), the author indicated that the presence of bones of saluki dogs was a certain sign of royal tombs. This is attested in Egyptian royal burials (eg Emery 1961: pl 26).

An important aspect of establishing a methodology was to search unopened tombs to answer specific questions, as is seen in Al-Baghdadi (*Al-Ifadah*: 115) in his quest for an answer to the problem of the absence of camel, horse and donkey burials, having first questioned the local people who could not provide him with a convincing answer. He also examined hundreds of ancient Egyptian mummies to settle medical and anatomical questions (*ibid*: 150).

Al-Baghdadi (*ibid*: 110f) also demonstrates another important methodology, that is, his ethno-historical approach based on observing contemporary practices and tracing them back to the past. Of equal importance to him was the obtaining of information from the local peasants in the countryside, not only from the educated city dwellers (cf Al-Qazwini *Athar*: 138).

In medieval Arab descriptions of countries, maps came to play an important role in illustrating the country under study. Examples are to be found in the books of Al-Iṣṭakhari, Ibn Ḥawqal and Al-Muqadasi, where their accounts of Egypt are accompanied by national maps with varied details of its landscape. In the case of Al-Iṣṭakhari, the map of the country actually forms the basis of his study. These maps are often in different colours that distinguish different features of the landscape. Al-Muqadasi coloured his maps according to a standard colour code in which he used red for the main roads, yellow for sand, green for seas, blue for rivers, and dust-colour for famous mountains, which he said was 'to enable the specialist as well as lay people to understand them' (*Aḥsan*: 9). This high regard for regional maps was not known in medieval Europe until much later (Harvey 1987: 464).

DESCRIPTIONS OF SITES

The works of some of the early Arab writers and travellers contain detailed descriptions of actual monuments which they visited but which have long since disappeared. Such descriptions were sometimes accompanied by a drawing of the monument. Descriptions of monuments still standing are certainly accurate and this would suggest that we can reasonably rely on descriptions of monuments no longer visible today. But even when a writer quotes an earlier account of a witness to an archaeological find, we get tantalising glimpses which may initially sound fantastic but could at least be indicative. For example, Al-Nuwairi (*Nihayat* 14:

134–35) (d 1331) gives an account of the discovery of the tomb of the South Arabian Queen of Sabaa in the time of the Umayyad Caliph Al-Walid Ibn ᶜAbd Al-Malek Ibn Marwan (ruled 705–15) in the town of Tadmur (Palmyra), Syria. The witness, Musa Ibn Nuṣair, said her tomb was uncovered after heavy rain demolished part of the town wall, and an inscription on her sarcophagus, which was found intact, tells that she died in year 21 of King Solomon's reign; when they wrote about this to Caliph Al-Walid he ordered the tomb restored. This quotation is useful as an indication of a respectful attitude towards ancient burials, and of an attempt to conserve the tomb by restoring it.

THE PYRAMIDS

Probably the most visited monuments in Egypt have always been the pyramids of Giza, and much poetry has been composed in their shadow. Al-Suyuṭi (d 1505) wrote a treatise on the pyramids in his book *Ḥusn*, translated by Nemoy (1939), in which he copies older poems.

One of the fullest descriptions is found in Al-Baghdadi, who was greatly impressed with the pyramids of Giza, viewing them as evidence for the great and brilliant past of the Egyptians. He said:

> If you reflected upon them you find that the most noble intellects were put into them and the highest minds were behind them. The most enlightened souls had given them their utmost efforts. The engineering skills brought them to realisation as an example of their best endeavour. They [the pyramids] are almost capable of talking of their people and telling of their status and speak of their sciences and intellects and expose their biographies and chronicles. (Al-Baghdadi *Al-Ifadah*: 96)

Al-Baghdadi explained their shape as the form:

> which has its central weight point in its middle and thus its parts/stones support each other by leaning inward on each other. Also the choice of design of the four corners/angles to face the four winds diverts the winds away from the surfaces of the four façades. (Al-Baghdadi *Al-Ifadah*: 96–97)

Al-Baghdadi (*ibid*: 96) noted that the three pyramids were in a straight alignment, and even produced speculative reasons for their protection and conservation, for example that two of the Companions of the Prophet who settled and died in Egypt had visited these pyramids and had written pious graffiti on them.

Al-Baghdadi tried to explain why the pyramids are not mentioned in the Qur'ạn, and placed them in a historical and religious context, taking up an ongoing debate as to whether they were built before or after the Flood, and even entertaining the idea that they could be pre-Adam, thus implying the presence of earlier forms of life and activity on earth.

Wishing to check on measurements that he had previously taken, he asked a local person to climb up the pyramid to carry out a fresh measurement on his behalf, hoping to be able to do this again himself in the future. He then entered the pyramid noting that this was not the original entrance, and admired the size and quality of the stones, noting how tightly cut and built they were and that it was impossible to pass a needle or a hair between them. He also noted that there was some kind of clay mortar as thin as paper between the stones. He described extensive writings on the pyramid that 'could fill ten thousand pages'. He speculated that the pyramids were the burial place of two great prophets, Hermes and Agathodaimon, and said that the site was a centre of pilgrimage. He recorded that to the east of the pyramids were countless numbers of deep interconnected caves, some with three storeys (*ibid*: 99) and that this place was known as The Town – *Al-Madinah*. Al-Baghdadi assumed this to be the quarry for the pyramid stones, saying the quarry for the granite was either in the Al-Qulzum area (Suez) or at Aswan. Around and between the pyramids, he noted many tombs and the writings on their walls.

Al-Suyuṭi (*Ḥusn* 1: 70) referred to the pyramidions that once adorned the top of the pyramids, noting that winds had blown them down, an observation made about the Giza pyramids. At that time the pyramidions must still have been visible lying on the ground next to the pyramids, as recent archaeological work in the area found one such pyramidion to the east of the pyramid of Khufu/Cheops. Today visitors to the Red/North pyramid of Dahshur can still see its pyramidion on the ground to the east of the pyramid.

Describing the Great Pyramid of Giza, Al-Suyuṭi used the phrase *wa yuqal: inahu kan ᶜalyih ḥajar shibih al-mikabah*, which means: 'It is said: it was topped by a stone similar to *al-mikabah*.' Nemoy, who edited and translated the text of Al-Suyuṭi on the pyramid, translated this as 'a ball of thread' (Nemoy 1939: 28). But the word *mikabah* has the meaning 'inverted bowl' which is how the pyramidions appeared to Al-Suyuṭi.

THE SPHINX

In the medieval Arab sources the Sphinx is known under the names *Belhaib* and *Abu Al-Haul/Hol*, names derived perhaps from its Coptic name *Balhoub* (Zivie-Coche 2002: 16), meaning 'Terrifying', 'Great Terror', 'Father of Terror'. It is commented upon by very many Arab travellers and writers who show a great interest in its form and function.

Al-Maqrizi (*Khiṭaṭ* 1: 323) reported that standing in front of the Sphinx was a small human figure claimed by people to be a concubine of the Sphinx. It is not clear from Al-Maqrizi's text whether this is a description of the Sphinx of Giza or of a similar one reported on the East Bank of the Nile, in direct alignment with the one at Giza, also facing east with his back to the Nile. But, if true, it will be the only Arabic description we have of the royal figure that once stood below the head of the Giza Sphinx. This account from Al-Maqrizi may also have been as a result of seeing one or more of the stelae set up in the area by Prince Amenhotep (later King Amenhotep II) which show a small standing figure below the head of the Sphinx (**Figure 4**). This has been supported by recent archaeological research on the Sphinx (Lehner 1997: 130–32).

A long paragraph in Al-Baghdadi's account of the pyramid area is devoted to describing the Sphinx (*Al-Ifadah*: 100). He noted its size and its handsome, almost smiling face which had on it red paint still shining as if fresh. He admired in particular the perfect and harmonious proportions of the different elements of the face, nose, eyes and ears. He marvelled at the skill of the ancient Egyptian sculptors who produced such a perfect statue without a natural model to copy.

At the end of this section he noted the presence of two sphinxes in Memphis, facing each other and broken and buried in the earth. This is of particular note as we now of course have only one, while the other sphinx, of granite, found by Petrie (Engelbach *et al* 1915: 33 and figs 19, 20) is now in Philadelphia. He also noted that a section of the ancient wall that surrounded Memphis was still standing, that its mud-bricks were dry and elongated, and that their size was half that of those in ancient Iraq where bricks had continued to be unchanged in size until his own day (*Al-Ifadah*: 107).

Arab sources widely reported a connection between ancient monuments such as the pyramids and the Sphinx, and the stars. Al-Idrisi (*Anwar*: 151) reported alignments between the sun as it rises and a special spot between the eyes of the Sphinx, because the statue was considered to be a major manifestation or idol of the sun.

TEMPLES

Temples were the most visible monuments in Egypt after the pyramids. Many were still intact and regularly visited by medieval travellers, while some continued to be used either as religious sanctuaries or for habitation. Medieval Moslems/Arabs use the word *birba* or *barba* (pl *barabi*) for an Egyptian temple. It is an ancient Egyptian word *p3-r3-pr* meaning 'the temple', used also in Coptic (Spencer 1984: 37ff; Vergote 1964). Occasionally in the medieval sources *birba* was also used to denote pyramids, as can be seen in the 12th century book *Al-Istibṣar* (53); in which case the sources may have associated the pyramids with royal cult functions and thus viewed them as temples. The medieval perception that the *birba* is also a pyramid would accord with the Coptic word *brbr*, which means 'pointed top of a pyramid or obelisk' derived from the ancient Egyptian *bnbn* (Černý 1976: 26).

In Ancient Egypt, there is a connection between the pyramid, the obelisk and magical power (Garven 1993: 14). A typical description of the *birba* is that of the 10th century writer Al-Nadim:

> In Egypt there are buildings called *barabi* made of immensely large great stones. The *birba* are [*sic*] temples of different designs, and have places for grinding, pounding, dissolving, assembling and distilling, showing that they are built for the craft of alchemy. In these buildings are reliefs and inscriptions in Chaldean and Coptic; their meanings are not known . . . the known *barabi* are the temples of Wisdom. (*Al-Fihrist*: 418, 425)

According to Al-Qazwini (d 1283), a *birba* is:

> a temple in which a tree or talisman was established. The *birba* of Akhmim is a temple which has images depicted in the stones, high reliefs, still visible until now. (*Athar*: 139)

Yaqut (d 1228) (*Mu^cjam* 1: 362) gives a somewhat different account, namely that *birba* or *barba*, pl *barabi* is:

> a Coptic word, I think it to be the name of the place of worship or the well-ordered closed building, or the place of magic.

There is another word in Arabic which seems to denote the concept of a temple where idols were worshipped, *al-azon* (Yaqut *Mu^cjam* 3: 159; Al-Kalbi *Al-Aṣnam*: 109). The shrines of Isis were known as Iseia (Plutarch, Moralia, tr Babbit, V, pp 10–11). Shrines for Isis were erected in Arabia under the Arabic name *Al-^cUza*. This word can also mean 'idol' and survived in the old Arabic proverb *'aḥsan mn al-zon'*, which means 'Better than the Idol' (Abdul-Rahman 1986: 72).

As we know, Egyptian temples did indeed contain numerous workshops and were hives of commercial activity (Drenkhahn 1976: 154–55; Derchain 1990; DuQuesne 1999: 33; cf Nock 1944: 24). Many medieval Arabs were familiar with Egyptian temples, which dotted the landscape around them; some were regular visitors and some even took up residence in them.

Ibn Umail (10th century CE), an Egyptian alchemist, was a regular visitor to ancient Egyptian sites, as is seen in his account of his visits with friends to a chapel at Abu Sir known as *Sijn Yusuf*, the Prison of Joseph (Stricker 1942). In his book *Al-Ma' Al-Waraqi*: 1, Ibn Umail said:

> I and Abu Al-Qasim ^cAbd Al-Rahman, brother of Abu Al-Faḍl Ja^cfar Al-Naḥawi, went once before into [a chapel], and later on I went [into it] once more together with Abu Al-Ḥassan ^cAli Ibn Ahmad Ibn ^cUmar known as Al-^cAdawi.

(For a full translation of the text see Stapleton *et al* 1933: 119ff; and for a recent study Ronca 1995.)

It is clear from this introductory note that he had been at least twice, in different company, to visit this monument in Abu Sir. Following the introduction he gives a detailed description of the chapel, and from this Stricker (1942) was able to study, identify and reconstruct it, assigning it to the cult of Imhotep which was very popular in the area (Wildung 1977a: 31ff).

Some ancient Egyptian temples were used for habitation by Moslems, as indeed was the case before the advent of Islam. It was widely reported that Dhu Al-Nun Al-Miṣri of Akhmim in Upper Egypt (d 861) actually lived most of his life inside the *birba* of Akhmim where he studied its ancient script. It was he who established the links between ancient Egyptian religious ideas and Moslem Sufism. The temple of Akhmim was a popular destination for travellers in Upper Egypt as well as being popular with local people because of its famous statue of the god Min. The temple was still there and almost intact when visited and described by the Andalusian traveller Ibn Jubayr in May 1183. His detailed description enabled Sauneron (1952) to study it and calculate its dimensions to be 115 x 85m based on a cubit that is 52 cm. The account by Ibn Jubayr of this temple serves as a good example of the reliability of some medieval Arab accounts and is worthy of full quotation here:

> The most remarkable of the temples of the world talked of for their wonder is the great temple east of the city and below its walls. Its length is two hundred and

> twenty cubits, and its breadth one hundred and sixty. The people of these parts know it as *birba*, and thus too are known all their temples and ancient constructions. This great temple is supported by forty columns, beside its walls, the circumference of each column being fifty spans and the distance between them thirty spans. Their capitals are of great size and perfection, cut in an unwonted fashion and angulated in ornate style as if done by turners. The whole is embellished with many colours, lapis lazuli and others. The columns are carved in low relief from top to bottom. Over the capital of each column and stretching to its neighbour is a great slab of carved stone, the biggest of which we measured and found to be fifty six spans in length, ten in width, and eight in depth. The ceiling of this temple is wholly formed of slabs of stone so wonderfully joined as to seem to be one single piece; and over it all are disposed rare paintings and uncommon colours, so that the beholder conceives the roof to be of carved wood. Each slab has a different painting. Some are adorned with comely pictures of birds with outstretched wings making the beholder believe they are about to fly away; others are embellished with *human images*, very beautiful to look upon and of elegant form, each image having a distinctive shape, for example holding a statue or a weapon, or a bird, or a chalice, or making a hand sign to someone, together with other forms it would take too long to describe and which words are not adequate to express.
>
> Within and without this great temple, both in its upper and its lower parts, are pictures, all of varied form and description. Some are of dreadful, inhuman forms that terrify the beholder and fill him with wonder and amazement. There was hardly the space of an awl or needle-hole which did not have an image or engraving or some script which is not understood. This remarkable decoration which can be wrought from hard stone where it cannot be worked in soft wood, covers the whole of this vast and splendid temple, in wonder at which the beholder might conceive that all of time spent in its adornment, embellishment, and beautifying would be too short.

(Broadhurst 1952: 53–55. The italicised words are my translation of the original Arabic (*Rihlah* 68) which is '*taṣawir adamiyah*', translated by Broadhurst as 'images of men' rather than 'human', as the images are actually of both males and females.)

A century and a half or so later, Akhmim temple was again described in detail by Al-Tujibi (d 1329) (*Mustafad*: 169–71). His description reinforces that of Ibn Jubayr. He described it as having seven halls, showing that the main part was still complete. He was particularly amazed at the size of the blocks of stone of the ceiling which he measured as 47 hand-spans in length, 10 in width and 7 in height. He counted 38 columns in the first hall, whereas Ibn Jubayr had found 40. He was particularly impressed by the painted reliefs on the walls, noting their human and animal forms. He said it was claimed by 'ignorant people' locally that these figures could perform magical acts if one made offerings to them and was patient enough, as it took a long time for magic to be effected, but Al-Tujibi was scornful of this story. This may explain the popularity of the temple of Akhmim, as can be seen from one medieval Arabic manuscript, a book on astrology, where an astrologer is shown offering incense under the heading 'On the Description of the Temple of Akhmim' (**Figure 5**), perhaps to gain Hermetic knowledge (cf Carboni 1988: 70f and pl 18). Such veneration and offerings at sites of ancient Egyptian temples seem to have been widespread in medieval Egypt. Al-Nabulsi (*Tarikh*: 66–67), in the 13th century CE, referred to the popular tradition at Biyahmu in

Fayum, where people visited the Middle Kingdom colossal royal statues, of using the water beneath them for medical treatment, and throwing offerings, including money, into it, and burning incense at their feet.

Al-Tujibi then tells us that he read in the works of the masters of his teachers (ie an early book) that the temples of Egypt were built by a King called Aq who lived in an Upper Egyptian city known as Aqsur, named after him. There was indeed an Upper Egyptian king of similar name about whom little is known (Dodson 1981), but we have not as yet found in Egyptological records a linkage between him and any known temples.

To sum up, here are some aspects of Egyptian temples:

- Large buildings of different designs.
- Well-built and enclosed.
- They had workshops for various crafts.
- They had inscriptions in what was believed to be Chaldaean (one of the writings of Mesopotamia) and Coptic (Egyptian).
- They are Houses of Wisdom.
- The pyramids are also sometimes regarded as temples.
- They had sacred trees.
- They had amuletic value as talismans.
- They had bas-reliefs.
- They were places of worship.
- They were places of magic.
- They were pure and clean places only to be entered in a state of purity.

THE LIGHTHOUSE OF ALEXANDRIA

A good example of an apparently accurate drawing based on personal observation is the sketch of the famous Lighthouse of Alexandria by the Andalusian traveller, Abu Hamid Al-Gharnaṭi. He visited Alexandria first in 1110 and again in 1117. He described the lighthouse as having three tiers:

> The first tier is a square built on a platform. The second is octagonal and the third is round. All are built of hewn stone. On the top was a mirror of Chinese iron of seven cubits wide (364 cm) used to watch the movement of ships on the other side of the Mediterranean. If the ships were those of enemies, then watchmen in the Lighthouse waited until they came close to Alexandria, and when the sun started to set, they moved the mirror to face the sun and directed it onto the enemy ships to burn them in the sea. In the lower part of the Lighthouse is a gate about 20 cubits above the ground level; one climbs to it through an archway ramp of hewn stone.

Here Al-Gharnaṭi refers the reader to a sketch he made (**Figure 6**) (Al-Gharnaṭi *Tuḥfat*: 99–100; cf Hamarneh 1971: 86, 87. For other detailed medieval Arabic accounts of the Lighthouse with various measurements and other monuments of Alexandria see Toussoun 1936; Hamarneh 1971). This drawing of Al-Gharnaṭi can be shown to be reliable in the light of recent research (compare this with a modern reconstruction in Empereur 1998: 83).

The Lighthouse was particularly admired and was often visited and described by Arab writers, much more so than by their Greek/Roman predecessors, partly because of its mighty size but perhaps also because of their interest in its technology as seen in the function of its mirrors (see Chapter 8 on Science). The reference to a mirror of Chinese iron is not a fantasy but reflects the fact that medieval Arab authors were familiar with Chinese sciences and the popularity of Chinese products, in particular the so-called 'kharsini' in Arabic which means 'Chinese iron', or perhaps 'steel' from which mirrors were made (Needham 1980: 429–30). As for the military use of these mirrors to burn attacking enemies, stories about this are also known from pre-Islamic literature (Temple 2000: 218ff) and may have played a part in the Arab perceptions of the function of the Lighthouse mirror.

DESCRIPTIONS OF ARTEFACTS

With all these Egyptian antiquities scattered around them, many Arabs, whether native Egyptians or not, were curious about their functions and possible hidden meanings. In spite of limited available information on the objects, many tried to see in them secrets of ancient Egyptian sciences and magic. In particular, alchemists speculated that Egyptian objects represented lost alchemical knowledge, and a process to recover such valuable lost knowledge was established among Arab alchemists, following in the footsteps of their fellow alchemists in the Greco-Roman/Coptic tradition.

One such alchemist was Ibn Umail, who presented in one of his works (*Kitab Al-Ashkal wa Al-Taṣawir*, MS Arabe 2609 Bibliothèque Nationale, Paris: fol 32bff) an account of meetings held with colleagues to discuss ancient Egyptian objects obtained from a temple and presumed to hold the secrets of alchemy. In this work, he included a poem inspired by these ancient objects, and his poem reveals his intellectual curiosity about the statues of the temples and his desire to gain scientific knowledge about them. In the poem, he also described reliefs and paintings from the temples, which he associated with alchemical symbols.

Ibn Umail explained that he was moved to write this poem because he once attended a meeting at the house of Abu Al-Ḥassan ^{c}Ali Ibn Ahmad where he found two colleagues, Sa^{c}adah Al-Shu^{c}abi and Abu Al-Qasim Al-Nahawandi, discussing an ancient Egyptian temple stela (*ṣurah barbawiyah*). These colleagues had asked for his opinion of the stela, informing him that a group of astronomers, with knowledge of the functions of the stars, had previously suggested that the stela depicted images of planets. Ibn Umail's colleagues complained that they could not comprehend the mysterious language used by those astronomers. Ibn Umail suggested that the reason for interpreting the images as planets was a picture on the stela of a person holding a sword and about to strike the neck of another person whose head he is holding (presumably a tied prisoner). These are images traditionally associated with astrological symbols. When Ibn Umail gave an alchemical explanation they asked for evidence to support his claim, which they doubted. Ibn Umail then said:

> Our friend Abu Al-Ḥassan Al-Ṣiqili (of Sicily) brought that book which has the paintings and statues from Upper Egypt, where he found it in the possession of a Byzantine monk – (*rahib min al-rom*) – and he took it from him.

Ibn Umail departed and returned the following day with his poem. His account demonstrates that:

- a group of like-minded scholars was interested in ancient Egyptian temples and objects;
- some of these scholars were hoping to further their knowledge of alchemy by studying Egyptian materials.

Indeed Arabic alchemists generally, but particularly those who lived in Egypt, found in ancient Egyptian monuments a limitless source of illustrations for their works, as can be seen in the many manuscripts of the alchemist Abu Al-Qasim Al-^{c}Iraqi.

Al-Baghdadi described the perfection of some of the artefacts he saw. He expressed wonder at the 'colossal statues' of Memphis, where he also noted that the ancient gate of the city was still standing. He wrote in detail about the perfection of the statues from the stance of an expert on anatomy, explaining how meticulous were the ancient artists in their detail, even down to wrinkles and skin appearance, and in particular the poses (*Al-Ifadah*: 106–07). He may be the first Arab art historian to have noted that Egyptian artists had been following a particular canon of measurement to maintain a perfect harmony of proportion in the parts of the statue. He gave us a detailed account of the size and measurement of each part of the body according to the Egyptian artists. He referred to Aristotle's study of human anatomy, comparing it to the work he was observing of the Egyptian sculptors, but he made no mention of other Greek writers such as Pythagoras and Plato on the subject of an Egyptian 'golden mean' (cf Davis 1989: 48f; Robins 1994). But Al-Baghdadi did say that he wanted this book to be limited to what he personally had observed.

There is no indication that museums were built to house pharaonic artefacts, but there is evidence that the idea of a museum housing belongings of dead rulers was known in medieval Egypt. The Mamluk queen Shajar Al-Durr built one to house the personal belongings of her late husband Sulṭan Al-Saliḥ Najm Al-Din Ayyub (d 1250). Sulṭan Qalawun (d 1290) built one in his own complex in Cairo which included, in addition to his tomb, a school, a library and the museum (^{c}Abd Al-Wahab 1994: 119, 316).

CHAPTER 5

MEDIEVAL ARAB ATTEMPTS TO DECIPHER ANCIENT EGYPTIAN SCRIPTS

INTRODUCTION

In this chapter I demonstrate the medieval Arab interest in ancient Egyptian scripts and investigate attempts to decipher them. To this end I survey the Arabic sources, the probable motivations behind their interest and the degrees of their success.

Nowhere in recently published Egyptological literature do we see any recognition or investigation of the contributions made by medieval Arabic scholars to the decipherment of Egyptian scripts. Yet these contributions were recognised long ago by European scholars in the field of Arabic studies. In 1806 the Orientalist Joseph von Hammer published in London the full Arabic text and English translation of an incomplete copy of Ibn Waḥshiyah's book on deciphering ancient scripts (ca 900 CE). From 1909 Blochet published a series of studies on Moslem Gnosticism in which he too maintained that certain medieval Arabic writers had succeeded in identifying some hieroglyphic letters.

My brief survey of the available materials reveals wide use of Egyptian hieroglyphs by medieval Arab scholars and artists. The sources also show a continuous process of attempting to decipher Egyptian scripts, sometimes through a medium or third script in the same way as later European scholars. The material shows that several scholars succeeded in deciphering at least half of the Egyptian alphabetical signs.

Demotic must have been much easier for medieval Arabs, as materials in more than one script and language – Coptic/Greek/Demotic – were still available and readable. It is interesting to note that nearly all the sources I refer to in this chapter were alchemists, many also called Ṣufis or Mystics (eg Jabir, Dhu Al-Nun and Ibn Waḥshiyah). This may be due to the fame of Egypt as the land of science, wisdom and mysticism, which drew people with such interests.

CONTINUITY OF INTEREST IN EGYPTIAN SCRIPTS

Greco-Roman writers' interest in the scripts of ancient Egypt is well documented (eg Budge 1929; Iversen 1993; Parkinson 1999; Pope 1999; Solé and Valbelle 2001). In general it seems that the classical commentators believed that hieroglyphic signs were symbols, each representing a single concept. The same could be said of early European attempts to decipher Egyptian scripts (for the most recent surveys of this history see Parkinson 1999; cf Gauthier 1906; Dawson 1932; Vercoutter 1992; Aufrère and Bosson 1998).

Arabic manuscripts from the 12th century, and perhaps earlier, containing Coptic grammars and vocabularies (eg *Scala Magna* by Abu Al-Barakat, also known as Ibn Kepir (Ibn Kabr): MS Orient 1350 British Library; cf Budge 1928: 79–81; MS Add 24, 050 British Library) were brought to the West by Pietro della Valle, and first studied by Thomas Obicini (Thomaso di Nova) in the early 17th century (Shore 1971: 418ff; Pope 1999: 37).

The view that each hieroglyph represented a single concept prevailed in Europe until the work of Athanasius Kircher in the mid-17th century, when he started to question the belief of the classical commentators that hieroglyphic signs were merely symbols. He suggested that hieroglyphs might represent sounds as well as ideas, and his work began to influence other European scholars, culminating in the work of Thomas Young and Jean-François Champollion. The debt owed to Kircher in this process has been acknowledged by Allen:

> Only with the work of Athanasius Kircher, in the mid-seventeenth century, did scholars begin to think that hieroglyphs could represent sounds as well as ideas. . . . It was not until the discovery of the Rosetta Stone, in 1799, that scholars were able to make practical use of Kircher's ideas. (Allen 2000: 8)

We should not underestimate the importance of Kircher's Arabic sources, nor the importance of a good knowledge of Coptic which enabled him to produce the first Coptic Grammar in a European language. In 1636, he published his first essay on Coptic, *Prodromus coptus sive aegyptiacus*, a study which he later developed and enlarged in *Lingua Aegyptiaca restituta* (Rome 1643) (Iversen 1993: 92–93). In this book, *Egyptian Language Restored*, he included a complete Coptic grammar and lexicon translated from the Arabic manuscripts brought by Pietro della Valle (Curran 2003: 127). This led in turn to the later success of Champollion (Pope 1999: 39), whose excellent knowledge of Coptic enabled him to beat Thomas Young to the trophy of deciphering Egyptian script (Shore 1971: 419).

In his vast work of some 2,000 large pages, *Oedipus Aegyptiacus* (1652–54), Kircher quotes over 40 different Arabic sources, on subjects as varied as religion, monuments including obelisks, and *mummia*, in addition to Egyptian scripts. I have not been able to identify all of the Arabic writers he quotes. It may be that he had a problem with the transliteration of some of the Oriental names. Some manuscripts may have perished, and it is also possible that there are some manuscripts still to be identified in Europe, for example in the Vatican. It is, however, quite clear that the medieval writings of, among many others, Gelaledden, Aben Regal and Aben Vahschia (Ibn Waḥshiyah) formed the basis for his studies on hieroglyphs.

Iversen (1993: 161 n 32) ignores these Arabic sources of Kircher, and refers in his note to only one Arabic writer, named Barachias Albebenephi, who is quoted extensively by Kircher but has not yet been identified with certainty. I believe he may be the well-known Egyptian/Coptic scholar Abu Al-Barakat Ibn Kepir (Ibn Kabr) referred to above, who wrote several treatises on the Coptic language including the Coptic/Arabic Scalae – 'dictionary/name-lists' (**Figure 7**).

ARTISTIC AND RELIGIOUS REASONS FOR ARAB INTEREST IN ANCIENT SCRIPTS

Jakeman (1993 1: 123ff) has discussed a number of reasons for the interest on the part of Arabs in the ancient scripts. She suggests two main reasons: the esoteric quality of the Egyptian script, and the alchemical meanings attached to the characters. This view of the esoteric association of Egyptian letters was not limited to Arabic writers, as it became popular later in Europe (Dornseiff 1925: 52ff). Alchemists closely associated with Sufism took a great interest in Egyptian scripts. Also important is the Ṣufi interest in calligraphy, for which Egyptian hieroglyphs met all the criteria laid out in Ṣufi circles (Abi Khuzam 1995: 65–80):

- Proportion in lettering, which should have balance, symmetry and similarity.
- Parallelism, where the forms of letters face in the same direction, and are the same distance apart, like Arabic *Kufic*.
- Straightness of arrangement, which in Arabic calligraphy means the harmony between the diversity of letter forms and the unity of the overall work, and the creation of lines of texts facing each other, also a common feature of Egyptian hieroglyphs.
- Graceful regularity, by keeping the order and form of the letter throughout the text.
- Aesthetics of 'Enigma', which is the challenge posed by the unknown script. It also invites the viewer to think and inspires his sense of curiosity.
- Surpassing the 'Horror of the Void', where every available space is filled.

To these criteria I would add the vividness of the colours that distinguishes Islamic calligraphy and which is also seen in Egyptian hieroglyphs.

There is a widely held misconception that Islamic rules of art disapprove of the representation of the human form and, because of this, many hieroglyphs would be unacceptable to Moslem artists/calligraphers. This is untrue, as a visit to any Islamic art collection shows, and it is clear that the ancient Egyptian arts were major sources of inspiration for Moslem artists (Grube 1962). I have been unable to trace any Islamic injunction against appreciation of the aesthetics of hieroglyphs. Moreover, in textiles from the Fatimid period (909–1171), there are many examples of Arabic script clearly emulating hieroglyphs **(Figure 8).** The copyists of many of the Arabic manuscripts on deciphering hieroglyphs were themselves most pious Moslems, to judge from their own statements. The copyist of the unique manuscript of Dhu Al-Nun Al-Miṣri signed the cover of his copy as Sheikh ᶜAli Al-Ḥamawi Al-Khalwati and dated it 1130 H = 1718 CE.

From an Islamic viewpoint it is easy to see why Egyptian hieroglyphs would be attractive to Moslem Ṣufis. Moreover, the passion of Ṣufis for metaphor (Abou-Bakr 1992) would encourage them to feast on hieroglyphic, known for its rich metaphor (Goldwasser 1995), and Ṣufi alchemists such as Jabir Ibn Ḥayan wrote treatises on the subject of the forms of letters (see below), as did the prominent Ṣufi Ibn Al-ᶜArabi (Fouad 1992).

But perhaps a more important reason for the study of Egyptian language and scripts is the curiosity of intellectuals that manifested itself in study seminars held by medieval Arab scholars to discuss ancient Egyptian materials and inscriptions (Ibn Umail, MS Arabe 2609 Bibliothèque Nationale, Paris: fols 32b and 33a). Also, in the introduction to various ancient scripts, the writer of the Arabic manuscript attributed to Ayub Ibn Maslama (see below) echoed this idea of learning the ancient scripts to acquire knowledge and wisdom:

> And keep what had reached you of the science of these scripts. For even if the virtues of this science was limited to its carrier, the one who deals in it is able to reach the secrets of the Sages and Philosophers and what they wrote to the Kings and Caliphs, which they kept from the ordinary and ignorant, and he does not miss out on any of their affairs, for this is the science that must be passed on and only kept from those who are not worthy of it. (Ayub Ibn Maslama *Aqlam*: fol 3)

SOURCES AVAILABLE TO ARAB SCHOLARS

Arab studies of ancient scripts started as early as the first century of Islam (7th century CE) (Sezgin 1967 1: 934). In some cases, the medieval Arab writers studying such scripts succeeded in achieving the correct identification of a number of the Egyptian signs.

Some Arab scholars recognised that the ancient Egyptian language was written in three different scripts. One of the earliest to do so was Ibn Fatik (10/11th century), who wrote of Pythagoras' quest for knowledge during his stay in Egypt:

> He attached himself to the priests in Egypt and learned wisdom from them. He excelled in the language of the Egyptians with the three types of script: the script of the commoners, the script of the elite which is the cursive one of the priests, and the script of the kings. (Ibn Fatik *Mukhtar*: 54)

This was copied by later scholars such as Ibn Abi Uṣaybiᶜah (d 1270) (*Ṭabaqat*: 53).

It is therefore clear that some Arab scholars were able to describe correctly the scripts of Demotic, Hieratic and Hieroglyphic. One important source for this, besides personal observation, may have been Clement of Alexandria (d 220 CE), who stated that the Egyptians used three kinds of writing: Demotic, Hieratic which he calls the writing of the priests, and Hieroglyphic (Cory 1840: 169). Ibn Fatik follows the same order and uses the same terminology.

The Coptic language played an important part in this process. Coptic is a hybrid of Greek and Egyptian language written in a script of 24 Greek and seven Egyptian Demotic letters. The language and script are still partly in use today in some of the services of the Coptic Church, though perhaps not understood by most worshippers. The adoption of new alphabets (Greek and Latin) to replace Egyptian was initially resisted by the Copts, but gradually Coptic established itself in its many dialects as the vehicle of liturgy, literature, and sciences such as alchemy and mathematics (Roccati 1992: 292). Much Demotic material was preserved in Coptic since the relationship between these two scripts/languages is so close that, as Roccati (*ibid*) put it: 'Late Demotic and early Coptic are so similar that they should not be treated as two distinct languages.' The Egyptian resistance to Greek may lie behind attempts to reconcile the two languages by producing Egyptian hieroglyphic texts, phonetically transcribed into Greek characters (cf Crum 1942).

Egyptologists have underestimated the depth of multilingual ability among the Egyptian people of the time. Al-Maqrizi gives us some clues while displaying his accurate knowledge of this linguistic diversity among medieval Copts. In his account of the Coptic monasteries in Asyut (*Khiṭaṭ* 4: 2: 1045) Al-Maqrizi includes an important linguistic observation about the local dialects. He notes that in the early 15th century, while Upper Egyptian Copts conversed in Ṣai^{c}dic Coptic, they also had a perfect knowledge of Greek but they preferred Ṣai^{c}dic which was the 'original Coptic dialect'. Al-Maqrizi (*ibid* 4: 2: 1083) made another important observation about the people of Daranka, also in Asyut province, that 'they all, young and old, speak Coptic, and explain it in Arabic'. This clearly shows bilingual, and even trilingual, abilities among the ordinary population.

Indeed, when Arabic eventually started to replace Coptic, concerned Coptic scholars ensured the survival of their script and language by producing Coptic Grammars in Arabic together with Coptic/Arabic dictionaries, often with Greek as well (Sidarus 2000), thus transmitting much Demotic/Coptic material into Arabic and thereby making it available to a wider readership.

Fascination with ancient Egyptian scripts, even among the Copts, can be seen in the Coptic Gnostic papyri of Nag^{c} Hammadi, in which Hermes advised his disciple to write his teachings on 'a stela of turquoise, in hieroglyphic characters' (Discourse on the eighth and ninth VI, 6, in Robinson 1996: 326). This idea that connects Hermes and hieroglyphs was popular in medieval Arabic sources, especially in the works of alchemy, so Abu Al-Qasim Al-^{c}Iraqi mentioned (*Al-Aqalim*: fol 11b) that he used a hieroglyphic text 'copied from writings found in the hall of Hermes who is thrice endowed with wisdom [Trismegistus] and crowned with blessing'.

It has been suggested that knowledge of hieroglyphic writing survived among the Copts until at least the 7th century (Amélineau 1888: xxxix; 1887: 140). This interest must have continued, and perhaps even expanded, so much so that it was at times a cause of concern for some in the church hierarchy. In an earlier work ascribed to the Coptic monk Shenoute (d mid-5th century CE), there is a monastic invective against hieroglyphs:

> And if previously it is a prescription for murdering man's soul that are therein, written with blood and not with ink alone – there is nothing else portrayed for them except the likeness of the snakes and scorpions, the dogs and cats, the crocodiles and frogs, the foxes, the other reptiles, the beasts and birds, the cattle etc; furthermore, the likeness of the sun and the moon and all the rest, all their things being nonsense and humbug . . . and where these are it is the soul-saving scriptures of life that will henceforth come to be therein, fulfilling the word of God, with His name inscribed for them and His son Jesus Christ. (Young 1981; Thissen 1994: 256)

This continuing Coptic interest in ancient Egyptian may explain why, in medieval Arabic writings, Coptic monks were perceived as the keepers of the wisdom and knowledge of the ancient priests. Al-Jobry, a Syrian who wrote a number of books on astrology, visited Egypt several times in the first half of the 13th century, and was a regular visitor to Coptic monasteries. On one visit to a monastery in Al-Bahnasa in Middle Egypt, he encountered a monk named Ashmonit, and wrote of him:

> This Elder (monk) is a brilliant philosopher who knows the secrets of the ancient priests, and uncovered their symbols and understood their sciences. (Al-Jobry *Al-Mukhtar*: 144)

The role of the Coptic monk/priest as a keeper of knowledge, of libraries and even of Nilometers is similar to that of the Egyptian priest in pre-Christian Egypt, as evidenced by the content of the vast hoards of papyri found in temples and the associated priests' houses in various parts of the country, for example the Fayum (Tait 1996: 179). Temple libraries contained books covering the various branches of religious and secular knowledge (Redford 1986: 215ff; Haiying 1998: 517).

There is no doubt that much pharaonic/Coptic magic passed into Arabic, with the result that many of the ancient Egyptian symbols were known to a wide Arab audience (Bilabel *et al* 1934; Haarmann 1980: 65; Fodor 1992).

Coptic magic spells invoked ancient Egyptian deities (DuQuesne 1991; Meyer and Smith 1994: 22–25), and Coptic scribes can also be seen to reflect some continuity with ancient Egyptian temple culture (Meyer and Smith 1994: 260). It is probable that many of the Coptic magic texts were translations of more ancient Egyptian ones and indeed, in some cases, Demotic parallels to these Coptic texts have been established (DuQuesne 1991: 11). There are numerous claims for pre-Christian survivals of some of the ritual and magic practices of ancient Egypt into Coptic Egypt, as can be seen in the works of many scholars (eg Zimmermann 1915; Lexa 1925, I: 139–53; Wassef 1971; Viaud 1978: 13; Vycichl 1991: 1503; Scholz 1993; Behlmer 1996; Kákosy 1989b, 1990, 1999: 33ff). Even outside Egypt, in Iraq for example, there is evidence for the magical use of Egyptian symbols as displayed in some of the Ṣabaean magic talismans which seem to show Egyptian hieroglyphic signs (McCullough 1967: 43).

Knowledge of ancient Egyptian also came from Arabic translations of many of the classical writers, whose works included references to ancient Egyptian language and scripts. These included Homer, Herodotus, Plutarch, Chaeremon, Plotinus, Porphyry and Iamblichus (Budge 1929: 179ff; Iversen 1993: 38ff). These classical writers were widely quoted by Al-Nadim (*Al-Fihrist*: 315), Ibn Fatik (*Mukhtar*: 54), and Ibn Abi Uṣaybiᶜah (*Ṭabaqat*: 50).

Among the early important contributions on Egyptian language is the now lost work on hieroglyphs by the Egyptian priest, Chaeremon (1st century CE) (Budge 1893: 113ff; van der Horst 1984). He was widely quoted by later classical writers such as Clement of Alexandria (flourished 191–220 CE), and Porphyry (d ca 305 CE), both of whom were well known to medieval scholars.

Many documents from pre-Islamic Egypt were written in more than one language, often a text with its translation into another language or its transcription into another script, the best known example being the Rosetta Stone. The obelisks of Philae are inscribed in Hieroglyphic and Greek (Briere 1935–38: 451). There are also mummy labels and various other documents in Demotic and Greek or in Hieroglyphic, Demotic and Greek (Clarysse 1978; Pezin 1978; Depauw 1997: 42). There are many such combinations of scripts, making it possible for an Arab scholar versed in Greek or Coptic, with some application, to read bilingual texts. A visiting Arab scholar could also draw on local knowledge, since among native Egyptians there were those who used Greek and Coptic and perhaps also Latin (Clarysse 1983: 56).

Dioskouros, a native Egyptian from the latter part of the 6th century CE, composed a Greek-Coptic glossary which undoubtedly served as a manual for bilingual work (Clarysse 1983: 57). Demotic texts from the library of Dioskouros suggest that he may have been able to use Demotic as well (Clarysse 1983: 59). The papyrus *Casati*, for instance, is in Demotic characters with a Greek translation. There are a few texts which combine more than three languages, in which we have Demotic, Greek and Latin in addition to an as yet unidentified language (Coles 1981). Another good example of multilingual material, including Egyptian hieroglyphs, is a statue of the Persian King Darius I from Susa, Iran (**Figures 9–11**) which has a text in four languages: Akkadian, Elamite, Old Persian and Egyptian Hieroglyphs (Kervran 1972; Yoyotte 1972; Myśliwiec 2000: 146–55; Razmjou 2002). There are other texts with multi-language scripts from the period of Persian domination of Egypt; these include cuneiform and hieroglyphs (eg Ménant 1887; Posener 1936) and even a cuneiform vocabulary of Egyptian words (Smith and Gadd 1925). We also find Latin, Greek and Coptic conversation manuals, as well as Greek-Coptic wordlists (Diethart and Satzinger 1983). Texts showing a mixture of two languages or scripts are also known, for example Phoenician and Hieratic (Shisha-Halevy 1978); Hebrew and Hieratic (Aharoni 1966; Kaufman 1967; Yeiven 1969); Old Coptic and Greek (Satzinger 1994); and Aramaic texts in Demotic script (Bowman 1944).

Many of the Copts who converted to Islam were probably able to converse in both Coptic and Arabic (Sobhy 1950: 3) and some Copts wrote Arabic texts in Coptic characters (Blau 1979: 216 and his bibliography for other works).

Some of the Arab scholars learned Coptic in their general quest for knowledge (ᶜAbdeen 1964: 90). Ibn Al-Dawadari (14th century) (*Kanz* 3: 214, 215) referred to the 'The Coptic Book' (*Al-Kitab Al-Qibṭi*), widely available for those interested in the history of Egypt, and said that Al-Masᶜudi had used it, as had he himself (*ibid*: 36; Haarmann 1982b: 207). There was indeed such a book in existence dealing with some biblical events, for example the creation story (Schenke 1999), which was a major topic of interest for most medieval Arab writers. It is also possible that some of the Coptic prophecies which referred to the Arabs and the Moslem prophet Muhammad (Martinez 1990: 248) were circulated by the native Copts to impress Moslem readers and interest them in Coptic literature.

Coptic was known not only in Egypt but also, for example, in Syria, according to the medieval Coptic legend of Apa Jeremias, who conversed with the Syrian king in Coptic (Esbroeck 1998: 3, 19). Even if allowance is made for the perhaps legendary nature of such a story, the perception that Coptic was known outside Egypt is an indication that it was not limited to Egypt. Indeed, we have evidence for well established contacts between the Coptic and Syriac churches (Fiey 1972/3: 320ff; van Rompay and Schmidt 2001). Coptic was also the language of religious services and was thus used wherever a Coptic mission was established or a Coptic service took place, one obvious example being Ethiopia.

During the first two centuries of the Roman Empire there was some occasional demand for translating Latin or Greek into hieroglyphs for obelisks and other monuments (Roccati 1992: 292), thus maintaining some knowledge and use of hieroglyphs, albeit in a limited way.

Some native Egyptian writers were familiar with Coptic, Greek and Arabic (Atiya 1986: 92). This process was undoubtedly helped by the fact that the ancient Egyptian and Arabic languages have so many roots and features in common that it has even been suggested that ancient Egyptian was the basis of Arabic (Kamal 1917: 331). That Ancient Egyptian and Arabic are related (cf Youssef 2000) should not be more surprising than that Egyptian and Hittite are related. As John Ray has suggested: 'It is becoming more and more likely that the Semitic, Hamitic, and Indo-European languages were originally one' (Ray 1992: 132), a view supported by earlier extensive research on the relationship of Arabic to other language groups (Ismail 1989; Kubaissi 2000). The nature of the relationship between Egyptian and Semitic languages including Arabic is a complex one, as can be see in the recent discussion by Takács (1999: 1ff, 333ff; Breyer 2003), but it is clear that roots of many Egyptian words can be traced in Arabic, as is demonstrated in the dictionary of Egyptian by Kamal (2002) and in the works of Bakir (1978), ᶜAbd Allah (1995) and Khashim (1998).

ARABIC NAMES OF EGYPTIAN SCRIPTS

From the many Arab sources I have studied I have identified a number of different names used to refer to Egyptian scripts:

- *Al-Qalam Al-Barbawi* البرباوى – The Pen of the Temples.
- *Qalam Al-Ṭayer* الطير – The Pen of the Birds.
- *Al-Qalam Al-Kahini* الكاهنى – The Priestly Pen (Hieratic?).
- *Al-Qalam Al-Musnad* المسند – The Pen of South Arabia/Yemen.
- *Al-Qalam Al-Ḥimiyari* الحميرى – The Pen of South Arabia/Yemen.
- *Al-Qalam Al-Qibṭi* القبطى – The Coptic Pen.
- *Qalam Hermes* هرمس – The Pen of Hermes.
- *Qalam Al-Simiya* السيمياء – The Pen of Natural Magic.
- *Qalam Al-Nirinjat* النيرنجات – The Pen of Magical Incantations.

- *Qalam Al-Ṭalișmat* الطلسمات – The Pen of the Talismans.
- *Qalam Al-Qalfaiṭriat* القلفطريات – The Pen of Magical Spells?
- *Al-Lisan Al-Miṣri* المصرى – The Egyptian Tongue.
- *Al-Qalam Al-Laqmi* اللقمى – (?).

The medieval Arab use of the South Arabian scripts *Musnad* and *Himiyarite* is not inappropriate, as we now appreciate the close relationship between not only the languages of South Arabia and Egypt but also their scripts (Quack 1993). In addition, medieval Arabs would have observed the finds of objects inscribed in South Arabian scripts and found in an Egyptian context, such as those discovered by Petrie (1914: pl 22, no 136e and p 32).

ARAB WORKS ON DECIPHERMENT

The interest of medieval Arabs in ancient scripts was not limited to those of the lands of the Islamic Empire, as can be seen particularly in Al-Nadim (d 920). A number of scholars refer to and attempt to decipher old scripts as far apart as Chinese, Old Persian and Anglo-Saxon.

The Arab sources show that Egyptian hieroglyphs were thought to have two aspects: they were letters of a language with phonetic value, and they were used as symbols representing ideas. In this they were perhaps influenced by the Egyptian philosopher Plotinus (d 270 CE), who suggested this in his *Enneads* (V 8.6). These different levels of understanding of hieroglyphic signs are common to the way ancient Egyptians themselves thought of them, according to Lacau (1913: 1), whose words deserve to be quoted in full:

> Aux yeux d'un Égyptien, toute image est un être vivant, une réalité agissante qui jouit d'un pouvoir magique et d'une efficacité propre. Or tous les signes de l'écriture hiéroglyphique sont des images. Ils ont, en tant que lettres, une valeur de son, mais comme ils conservent avec netteté leur forme precise et définie, ils gardent également leur pouvoir d'image.

Al-Nadim (*Al-Fihrst*: 423) said that he saw books by Ibn Waḥshiyah written in the latter's own hand, containing ancient scripts, and also saw them copied by Abu Al-Ḥassan Ibn Al-Kufi who collected them from the library of Ibn Al-Furat. Al-Nadim was impressed with that copy, a sign of the popularity of Ibn Waḥshiyah's works even at that time. He then referred to two different scripts which are called 'Letters of the Copts(?)' or 'Letters of the Alphabet(?)' (*ḥuruf al-faqiṭus/alphabetus*) and 'Letters of South Arabia/Hieroglyphs' (*ḥuruf al-musnad*), plus a third one, *ḥuruf al ᶜanbath*, which he suggested were the letters that should be used as keys to decipher the (other two) ancient scripts (Al-Nadim *Al-Fihrist*: 423–24 and Dodge 1970 2: 864 with notes 185–86). Al-Nadim's idea that one language could be used as a key to decipher another is the very principle on which the later European decipherment of Egyptian scripts was based, using a known language, in this case Greek, to help decipher the unknown hieroglyphic and Demotic signs.

Others such as Al-Idrisi (*Anwar*: 100f) and Al-Qalqashandi (*Ṣubḥ* 3: 20) knew that the ancient Egyptians, whom they call *al-qibṭ al-awal*, had 32 to 36 letters in their alphabet. They both referred also to the fact that Coptic was linked to the ancient Egyptian language by calling the latter *al-qibiṭiyah al-ula* (the First Coptic [language]).

This link was made as a result of observing that some Coptic monks were able to read old texts, or were at least perceived to have such knowledge. Al-Minufi (d 1524) (*Al-Fayḍ*: fol 49b) quotes the 10th century account by Al-Masᶜudi (*Muruj* 1: 347ff) of the story of the Old Copt hosted by Ibn Ṭulun in the 9th century to help to quench his thirst for knowledge of the past of Egypt. The Old Copt told him that:

> Coptic script is a mixture of the ancient native letters and those of Greek. (Al-Masᶜudi *Muruj* 1: 350–51)

So at least some medieval Arab scholars were aware of the connection between the Coptic language and its ancient Egyptian predecessor and were able to pass this knowledge down from one generation to another.

It became fashionable on the part of some Arab writers to include in their descriptions of ancient Egyptian matters either a few lines of an Egyptian script, or what was perceived as an Egyptian alphabet, with its phonetic value in Arabic. This can be seen in the 13th century anonymous book *Al-Istibṣar* (58–59). In this case many of the letters resemble Hieratic/Demotic.

The medieval Arab use of hieroglyphic signs spread to other areas, as scientists found them inspiring as symbols in designing alchemical tools and equipment (**Figure 12**), or useful as signs for their drawings of mechanical devices (Blochet 1907: 210), such as the automated devices designed by Al-Jazari (12/13th century) (**Figure 13**). Hieroglyphic signs were also used in Islamic arts for their symbolism as well as for their aesthetic value and, according to Blochet (1907: 222), with full understanding of their original meaning, a view also supported by later scholars (Mayer 1933: 13) (**Figure 14**). Those shown in Figure 14 resemble the ancient Egyptian symbols of *Nb M3ᶜt Rᶜ* and perhaps also *T3wy*, all significant parts of royal epithets which denote in Ancient Egypt a range of meanings: The Sun, Lord of Justice, Lord of the Two Lands. These all fit well with the Mamluk views of themselves as rulers, as exemplified by Baybars I for instance. These blazons may also have been inspired by some Christian symbols (Kurz 1977).

But my main interest here is with attempts to decipher the scripts, and to this end I have succeeded in obtaining and studying most of the known manuscripts on this subject. These are:

- Ayub Ibn Maslama (attributed) (first half of the 9th century) *Kitab Aqlam Al-Mutaqadimeen*. MS 10244 in Al-Assad Library (formerly known as Al-Ẓahiriyah), Damascus.
- Dhu Al-Nun Al-Miṣri (first half of the 9th century) *Ḥall Al-Rumuz wa Bar'Al-Asqam fi Kashf ᶜUlum Uṣul Lughat Al-Aqlam*. MS Muallim Cevdet K 290 in Ataturk Kitapligi, Istanbul.

- Ibn Waḥshiyah (9th/10th century?) *Kitab Shauq Al-Mustaham fi Maᶜirfat Rumuz Al-Aqlam.* MS Arabe 6805 Bibliothèque Nationale, Paris.
- Abu Al-Qasim Al-ᶜIraqi (13/14th century) *Kitab Al-Aqalim Al-Sabᶜah.* MS Add 25,724 British Library, London.
- Abu Al-Qasim Al- ᶜIraqi *Kitab Ḥall Al-Rumuz wa Fak Al-Aqlam.* MS Arabe 2676 Bibliothèque Nationale, Paris (cf MSS Arabe 2657 and Arabe 2703 in the same library and British Library Add 23, 420; MS 10244, Al-Assad Library, Damascus, cited above. I comment further on this below).

It must of course be said that many of these manuscripts are not in the original handwriting of their authors; some are copies made sometimes centuries later. Occasionally the copyist was not familiar with the shape of the ancient scripts and unwittingly distorted them. There are a few other Arabic manuscripts which are reputed to contain hieroglyphs, but I have not yet been able to study them, due to their inaccessibility.

The first Arab scholar known to take an interest in Egyptian scripts is Jabir Ibn Ḥayan, who lived between the mid-7th and mid-8th centuries CE. His study of Egyptian scripts was so widely known that later writers (eg Dhu Al-Nun, *Ḥall* fol 78; Ibn Waḥshiyah, *Shauq* fols 47–48) ascribed to him an ancient script assumed to be Egyptian and called it 'The Script of Jabir Ibn Ḥayan' (*Qalam Jabir Ibn Ḥayan*). And indeed Ibn Waḥshiyah (*ibid*) referred his own readers who wanted to learn more about ancient scripts to a much more detailed work of Jabir on this subject under the title *Ḥall Al-Rumuz wa Mafatiḥ Al-Kunuz.* Unfortunately, no work of Jabir on Egyptian scripts has yet been located. But it is clear from his other writings that he knew several ancient languages. He cited several languages in his book *Al-Ḥaṣil* while discussing alchemical terminology (Ryding 1997: 236). These languages are Arabic, Greek, Alexandrian, Persian and Himiyarite (South Arabian). The Alexandrian script (*Al-Khaṭ Al-Iskandarani*) is certainly not Greek, since the latter is listed as such beside it (Kraus 1986: 261). Jabir developed what may be termed a 'philosophy of letters' which he called Balance of Letters (*Mizan Al-Ḥuruf*). He believed that the forms of letters were indications of the nature of things, and therefore the forms were of equal importance to the ideas and meanings they denoted. This is one reason why he took so much interest in Egyptian scripts with their very rich and varied forms. For him, the letters of the alphabet were designated figures for the notation of sounds, and the ordered composition of these figures signified meanings (Haq 1994: 85). This is indeed a major aspect of Egyptian hieroglyphs (Goldwasser 1995).

Another early scholar whose main interest was in ancient scripts is Ayub Ibn Maslama, described by Al-Idrisi (*Anwar*: 61) as an Egyptian scholar with great knowledge of ancient Egyptian scripts, and said to have translated various texts inscribed on the pyramids and other places for the Caliph Al-Ma'moun during his visit to Egypt in the year 831 CE. We are not told how Ayub translated these texts other than that he had 'knowledge of deciphering the letters of the hieroglyphs' (*Maᶜrifat Ḥall Ishkal Ashkal* [*sic*] *Ḥuruf Al-Aqlam Al-Birbawiyah*). Al-Idrisi also noted that if these writings on the pyramids had been in Greek or Syriac, then the Caliph would not have needed to seek out Ayub since he already had with him translators of these languages.

Al-Idrisi also describes an old, badly damaged book by Ayub Ibn Maslama entitled *Priestly Talismans* (*Al-Taliṣmat Al-Kahiniya*) which contained translations of many ancient Egyptian inscriptions. The book itself cannot be traced. The manuscript in Damascus cited above, *Aqlam Al-Mutaqadimeen* 'Pens/Scripts of the Ancients' and attributed to Ayub Ibn Maslama by Sezgin is, I believe, not his work. On studying MSS Arabe 2676, Arabe 2657, Arabe 2703 Bibliothèque Nationale, Paris and MS Add 23, 420 British Library, it became clear to me that they are copies of the same document, and should certainly be attributed to the alchemist Abu Al-Qasim Al-ᶜIraqi as his name is cited in MSS Arabe 2676 folio 45a and Arabe 2703 folio 23b Bibliothèque Nationale, Paris, and elsewhere in the same manuscripts, as the author.

The next author credited with a knowledge of Egyptian scripts and books on the subject is Dhu Al-Nun Al-Miṣri, who was probably a contemporary of Ayub Ibn Maslama or perhaps slightly later. The book *Kitab Ḥall Al-Rumuz,* attributed to Dhu Al-Nun Al-Miṣri, is known only from a unique manuscript in Istanbul. On folio 96a it is stated that 'this book is called Ḥall Al-Rumuz of Dhu Al-Nun Al-Miṣri' (Deciphering Symbols/Signs), so the attribution of the book here confirms that on the title page to Dhu Al-Nun, but it is possible that copyists added sections to his original material as a script is named after him in the book (eg folio 67a). It contains at least 112 folios, but unfortunately the copy I obtained from the library in Istanbul seems to lack some folios, as the last one, folio 112, does not seem to have a normal ending. It is possible that the manuscript was much longer.

Between folios 3a and 9b there are 14 pages, each containing two tables, each headed by a letter of the Arabic alphabet with its phonetic value. Below the Arabic letter are 28 squares containing the form of that letter in 28 different scripts. All the tables include signs which bear a close resemblance to the equivalent Egyptian scripts. There are in addition to Egyptian scripts, South Arabian Himyarite, Persian, Old Greek and Old Latin to name but a few; to try to identify the languages and all the symbols would be a major research project as the book contains more than 300 scripts.

The next major work on Egyptian scripts known to date is that of Ibn Waḥshiyah. Al-Nadim (*Al-Fihrist*: 423f) mentioned that he saw works in the handwriting of Ibn Waḥshiyah and that the latter had corresponded with a disciple of Dhu Al-Nun called ᶜUthman Ibn Suwaid Al-Akhmimi (cf Fück 1951: 105f).

This work of Ibn Waḥshiyah is now known from three copies: MS Arabe 6805 (cited above), which was bought in Malta and used by Kircher. The second is now in the Library of Sipahsālār, Tehran (El-Ṭabaᶜ 2003: 126). The third is the one used by Hammer, bought by him in Cairo. Hammer published its Arabic text together with his English translation in London in 1806 under the title *Science Alphabets and Hieroglyphic Characters Explained; with an Account of the Egyptian Priests, their Classes, Initiation, and Sacrifices, in the Arabic Language by Ahmad Bin Abubekerr Bin Wahshih; and in English by Joseph Hammer, Secretary to the Imperial Legation at Constantinople.* The present whereabouts of Hammer's Arabic manuscript is unknown, and it was not easy to find a copy of the English translation. In the introduction, under the title 'Translator's Preface' (pp xviiff, especially xix),

Hammer referred to the other copy used by Kircher, which is the one now in the Bibliothèque Nationale, Paris. The latter is the one used by me here and it is also the more complete.

Hammer's work deserves some attention. His introduction starts with how his copy had:

> escaped the researches of the French Savants, who, though successful in collecting many valuable Oriental books and manuscripts, failed in their endeavours to produce a satisfactory explanation of the Hieroglyphics.

This shows his awareness that French scholars were searching for Arabic manuscripts that might shed light on deciphering hieroglyphs, and indeed Arabic manuscripts were among the loot confiscated from the defeated French by the British forces (Budge 1929: 25). Hammer had problems trying to establish the date of Ibn Waḥshiyah. But it is clear that he was still alive in 903 CE when he dictated his famous book *Nabaṭaean Agriculture* (*Al-Filaḥa Al-Nabaṭiyah*) (Fahd 1971 and 1993 1: 5; Al-Zerekly 1999 1: 170–71). It is interesting to note that this English translation of Ibn Waḥshiyah was regarded by Solé and Valbelle (2001: 102) as the 'English contribution' to the process of the decipherment progress without any mention of the original Arab author.

Ibn Waḥshiyah's work on ancient scripts covers more than 80 different scripts, including the Egyptian ones. Following the introduction he gives the name of each script, generally named after kings, priests or philosophers. He then gives a list of hieroglyphic signs with their meanings, and it is quite probable that he was here using works such as Horapollo since he followed the same pattern.

These books on the decipherment of ancient scripts may have been a source used by later writers attempting to give translations of various ancient texts. For example, Al-Maqrizi (*Khiṭaṭ* 2: 425–29) gave an account of the demolition of some old walls and gates of Cairo during which ancient objects with inscriptions were found. He described these objects and left us a translation of the texts. His description is fairly detailed and probably accurate but he does not claim that the translation was his own. He refers to 'Script Readers' being called upon to read it.

The account of demolishing the gate 'Bab Al-Baḥr' (Gate of the River) of the Fatimid palace in Cairo, built by Al-Ḥakim Bi-Amr Allah at the end of the 10th century and demolished in 1273 CE during the reign of Al-Ẓahir Rukn Al-Din Baybars, has been recalled by Al-Maqrizi (*ibid* 2: 425–27) as follows:

> While demolishing this gate to take away some of its columns for some Sulṭanate building, they uncovered a box in a wall built around it and immediately witnesses and a large crowd came and the box was opened. A statue was found in it. It is hollow yellow copper on a seat similar to the pyramid, its height is about a hand span with four legs supporting the seat. The idol sits cross-legged with his hand raised high. He holds a scroll (*ṣaḥifah*) about three hand spans wide and in this document are standing figures. In the middle there is a picture of a head without a body encircled with writing in Coptic and *Qalfeṭeriat* (magical signs?).

(For the translation of *Qalfeṭeriat* as '*signes magiques*', magical signs, see Henein and Bianquis 1975: 29 (French text) and 16 (Arabic text); cf Ibn Waḥshiyah, MS: fol 112 where one of the ancient Egyptian scripts is called Script of the Sage Qalfeṭerius – *Qalam Al-Ḥakeem Qalfeṭrius*.)

Next to it in the document is a figure in the shape of an ear of wheat bearing two horns. On the other side is a figure with a cross on his head, and another with a walking stick in his hand and a cross on his head. Under their feet are figures of birds. Above the heads of the figures, is some script. Also found in the box with this idol, was a boy's writing palette of the type used for writing in the Makatib (plural; small classes to teach children The Qur'an with lessons in reading, writing and reciting poetry). One of its sides was painted white and the other red, from which most of the writing has fallen off because of the long passage of time. The palette has deteriorated and so has the writing, hence I am leaving spaces of lacunae free where writing has disappeared.

The white side was written in the same Coptic script as the written remains on the red side, in the following order [of lines]:

1st line – Alexander ...

2nd line – the land he gave to him ...

3rd line – he tried for all ...

4th line – companions ...

5th line – and he guards ...

6th line – and his strong holding ...

7th line – the king is begged and gates ...

8th line – changed his house seven ...

9th line – a wise scholar knowledgeable in his mind ...

10th line – its description [so do] not spoil ...

11th line – remover of every evil and the one who shaped it/them [are] women ...

12th line – walled also all Lion's antiquities of Baybars and it is one ...

13th line – Baybars king of all time and wisdom, the Word of Allah, the Glorious.

This was the picture of what was found on the palette.

It was said that this palette is in the handwriting of Caliph Al-Ḥakim. The most peculiar thing about it is that it contains the name of Sulṭan Baybars, who saw it and ordered it to be read, so it was shown to the Readers of the Scripts (*qura' al-aqlam*) and was read. It is in the Coptic script and its content is a talisman made for Al-Ẓahir, son of Al-Ḥakim, in which his mother's name was written together with names of angels, spells (*ᶜazaim*), incantations (*ruqi*) spirits' names (*asma' ruḥaniya*) and images of angels most of which were for the protection of the land of Egypt and its ports and to repel enemies. This talisman was carried to the Sulṭan and remained among his treasures. It was also seen in an old book called by its writer 'The will of The Imam Al-ᶜAziz Bi-Allah, father of the Imam Al-Ḥakim Bi-Amr Allah for his above mentioned son'. He mentioned in it the talismans made on the palace gates to give power to the Sun King (*al-shams al-malik*) over his enemies.

Al-Maqrizi (*Khiṭaṭ* 2: 427–29) also narrates what was found during the demolition of another gate of the same palace, 'Bab Al-Riḥ' (Gate of the Wind):

A statue of a person was found and when that news reached me I went to the Emir in charge of the demolition, Emir Jamal Al-Din Yosef Al-Istadar, and asked him to

> bring it. He told me that he was brought a person of stone, short, with one eye smaller than the other. I said, I have to see it, so he ordered the man in charge of constructions to bring it while I was with him at the site of the gate, after the demolition of the whole building. The man said he had thrown it into the building stones and that it broke and was mixed up with the rest of the stones and that he could not distinguish it. The Emir pressed the man hard but they failed to bring it, so I asked the man to describe it. The man said that they found a circle with writing in it, and in the middle was a short person with one of his eyes smaller than the other. This sounds very much like the Emir Jamal Al-Din just mentioned.

These quotations from Al-Maqrizi show his awareness of the many issues that an archaeologist nowadays will take into account: provenance and context of the find, description of the object, offering an interpretation, and postulating reasons, purpose and function for the object. Al-Maqrizi's analysis is attempted within the framework of the then available understanding of magic and angels. His limited historical knowledge did not stop him from sharing his interest with his readers. The most important feature of his description of the palette is his attempt at accuracy in recording the words in every line and noticing the breaks, lacunae and damage. There is also an attempt at internal textual criticism if only in the form of wondering at the supposed existence of the current ruler's name on the palette '*wa a*^{c}*jab mafih ism al-Sulṭan Baybars*'. It may be that Baybars' fascination with things ancient Egyptian such as sphinxes, lions being his emblem, caused him to commission the addition of his name to already existing ancient objects. Baybars also became the hero of one of the most popular folktales in medieval Egypt, known as 'Sirat Al-Ẓahir Baybars', which remained popular well into the 20th century, as seen in the account of Ṭaha Ḥusayn (Reynolds 1995: 23).

EGYPTIAN SCRIPTS CORRECTLY DECIPHERED

Here, for reasons of simplicity, reference will be made to the folios/figures which show Egyptian signs correctly identified as letters or determinatives.

Correctly cited Coptic with the correct phonetic values can be seen in the work of Dhu Al-Nun in *Ḥall* folio 12a, b (**Figure 15**). (For comparison with the arrangement of Coptic letters and phonetic values see Layton 2000: 13.)

In the work *Shauq* (MS Arabe 6805 Bibliothèque Nationale, Paris), Ibn Waḥshiyah distinguishes certain hieroglyphic signs as phonetic symbols, with several letters correctly identified in folios 92b, 93a (**Figure 16**) and 93b (**Figure 17** right). Ibn Waḥshiyah talks of the Egyptian alphabets according to the Hermetics (*ra'i al-haramisah*), in which there are a total of 38 letters (Arabic has 28 letters), and he then gives the hieroglyphic sign with its phonetic value below it. All 38 of the signs are correctly copied and 12 of these are certainly used in the Egyptian alphabet, and perhaps more, if we assume that he was using the hieroglyphs of the Greco-Roman period, as almost all the still intact temples accessed by medieval Arabs belonged to this period, for example Dendera, Esna and Edfu. On folios 94a (**Figure 17** left) and 94b (**Figure 18** right) he gives the names of these letters and this shows the need for a separate, detailed study which may help

Egyptologists to establish the correct vocalisation of the ancient alphabets, notwithstanding natural changes to the phonetic value of letters that occur over such a long period of time.

In an earlier section of his book, Ibn Waḥshiyah gives long lists of words, which are written with hieroglyphic signs, each representing an epithet. Folios 56–57 (**Figures 19, 20**) are good examples of where he correctly identifies determinatives, which he distinguishes from alphabetic letters. When compared to the sign list of Sir Alan Gardiner (1957: 438–548), it is clear that Ibn Waḥshiyah had indeed studied genuine Egyptian sources and perhaps also studied works such as Horapollo's *Hieroglyphica*, as he emulates its style. For example, in folio 56a (**Figure 19** left side) the sign in the middle of the top line is identified as *al-ᶜadl*, 'Justice', a correct identification according to Gardiner (1957: 493–95) as sign lists O 9 and O 20 are both associated with temples or shrines where justice was dispensed to local communities (van den Boorn 1985; Derchain 1995). The sign in the middle of the bottom line of the same folio shows a forearm with two signs of the letter *t*, with the meaning *al-tadbir*, 'provisions, preparations . . . etc'. Again this tallies with Gardiner's (*ibid*: 454f) sign list D 36ff.

On folio 56b (**Figure 20** right side), the first sign on the right of the second line shows a seated figure with a flagellum – meaning authority, *al-salṭanah*. Again, when compared with Gardiner (*ibid*: 446) sign list A 42, it is a correct identification.

Finally, the works of Abu Al-Qasim Al-ᶜIraqi show several correctly copied and sometimes also correctly identified hieroglyphs. In his manuscript (*Al-Aqalim*, Add 25,724 British Library), on folios 21b (**Figure 21**) and 22a (**Figure 22**) he gives a list of hieroglyphic signs with their phonetic values below in a different colour. It is possible to establish that he identified four hieroglyphic letters correctly. **Figure 21**, top line, shows that the sign for *h* is correct and the last sign on this line may well be the letter *k*, written in Egyptian as a basket with a handle. On the bottom line of the same plate the sign for *a/i* is given as a stroke, which is also correct. In **Figure 22**, the top hieroglyphic line shows the letter *sh* correctly identified. Abu Al-Qasim gives us in his MS Arabe 2676, folio 18b Bibliothèque Nationale, Paris, a table with the whole hieroglyphic alphabet (**Figure 23**). It is clear that he identified correctly the first three signs on the top line, *a*, *b* and *t*. On the second line, the third sign from the right is correct – *kh*. On line three, the third sign from the right, that for *z*, is correct.

Abu Al-Qasim (*Al-Aqalim*: fol 50a) also copied an entire stela from which it is easy to identify the name and titles of King Amenemhat II of the Twelfth Dynasty (**Figure 24**).

Among the hundreds of scripts cited by Dhu Al-Nun (*Ḥall*: fol 36b top), one is named after Jabir Ibn Ḥayan, and many of its signs may be identified as Demotic. On comparing the script of Jabir (**Figure 25**) to the Demotic letters from a modern work (eg du Bourguet 1976: 75), many signs can be seen to have been correctly written and identified by Dhu Al-Nun. In spite of the number of changes the original handwriting must have gone through during the process of copying over hundreds of years, we can see that the letters *a, b/p, t, g, h/ḥ, kh, d, r, sh, q/k l, m, n, w, i/y* have, on the whole, been correctly written and deciphered.

There is still an enormous amount of research required before one can speak authoritatively on the subject of medieval Arab processes of decipherment, and issues such as motive and extent also require further study. It should also be noted that some of the phonetic values given to certain hieroglyphic signs in the above cited manuscripts may at first seem questionable, but could well be based on some knowledge on the part of the Arab authors of ancient Egyptian cryptographic values, similar to those studied recently by Darnell (2004). I suggest that there is a need for a comparative study of the values used by the Arab writers and those in the list of cryptographic values in an appendix compiled by C Manassa in Darnell (2004: 587–617), because of the known interest in cryptography among the medieval Arab alchemists who wrote about Egyptian hieroglyphs. It would also be of interest to explore the idea that hieroglyphic signs may hold the key to understanding the enigmatic letters at the beginning of a number of *suras* in the Qur'an. This has been advocated in a recent controversial study published in Egypt with the provocative title 'Hieroglyphic Explains the Holy Qur'an' (Al-ᶜAdl 2002).

CHAPTER 6

MEDIEVAL ARABIC CONCEPTS OF ANCIENT EGYPTIAN RELIGION

INTRODUCTION

Pre-Islamic religions received extensive coverage in medieval Arabic sources, a phenomenon which was no doubt prompted by the prominence given to the subject in the Qur'an and Ḥadith on the one hand, and by the continued visible presence of many practitioners of these religions on the other. This is evidenced by works on such religions by prominent Moslem scholars such as Al-Nadim, Ibn Ḥazm and Al-Shahrastani.

It would seem that these writers found affinities between their own beliefs and those they perceived to be ancient Egyptian, and that they ascribed this to a common origin or source of religious ideas represented in the form of the prophet Idris/Hermes/Thoth. Magic was seen as an integral part of Egyptian religion and much ancient Egyptian magic material remained in wide use throughout the medieval period, not only within Egypt but also far beyond it. The Arab sources were familiar with Egyptian deities, particularly Osiris, Isis, Horus, Min and Amun. They also show serious attempts to understand the concepts and origin of oracles, healing, and the royal and animal cults of Ancient Egypt. The influence of Egyptian religion on the development of Islamic Sufism through Egyptian masters like Dhu Al-Nun Al-Miṣri awaits a separate study.

WHAT IS 'RELIGION'?

The word for religion in Arabic, *din,* دين has a wide spectrum of meaning and covers extensive areas of human activity that may at first seem unconnected. In the Arabic dictionary *Al-Muᶜjam Al-Waṣeeṭ* under the word *din* we find: a name for all worship of God, biography, custom, state, affair, piety, accountability, kingship, authority, ruling, jurisdiction, and management (cf Al-Fakhri *Talkhis*: 35). These varied uses and meanings of *din* may explain the wide interest in the subject among these writers.

In their study of ancient Egyptian religion the Arab writers had a wealth of sources to draw upon:

- Jewish sources *'Al-Israiliyat'* (Judaica), especially appreciated by some commentators on the Qur'an (*Al-Mufasrun*) (Al-Dhahabi 1976 1: 169ff). A measure of the extensive use of these Judaica by Moslem scholars can be seen in the exegesis of Al-Ṭabari (d 922) (Rabiᶜ 2001).

- Greco-Roman sources which gave extensive coverage of Egyptian religion in both Greek and Latin (Hopfner 1922–25) by many authors familiar to Arab writers, such as Herodotus, Pliny, Josephus Flavius, Clement of Alexandria, Porphyrius and Plotinus, to name just a few.
- Egyptian/Coptic sources.
- Observation of contemporary Egyptian practices, which were perceived by some Arab writers to originate in Ancient Egypt.

So we find one writer, Al-Baghdadi (*Al-Ifadah*: 110), who lived in Egypt for a number of years and who, having observed the manners and customs of his contemporary Egyptians, described religious practices and representations of the deity among Egyptian Christians as being derived from their ancestors (*sunat aba'ihim al-qadeemah*). Another writer and contemporary of Al-Baghdadi, Al-Makhzumi (d 1189), who wrote a detailed study on Egyptian agriculture and the collection of taxes (*kharaj*), tells us that in the month of Tut, the Nile reached its highest level and canals were opened on day 17, and that during this month 'Ancient Egyptians did not lay the foundations of any building' (Al-Makhzumi *Al-Minhaj*: 6). He also tells us (*ibid*: 7) that Hator was the month when Ancient Egyptians did lay their building foundations. He was citing this in the context of contemporary Egyptian timetables of agriculture, building works and religious ceremonies, thus linking past and contemporary practices.

THE TEMPLE DOMAIN

In Chapter 4 I showed that the Arabic sources called the temples *birba*, and that Arabs visited them often and associated them with science, wisdom, magic and alchemy.

As houses of worship they were the abodes of images of deities, which were a focus of veneration. As such, ancient Egyptian temples were places where the concept of purity and cleanliness was significant. Arab descriptions often refer to this; for example, according to the author of *Akhbar Al-Zaman*, an ancient Egyptian king named Ashmoun built a temple to the east of his town, which had four gates decorated with faces talking to each other:

> Whoever enters that temple impure (these faces) blow at him, afflicting him with an illness that stays with him until death. It is said that in the middle (of this temple), there is a constant column of light and whoever embraces it never fails to see and hear the spirits. (*Akhbar Al-Zaman*: 176)

Herodotus (II: 64) made a similar comment, recording that the Egyptians were the only people to avoid copulating in places of worship, and after such an act would not enter them without first washing (Budge 1898: 191; Manniche 1987: 10). Moslems may have taken a special interest in this subject as they too are commanded not to enter places of worship unless cleansed (Q2: 187; Q4: 43).

It is clear also that Arab writers were aware of the function of offerings and of burning incense in the temples for the benefit of the gods.

Another function associated with temples in the Arabic sources is their oracular aspect, based perhaps on the fame of many ancient Egyptian rulers who are often depicted in the sources as magician/astrologers. For example, Al-Mas^cudi wrote about an ancient Egyptian queen who built:

> temples and equipped them with magic tools and pictures of whoever may come from any direction and their animals, camels or horses, and the ships that may come from the sea of Morocco or Al-Sham (Syria), and she assembled in these great, glorious monumental temples, the secrets of nature, the properties of stones, plants and animals ... All was done at certain times of astronomical movements and contacts with higher influences. If an army invaded, she damaged their picture on the temple wall so those who are in that army are wounded. This is why the kings and nations feared and respected Egypt. (Al-Mas^cudi *Muruj* 1: 359)

Al-Mas^cudi's reference to camels may have been a mistake, as this animal is almost totally absent from such Egyptian scenes. But walls of ancient Egyptian temples are frequently covered with scenes of pharaohs battling foreign enemies, so we cannot identify with certainty the site described here; nevertheless it is a very good description of similar scenes at the temple of Queen Hatshepsut at Deir El-Bahri, where boats, animals, soldiers and the people of Punt are represented. It is known that many of them had been disfigured long before Al-Mas^cudi would have seen them in the 10th century. Another good example of ritual magic against the enemies of Egypt is to be found on the walls of the Red Chapel of Queen Hatshepsut at Karnak, where effigies of the enemies are destroyed by fire (Lacau and Chevrier 1977 1: 321–22). This magical destruction by fire of the figures representing the enemies of Egypt was an established magic ritual in Ancient Egypt (Étienne 2000: 21).

THE ROLE OF MAGIC

Magic was treated in Arab sources as a scientific discipline that was a fundamental part of ancient Egyptian religion. Modern Egyptological studies have tended to treat magic as a marginal subject, with widespread disagreement among scholars as to its definition (Ritner 1993: 7ff), in spite of the fact that medieval Europeans, just like their Arab counterparts, treated it as a science (Burnett 1996: 2). The ancient Egyptians did not make a distinction between religion and magic, and both were the responsibility of the ruler as well as of the priests. Arab writers seem to have had a deep understanding of ancient Egyptian magic and saw its connection with the role of the ruler as well as with that of the temple and the priest. In the sources, magic (*siḥr*) is the word most often used to refer to the arts and sciences, which were part of the duties of kings, priests and priestesses in the service of society. In the 15th century, Ibn Khaldun defined *siḥr* as follows:

> These [magical practices] are sciences showing how human souls may become prepared to exercise an influence upon the world of the elements, either without any aid or with the aid of celestial matters. The first kind is sorcery. The second kind is

talismans. (Ibn Khaldun *Muqaddimah,* trans Rosenthal 1967, 3: 156. For other definitions in Arabic and for Qur'anic references to *siḥr* see Yakan 1994: 17ff; Al-Sha^crawi 1995: 16ff; Ittig 1982: 79; Pielow 1995: 23ff)

In ancient Egyptian, the word for magic, *ḥk3,* looks, and possibly sounds, very similar to *ḥq3* 'to rule' and 'ruler', and indeed the association between king and magic is well attested (Depauw and Clarysse 2002). This may have been one reason for Arab writers making a connection between magic and kingship, often describing ancient Egyptian rulers as magicians and healers (eg *Akhbar Al-Zaman*).

Such a link is also found in Arabic. The root *ḥkm* حكم means 'rule' or 'govern'; its derivatives *ḥakim* حاكم means 'ruler', and *ḥakeem* حكيم means 'sage, philosopher, and healer'. This linkage in Arabic suggests an understanding of the wide role of magic (Khashim 1998 1: 104). Ritner's views on the subject of religion and magic are also helpful here. He argues for a rethinking of the current view of magic in Egyptological studies and puts forward a new evaluation of its role, suggesting that:

> Egyptian *ḥk3* was a most complex theological concept; only the superimposition of Christian theology demoted it to 'magic'. (Ritner 1992: 197)

A similar view has also been expressed by Goelet (in Faulkner *et al* 1994: 145). There are many examples in the Arab sources of the role of magic in the administration of justice in Ancient Egypt. One of these is the story from the book *Akhbar Al-Zaman* of an ancient Egyptian priestess, Qunia, acting as a judge:

> She sits in her court on a throne of fire. If a person seeking her judgment was truthful, he would walk through the fire unaffected. She built a palace with hollow walls of copper, and on each of its pillars wrote the name of a specific craft on which people would seek her advice. People will come to the pillar and speak their mind, asking questions, and they will be answered. (*Akhbar Al-Zaman*: 104)

Many elements in this account are familiar from ancient Egyptian materials on the performance of oracles; for example, the Lady's oracle as attested in the cult of Queen Ahmose Nefertari, written requests for oracles to the gods who hear them, prayers made outside the rear walls of temples, and the 'ear stelae' which were sometimes decorated only with ears to emphasise this aspect of the hearing deity (Morsy 1986: 244ff; Sadek 1987: 16ff and his pls I–II; Pinch 1993: 251). Listening to or calling for the deity is also known from chapels at the rear of Egyptian temples such as that of Hathor at Dendera (Derchain 1972: 11, 17). As for walking through fire, presumably those who are guilty will be burnt by it, another attested punishment in Ancient Egypt (Leahy 1984).

Some of the writers also knew of specific functions of certain divine images, some of which were used to pass judgments to disputants who were to:

> stand before a statue of black stone (basalt?) called ^cAbd Afroys which means Servant of Zuḥal (Saturn); if the disputant strayed from the truth he got stuck in the place and could not move. (*Akhbar Al-Zaman*: 105)

This shows a perception on the part of the author of *Akhbar Al-Zaman* that a link did exist in Ancient Egypt between oracles and astronomy, and such connections are indeed attested in Ancient Egypt (von Lieven 1999: 99ff).

Using similar objects, this same ancient magic/oracle seems to have continued to be practised by various medieval Egyptian Caliphs and Sulṭans. For example, Ibn Iyas, quoting Ibn Khalkan, gave this account of Al-Ḥakim, the most famous of the Fatimid Caliphs who ruled from 996 to 1020 CE:

> The Al-Ḥakim Bi-Amr Allah was a star worshipper like his grandfather, Al-Muᶜizz, and he was involved in hunting treasures. He obtained an idol, it is hollow and inside it is the spirit (*ruḥani*) who looks after it. It spoke like humans, and this statue used to recover lost objects by telling where they were. ... Then people who lost objects were called to Al-Ḥakim, the idol was brought out and everyone who had lost anything stood before it and said: 'O Abu Al-Haul (Sphinx) I have lost such and such a thing'. The spirit inside the statue then says: 'Your lost object was taken by X and it is in such and such place at such and such address'. So Al-Ḥakim sent his servants to the place, they brought back the lost item and all the thieves were then hanged. From then on nothing was ever stolen. (Ibn Iyas *Badaiᶜ* 1/1: 202)

The Fatimid Dynasty was particularly interested in astronomy and astrology with their natural associations with magic and oracles, and a number of its rulers were themselves practitioners of these sciences. This case of an oracle statue is based on well attested ancient Egyptian practices in which questions were addressed to statues (Černý 1935) which would answer them with a human voice (Loukianoff 1936; von Lieven 1999: 79–83).

The Arab writers recognised at least some of the ancient Egyptian beliefs in the relationship between Egyptian deities and the healing of illness, good health and, most importantly, the connection between magic and childbirth, in addition to deities being the source of creation. All of this is based on the central ancient Egyptian theme of creation, birth, and the importance of good health to maintain order (Hassan 1999).

In *Akhbar Al-Zaman*, we read of a King whom the Arabs called 'Shadat' who built new towns on the East Bank of the Nile. In one of them he erected what was presumably a statue of the god Min, the symbol of sexual potency, who was Lord of the Eastern Desert and Protector of the Road to Arabia (Saleh 1981: 116); his main cult centres were on the east bank of the Nile at Qift and Akhmim, north of Luxor (Gundlach 1982: 136ff). According to the author of *Akhbar Al-Zaman*, Min was well known to medieval Arab writers, and he gives this description of him and attributes to him a healing function:

> a standing statue with an erect phallus; if one who is impotent and cannot have an erection for any reason, came to this statue and held it with both hands, he will recover and obtain the desired erection and the strength to copulate. (*Akhbar Al-Zaman*: 166)

Al-Maqrizi (d 1442) quoted a description of this statue as:

> Standing on one leg and has only one arm which is raised high. There are inscriptions on his forehead and around the body. He has a prominent phallus. (Al-Maqrizi *Khiṭaṭ* 1: 651)

He then referred to the popular use of this stone phallus for treating male impotence, provided the petitioner succeeded in removing it from the statue without damaging it and wearing it around his waist. This may be also a reference to the images of Min carved on the walls of the temple.

The same king, Shadat, also erected in another town:

> A (statue of a) cow with two large udders; if a woman whose milk has decreased or dried up touches it, her milk will flow. (*Akhbar Al-Zaman*: 167)

According to the same book, another ruler who appears often in medieval Arabic sources, King Menqaus:

> built a House with statues that cure all illnesses, and wrote on top of the shrine of every statue what it would cure, so people benefited from this House for a time until some kings spoiled it. (*Akhbar Al-Zaman*: 169)

Also in *Akhbar Al-Zaman*, we encounter another ancient Egyptian ruler, King Shasta, who shows his care for the mental health of his people by erecting in his city a stone statue of a woman which people suffering from depression could visit to be healed:

> As soon as a depressed person sees it, he smiles and forgets his care. People hold it and circumambulate it. At a later date they worshipped Her. (*Akhbar Al-Zaman*: 169)

All the above citations show that for some medieval Arab writers, ancient Egyptian kings were concerned with the social aspect of the function of magic, within Egyptian religion, as a tool to heal and improve the health of the population. But there is another important role for magic: it was put at the service of the state, king and country in order to ward off enemies; this perception is supported by evidence from Ancient Egypt, particularly in Demotic literature. For example, Imhotep is depicted in some late Demotic papyri using magic in a campaign with King Zoser against an Assyrian queen (Wildung 1977a: 54).

To summarise, the main ideas of Egyptian magic, as seen in the above Arabic sources, are as follows:

- Magic was associated with kings and queens, priests, priestesses and sages.
- Sacred images were used in magical practices.
- Magic was used in healing both physical and mental illnesses.
- The Arab writers also commented on the use and survival of ancient Egyptian objects in medieval magic.
- Magic was a discipline put to the service of the state and the community.

SUPERSTITIOUS BELIEFS RELATED TO ANCIENT EGYPT

Closely connected with magic is superstition. A number of Arab sources suggest that at least some of the writers discoursed not only with rulers and savants, but also with the fellaheen in the countryside, and that their views of the temples and idols were also recorded seriously. Interest in the ancient images shows a strong element of superstition and is sometimes the result of fear. For example, Al-Qazwini (d 1283 CE) tells us in *Athar* (138):

> In the village of Absoug on the west bank of the Nile, there is a *Baiᶜah* (بيعة a place of worship or temple) whose door has a picture of a mouse on a stone which keeps the mice out. People take a clay imprint of this to their homes to keep mice away.

Yaqut (*Mu^c^jam* 1: 73) tells a similar story of the mouse but locates the site between Al-Qys and Al-Bahnasa in Middle Egypt and puts it in a *ḍai^c^ah*, meaning an estate, rather than in a *bai^c^ah*.

The author of *Akhbar Al-Zaman* (171) quotes the people of Akhmim talking about a man from the East who visited the temple every day, bringing incense and perfumes to an image on the door frame and who in return daily collected a dinar from beneath its feet. He did this for a long time until he was arrested.

Al-Minufi (d 1524) quotes a story told him by a certain Yosef Ibn ^c^Abd-Allah that looking at the Sphinx reverses one's fortune so that:

> if seen by a person in command, he loses his command, and if a person lacks ability he becomes (ably) in charge. (Al-Minufi *Al-Fayḍ*: 52)

Ibn Duqmaq (d 1406) talks of an alley in Cairo named *Zuqaq Al-Ṣanam* (Alley of the Idol) after an image known as *Sariyat Fir^c^un* (Pharaoh's concubine), which was regarded as:

> A talisman to keep the Nile within its banks. It is said that the statue known as Abu Al-Haul (the Sphinx) at the pyramids, is aligned with the above idol, both facing east. (Ibn Duqmaq *Al-Intiṣar* 4: 21)

This icon was likened by Ibn Duqmaq to the Sphinx on the West Bank and both were facing east. He then described the demolition of this icon in the year 711 H (1311 CE) and said that the search underneath it uncovered large blocks of stone. These have all been reused as foundations for the granite pillars in the Naṣiri mosque in Cairo (*ibid*: 22). Unusually for a medieval Egyptian writer, he seemed to have no qualms about this act of vandalism, saying that the Roms, perhaps meaning the non-Moslem population, were of the belief that these statues were for the protection of Egypt, perhaps in the vain hope that they would be left undisturbed by quarrymen or treasure hunters.

Such medieval superstitious beliefs have been common in Egypt at all times and there has always been a belief that divine images have magical and protective powers, as can be seen in ancient Egyptian materials and in modern Egypt alike (cf Blackman 1927).

In Alexandria, two fallen pillars (obelisks?) were used by visitors in the medieval period for treatment of illness and were known as *^c^Amuda Al-I^c^iya'* (Pillars of Illness) (Al-Qalqashandi *Ṣubḥ* 3: 357). According to the account of Al-Qalqashandi, patients would come to the two fallen pillars, each bringing seven pebbles, and would lie down on one of the pillars and throw the seven pebbles behind them; they would then leave without looking backwards and would be cured.

DEITIES AND PROPHETS

A number of medieval Arab writers describe a relationship between ancient Egyptian religion and its deities, and the religious practices and deities of pre-Islamic Arabs. Some even suggested that ancient Egyptian deities were still being worshipped. For example, during his travels in Egypt, Al-Ya^{c}qubi (*Al-Buldan*: 337) reported that a tribe of Beja in the south was still worshipping an idol called 'Ḥeḥakhua idol'. This may be the one described by Al-Baladhuri (*Futuḥ*: 241 n) as a stone idol in the form of a boy carried by his company for the chief of Beja to pray to during his visit to Baghdad in the year 865 CE. A Nubian chief praying to an idol in Baghdad may have been an unusual sight in the city, but not out of place in the countryside with its various temples of other religions. Al-Hamadani, the Yemeni 10th-century scholar, recognised (*Ṣifat*: 42–49) that Amun was worshipped in the Western Desert between Egypt and Libya (Siwa). The fame of the cult of Amun in the Western Desert may have been known as far west as the Atlas Mountains (Camps 1994). Al-Hamadani also noted that Isis was widely worshipped in south-west Asia. He may also have been stressing the antiquity of these cults, as he stated at the outset (*ibid*: 37) that he was citing as his main source Ptolemy, the well-known geographer from Alexandria.

Isis was particularly popular in Arabia (Wagner 1976; Donner 1995; Hoyland 2001: 142f), and her worship continued in various guises even after the advent of Islam. Other deities common to Egypt and Arabia include, according to the Arabic Dictionary of Al-Fayruzabadi (*Taj* under bs and ḥr), Bes and Horus, well known in Arabia, where they were believed to have originated (Brugsch 1902: 54; Kamal 1902; on Bes see Dasen 1993: 55–83). Bes had a cult centre in South Arabia similar to the Ka^{c}ba of Mecca (Yaqut *Mu^{c}jam* 1: 412). Beeston (1962: 13–14; MS Bodleian, OX Arab d 221) noted that the name of Horus was common in Arabia, and his figure appears in medieval Arabic manuscripts clearly copied from an Egyptian context (**Figure 26**). In fact the Arabic word for falcon is *ḥr* حر pronounced *ḥor*, the same word as in ancient Egyptian, and there are other words in Arabic for falcons such as *ṣaqr* and *bazi* which may be found in Egyptian as well (Loret 1903: 10ff). Names of Egyptian deities formed elements of many Nabataean names, reflecting the influence of Egyptian religion, for example *^{c}bd ḥwr* 'servant of Horus' and *^{c}bd'sy* 'servant of Isis' (Graf 1997: 70–72).

Various Egyptian deities such as Osiris and Isis found their way into Arabic folklore and popular magic (Fodor 1992; Ray 1994). In the Arabian epic of Al-Zir Salim, his sister saved his body by floating him out to sea in a wooden chest, as did Isis with the tree coffin of Osiris (Lyons 1995 1: 97). Similarly, Baudy (1986: 15f) has argued for the survival of practices relating to Osiris in medieval Arabic traditions as described by Al-Biruni (*Al-Athar*: 368f), where Egyptians celebrated a combination of the resurrection of Osiris and of foretelling the future on the night of ca 25 July, by sowing seeds on a plate and watching their growth; this ritual is still celebrated in the same manner by present-day Egyptians and some still believe that trees grow from the bodies of saints. The tombs of most saints are in fact associated with sacred trees (Hassan 1936: 10–13; Naẓeer 1967: 31). The present writer, as a child, together with friends and neighbours, used to celebrate this occasion by planting fenugreek seeds in a pot, which was then left in the open. This image of the dead being resurrected like growing plants is familiar to Moslems through a Ḥadith of the Prophet which describes the Day of Resurrection: 'Water will fall from the sky and they [the dead] shall sprout like greens (*Al-Baql* البقل)' (Ewais 1966: 113).

Egyptian influence found its way through medieval Arabic, and was carried by Islam into epic folklore as far away as Azerbaijan, where studies show the presence of ancient Egyptian words in their famous epic of 'Dada Ququrd [*sic*]' (Ḥamidov 2002: 100). (For this epic, known in the West as Dede Korkut, see Lewis 1974.)

The influence of some aspects of Egyptian religion on Islamic ritual has been noted by Stetkevych (1996). In my opinion, Islamic Sufism is firmly rooted in Egyptian religion, but this is a major subject which requires separate study.

In some cases Egyptian deities were translated into prophets or angels, in order to ally them more closely to Islam, Christianity and Judaism. A good example is the explanation given by Ibn Al-Wardi of the creation of earth:

> Following the rule of the theory of the ancients, there must be a sky under the earth like the one above it. It is said that when glorious God created the earth, it was tilting like a ship so God sent an angel who went down until he was underneath the earth and carried it upon his shoulders. Then he put his hands out, one towards the east and the other towards the west and held the seven earths (Earth and its spheres) and restrained it [until it] was stable. But the angel's feet did not have a platform [to stand on] so God sent a bull from heaven for the angel to stand on. (Ibn Al-Wardi *Kharidat*: 14–15)

In this text, we see a mélange of ancient Egyptian iconography relating to the primeval god Nun and the common image of him carrying the ship of the Sun God at the beginning of creation, with an attempt to explain the disappearance of the feet of Nun into the earth (**Figure 27**). There are ancient Egyptian texts referring to the creator, the Sun God, in one of his manifestations as one 'who fixed the sky on his head' (Assmann 1997: 202). These Arab sources show a familiarity with ancient Egyptian religious scenes encountered during visits to tombs, chapels and temples.

Another early Arab scholar to remark on the continuous thread that connected the different phases of Egyptian religion was Al-Baghdadi:

> And as for the idols, they were very common in the ancient world even with the Christians, most of whom, Copts and Ṣabaeans [of Ḥarran] were inclined towards their origin in the old tradition of their ancestors of adopting icons in their places of worship. They can even go as far as depicting their god surrounded by angels. All these are remains of the traditions of their predecessors, although the predecessors elevated god beyond any logical or physical reach or comprehension, let alone depiction. (Al-Baghdadi *Al-Ifadah*: 109–10)

The writer of *Akhbar Al-Zaman* also seeks to bring the Ancient Egyptians closer to Islam, claiming that the Ancient Egyptians:

> believe in the Oneness of God, and their praise of functionary mediums (like stars), does not affect their Creator for they glorify these mediums to worship God and get nearer to him as do the Indians, the Arabs and many other nations. (*Akhbar Al-Zaman*: 166).

Indeed, the interest of ancient Egyptians in celestial bodies and their association with known deities such as Osiris are well documented (Wallin 2002).

Al-Shahrastani, in keeping with his preferred style of writing, records a dialogue between the Ṣabaean and the Ḥanifeen (followers of primordial religion) and then says:

> It was in my mind to (cover) other angles and dictate them, still in my heart, hardly hidden (but) I left (them) out to talk about the wisdom of Hermes the Great, not as one of the Ṣabaeans, far be it from him, but because his wisdom shows what the sect of the Ḥanifeen say of perfection in human beings, and the necessity of following the divine ordinance, contrary to the Ṣabaean sects. (Al-Shahrastani *Al-Milal* part 2: 345)

This text shows Al-Shahrastani's awareness of the existence of different sects among the Ṣabaeans and is yet another attempt to bring Hermes into the fold of Islam as a natural believer – *ḥanif*. This Arabic word is derived from the root *ḥnf* meaning someone who has a natural/innate belief in, and submits to, god, and it is used several times in the Qur'an in this sense (eg Q2: 135; Q3: 67; Q30: 30). There were groups in Arabia before Islam, known as *Aḥnaf*, who had diverse practices but shared this belief in the unity of the deity (Lyall 1903; Al-Ṣabagh 1998: 63). The word is also attested in Egyptian with a similar meaning of 'veneration/ submission' (Badawi and Kees 1958: 161).

HERMES/IDRIS

Almost all Arabic sources link Hermes [Thoth] in any one of his forms – Hermes the First, or the Second or the Thrice Great/Endowed with Wisdom, known also as Trismegistus – with the Qur'anic Prophet Idris (Q19: 57) who is highly praised in the Qur'an and credited with great honour (Q19: 56–57). A good example of this from the Arab sources is Al-Mas^c^udi, who had a good knowledge of different cultures and creeds, and who also made the link between Idris, known also by his Hebrew name Enoch/Akhnukh, and Hermes. He says of Akhnukh ibn Anush ibn Shith ibn Adam:

> then came his son Akhnukh who is Idris the Prophet, peace be upon him. The Ṣabaeans claim that he is Hermes; the meaning of Hermes is Mercury (c*Aṭarid*). It was he of whom Allah Most Glorious, said in his Book that he 'elevated him to a higher place'. He was the first tailor, the first to sew with needles. And thirty Books of Scriptures were revealed to him. (Al-Mas^c^udi *Muruj* 1: 39–40)

As seen from these examples from Al-Shahrastani and Al-Mas^c^udi, at least some of the Arab writers saw close ties between Islamic teachings and ancient Egyptian ideas and sought to explain these ties by tracing the origin of the earliest messengers of God back to Ancient Egypt. Thus Idris was born in Egypt and is identified with Enoch, one of the earliest, if not the earliest, of the prophets, and the originator of prophethood (Q19: 56; Al-Sayyar 1995: 154), who conveyed the message of God to the Egyptians. Through such connections, Hermes and writings attributed to him exercised great influence on both Jewish thought (Doresse 1960: 13; Mussies 1982), Moslem thought (Affifi 1951; Gilis 1984) and beyond these to the African culture of the Dogon people (Lambert 1988).

This Hermetic influence on Islamic thought can be traced through medieval Arabic sources, as illustrated for example by Al-Ya^c^qubi (*Tarikh* 1: 11), who says that Akhnukh/Idris 'was the first to write', just as the Egyptian origin of this figure, Thoth, was believed by ancient Egyptians to have been the first to write and teach writing, as Lord of the Divine Words who founded the hieroglyphs (Boylan 1922: 92–93; Burnett 2003: 81ff).

Al-Yaᶜqubi also gives a detailed account of this figure:

> The Sage (Ḥakeem) of the Copts is Hermes the Copt. They are the builders of the temples who write in the script of the temples (*khaṭ al-barabi*/Hieroglyphs) and here is how it looks. [No hieroglyphs are shown in the edited work.]
>
> And in our time, nobody knows how to read it, because only the elite among them were writing in it; they would not allow the common people to do so. The ones in charge of it were their sages and priests. It had the secrets of their religion and the origins of sciences which nobody was allowed to see but their priests, who did not teach it to anyone unless ordered to do so by the king. . . . Their religion was the worship of planets/stars. From their sayings: The souls are old and were in Upper Paradise (*al-firdaus al-aᶜla*) and every thirty six thousand years, all that is in the world will perish either from dust (*turab*) meaning the earth, its earthquakes and eclipses, or from fire and burning, destructive poisons, or from a great and noxious wind, in which animals, plants and humans shall perish. Then nature will bring back to life from every kind and the world will return after its demise. They had of these spirits, deities who descend into the idols, causing the idols to speak, but that is how they used to deceive their commoners, and hide what causes the idols to speak, which was a craft made by the priests and the drugs they use; tricks they utilise until it whistles and screams as if the idol was indeed a bird or an animal. Then the priests translate that sound of the idol according to whatever they like to judge, according to their astronomical signs and physiognomy. They tell that when souls depart, they go to these deities who are the planets, so they wash them and purify them if they had sins. The souls then go up to paradise where they belong. They say that their prophets were spoken to by the planets which informed them that the Spirits descend into the idols and take residence inside, and foretell events before they happen. They had such precise and wondrous astuteness with which they instilled into the common people the illusion that they were conversing with the planets, which then foretell to them what will happen. This was possible only because of the perfection of their knowledge of the secrets of the signs of the zodiac, and their exact physiognomy. They were seldom wrong and they claim to have acquired this knowledge from the planets which tell them whatever happens. (Al-Yaᶜqubi *Tarikh* 1: 187–88)

Al-Yaᶜqubi, who is one of the few writers to comment critically on ritual practices, said that such beliefs are 'irrational', in an attempt to convey to the reader that he himself did not share such beliefs, in spite of his apparent admiration for the knowledge of the ancient priests. The passage quoted, however, suggests that he did in fact believe the knowledge and beliefs to be valid; it was the trickery in the use of the sacred images that he was exposing as irrational. This is no different from the attitude to Egyptian religion among eminent Egyptologists such as Erman, who is said to have ended a lecture on ancient Egyptian religion with, 'but it's nonsense all the same, gentlemen' (te Velde 2003: 43). This text reflects a number of themes of ancient Egyptian belief:

- the keeping of sacred knowledge within certain circles, mainly of learned priests;
- the cycle of creation which is the basis of the Egyptian genesis;
- priests using mechanical devices to make divine statues move and talk during oracles, which has been demonstrated by current research (DuQuesne 2001a: 16 n 67);
- the concept of the souls of the dead united with the stars in the heavens.

Al-Yacqubi also apparently admired the knowledge and beliefs of the ancient Egyptian priests. He, like many other Arab writers, was familiar with Hermetic and Gnostic literature and ideas, which had a long tradition in Islam (Corbin 1986: 1) and was a great influence on the Arabs (Plessner 1954; Fodor 1974; Massignon 1981; Scott 1985 4: 248ff).

PILGRIMAGE SITES

Medieval Arabs regarded many ancient Egyptian sites as holy places, some of which continued as pilgrimage sites during the medieval period. Feasts and ceremonies were celebrated by medieval Egyptians and others at and around these ancient holy sites. Contemporary writers described many of these festivals and suggested that they originated in Ancient Egypt. The Nile has a special place in the Egyptian calendar and was celebrated as a holy river in medieval Egypt (Margoliouth 1896: 688–94; Lutfi 1998).

THE PYRAMID AREA AT GIZA AND THE MEMPHITE NECROPOLIS

This is the most revered site in medieval Arabic sources for a number of reasons. Al-Idrisi (*Anwar*: 28) was told by Al-Sharif Ibn cIsa Al-Ḥusani, a friend of his, that he found in various books on and by ancient Egyptians that the pyramid site was known as The Holy Land, and that it was because of its sacred nature that the Egyptians had chosen it as a burial site for their greatest kings and noblemen.

Al-Mascudi (*Muruj* 2: 243) refers to Egyptian pyramids as among the three most sacred sites or temples of the Greeks. According to Al-Idrisi (*Anwar*: 89) quoting Ibn Krion, the Greek philosopher Aristotle was buried in one of them, while the pyramid next to it was prepared for Alexander. Even though Alexander was in fact known not to be buried there, both pyramids became pilgrimage centres for the Greeks.

There is a long tradition about the pyramid builders in medieval Arabic that perhaps became available to Arab writers from Greek and Coptic sources (A Fodor 1970: 350), but direct observation and personal enquiry seem to have played a larger role in the Arabic legends. It is also common in these medieval Arab stories about the pyramids to cite a guardian spirit in the shape of a woman who protects the pyramids against ill-intentioned visitors (eg Al-Idrisi *Anwar*: 133,

136), and this may be a memory from a distant past when a shrine was erected beside the pyramid for Isis, Mistress of the Pyramids, which was popular with visitors to the area during the Saite period ca 672–525 (Peden 2001: 279).

Just as the pyramids of Giza were popular with ancient Egyptian visitors, they continued to attract them no less in medieval Egypt. The Scribe of Saladin, Al-ᶜImad Al-Iṣfahani (latter part of the 12th century) (*Sana*: 118), tells of a leisure trip spent in the pyramid area at the invitation of the Chief Judge Ḍiau' Al-Din Al-Shahruzuri, where they toured the pyramids and debated, among other issues, the identity of their builders and their functions. On their way to the site, Al-Iṣfahani saw a group of people dressed in the manner of Iraqis and Syrians, wearing headscarves, and he thought they were students, from the manner of their gathering in a circle, but as his company approached them, they fled. It is possible that these may have been Ṣabaean (from Ḥarran, Iraq) worshippers, of whom Al-Maqrizi (*Khiṭaṭ* 1: 334) much later says that they did not cease to worship Abu Al-Hul (the Sphinx), to whom they sacrificed white roosters and burned incense of sandarac-wood, a recognised ritual among the Ṣabaeans (Scott 1985 4: 254 n 4). White roosters were also used in ancient Egyptian magic (Betz 1992: PGM III 633–731 and PGM IV 26–51). These Ṣabaeans must not be confused with the people of the ancient South Arabian Kingdom of Saba. The former are mentioned in the Qur'an among 'Believers in God' who are respected in Islam, as we can see from the following verse:

> Those who believe (in the Qur'an), and those who are Jews, and the Christians and the Ṣabaeans, anyone who believes in God and the Day of Judgment, and works righteousness, shall have their reward with their Lord. And on them shall be no fear, nor shall they grieve. (Q2: 62)

The Ṣabaeans are the subject of endless debates as to their origin, the meaning and definition of their name, and their worship and sects, as exemplified in one of the longest chapters in Al-Shahrastani (*Al-Milal* part 289–363) (cf Tardieu 1986). In Arab sources, their name is usually said to be derived from the Arabic root *ṣaba'* with the meaning 'deviated from the orthodox path/belief' (eg Al-Shahrastani *ibid*: 289; Abada 2003). But others took it to mean 'philosophers', and according to Al-Sayyar (1995: 208f) the name is derived from the Egyptian word *sb3* which is written with the determinative of a star with the meaning 'Star/Light', and with the additional determinative of a man carrying a stick meaning 'teach, teaching'; *sb3* also means 'pupil' and *sb3yt* means 'instructions of wisdom, guiding to the right path' (Badawi and Kees 1958: 216; Faulkner 1962: 219; Saleh 1966: 343f). This Egyptian origin of their name *Ṣab'a* (Al-Sayyar 1995: 208) is plausible in view of the fact that these Ṣabaeans regarded themselves as descendants of the Egyptians (Al-Masᶜudi *Al-Tanbih*: 161) and until now, they claim links with ancient Egyptians, asserting that they were co-religionists and that they originally came from Egypt (Drower 1937: 10, 261; Bringi 1997: 23). Moreover, they commemorate the souls of Egyptians who were said to have drowned during the Exodus – 'for these Egyptians are thought to have been Mandaean by creed' (Drower 1956: 234–35). This echoes some medieval Arab examples (eg *Akhbar Al-Zaman*: 126), where the Egyptian priests were presumed to teach people their religion which was that of 'the first Ṣabaeans'.

This medieval continuity of veneration was also extended to the Sphinx, venerated as a god by the ancient Egyptians, and the area was known as a place of pilgrimage well into the 4th century CE (Hassan 1951: 10). Some foreigners living in Memphis saw in the Sphinx their god Ḥurun/Ḥauron (Horon) and worshipped it under this name (Sauneron 1950; Wildung 1977a: 19). The reason for associating Ḥurun and the Giza Sphinx may be that both are linked to the desert, the former as its patron and the latter as its inhabitant (van Dijk 1989: 65). This idea survived in medieval Arabic sources which regarded the Sphinx as a talisman against the dangers of the desert (Al-Idrisi *Anwar*: 151). Urn-burials, which may have belonged to Babylonians, were found around the Sphinx by Hassan (1951: 33), who also found that many of the offerings presented to the Sphinx were from foreign worshippers who lived in the vicinity, in the area now known now as Ḥarrania (Hassan 1951: 96). This may well have been the place where Ṣabaeans from Ḥarran gathered during their pilgrimage and the present name alludes to such a connection. Hermes was of great importance in Ṣabaean thought (Yates 2002: 52f; Al-Ḥamd 1999) and it was therefore natural for them to believe that he was buried in a holy area such as the Giza Pyramids and Sphinx.

A Babylonian presence and worship is attested also in other parts of Egypt, a testimony to the religious tolerance and multicultural nature of ancient Egyptian society (Horn 1969: 39, 42). Ḥoron was widely worshipped in the ancient Near East and traces of his cult may be found in the Phoenician god of healing named Eshmun (Gray 1949: 31; Gese *et al* 1970: 145f), who may well be associated in the minds of medieval Arabs with Eshmun/Ashmun of Egypt (Hermopolis), where the god Thoth resided.

According to some writers (eg Ibn Al-Kindi *Faḍail Miṣr*: 66; Al-Idrisi *Anwar*: 28; Al-Suyuṭi *Ḥusn* 1: 71), the pyramids were regarded as a pilgrimage centre by the Ṣabaeans (of Ḥarran), because they were the tombs of their prophets Agathodaimon and Hermes (Al-Baghdadi *Al-Ifadah*: 98). Al-Kindi (*ibid*: 48) said he actually met Ṣabaeans who performed their rituals at the pyramids. The people of Ḥarran spread the veneration of Hermes beyond their city, making him popular among various Moslem groups (Peters 1990). As for Agathodaimon, a Greco-Egyptian god, he was regarded in Arabic sources as an ancient Egyptian sage or prophet and some even regarded him as the teacher of Hermes (Plessner 1960). The traditional image of Agathodaimon is as a guardian whose name means 'The Good Spirit'; in Greco-Egyptian sources he is a bearded serpent with the Atef crown of Osiris on his head (see plate and description in Hassan 2002: 168). His origin may be sought in the ancient Egyptian Ouroboros, the serpent with its tail in its mouth, called *Mḥn* in Egyptian, which represented protection and eternal regeneration (Kákosy 1995; Hornung 1999: 38, 78f) (**Figure 28**). *Mḥn* was a god closely associated with recondite knowledge, protection of the sun god, and resurrection (Piccione 1990: 43), which may explain his visible presence and popularity in medieval Arabic alchemy with its interest in the mystery, the sun and in alchemical transmutation and resurrection. The image of the Ouroboros with hieroglyphs in Abu Al-Qasim Al-ᶜIraqi (*Al-Aqalim*: fol 4a) is clearly copied from ancient Egyptian sources (**Figure 29**).

It is clear from the above cited Arab sources that this veneration continued throughout the medieval period (Haarmann 1978).

The pyramid shape itself remained a favourite form for tombs and we know of one medieval Moslem Sheikh, a scholar of Islamic jurisprudence and the Ḥadith named Naṣir Al-Din, who chose this form for his tomb at Al-Qarafah Al-Kubra (The Great Necropolis), east of Cairo but within sight of the great pyramid of Giza (Al-Sakhawi *Tuḥfat*: 163).

Al-Idrisi (*Anwar*: 151) informs us that the Sphinx:

> has a certain day of the year when visitors who aspire to senior jobs with the Sulṭan offer incense to the Sphinx.

It may have been this popular practice of ordinary people venerating, as did their ancestors, what was perceived by others as a pagan symbol, that angered a certain pious Sheikh from a Ṣufi establishment, Khanqah Sa^c^id Al-Su^c^ada, who went up to the Sphinx and disfigured his face. Shortly afterwards, Alexandria was sacked for a week in October 1365 CE by the Crusader ruler of Cyprus, Pierre I of Lusignan, an event described by Al-Minufi (d 1524) (*Al-Fayḍ*: fol 52a) as a divine retribution for the desecration of the Sphinx. Al-Minufi went on to remind his readers that monuments should be left intact, following the guiding example of the Companions of the Prophet who had visited the area and had not, in spite of their religious piety, objected to any of its monuments, thus echoing the same sentiments as expressed by Al-Idrisi (*Anwar*: 45f). Al-Minufi does not give us the name of this Ṣufi Sheikh but Al-Maqrizi (*Khiṭaṭ* 1: 333) gave his name as Ṣaiem Al-Dahr, reporting the views of the local people that the sand had taken over their land as a punishment for the disfigurement of the statue. More detail of this Ṣufi Sheikh is given by Ibn Qadi Shuhba (d 1448), who recorded his name among notables who died in the year 1384 as Muhammad Ibn Ṣidiq Ibn Muhammad Al-Tibrizi Al-Miṣri, also known as Ṣaiem Al-Dahr. According to Ibn Qadi Shuhba, he disfigured the sphinxes of Qanaṭir Al-Siba^c^, and he may well also have been responsible for disfiguring the one at Giza. The Qanaṭir Al-Siba^c^ was actually an avenue decorated with sculptured lions (like a row of sphinxes) set up by order of Sulṭan Al-Ẓahir Baybars (known also as Baybars I, reigned 1260–77) (Sayyid 1995: 16 n 2) as lions were his emblem and feature prominently on all his monuments (Creswell 1926: 147, 150f, and pls VIII–XII). The lions cited in Creswell are carved on the sides of another bridge also built by Baybars, while the lions of Qanaṭir Al-Siba^c^ must have been actual sphinx-form ones which were regarded as offensive by a later Sulṭan, Al-Naṣir Muhammad (d 1309), who had them destroyed. But they must have been reinstated as they were disfigured yet again by the above mentioned Ṣufi Sheikh Ṣaiem Al-Dahr (Al-Shishtawi 1999: 199). We do not know where these lions/sphinxes came from, but they were likely to have been brought from nearby Heliopolis. It is interesting that a Moslem Sulṭan should be so enamoured of the Sphinx, but this particular Sulṭan was associated by Al-Maqrizi (*Khiṭaṭ* 2: 426) with several stories in which the name of Baybars I was found on ancient Egyptian idols and talismans. Qanaṭir Al-Siba^c^ (in what is now Saydah Zaynab Square) was very popular among the people of Cairo as a destination for leisure outings (Al-Shishtawi 1999: 198–200).

The site of the Sphinx at Giza was popular with many of the rulers of Egypt, such as Ibn Ṭulun (ruled 868–84), who was said to be a regular and frequent visitor (Al-Balawi *Sirat*: 194; Al-Idrisi *Anwar*: 35f), Al-Ḥakim (ruled 996–1021) (Al-

Maqrizi (*It^{c}az* 2: 45), Qaitbay (ruled 1468–96) and Al-Ghouri (ruled 1501–16) (Ibn Iyas *Badai^{c}* 3: 55 and 4: 290–92). During the Fatimid Dynasty, at the national celebration known as Night of Fire, the ceremony was started by lighting a huge fire on the top of the pyramid (Al-Idrisi *Anwar*: 38).

Pilgrimage and national celebrations at venerated sites where eminent holy persons or animals were buried were seen by some Arab writers as dating back to Ancient Egypt. For example, the writer of *Akhbar Al-Zaman* reported that once the cow/bull cultic rite had been established, its tomb also became a pilgrimage site:

> later on after the Holy Bull was buried people from all over Egypt and neighbouring areas flocked to his shrine with offerings to his statue and he would tell them whatever they wanted. (*Akhbar Al-Zaman*: 174)

Such ceremonies accompanying burial are well known from Ancient Egypt, where they included large processions of people gathering to consult the oracle. The Serapeum in Saqqara was just one such site (Smith 1974; Sadek 1987: 270–73). This particular pilgrimage may well have continued until the author's time in the 12th century and even beyond.

In the Memphite necropolis we have the site of Sijn Yousuf (The Prison of Joseph) at Abu Sir, named after the biblical/Qur'anic prophet Joseph because of the belief that he received divine revelations whilst imprisoned there. The site became in medieval times a pilgrimage centre, with annual ceremonies lasting for three days (Ibn Iyas *Badai^{c}* 1/1: 35). It was very popular among Moslems in general as a holy place where God would answer requests favourably (Al-Qalqashandi *Ṣubḥ* 3: 307). This site has been identified by Stricker (1942) as a cult centre of Imhotep (Imouthes) who was perceived throughout Egyptian history as a symbol of wisdom, and was associated with oracular practices as well as being venerated as a healer (Wildung 1977a: 44–46; Allen 1999; cf Smith 1974: 28). Joseph also foretold future events and interpreted dreams. The common features in the veneration of these two characters made it possible for medieval pilgrims to continue using the ancient cult of Imhotep under the biblical/Qur'anic name of Joseph. The surrounding area was also associated with the Oracle of Hermes Trismegistus (Skeat and Turner 1968), a very popular figure in Arab writings (Massignon 1981; Plessner 1954). All these medieval practices, assimilating different venerated figures, stem from ancient Egyptian practice, as Egyptians made no differentiation between these divinities (Wildung 1977a: 47).

HELIOPOLIS

The ruined city was known in medieval Arab sources as ^{c}In *Shams,* meaning 'Eye/Spring of the Sun'. Its important holy site was the 'Grand Shrine at Heliopolis' which, according to Al-Idrisi (*Anwar*: 109–10), was venerated by both Ṣabaeans (of Ḥarran) and Egyptians. Al-Maqrizi (*Khiṭaṭ* 1: 617) also referred to it as a pilgrimage centre not only for ancient Egyptians, but for people from all over the world. He records that the Shrine was dedicated to seven deities associated with seven heavenly bodies, headed by the Sun God called Lord of the Gods. Al-

Maqrizi (*Khiṭaṭ* 1: 618) quoted earlier Arab sources, then presented an account of the daily service which included prayers performed three times a day: the first at sunrise, the second at midday and the third at sunset. He also quoted (*Khiṭaṭ* 1: 623) from a book, now lost, by Ibn Al-Kalbi (not his *Kitab Al-Aṣnam*) that the Arabic name of the city ᶜIn Shams (which in Arabic means Eye of the Sun) was derived from the old Sun God. Ibn Al-Kalbi (d 820 CE), an early Arab historian of religions who wrote several books on different aspects of pre-Islamic Arabia, was clearly aware of the sun cult at Heliopolis. These writers also commented on the ancient Egyptian royal visits to perform religious duties at the Grand Shrine of the city, staying there for seven days. Some Egyptian kings were said to have ordered private chapels to be built at the Grand Shrine especially for their visit (Al-Maqrizi *Khiṭaṭ* 1: 619). (For this Grand Shrine and the sun cult see Quirke 2001.) The notion of the holiness of this area has continued up to the present day, as can be seen from pilgrims flocking to The Holy Tree of Mary (Shajarat Maryam) at Maṭariah to the south of the walls of Heliopolis.

AL-MUQAṬAM

A further site connected with Heliopolis is Jabal Al-Muqaṭam (Muqattam Mountain) to the east of Cairo. According to Ibn ᶜAbd Al-Ḥakam (*Futuḥ*: 157f), the Copts told ᶜAmr Ibn Al-ᶜAṣ, who led the Moslem campaign and became the first Moslem ruler of Egypt, that Muqaṭam was their holy site and so Moslems treated it with reverence, and even came up with reasons of their own to justify its sanctity (Al-Maqrizi *Khiṭaṭ* 1: 335ff and the sources cited there). This mountain was regarded as so holy by Moslems that it became the most desirable burial ground for their dead, including ᶜAmr Ibn Al-ᶜAṣ himself and a number of the Companions of the Prophet (Ibn ᶜAbd Al-Ḥakam *Futuḥ*: 253). Its soil was used to treat diseases after a woman with a severe eye problem alleged that the Prophet Muhammad had recommended it to her in a dream (Ibn Qadi Shuhba *Tarikh* 1: 522).

According to Ibn ᶜAbd Al-Ḥakam (*Futuḥ*: 253) and Al-Maqrizi (*Khiṭaṭ* 1: 335), Egyptian kings had built a rest-station on the top of this mountain en-route between their palace at Memphis and the cult centre at Heliopolis. This way-station was also used to announce the arrival and departure of the pharaohs for their regular visits to Heliopolis. These accounts show a knowledge of the lines of vision connecting Memphis, the Muqattam Mountain and Heliopolis as well as of the religious ties; this too is in accordance with recent archaeological work (eg Jeffreys 1998: fig 3; Verner 2000: 600). When the Nubian King Pi(ankh)y (reigned 747–716 BCE) visited Heliopolis on pilgrimage during his campaign in Egypt, he took this traditional route from Memphis via the area known now as Old Cairo and Muqattam Mountain (Grimal 1981: 130; Goedicke 1998: 113–22). An interesting observation made in some Arab sources (eg Ibn Saᶜid Al-Maghrabi *Al-Nujum*: 375) is that the area between present day Old Cairo (Fusṭaṭ) and Heliopolis was settled with buildings in ancient times, an observation supported by later archaeological investigation (Hamza 1937). There is potential here for further archaeological work.

For Arab geographers, the Muqattam Mountain stretched along the Eastern Desert all the way to Nubia (eg Ibn Ḥawqal, **Figure 2**).

Stone was quarried in this area by ancient Egyptians for building and sculpture, and unfinished monuments are still visible there today.

In general, many of the ancient Egyptian holy sites continued to be treated as such by Moslems, even if new myths had to be woven to explain their sanctity. A well known example is the Temple of Luxor, part of which later served as a church, and where later still the Mosque and Tomb of Abu Al-Ḥagag, a Moslem Sheikh (Saint), was built. A special festival, still held every year for this Sheikh, recalls the Opet Festival of pharaonic Egypt. This Egyptian reverence for their immortal ancestors was rooted in Ancient Egypt (Malek 2000) and was still attested in the Greco-Roman period (McCleary 1992). The same process can still be seen in Egypt today, where ancient tombs or temples may still serve as shrines for local saints (eg the tomb of Sheikh Al-Saman on the Giza Plateau was originally an Old Kingdom tomb, Porter and Moss (1974) 3:1: 235; for other examples see Yamani 2001: 395).

ROYAL CULTS

A description of royal cult chapels and royal processions is to be found in the book *Akhbar Al-Zaman* (171–72):

> It is said that King Menqaus built a shrine for the priests on the Mountain of the Moon, headed by one of them called Mustuhmus; they did not allow wind to the departing ships without their paying a due ... Whenever the king rode out, they made before him colossal statues; people would gather to marvel at their works. He ordered a cult chapel built especially for himself and had in it images of the sun and planets. He surrounded it with idols and marvels. The king used to ride out to it and he would stay there for seven days and then leave. He erected two columns in it with the date of their erection; they are still there in the place called ᶜIn Shams (Heliopolis). King Menqaus reigned for 71 years and died of the plague, though it is also said that his food was poisoned. A tomb (*naous*) was made for him in the desert of the Copts, to the west of Quṣ (possibly the Valley of the Kings in Luxor?).

The author then went on to say that a maiden, who was the most favoured of the king and whom he greatly loved, died before him and so the king, in an act recalling the well established New Kingdom burial practice where either Nut or Isis is depicted at either end of the sarcophagus or on the lid:

> ordered her image to be placed in all the chapels. A statue was made of her with two ringlets of black, gold-dressed in ordered jewels seated on a golden chair, and was placed before him wherever he sat to give him solace. Her image was buried at his feet as if he is speaking to her. (*Akhbar Al-Zaman*: 172)

Attempts were made by some Arabs to see in pre-Islamic materials prophecies of their own later prophets, as if one of the functions of the artefacts was to foretell the coming of the three related religions. For example, Ibn Khurdadhiba tells us that he heard a story about:

> the journey of the scribe of Ahmad Ibn Ṭulun (reigned 868–84 CE), to the pyramids of Giza accompanied by some workers who then opened one of the ten small pyramids there. They found a basalt or black granite sarcophagus. They had to set fire to it and when they opened it they found a dead old man. Under his head was a white alabaster stela which had cracked in the fire. It had two golden images on one side, one of a man with a serpent on his hand; the other an image of a man on a donkey, with a walking stick in his hand. On the other side of the stela an image of a man on a she-camel with a stave in his hand. This was taken to Ahmed Ibn Ṭulun, where the people present all agreed that the images were those of Moses, Jesus and Muhammad. (Ibn Khurdadhiba *Al-Masalik*: 160)

Some writers were aware that ancient Egyptian royal cults survived and were still popular. For example, Al-Nuwairi (*Nihayat* 1: 395) is likely to have visited the South tomb of the Step Pyramid complex in Saqqara, as he described the lapis lazuli decorated vault (*ḥinyat al-lazaward*) and the large court with a high building which had a black granite door inscribed with 30 lines of hieroglyphs. He correctly identified it as the tomb of Zosara [Zoser/Djoser], 'a king who was a wise ruler of Egypt'. He tells us that the Copts had a feast in honour of this king called the Vine Festival, which recalls perhaps the Osiris/Dionysus festivals. The lapis lazuli he describes in the South tomb refers in fact to the blue faience tiles which were found covering its walls (PM 3: 2: 400, 408). Such festivals were perhaps held throughout the history of Ancient Egypt when visitors might come to Saqqara to honour the memory of ancient kings such as Zoser, leaving behind graffiti expressing their respect for Zoser and his pyramid, some describing it even then as a 'wonder' where petitioners asked the king to intercede with god on their behalf (Peden 2001: 61–63, 96ff, 279f). Zoser was a popular hero in late Demotic literature, as can be seen from the *Michaelides* papyri in Copenhagen, where he is shown conducting campaigns to protect the country (Wildung 1969: 57–93, 91ff; 1977a: 54).

These sites of royal monuments, especially those at Saqqara, became pilgrimage centres and pleasure-walks for ordinary people throughout Egyptian history, as can be seen from visitors' graffiti and what has been described as 'enthusiasm for Old Kingdom monuments' (Peden 2001: 96, 100).

ANIMAL CULTS

One of the oldest forms of worship was that of animals, in particular that of the cow and the bull. Some medieval Arab writers show a good understanding of these cults and how they developed. The medieval Arab attitude to the subject shows a marked difference to that of the Roman writers, many of whom were scornful of the idea of worshipping animals (Juvenal: xvi), stemming perhaps from the general incomprehension on the part of Roman authors of the subject of Egyptian animal worship (Smelik and Hemelrijk 1984: 1859).

In contrast to the general Roman attitude, medieval Arabic accounts are more sympathetic. For example, the author of *Akhbar Al-Zaman*, in spite of his treatment of cows and bulls as one, illustrates some ideas which are familiar from Egyptian religion. He relates the case of King Menaus, whom he regards as the first pharaoh to worship cows, and then goes on to cite the reasons that caused this king to establish the cult of the cow:

> The reason for this was that he became ill and despaired. He saw in his sleep a great Spirit speaking to him thus: 'Nothing will cure you but your worship of cows', because the zodiac at the time was in the sign of the Bull which is in the image of a bull with two horns. When the king awoke he gave orders and they got a handsome piebald bull and made for it in his palace a shrine with a gilded dome . . . and he worshipped him secretly and he was cured. Later on, a bull talked to the King and directed him to worship and look after the bull and in return the bull will look after the King's interests and strengthen him and cure him. So the king established a shrine for the bull and arranged servants to care for it and hold the service of its cult. According to some of their books, that bull, after they worshipped him for some time, ordered them to make an image of him in gold, a hollow one, and to take some hair from his head and tail, and a scraping of his horn and hooves, and put it all in the statue. And he informed them that he would join his (heavenly) world and that they were to place his body in a stone sarcophagus and establish it in the shrine with his statue on top, when the planet Saturn was in his sign and the sun was looking upon him in trine (*tathlith*). And the statue was to be inscribed with the signs of the images of the seven planets and they did that. Later on after the Holy Bull was buried people from all over Egypt and neighbouring areas flocked to his shrine with offerings to his statue and he would tell them whatever they wanted. (*Akhbar Al-Zaman* 172–74)

This is a good example of Arab interpretations of ancient Egyptian material about the burial of the bull and the origins of its cult, which are based on sound knowledge as attested from our current archaeological record (eg Davies and Smith 1997).

CHAPTER 7

EGYPTIAN *MUMMIA*, MUMMIFICATION AND BURIAL PRACTICES IN MEDIEVAL ARABIC SOURCES

INTRODUCTION

The word *mummy* has passed into many languages of the world, first to describe the ancient Egyptian corpses preserved by active human intervention, and later to denote more recent discoveries of bodies preserved naturally in dry desert conditions or in ice. But the word *mummia* was originally used to describe a substance used for the embalming process which I describe in some detail below. There was a great deal of interest in animal mummies and burial practices.

The substances used for mummification were also used for medicinal purposes into the medieval period. Eventually it became easier and cheaper to obtain these substances from mummified corpses and it was this that led to both the idea of consuming mummies for cure and protection and the widespread trade of mummies in the West. Whether as a result of linguistic confusion between the names of the substance and the Egyptian bodies, or a conscious quest for the magical power of Egyptian mummies as *holy relics*, thousands of ancient Egyptian mummies have been lost to us through their use in medicine and magic. The Arabic sources show an awareness of the difference between *mummia* from natural sources and that obtained from Egyptian mummies, and describe a range of its contemporary medical uses to treat various conditions. The Arab sources show a keen interest in mummification and burial practices of both animals and humans. On the whole, the Arabic sources display an accurate knowledge of the subject from direct observation, supplemented by earlier classical sources.

TYPES OF *MUMMIA*

The word *mom* موم or *mummia* موميا is sometimes used in Arabic writings to describe 'honeybee wax', but more often to describe the pissasphalt which oozes from the rocks in certain places such as Persia and Yemen. The same word is also used for natural bitumen obtained from the Dead Sea, as well as for the resin from cedar and pine trees. The 10th century anonymous writer of *Akhbar Al-Zaman* (66), describing the 'Kingdoms of the Black', south of Egypt, tells that in the kingdom of Twan, possibly in the southern part of Sudan, were wells which contained *mummia* that moved like quicksilver and which was used by the local people, though we are not told for what purpose. This area of wells was surrounded by fortifications (see Hopkins and Levtzion 1981: 36; for location of Twan in the

Fezzan Oasis, Libya, and translation of '*mummia*' as sodium salt see Vantini 1975: 142).

In early Arabic sources there are five different materials that are similar to each other in appearance and use and all are associated with *mummia*:

- ***Mom***, produced by honeybees in two colours, white and black, which can be used as medication and as a preservative (Al-Kindi *Aqrabadhin* 294–95; Ibn Al-Bayṭar *Al- Jami*^{c} 2: 90–91 under the name *sham*^{c}, meaning beeswax; cf Majino 1975: 117–18).

- ***Mummia***, which is a natural mineral product from Persia, Yemen, North Africa and other places (Al-Ḥosni 1986: 129). It comes in two colours; black and white. The latter is said to be of better quality (Ibn Al-Faqih *Al-Buldan*: 407). This *mummia* was widely used in Arab medicine. I shall call it *natural mummia* to avoid confusion with Egyptian *mummia* derived from corpses. The latter is referred to by Ibn Al-Bayṭar (*Al-Jami*^{c} 2: 463) as *al-mummia al-quburi*, meaning *mummia* of the tombs.

- ***Qifr al-yahod*** (known also as red *mummia*) means bitumen Judaicum and is so called either because it was extracted from the Dead Sea (Ibn Al-Bayṭar *Al-Jami*^{c} 2: 274; Reichman 1997: 31) or, according to the 13th century Egyptian herbalist Cohen Al-Haroni (also known as Al-^{c}Aṭar) in his book *Minhaj Al-Dukan* (130), *qifr* is derived from the Hebrew word *kifar*, which means estate/small village, and this product is also known as red *mummia*. Classical writers such as Dioscorides described the medicinal use of this natural bitumen for treating various illnesses, and early medieval Arabic writers followed him (cf Ibn Al-Bayṭar *Al-Jami*^{c} 2: 463; Dietrich 1991: 61). Ibn Al-Bayṭar (*ibid*) also suggested that the people of Bilad Al-Sham (Greater Syria) used this *qifr* mixed with oil to protect their vines from insects, hence they called it *qifr al-khamr*, meaning wine bitumen. Bitumen was found at Maadi, Egypt, from the 5th millennium BCE (Serpico and White 2000: 456), but we are not certain what it was used for. Bitumen from the Dead Sea was still popular for mummification in Egypt in the Greco-Roman period (Altheim and Stiehl 1964 1: 34). (For other sources see Aufrère 1984.)

- ***Qiṭran***, which is cedar-pitch, a black aromatic resin extracted from the tree. Among its varied uses is the embalming of the dead (Ibn Sina *Al-Qanun* 1: 419; Ibn Al-Bayṭar *Al-Jami*^{c} 2: 80–82 under the name *shirbib*).

- ***Zift***, a resin that is found in the sea or extracted from various kinds of trees such as pine (Ibn Sina *Al-Qanun* 1: 306; Ibn Al-Bayṭar *Al-Jami*^{c} 1: 470–71).

The above sources are all medical, but natural *mummia* was also referred to in other Arabic sources, such as accounts of geographers. Ibn Al-Faqih (d ca 902) left perhaps the most detailed account of Persian *mummia* and the method of extracting it: using a naked man supervised by a number of public officials (Ibn Al-Faqih *Al-Buldan* 407–08; for a similar but much later account by a European traveller from 17th century, see Carrubba 1981: 464ff). Al-Iṣṭakhari (d ca 934) in his book *Al-Masalik* (93) gives a brief account of this *mummia* and his account is copied later by Ibn Ḥawqal (d 988) (*Ṣurat Al-Araḍ*: 262). Other Arab travellers wrote about the same substance in varying detail (eg Al-Muqadasi (d 985) *Aḥsan*: 438; Al-Idrisi *Nuzhat* 1: 408).

The oldest reference that I have found so far in Arabic sources which associates *mummia* with Egyptian bodies dates from the mid-10th century and is by Ibn Waḥshiyah (*Shauq*: fol 77a). In a list of Egyptian signs indicating names of materials grouped together by subject, such as fruits, herbs and minerals, he includes *ladin* (laudanum), *zift*, *napht* and *mummia*. The latter is written with a human upper body, showing that already, by then, the material was extracted from human bodies (**Figure 30**). Eventually Egyptian mummies became the main if not the only source of *mummia*, with a growing international trade. Many Arabic sources give detailed accounts of this trade. The account given by Al-Baghdadi is the most detailed and is worth quoting in full:

> As for that which is inside their bodies and heads which is called *mummia*, there is a lot of it. The people of the countryside bring it to the city and it is sold for very little. I bought three heads full of it with half a dirham. The seller showed me a sack full of this with a breast and belly with a filling of this *mummia*, and I saw that it was inside the bones which absorbed it until they became part of it. I also saw on the back of the head traces of the shroud and the imprint of its fabric inscribed upon it, like drawing on wax if you stamped it on cloth. This *mummia* is black like tar, and I saw that if the summer temperature gets very hot, it runs and sticks on what ever comes near it, and if thrown into fire it boils and produces a smell of tar; it is most likely pitch and myrrh. The real *mummia* is something that comes down from the top of the mountains with water, then dries like tar that produces a smell of pitch, mixed with myrrh. (Al-Baghdadi *Al-Ifadah*: 112–13)

The *mummia* obtained from the heads of Egyptian mummies was considered by some to be 'better than the Persian mineral one' (Al-Harawi (d 1215 CE) *Al-Isharat*: 42).

Al-Bakri (d 1094) (*Masalik* 2: §1030), in his description of Quṣ in Upper Egypt, mentioned rock-cut tombs (*ghiran manḥouta*) in the mountains between Quṣ and Aswan where the finest *mummia* was obtained from the dead buried there. This was repeated by the 12th century anonymous author of *Kitab Al-Istibṣar* (85) (cf Garcin 1976: 12 and n 2; Al-Idrisi *Nuzhat* 1: 129).

The high reputation of Egyptian mummies as a source of good *mummia* was behind the massive demand which led even to local merchants fabricating mummies to satisfy the market. Ibn Iyas (*Badai*ᶜ 2: 91–92) recalled a trial that had taken place under Sulṭan Al-Ashraf Barsbay (reigned 1422–37), in which the accused had been found mummifying the newly dead and selling them to Europeans as *mummia* at the price of 25 dinar per qinṭar. In this case the men had their hands cut off and hung around their necks and were marched through the streets of Cairo before being imprisoned by the Sulṭan in the hope of putting a stop to such trade. But the *mummia* trade clearly continued: Ibn Iyas (*Badai*ᶜ 4: 275) reported that in the year 1513, a man was arrested for desecrating ancient tombs and selling the dead to foreigners from Europe for *mummia*. In this case the accused was sentenced to death.

In summary, there are many and varied sources detailing the different substances, looking and smelling alike, which in Arabic and Persian are called *mummia*.

DESCRIPTIONS OF MUMMIES

Some Arab writers dwell on the vast number of mummies to be seen, and endeavour to date them and to identify the substances and plants used in the mummification process. Reading these accounts leads one to question just how many humans and animals must have been mummified in Ancient Egypt, as hundreds of thousands must have been destroyed by medieval traders.

Al-Mas^{c}udi saw in the town of Tinnis, 9 km south-west of Port Said (Ramzi 1993 1: 197–98):

> Well arranged mounds of (dead) people, young and old, males and females like great mountains, known as Abu Al-Kuom. And there are also in Egypt stacked (dead) people on top of each other inside caves, grottoes and tombs and many sites in the land; it is not known from what peoples they are. Neither Christians mention them as their ancestors nor do Jews speak of them as their predecessors, nor do Moslems know who they are. No history to tell about their affairs; [they are left] with their clothes on, and often their jewellery is found in these hills and mountains. (Al-Mas^{c}udi *Muruj* 1: 361)

Al-Iṣṭakhari (d ca 934), who also visited the Tinnis mummy mound, gives the name of the mound as 'Boton/Botom', then attempts to date it:

> It is likely to date back to [an era] before Moses, peace be upon him, because the land of Egypt in the time of Moses had the custom of burial. Then it became Christian and they too had burials. Then it became Moslem [who did likewise]. (Al-Iṣṭakhari *Al-Masalik*: 42)

Al-Iṣṭakhari means by burial just burying the dead without mummification, explaining that since neither Jews nor Christians nor Moslems practiced mummification, the mummy mound of Tinnis must predate them. Al-Iṣṭakhari's account and dating method is repeated by his student Ibn Ḥawqal (Ṣurat: 149–50).

Al-Baghdadi was so impressed by the state of preservation of Egyptian mummies that he wrote:

> I saw some human bones so old, they had turned white like loofah. Yet most of the bodies I saw were very firm and looked more fresh than those who died in the famine of year 597 H [ie just recently 1200/1 CE], and specially those bodies dyed by naphtha and tar, you find them with the colour of iron and equally solid and heavy. (Al-Baghdadi *Al-Ifadah*: 115)

MUMMIFICATION AND BURIAL PRACTICES

Ibn Khurdadhiba, one of the earliest Moslem geographer travellers (d ca 885 CE), is the earliest Arabic source yet known to mention *mummia* in an Egyptian context. He says he heard the following from a man who was involved in the event:

> In the time of Ahmed Ibn Ṭulun, his scribe went into one of the ten small pyramids at Giza accompanied by some workers. They found an onyx/alabaster jar (*jarat jaza^{c}*

> (جرة جزع), with a stopper of the same material in the shape of a pig, full of *mummia*. There were three more but with different tops. (Ibn Khurdadhiba *Al-Masalik*: 159–60)

As Ahmed Ibn Ṭulun ruled between 868–84, this must be the oldest, and possibly the only, known description of Canopic jars in medieval Arabic, and what is described as a pig is very likely the Canopic jar with the monkey's head of Ḥapy with the other known heads of Imesty (human), Duamutef (jackal), and Qebeḥsenuf (falcon). When the scribe took one of the jars home, he emptied out its contents and found:

> pieces of cloth folded together and when he unfolded them all he found was a piece of bull skin and a drop of clotted blood [?] (*ᶜabeeṭ* عبيط) fell.

This puzzled the scribe because of the complex wrapping, which had led him to expect something more precious.

The traveller and historian Al-Masᶜudi (d 952) described the finding of coffins in the pyramid area of Giza in the time of the ruler Al-Ikhshid (935–46), noting that next to each coffin:

> was a jar, along with other equipment of marble and alabaster, which contained a substance used for painting the dead in their coffin. The rest of the substance was left in that jar. This paint (*al-ṭala'*) is a powdered drug and mixture which is odourless and when burnt it produces different beautiful smells not known from any of the usual perfumes. (Al-Masᶜudi *Muruj* 1: 368)

Najib Effendi, an Egyptian archaeologist who worked with De Morgan at Dahshour, described a similar experience when a large jar was discovered in one of the tombs. When some of its content was burned to establish whether it was incense, it turned out to be the tar material known as *mummia* used for embalming. Najib commented that this was the substance described in Arab sources (Najib 1893–94: 469).

Another very early account in Arabic of ancient Egyptian mummification and a description of the alchemical properties of *mummia* is that found in the book *Akhbar Al-Zaman*. When an Egyptian King named Piqrawis (?) died:

> They anointed his body with preserving medicines and placed him in a sarcophagus of gold and made for him a *naos* plaited with gold and buried him in it with endless treasures and plenty of the Elixir of the Alchemical craft and gold. Then they inscribed on the tomb his date of death and placed on top talismans against harmful insects. (*Akhbar Al-Zaman*: 113)

In the same book (p 155) we find names for some of the materials used to preserve the body: *marmar* (lit white marble but may be natron or travertine?), camphor and *mummia*. In addition to the grave goods described above, placed in one royal burial (*ibid*: 163) were 170 scriptures and seven tables made of precious materials laden with vases of the same materials. This is a most interesting text, since it may refer to spells of the Book of the Dead, which was divided by Lepsius into 165 chapters (Faulkner *et al* 1994: 18). It is also important to note that the number of tables carrying vases were seven, as this may relate to the ancient Egyptian seven holy oils used in the funerary service and in embalming (Wilkinson 1994: 136; Ikram and Dodson 1998: 106; cf Sandison 1975: 613).

Al-Baghdadi gives many accounts of mummification and burial customs:

> People find underground tombs with many of the dead of the Ancients, wrapped in shrouds of linen cloth, which may be of a thousand arms-length; each limb is wrapped separately, hand, leg, and the finger in fine pieces, then the body is wrapped as a whole. (Al-Baghdadi *Al-Ifadah*: 112ff)

This description is accurate and shows that Al-Baghdadi must have carried out his investigation aided by his knowledge as a physician, because the practice of wrapping the limbs separately during mummification is certainly known from Ancient Egypt (Taylor 2001: 80).

Al-Baghdadi was told of an incident by a treasure hunter in the pyramid area who had found a sealed jar. When they opened it, they found honey, so they started eating it. Suddenly someone's finger became caught in human hair, and when he pulled it up a small boy appeared:

> with firm limbs and tender body on which was some jewellery. These dead may have on their foreheads, eyes and noses, leaves of gold; there may be some also on a woman's vagina; leaves of gold may also cover all the body like a skin, and may be accompanied by gold and jewellery. The deceased may be accompanied by his tools which he worked with while alive; a trustworthy person told me that he found by one of them an implement for a beautician, a sharpener and a razor, and by another the tool for blood letting, and by another the tools for sewing. And it appears from their state that it was traditional to bury with the man his tools and money.

Al-Baghdadi also describes the custom of burying gold with the dead:

> I heard of some groups of Abyssinians that this was their tradition and they believed evil would befall them [if they kept] the goods of the dead; they will not touch it or change it. And we had a relative who went to Abyssinia and earned money, 200 ounces of gold. When he died they forced an Egyptian man who was with him to take his money, so he gratefully took it. It was the tradition of Egyptians to place some gold with the dead. Some judges from Abuṣir [who live] next to their tombs told me that they excavated graves and found on every corpse very thin leaves of gold, and in each one a band of gold. He collected three bands and they measured nine *mithiqal* (ca 42 grammes, Hinz 1955: 2). These are very common stories [*sic*].

All these observations by Al-Baghdadi are attested in archaeological works in this area and indeed elsewhere in Egypt.

ANIMAL MUMMIES

Arab writers were equally fascinated by the discovery of animal mummies and gave many detailed accounts of their burials.

Al-Harawi (d 1215) tells us that in Upper Egypt and its mountains (possibly Asiut):

> Grottoes full of dead people, birds, cats, and dogs, all still in their shrouds till now. The shroud is like the infant's garment; on it there are drugs in order that it does not disintegrate, so if you unwrap the shrouds from the animal you find that nothing had changed. (Al-Harawi *Al-Isharat*: 42)

Al-Baghdadi gives the most detailed and learned account of animal mummies from his lengthy visit to the Memphite Necropolis:

> Among the wonders found in their tombs are all kinds of animals, birds, beasts and insects; each one is shrouded in many cloths, wrapped tightly around it. A trustworthy person told me that they found a building (a house) well sealed underground. When they opened it they found rolls of hemp cloth which had become very solid. They removed it in spite of its great size and found underneath it a complete bull, really solid. Another told me they found a falcon and when they unfolded the many cloth rolls until they tired they found not a single feather had dropped, and similar was narrated to me about a cat, a sparrow and a beetle . . . etc.
>
> I was told by the Al-Amir Al-Ṣadiq that while he was in Quṣ, some treasure hunters came to him and mentioned that they had fallen in a hole, suggesting that it has treasure, so he went out with them accompanied by an armed group and they dug down and found a large pitcher, its top sealed with gesso. With some effort they opened it and found finger-like things shrouded in rags. When they unwrapped one, they found *ṣir*, a small fish, which turned into dust. The pitcher was then transported to the governor of Quṣ, where about a hundred men gathered and unwrapped them all, but it was all the same, wrapped fish and nothing else. Later on I saw in their tombs in Abu Sir too many wonders to be included in this book. For example, I found in these tombs, grottoes well built underground which have wrapped bodies. There is a countless number in each grotto; some of the grottoes are full of bodies of dogs, some are full of cows, some have cats, and all are wrapped in shrouds of hemp wrapping; thus it dyes the flesh and preserves it, and wherever it reaches the bones, it dyes them with red and black.
>
> I saw a vast number of skulls of cows as well as sheep, and I distinguished between the heads of goats and lambs from those of cows and bulls. I found the flesh of cows stuck to the shrouds so that they became one piece which is more black than red, beneath which the bones appear white, some red, and some black; likewise with the bones of humans. There is no doubt that some shrouds were wet with aloe and tar, and were saturated with it . . .
>
> I found in many places, mounds of bodies of dogs which may have a hundred thousand dogs' heads or more, which are turned over by treasure hunters, for there is a group which makes its livelihood from these tombs taking whatever they find of wood and rags and other things.
>
> I searched through all the closed places but never found any head of a horse, camel or donkey, which puzzled me. I then asked the sheikhs of Abu Sir and they hastened to inform me that they too thought about that and queried it but never found any.
>
> Most of their sarcophagi are made of sycamore wood; some of them are strong and solid, and others became ashes. The Judges of Abu Sir told me wonders, one of which is that they found a stone naos. They opened it and found another naos, they opened it where they found a sarcophagus (*tabut*). They opened it and found a lizard, a wall gecko, very carefully wrapped and sealed. (Al-Baghdadi *Al-Ifadah*: 111–16)

The puzzlement expressed about the lack of donkey, horse and camel mummies is particularly interesting. There must have been, by the time Al-Baghdadi was writing, no cognition that in pharaonic Egypt the donkey was sometimes associated with the god Seth who later represented mischief, though this was also a popular belief among Moslems, as Satan ('*Iblis*') had smuggled himself into Noah's Ark inside a donkey (Al-Tha^{c}labi *Qiṣaṣ*: 56f). The ancient Egyptians may not have wished to preserve for eternity an animal which was associated with chaos, in spite of their wide use of donkeys in daily life as seen in wall paintings, and also because of the fact that the donkey was worshipped as a symbol of the god Seth. Very few donkey burials have been found so far in Egypt and the evidence shows that these were domestic, some dating back to the early dynastic period (Boessneck *et al* 1992) but others dating from later periods (eg in the Hyksos city of Avaris, see Bietak 1996: pls 10A, 10B; cf Houlihan 1996: 31). Horses and camels were not represented in Old Kingdom Egypt and camels are said to have been introduced into Egypt much later than horses. However, in various parts of the country some evidence for the presence of camels has been uncovered, associated with dates as far back as the predynastic period (Free 1944: 191). In the 9th century BCE, two-humped Bactrian camels were counted by the Assyrian King Shalmaneser amongst the tributes brought by the people of 'Musri' – Egypt; these are seen on the so-called Black Obelisk at the British Museum (Kitchen 1986: 327; cf Kuhrt 1999). As for horse burials, there are a few but these occurred mostly in the south (Nibbi 1979: 160; Houlihan 1996: 35) and none has as yet been found in the Memphite Necropolis.

In his account of the animal burials at Saqqara, Al-Baghdadi makes it clear that they were a major attraction for visitors, just as they were throughout the history of Egypt and, indeed, still are today (Smith 1974; Martin 1981: 3).

MEDICINAL USE OF MUMMIES

The literature on the medicinal use of Egyptian mummies in Western sources is readily available (eg Pettigrew 1834; Wiedemann 1906; Dawson 1927; Zimmels 1952: 126ff; Patai 1964; Dannenfeldt 1985; Reichman 1997; Ikram and Dodson 1998; Camille 1999). These works are concerned mainly with the origin of the word *mummia* and the various bituminous substances called *mummia,* and their uses as medicinal remedies in the West. Bitumen was regarded in classical and medieval medicine as a potent cure. According to medieval European alchemists, *mummia* was the 'arcanum and secret of the microcosm' (Thorndike 1958 8: 106). It was also stated that the common *mummia* was 'the spirit of life for all men' (*ibid*: 355).

These Western works also list the medical conditions treated by *mummia* in the West well into the 19th century (Patai 1964: 7–8) and show its persistence in spite of the opposition of well-known medieval medical authorities such as Ambroise Paré (d 1590) and others (Dannenfeldt 1985: 174ff). Paré wrote a treatise refuting the benefits of *mummia* (Paré 1951: 143–46). The same substance was called *mummia* in Arabic, to denote the embalming materials used by the ancient Egyptians.

In medieval literature the extensive consumption of Egyptian mummies crossed all secular and religious barriers. The trade was mostly dominated by Jewish merchants (Reichman 1997: 30, 51; Patai 1964: 8), some of whom were *kohanim,* priests (Reichman 1997: 50), which led some worried individuals involved in the trade to seek religious clarification and permission from the

Jewish religious authorities, sending questions to the Chief Rabbis in Egypt and elsewhere asking whether it was *halakhic* (permitted) to eat and trade in the Egyptian *mummia* (*ibid*: 47). The answer varied from one authority to another.

The earliest physician in Arabic sources to refer to the medicinal use of natural *mummia* is Girgios. He attended the Abbasid Caliph Al-Manṣur, who ruled from Baghdad between 754 and 775. This physician prescribed it as a plaster, and for problems of the lungs, general weakness of the body, penile ulcers, the bladder (as quoted in Ibn Al-Bayṭar *Al-Jami*ᶜ 2: 464) and for convulsion of nerves of the head (facial paralysis) (as quoted in Al-Razi *Al-Ḥawi* 1: 113). The next physician to prescribe the natural *mummia* is Ibn Ribn Al-Ṭabari (lived between 770 and 850), who used it as a remedy for haemoptysis (as quoted in Ibn Al-Bayṭar (*ibid*) 2: 464). The next Arabic source is a woman physician called Al-Khuz, cited by Ibn Al-Bayṭar (*ibid*) as having prescribed it also for haemoptysis. Then we have Ibn ᶜAbdous, a physician who treated the Abbasid Caliph Al-Muᶜtaḍid (ruled 892–902). Al-Razi (d 925) related that Ibn ᶜAbdous prescribed, in his medical book *Al-Tadhkirah fi Al-Ṭib*, the natural *mummia* for facial paralysis (Al-Razi *Al-Ḥawi* 1: 168). Al-Razi himself prescribed it for migraine (*ibid* 1: 263) and also for conditions of the lungs (Al-Razi *Ṭabib*: 80).

Ibn Sina (Avicenna, d 1037) prescribed *mummia* for a wide variety of diseases: tumours, ulcers, phlegmatic tumours, dislocated and fractured bones, hemiplegia, convulsion of head nerves, migraine, chronic and simple headache, epilepsy, vertigo, ear problems such as otitis, haemoptysis, slow tongue, angina, throat pain, cough, palpitations, disorders of the spleen, lungs, stomach, liver and bladder, penile ulcers, and as an antidote to poison (Dannenfeldt 1985: 173). Ibn Sina makes no mention of Egyptian *mummia*.

From then on *mummia* appears regularly in Arabic medical prescriptions. Among those who prescribed it was Al-Biruni (d 1051), who gave a description of it and ways of testing its quality (Al-Biruni *Al-Ṣydanah* 2: 311), and who also referred to the *mummia* and its sources in his book on precious stones, *Al-Jamahir* (331–35). It was also prescribed by Moses Ibn Maimun (Maimonides) who died in Cairo in 1204 (Rosner 1995: 182–83; Reichman 1997: 38–40); by Ibn Zohr (Avenzoar) (d 1162) in his book *Al-Taisir* (index 535); by Ibn Al-Quff (d 1286) (Ḥamarneh 1989: 630); by Ibn Al-Khaṭib (ᶜ*Amal*: 34, 77 and 84); and by Dawoud Al-Anṭaki (d 1599) (Al-Ḥosni 1986: 129).

The most direct and earliest Arabic source that specifically describes Egyptian *mummia* and its use as a drug is by the Andalusian geographer Al-Zohri (db 1161). He described the ancient burials of Alexandria where:

> In each tomb there is a dead body of a human being, still looking as on the day he died, nothing changed in him. Some had their skin dried on their bones with his oil leaked into the sarcophagus. From these sarcophagi, *mummia*, which is the oil of those dead persons, is extracted and this the physicians give to the sick patients with fractures, so this fat is most beneficial to him [the patient] and he heals with Allah's grace. (Al-Zohri *Al-Jughrafyiah*: 47)

Egyptian mummies were put to other uses as well. An interesting argument about the anatomy of the human lower jaw was settled by Al-Baghdadi, who examined hundreds of Egyptian burials to prove that the lower jaw is composed of one single bone, contrary to the view of Galen (2nd century CE Greek physician) that there were two bones (Al-Baghdadi *Al-Ifadah*: 150). Whilst Galen was using apes for anatomical lessons, Al-Baghdadi had the benefit of studying humans (Al-Baghdadi *ibid*: 153–88, a comment made by his editor Ghalioungui). In doing so Al-Baghdadi followed a recommendation he attributed to Galen that anybody studying bone structure should go to Alexandria and observe the ancient dead (Al-Baghdadi *ibid*: 116). This educational use of Egyptian mummies is indeed one of the observations made by Galen, who himself went to Alexandria to study (Galen; On Anatomical Procedure: xiv, 2–3).

Al-Baghdadi (*ibid*) quoted Galen, who said: '*Mummia* comes out of springs like tar and naphtha.' He also quoted unnamed 'others', saying:

> It is a kind of tar and called menstruation of the mountains, and this which is in the bodies of the dead in Egypt is not very different from the natural *mummia*, and is used instead when (the latter is) not available.

This last remark is interesting as Al-Baghdadi puts the use of Egyptian *mummia* down to the lack of natural *mummia*, while Al-Harawi (*Al-Isharat*: 42) a few years earlier had suggested that it was the better quality of the Egyptian *mummia* that was behind the demand. The latter may well be true, if only for the magical power which people frequently attach to the ancient dead. This may have originated in the ancient Egyptian idea of the mysterious and sacred nature of mummification (Goyon 1988).

A belief in the qualities and healing power of ancient bodies is well known in the West as well as in the East, especially the powers of the relics of saints (Ball 1989: xxiv). This faith in sacred relics in the medieval West encouraged widespread trade in them as a commercial commodity and as such they became the target of thefts (Geary 2001: 184f), just as happened to Egyptian relics. In Coptic Egypt, veneration of human remains of saints as sacred relics was so common that St Shenoute (5th century CE) wrote a treatise against what he called 'those who honour bones of skeletons' (O'Leary 1937: 254–55). Places where such relics were kept were regarded as holy (MacCoull 1991: 127). Even dead Copts were thought to benefit from having amulets around their neck containing a small bone or even dust made from a saint's bones (Budge 1930: 15). The same beliefs continued in medieval Egypt, where magical powers were attributed to the bodies and to the tombs of the ancient dead. Ibn Rusta (da 913) refers to the village of Badrsanah Al-ᶜAra (modern Badrashien to the east of Memphis, on the west bank of the Nile) where in a room below the church there was a bed on which lay a dead body which generated an endless flow of oil. If a woman wanted to check whether she was pregnant, she laid the dead body on her lap. If she were pregnant, her child would move in her womb (Ibn Rusta *Al-Aᶜlaq*: 81–82).

Al-Maqrizi (d 1442), in his encyclopaedic *Khiṭaṭ* (1: 183–85), gives an account of a Coptic festival called Festival of the Martyr, during which a finger from a saint was placed in a sarcophagus and thrown into the Nile to ensure a good annual flood (Diab 1998: 250; Lutfi 1998: 263ff). Such use and veneration of the ancient dead continued into modern Egypt (Blackman 1927: 98–99), as seen from the numerous accounts of women, concerned about conception, using bones of ancient Egyptian mummies and performing rituals at the ancient tombs. This use of the dead is still to be found in contemporary Egypt, especially for love charms (Fodor 1992: 174). In medieval Arabic books of magic, *mum/mummia* was used to generate love or hatred between men and women (Al-Ghalani *Al-Dur* 2: 73, 112).

It seems that a belief in the power of those beyond the grave was always present in Egypt, to judge from 'letters to the dead' in Ancient Egypt (Gardiner and Sethe 1928; Wente 1990: 210ff), a custom which can still be seen in modern Egypt, where people write letters to the dead seeking help with all sorts of social, economic and political problems, including legal disputes as well as daily life matters (Ewais 1978). Such interaction between the living and the dead was not a one-way process in which the living sought the help of the dead, as the dead also asked for help from the living. Thus we find ancient Egyptian funerary texts appealing to the living for a prayer, or even to weep for the deceased, a tradition which survived into Coptic times (Behlmer 1996: 574). Also from Coptic literature we have a 7th century story of a Coptic bishop, Piscentios, who, while living in an ancient Egyptian tomb, witnessed a mummy leaving its case and demanding the bishop's intercession (Butler 1978: 86f).

Egyptians consciously kept alive a belief in the power of the dead by recalling ancient Egyptian practices, as seen for example in the book *Akhbar Al-Zaman* (123), in a reference to an ancient Egyptian case:

> When the Queen Mother, who was also a magician, died, she used to tell them from her grave about marvels and answer all their questions.

This is a reference to oracles, for example that of Queen Ahmos Nefertari, mother of King Amenhotep I of the Eighteenth Dynasty (1526–1506 BCE). Both these rulers played an important role as patrons of the workmen's village of Deir El-Medina on the West Bank at Thebes. They spoke oracles, and solved disputes among the villagers from beyond the grave (on the oracle at Deir El-Medina, see McDowell 1990; Sadek 1987: 131ff).

The idea of making use of holy or dead bodies can be traced back to the Pyramid Texts of the Fifth Dynasty and appeared for the first time during the reign of King Wenis (ca 2351 BCE). In Pyramid Text (PT) Utterances 273–74, the 'Cannibal Hymn', we read:

> The King has appeared again in the sky,
> He is crowned as Lord of the Horizon;
> He has broken the back-bones
> And has taken the hearts of the gods;
> He has eaten the Red Crown,
> He has swallowed the Green One.
> The King feeds on the lungs of the Wise Ones,
> And is satisfied to live on hearts and their magic;
> He enjoys himself when their magic is in his belly;
> The King's dignities shall not be taken away from him,
> For he has swallowed the intelligence of every god.

(Faulkner 1969: 82. For a recent translation and study see Eyre 2002)

It is the idea that we eat of the gods to become like them, powerful and eternal, that lies behind this text. Another manifestation of ancient Egyptian belief in the protective power of mummies can be seen in the number of amulets that take the form of mummies (Petrie 1914: pl 6, no 82). This is surely what was in the minds of those who were excavating ancient Egyptian bodies for use as medicine, believing that they were endowed with powerful magical spells written among the wrappings, and that the magical effect would still be as powerful on those who consumed them. Moreover, the ancient Egyptians themselves associated human mummies with divine corpses of gods, using the same words for both (Yahuda 1944: 195), and this in turn may have led to the veneration of human bodies. There may also be a connection with ancient Egyptian ideas of the deification of certain members of the body (DuQuesne 2002a). Since every part of the body was protected by its own deity, special protection could be gained by eating these parts, in whatever form. This belief in the benefits of eating human bodies found its way into late medieval Arabic books of magic, as seen in the long chapter by Al-Ghalani (*Al-Dur* 2: 174–86) on the specific benefits of every part of the body in magical and medical treatments.

This knowledge, based on ancient practice, was still evident as late as the 17th century when an Egyptian Rabbi, Abraham Halevi, showed an extensive knowledge of the embalming process and the different uses of the mummy (Zimmels 1952: 127). He attributed medicinal value to the corpse itself, making the body the actual medicine with the embalming materials used solely to preserve the otherwise temporary medicinal value of the flesh (Reichman 1997: 48–49). Rabbi Halevi recommended only the upper parts of the mummy for medicinal use, as the flesh from below the hips is worthless (Zimmels 1952; Patai 1964: 9). His reasons for this recommendation are, first, that the upper parts absorb more balsamic drugs than the lower parts, and secondly, that the upper parts have more sympathetic power, and are therefore more effective (Zimmels *ibid*). The Rabbi also thought that 'in any case there is an enjoyment and usefulness in the mummy itself' (Patai 1964). Patai links this to the practice of barren Sephardi women, in Seattle during the 19th century, of swallowing foreskins in order to conceive, saying there was a possible confusion with *mummia*. This could be compared with an ancient Egyptian practice in which a mother who had given birth to a weak baby checked whether it was going to survive by mixing the placenta with her milk to feed to the baby. If the baby swallowed it s/he would live, but if the mixture were vomited up, the baby would die (Lexa 1925 1: 73). Lexa explained this on the grounds that the placenta is of prime importance in keeping the baby alive in the mother's womb, therefore if s/he vomits it up, this is a rejection of life. The ancient Egyptians certainly regarded the placenta as a twin or ghost of the individual (Blackman 1916). Among the Egyptian words for placenta, *mwt-rmt* literally means 'Mother of Mankind' (Nunn 1996: 149), which may help to explain the importance attached to it by ancient Egyptians who regarded it as the origin of human beings.

ETYMOLOGY OF THE WORD '*MUMMIA*'

I have referred above to the fact that the Arabic and Persian word *mom/mummia* can mean 'honeybee wax' and also 'pissasphalt'. This word was also sometimes used in Arab poetry as a compliment: for example, likening a physician who is most kind with his treatment to the mummia which heals broken bones (Ibn Khalikan *Wafiyat* 3: 599).

However, I believe that the ancient Egyptian word *mnnn, mnn, mnrw* or *mnni* is quite possibly the origin of the word *mummia* (for its various forms see WB 2: 82; Chassinat 1955: 65ff) with the meaning 'bitumen, natural asphalt and balsam' (Loret 1894: 161; Charpentier 1981: 332 no 520 and 336–37 no 527; Sternberg 1982: 213; Aufrère 1984: 1–2; Hannig 1995: 339). In suggesting this I do take account of the warning given by Quirke (1998: viii) on the danger of translating words out of context. But there is no word in either Egyptian or Arabic with three *n* following *m*. The Egyptian word could just as well be pronounced *mnmw* or *mmw* and, by adding vowel sounds, we arrive at the Persian/Arabic *mum* and *mummia,* bearing in mind that the letters *m* and *n* are interchangeable in both Egyptian and Arabic and often *n* is assimilated into *m* (eg WB 5: 132; Brockelmann 1938: 383). In Egyptian, cases where *nw/nnw* is pronounced *mw* and not *n* or *nw* are known (Fairman 1943: 278 no LXV).

A similar process exists in Arabic, for example *naṭar* and *maṭar* (rain); and *ᶜanbar* and *ᶜambar* (amber) (Ibn Manzur *Lisan* 14: 135). Often when a word has several consecutive *n,* one or two may disappear if only in script, eg: *mnnw* and *mnw* 'fortress' (Badawi and Kees 1958: 98–99; Faulkner 1962: 108–09). The Egyptian *n* can also become *l* and *r* in Coptic and Arabic (Vycichl 1990 1: 56). The Coptic word for *mummia* (pronounced *miolōn*), derived from the Egyptian *mnnn,* means 'bitumen extracted from embalmed corpses' (Loret 1900: 58; Crum 1939: 165; Westendorf 1977: 89).

Wilson (1997: 431) suggested that this Egyptian word *mnnn* is the origin of the Arabic, saying that it is the word thought to have become Arabic *mwmia* and thus 'mummy'. Here I have offered a hypothesis on the development of the word which supports Wilson's suggestion.

CHAPTER 8

EGYPTIAN SCIENCE IN MEDIEVAL ARABIC SOURCES

INTRODUCTION

Classical sources portray Egypt as the source of all sciences (Hornung 2001). Some of them were available in Arabic as early as the 8th century CE and helped to shape the medieval Arab view of Ancient Egypt as the land of wisdom and science.

Arab scholars were generous in their praise of the sciences of ancient nations, regarding scientists, irrespective of origin or creed, as ancestors who had contributed to a universal process to which every nation contributes its share in its own time. Almost all medieval Arab books on any science start with a chapter on previous scientists in the field and so establish a long, continuous chain of knowledge.

This is clear from the examples of Al-Nadim (*Al-Fihrist*), Ṣaᶜid Al-Andalusi (*Ṭabaqat*) and Ibn Abi Uṣaybiᶜah (*Ṭabaqat*). In these books, pre-Islamic Egyptian scientists are portrayed as being masters of science and wisdom who belonged to the land where science and wisdom originated. Two examples may serve to illustrate this point; Al-Nadim (*Al-Fihrist*: 425) said that:

> the origin of alchemy was in Egypt which produced many writers and scientists who obtained the knowledge from the temples of Egypt.

Al-Nuwairi, quoting Al-Ḥassan Ibn Ibrahim (Ibn Zulaq), said that:

> In antiquity, Egypt was the destination for students of science and scholars of exact science in order that they sharpen their brains, intellect and intuition. (Al-Nuwairi *Nihayat* 1: 353; cf Ibn Zulaq *Faḍail*: 20)

This acclaim may be due in part to the obvious remains of the material culture of Ancient Egypt which dominated the country's landscape, and it was logical for medieval Arab writers to assume that ancient Egyptians had advanced knowledge in the many fields required for erecting such magnificent buildings as the pyramids and for sculpting such great statues as the sphinx. The precision with which Egyptians engineered their monuments in terms of orientation and astronomical connections, as well as the materials used for their colours, were amongst the scientific achievements that most impressed the medieval Arabs.

It was common for long passages to be quoted from classical writers such as Homer, Herodotus, Iamblichus, Plato, and Plotinus even in Arab literary works, for example in the writings of Al-Sajistani and of Ibn Fatik.

Surprise at these early Arabic translations on the part of highly respected modern scholars seems to stem from a misleading presumption that Arabs translated only what was of direct practical use to them, such as medical books. For example, the eminent orientalist CH Becker (1931: 14–15) specifically commented on the enthusiasm of the Caliph Al-Ma'moun (early 9th century) whom he refers to as an 'enlightened despot', questioning his motives for translating a large number of works by Greek philosophers. Becker found such enthusiasm 'unknown and abnormal in the Orientals', suggesting that the Arab translations were not:

> as a result of an abstract desire to acquire science and knowledge, because if this had been the case then Homer or the Tragedies would have been translated as well, but the reality was that people did not take any interest in nor feel any need for them. (Becker 1931: 14–15, translated from German)

Becker's assertion that the Arabs did not translate Homer is easily disproved by looking at the long quotations from Homer by Al-Sajistani (*Ṣiwan*: 68ff) who referred to an Arabic translation of Homer produced by Stephanus the Elder (Ostanes). This is likely to be the Greek/Byzantine Alexandrian Ostanes, the philosopher and alchemist who, according to Al-Nadim (*Al-Fihrist*: 303f), also translated alchemical works for Prince Khalid Ibn Yazid (d 704) in the first century of Islam.

DEFINITION OF SCIENCE IN ARAB SOURCES

Science (*ᶜilm*) and wisdom (*ḥikmah*) were interlinked in Arab thought and both related to knowledge. The Arabic word *ᶜilm* and its derivations appear more than 700 times in the Qur'an, thus giving it a profound significance in Arab culture. The word has a wide spectrum of meaning, including knowledge, learning, reasoning and wisdom, and defies all attempts to define it in a nutshell (on this problem see Rosenthal 1966). Any attempt to narrow the meaning of *ᶜilm* is artificial (Article ᶜIlm in EI^2 3: 1133–34).

For Arab writers it seems to have been difficult to isolate the concept of science from concepts of philosophy, knowledge and general wisdom. Seeking knowledge is equivalent to an act of worship in Islam and it is therefore incumbent on every Moslem to seek out knowledge that is useful, not harmful, and almost everything worth learning is called *ᶜilm* (for a recent discussion on Moslem classification of knowledge see Jolivet 1996: 1008ff; Bakar 1998). A considerable number of medieval Arab writers produced a large body of work on the divisions of knowledge, and this has been well studied and analysed (eg Al-Tahanawi *Kashaf* 1: 5–70; Nasr 1968: 60ff; Rosenthal 1966, 1975: 52ff). Such was its importance that as eminent a scholar as Al-Ghazali (d 1111) devoted several works to the definitions and divisions of the sciences and started his most famous work *Iḥya' ᶜUlum Al-Din* with a chapter, the longest in the book, on this subject (*Iḥya'* 1: 14–118; Faris 1966).

In summary, sciences may be divided into two main types (Mahdi 1994):

- *Manqul* means transmitted sciences. It includes knowledge which is understood through study and by going back to the founder of the science and his/her followers through a recognised chain of transmission. It includes religious science, for example, ᶜIlm Al-Ḥadith, the Science of the Ḥadith.
- *Maᶜqul* are the rational or natural sciences which are learned through innate reason and intellect: for example logic, physics and mathematics.

It is not suggested that the *manqul* sciences are irrational or devoid of reason, because this is certainly not the case. But it may be said that the natural sciences have more of a universal nature, transcending linguistic, national and religious barriers (Mahdi 1994: 249).

This is an oversimplified summary of a complex issue, but it demonstrates the lack of religious prohibition on Moslems from seeking scientific knowledge as a universal quest, wherever it was to be found. One of the ways in which early Moslem scholars categorised scientific knowledge was on the basis of its necessity to humanity. So, for example, Al-Jaḥiẓ (d 771) in one of his treatises (*Rasail* 4: 51) recalled the instruction of his teacher, Abu Isḥaq Ibrahim Ibn Sayar Al-Niẓam (d ca 741), who divided knowledge into eight kinds. One was optional (*ikhtiyar* اختيار) – that of the knowledge of God, his prophets and exegeses of the Holy Books. Today it would be considered very radical thinking to include in optional knowledge the religious studies of God and his prophets, yet it was widely and amicably discussed during the 8th century, as demonstrated for example by Al-Jaḥiẓ. The other seven sciences were obligatory (*iḍiṭrar* اضطرار), and included the study of chronicles, histories of ancient countries, biographies and monuments (*al-siyar wa al-athar*). Generally but not exclusively, the word *athar* was used in medieval Arabic to mean 'Traditions of the Prophets', but it was also used to mean traditions and relics/monuments.

SOURCES FOR MEDIEVAL ARAB STUDY OF ANCIENT EGYPTIAN SCIENCE

Pre-Islamic Egypt was perceived in medieval Arab writings as the land where science and wisdom originated, as seen in the above cited example of Al-Nadim (*Al-Fihrist*: 425).

In many medieval Arabic sources, scientists from pre-Islamic Egypt and their achievements are described at length. These pre-Islamic scholars from Egypt were thought of as Egyptians but they wrote in Greek, and were thus often designated as Greek. They included Meton and Euctemon, from Alexandria, both of whom flourished in the 5th century BCE, Aristarchus the astronomer, who around 200 BCE devised the first heliocentric model of the universe, and Eratosthenes, who measured the size of the earth and calculated its diameter (Salem and Kumar 1991: 95 n 11). Another scientist well known from Arab sources is Zosimus (ca 300 CE), the alchemist from Akhmim in Upper Egypt (Holmyard 1957: 27; Mertens 1995, 2002; Stolzenberg 1999).

Al-Nadim (*Al-Fihrist*: 328) and Al-Qifṭi (*Ikhbar*: 53) refer to the scientist Hero (1st century CE), designated 'Heron the Egyptian, the Rumi, the Alexandrian'. Hero's book on Pneumatics, cited by Al-Qifṭi, survived only in its medieval Arabic translation (Farmer 1931: 159ff; Hall 1971: x). This book, dealing with mechanical devices, was very popular among medieval Arab scholars and was a main source for mechanics (*ᶜIlm Al-Ḥayal*) in the Moslem world (Hill 1993: 123).

Another famous Egyptian scientist was Apollinus the Carpenter (Apollonius of Perga) of the 2nd century BCE (Ṣaᶜid *Ṭabaqat*: 26), a mathematician who wrote a book on Conics – *Al-Makhruṭat*. He was from Alexandria, the city in which Euclid (the Father of Geometry) flourished much later (Al-Qifṭi *Ikhbar*: 44–48).

Another important Egyptian scientist was Ptolemy (2nd century CE), an astronomer and geographer whose book *Almagest* was the foundation for the mathematical astronomy and geography of Arab scholars (Hill 1993: index).

Most of these pre-Islamic Egyptian scientists belonged to and flourished in the Alexandrian school, which was still in existence and widely renowned when the Moslems arrived in Egypt in the 7th century (Meyerhof 1930: 389). Even if this Alexandrian school was no longer functioning when Moslems arrived, its scholarship formed part of the foundation upon which the famed scientific knowledge of Ḥarran and Baghdad was built (Lameer 1997: 182).

The fame of ancient Egyptian science was also due in part to the many classical writers such as Herodotus (mid-5th century BCE), Plato (ca 427–347 BCE), and Iamblichus (ca 300 CE), who wrote extensively about Ancient Egypt and were all admirers of its science and wisdom. Much is also recorded of famous Greek scholars who went to Egypt in search of knowledge. Not least of these was Pythagoras (ca 582–500 BCE) who appears in almost all the Arabic sources on the history of science and scholarship. His fame was credited to his stay and study in Egypt where, in particular, he studied geometry under the tutelage of Egyptian masters (Ṣaᶜid *Ṭabaqat*: 21; Iamblichus, Life of Pythagoras IV). Many of the classical sources praising ancient Egyptian sciences were well known to medieval Arab writers, for example Al-Nadim, Ṣaᶜid Al-Andalusi, Ibn Fatik, Al-Qifṭi and Ibn Abi Uṣaybiᶜah.

This may explain why key figures in Islamic alchemy such as Khalid Ibn Yazid, Jabir Ibn Ḥayan, Dhu Al-Nun and Ibn Umail all claim to have spent time in ancient Egyptian temples where they received their knowledge of alchemy from Egyptian sources, leading to their naming it *'ṣanᶜat al-barabi'* (صنعة البرابى) meaning 'The Craft or Science of the Egyptian Temples' (see a selection of such works in Shawqi 1990: 540, 549, 570, 575). There is a clearly established lineage from the alchemy of Ancient Egypt to that of Islam.

Al-Nadim (*Al-Fihrist*: 303) tells us that the first Arabic translations of scientific books, which were prepared in Damascus during the second half of the 7th century, were of Egyptian books written in Greek and Coptic. This task of translation, instigated by the Umayyad prince, Khalid Ibn Yazid (660–704), represents perhaps the earliest recognition of pre-Islamic Egyptian scholarship and advanced scientific knowledge (cf the detailed study of Khalid by Ibrahim 1984 and Sezgin GAS 4: 120–26).

The Andalusian judge and scholar Ṣaᶜid (d 1068), who in his book on the 'Categories of Nations' described particularly those ancient nations known for their sciences, gave an account of the eight nations which had contributed to scientific knowledge. These were the Indians, Persians, Chaldaeans, Greeks, Romans, Egyptians, Arabs and Banu Israel.

THE HERMETIC TRADITION IN ARABIC SCIENCE

The Egyptian Hermes, known as Hermes the Copt (Al-Yaᶜqubi *Tarikh* 1: 187), was perceived as the source of scientific knowledge. This followed earlier sources which treated the Egyptian Thoth/Hermes as the originator of many of the sciences (Kákosy 1981: 42).

Some Arab writers, for example Al-Nadim (*Al-Fihrist*: 345), quoting Isḥaq Ibn Ḥunain (*Tarikh*: 150), attributed the invention of certain sciences to the ancient Egyptians or to Hermes:

> Some say it was the Egyptians who invented medicine. Others say Hermes invented all crafts and philosophy and medicine.

In keeping with earlier Arab sources, Ṣaᶜid (*Ṭabaqat*: 35–37) speaks highly of ancient Egyptian science and reports that Hermes, a resident of Upper Egypt before the Flood, was the source of all science. Hermes was said to be the first astronomer, builder, doctor and poet. He was also:

> the first to predict the Flood and to foretell that a celestial catastrophe of water and fire would strike the earth, and he became concerned that science and other forms of knowledge would be lost; so he built the pyramids that can still be found in Upper Egypt. On the wall of the pyramids he drew all forms of technical equipment and devices and described all aspects of science, intending to preserve them for future generations, because he was afraid that they might be lost to the world.

This Egyptian Hermes was very popular in medieval Arab sources (Scott 1985 4: 248ff; Massignon in Festugière 1981 1: 384ff; Siggel 1937; Plessner 1954). He was claimed as a native by almost every country, including Yemen, Iraq and Lebanon (Sabanu 1982: 11; Blanco 1984: 2254). He was also associated with the Hebrew prophet Enoch and the Qur'anic prophet Idris (Q19: 57–58; Q21: 85–86), who was said (Al-Qifṭi *Ikhbar*: 229) to have taught the Greek Asklepios who travelled from Greece to Egypt especially to learn and transfer scientific knowledge back to Greece. Al-Qifṭi seems to have been aware of the nature of the relationship between the Greek Asklepios, the Egyptian Imhotep, and Hermes (Fodor 1974: 156; Burnett 2003: 81). In other words, Hermes was identified in Arabic sources with Imhotep as well as with Thoth following the Greek tradition (Fodor 1974; Fowden 1986: 22, 32, 216). Ibn Fatik (*Mukhtar*: 10) alluded to this in his description of the physical appearance of Hermes. Among many features he was:

> dark coloured (*adam al-lun*) all over his body, bald, handsome, with a thick beard, broad shouldered, large boned with little flesh, bright eyes painted with kohl, gently spoken, with long silences, and unmoving limbs. When walking, he often focuses his eyes on the ground and is mostly in deep thought. He is very serious and moves his index finger whilst talking. He lived on earth for 82 years.

The association in the minds of medieval Arabs of Hermes and Thoth is referred to by Al-Magriṭi (*Ghayat*: 310), who mentioned an Egyptian city founded by Hermes named Al-Ashmunin (Hermopolis), which is the main cult centre of Thoth.

Among writers other than alchemists, Hermes was already known for transforming lead into gold (eg Ibn Zulaq *Faḍail* 17): Moslem alchemists regarded him as the founder of the science of alchemy (Holmyard 1957: 82, 98–100). They claimed that he was the source of their own material and knowledge). It was believed to be Hermes who wrote the famous 'Tabula Smaragdina' (Emerald Tablet), which contained the key to all the secrets of the universe (for literature on this tablet see Kahn 1995 and the references therein). The name of this tablet in Arabic is *al-lawḥ al-maḥfouẓ*, which has a profound meaning for Moslems as it is referred to in the Qur'an: 'This is a glorious Qur'an [inscribed] in an [eternally] preserved tablet' (Q85: 21–22), meaning that the most revered book for Moslems has been in eternal existence. It has already been noted that Hermes was *Islamicised* in these Arab sources and that alchemists elevated his tablet to a revered status as the origin of their sacred knowledge. This concept of sacred or magical knowledge inscribed on tablets is rooted in ancient Egyptian materials. This can be seen in the rubrics in the Book of the Dead, where magical spells were believed to be found on tablets of 'real lapis lazuli' discovered 'under the feet of the majesty of this god in the time of the reign of King Menkaure' (Allen 1936: 151, §20).

Ṣaᶜid described another Hermes who lived in Egypt after the Flood whom he called 'Hermes the Second', a travelling philosopher, geographer and alchemist. This Hermes is often referred to (eg Ibn Juljul *Ṭabaqat*: 8) as Hermes the Babylonian. There is yet another Hermes, 'Hermes the Third', who also lived in Egypt (Ibn Julful *Ṭabaqat*: 19, 90 nn 5–6).

The main source in almost all Arabic materials for these various forms of Hermes is Abu Maᶜshar Al-Balkhi (d 885) in his book 'Thousands on Houses of Worship' (*Al-Uluf fi Byut Al-ᶜIbadat*) (Burnett 1976), which is now lost; only small fragments of it have been collected and edited by Pingree (1968). Long quotations from Abu Maᶜshar are found in many Arab books when referring to Hermes, for example in Ibn Juljul (da 994) (*Ṭabaqat*: 1–100) and in Al-Qifṭi (*Ikhbar*: 2–6, 227–29), who said that:

> Hermes the Third, the Egyptian, is known as Trismegistus because he is the third of the three sages. He was from Egypt after the Flood, a travelling philosopher, an ancient one who knew the countries very well, their cults and their peoples' characters. He wrote an excellent book on alchemy and another on poisonous animals. He was a native scientist of Egypt, a country among the esteemed ones. It had a great kingdom and ancient fame in old times as evidenced from their monuments, buildings, sanctuaries and science centres, most of which still stand in the country to this day and all of which, as agreed by all people, are unique on earth.

Knowledge of Hermes and his books was essential for the medieval Arab scholar, as attested by Al-Jaḥiẓ (*Rasail* 3: 72), who taunted one of his critics for not knowing the writings of Hermes (Netton 1991: 50ff). As Al-Jaḥiẓ died in 771 CE, knowledge of Hermes must already have been common among Arab scholars well before the 9th century, the earliest date given by Blanco (1984: 2255) for Arab knowledge of Hermes.

After the Flood, highly esteemed ancient Egyptian scientists were said to be knowledgeable in all science and philosophy, including mathematics, the physical sciences and theology. Ṣaᶜid tells us that the Ancient Egyptians dealt with the most complex of problems. He quotes a widely used source named Al-Waṣyfi on one such problem, the 'Theory of Creation':

> The ancient Egyptians believed that prior to the birth of the human race, the earth was populated by species of animals having strange forms and extraordinary appearances. Then came the human race, which fought and defeated all the other species until they were annihilated or dispersed in the wilderness and deserts. Among these animals were the ogres and the ghouls and others as mentioned by Al-Waṣyfi in his book on the history of Egypt.

Recent translators of the *Ṭabaqat*, Salem and Kumar (1991: 94 n 5), have suggested that this quotation from Al-Waṣyfi may have been a later addition to the work of Ṣaᶜid by a copyist, since Al-Waṣyfi died in 1202 some hundred and thirty years after the death of Ṣaᶜid (Kaḥalah 1957 1: 125). But we do not know the exact dates for Al-Waṣyfi and whether he might be the same person as Ibn Waṣif Shah, who is believed to have lived in the 10th century (Ferré 1991), or perhaps even Ibn Waṣif Al-Ṣabi' (Sezgin 1994). The quotation above seems to have been particularly popular since it is often repeated, and sourced to Al-Waṣyfi (eg Abu Al-Ṣalat *Al-Risalah*: 24; Al-Qifṭi *Ikhbar*: 228).

Arab thoughts on the origin and conflict of species and on natural selection leading to the evolution of humans can be seen in the works of Jabir (d ca 815), for example in his book *Tadbir Al-Iksir* (8–9), where he even hints at an evolutionary connection between fish and humans, warning his readers 'not to be surprised at such a connection' (*ibid*: 9). These discussions on evolution had become common knowledge by the 9th/10th centuries, as can be seen in the works of Ikhwan Al-Ṣafaa (Kruk 1996: 79 and n 55), Al-Muqadasi (d 950) (*Al-Bad'* 2: 75f), and Miskawaih (d 1030) (*Tahdhib*: 64ff). Salem and Kumar's suggestion that the quoted passage of Al-Waṣyfi is a later addition may be supported if they were referring to the comment on it, attributed to Ṣaᶜid, which questioned the intellect of the ancient Egyptians if they had truly been the advocates of such a theory of evolution. He said:

> If true, this will make them [the ancient Egyptians] as far as they could be from the discipline of wisdom and the laws of philosophy. (Ṣaᶜid *Ṭabaqat*: 94)

This quotation of Ṣaᶜid is in contrast to his obvious admiration for Egyptian scientific knowledge seen in his accounts of the many eminent Greek scientists who studied under Egyptian masters. Finally, it is worth pointing out that such 'species of animals having strange forms and extraordinary appearances' have been found in Egypt (Simons *et al* 1990; Nothdurft *et al* 2002) and are likely to have been noted by both ancient Egyptians and medieval Arabs.

THE NATURAL SCIENCES

Medieval Arab sources were well aware of their debt to pre-Islamic scientists, particularly in the area of the natural sciences – which included physics and mechanics. Of those pre-Islamic scientists particular mention is made of Archimedes (ca 287–212 BCE), originally a native of Syracuse, Sicily, but known in medieval Arab sources as Archimedes of Alexandria, an Egyptian Greek who according to Al-Qifṭi (*Ikhbar*: 48–49) was behind the building of dykes, dams and new villages in Egypt to alleviate the effects of the Nile floods:

> The reason was that for most villages in Egypt when the Nile flooded, the inhabitants left them and went up the nearby mountains where they stayed until the Nile receded, for fear of drowning. As the Nile started to recede, people began going down to their fields and started cultivation but they were prevented from reaching the higher fields because the lower ones would still be filled with water, so they had to wait until the water dried up completely, thus missing a lot of produce. Archimedes surveyed all the villages at the highest possible level of the Nile and filled in much land and built villages connected by bridges and dykes that allowed water to flow from one village to another so that they all benefit from the water and all are cultivated. He set up endowments, the income of which was designated exclusively for the upkeep of these bridges and dykes. This system is still in place even now and it has a separate Diwan known as *Diwan fidn al-jisur* (Department of Dyke Lands) which still receives special care, and I knew it since I was a child as it has been under my father's supervision with many deputies and a large staff. The work in this Diwan was harder than all others.

However effective was the work of Archimedes in trying to manage the effects of the annual Nile flood, this was obviously still causing problems some 12 centuries later, when Al-Baghdadi devoted much of his time to scientific observation and record-keeping to try to find a solution to the damaging effects of varying flood levels. He started his own observations in the year 1200, but included in his book details of flood levels from 622 CE. He tells us that the minimum level of the flood was 16 cubits, referred to as *dhira*ᶜ*- al-Sulṭan* (royal cubit ca 66.5 cm) which would trigger the taxation system. His records show that between the years 622 and 1200 the flood failed to reach this level in only 26 of these years. The level of flood for taxation purposes that he quotes may well have remained unchanged since pharaonic times.

Arab fascination with pre-Islamic Egyptian sciences and scholars was not limited to past Egyptians but included their contemporaries as well. For example, while Al-Masᶜudi's narrative on ancient Egyptian wonders is mainly concerned with marvels and the advanced scientific knowledge of the past (*Muruj* 1: 360), he also observed and admired contemporary Egyptian innovations:

> We mentioned the production in Upper Egypt, close to Abyssinia, where they produced crossbreeds from bulls and she-asses, and also from donkeys on cows. We gave an account of their genetic [?] engineering (*ḍroup al-tawlidat*), in animals and plants in our book titled 'Book of Matters and Experiments'. (Al-Masᶜudi *Muruj* 1: 363)

Al-Baghdadi (*Al-Ifadah*: 118f) too described with admiration Egyptian technology, for example the water system serving the public baths and also the artificial breeding of chickens in what was called a chicken-breeding factory (*ma^cmal al-firuj*), where eggs were stacked in their thousands in heated, sealed rooms with floors furnished with papyrus mats (Al-Baghdadi *Al-Ifadah*: 87–90).

MIRABILIA OF EGYPTIAN SCIENCE

Arab sources attributed to pre-Islamic Egyptian scientists many scientific innovations that can be called *Mirabilia*, including the following inventions and disciplines:

- Medicine, alchemy, magic and astronomy, which were taught for the first time by Hermes the Copt, who preserved these sciences on the walls of Egyptian temples.
- The Burning Mirror on the top of the Alexandria Lighthouse which, in addition to guiding ships into harbour, had two other functions: the first being an early-warning system enabling watchers to see ships long before arrival at the Egyptian coast; the second being in cases where ships turned out to be hostile – by directing the mirror at a certain angle to reflect and intensify the sun's rays and focusing it on incoming enemy ships, the ships would be set alight at sea (*Akhbar Al- Zaman*: 154; Al-Harawi *Al-Isharat*: 48; Yaqut *Mu^cjam* 1: 188; Al-Qalqashandi *Ṣubḥ* 3: 356). Ibn Ḥawqal (*Ṣurat*: 142) disagreed that those were the functions of the mirror, believing the whole structure to be an observatory to study astronomy (on the Burning Mirrors see Toomer 1976).
- Mechanical devices such as water-clocks, water-wheels, and automated devices used in the temples, such as those seen in the work of Hero of Alexandria (eg Hall 1971: 49 no 31; 50 no 32; 57 no 37; 83 no 60).
- A metal cannon which fired sulphur to protect Egypt against enemies (*Akhbar al-Zaman*: 113).
- A glass planetarium made for King Tosidon/Tomidon (*ibid*: 123).
- Decoration of tombs and ceilings with astronomical scenes (*ibid*: 133).
- Glass that bent without breaking – 'flexi-glass' (*al-zujaj al-ladhi yoṭwa fa-yanṭawi wa la yankasir*) (*ibid*: 136).
- An automatic public clock that sounded every hour (*ibid*: 136).
- A city lighthouse with a dome on top, painted with a special chemical which, when the sun set, illuminated most of the city. Neither wind nor rain affected this light, which faded only when the sun shone (*ibid*: 145).
- The Egyptian Hermes cut a new Nile and redistributed its water more evenly (*ibid*: 159).
- A dome was erected to announce the New Year, with smoke of different colours rising from it. If the smoke was green, it indicated that the New Year would be a good one for building, fertility, and good harvest. If the smoke was white, it would be a lean year. Red smoke meant bloodshed, wars and the

arrival of enemies. If it was black, it meant great rains and flash floods and damage to some of the land. If the smoke was yellow, it meant fires and cosmological disasters. If the colours came out mixed, this signified strife amongst the people and neglect of duty on the part of their rulers (*ibid*: 159).

- Sand attacking the western side of Egypt was stopped by erecting a statue with an inscribed body holding a basket and a hoe (*ibid*: 160–61).
- State monopoly of alchemy to enrich the kingdom of Egypt (*ibid*: 169).
- Production of healing statues to cure all kinds of ailments (*ibid*: 169).
- A statue of a woman, the seeing of which cured misery and depression (*ibid*: 171).
- A lighthouse that flooded the city with a different coloured light each day of the week. The lighthouse was in the middle of a pond with coloured fish. The city was protected by talismans with human bodies and baboon heads. Nearby, a special new city had in its centre a dome, above which a permanent cloud always rained lightly. At this city's gates were statues of priests holding scrolls of scientific works, and whoever wanted to learn a science went to its particular statue, stroked it with his hand and then stroked his own breast, thus transferring knowledge of the science to himself. These two cities were named after Hermes (*ibid*: 175–76). This is clearly a description of what was left of Ashmunein, the centre of Thoth/Hermes, and an attempt to explain the remaining monuments based on the ancient fame of this centre.
- King Ashmun built under the Nile a tunnel connecting the city of Ashmunein on the West Bank to the East Bank for the use of his women when they went to visit the Sun Temple. The tunnel was paved and its walls were covered with coloured glass (*ibid*: 176–77). This may be mainly a fantasy but there are some related historical facts. Across the Nile from Ashmunein lies the city of King Akhenaton and his Sun Temple. His city also had outlying areas on the West Bank. On both banks there are stelae depicting the king, his wife and daughters worshipping the sun. These were visible to passers-by and very clearly indicate a sun cult with the distinguishing sun disc extending its rays over the royal family. It would be interesting to test the possibility of the existence of the tunnel, though the story may merely be the medieval Arab attempt to explain the existence of the same type of stelae on both banks (cf Murnane and Van Siclen III 1993: pls 1, 17, 18).
- Inventions of advanced technology by Egyptian kings (*ibid*: 197).
- An oven that cooked without fire (*ibid*: 241).
- A blade that automatically slaughtered animals (*ibid*: 241).
- A system that converted water into air (*ibid*: 241).

Many Arab writers said that the ancient Egyptians designed their monuments with astronomical functions in mind. For example, according to Al-Maqrizi (*Khiṭaṭ* 1: 633), the temple of Dendera was said to have 180 niches; each day the sun entered the temple through each of them in succession until it reached the last niche, when it started again from the beginning for the second half of the year. This is an important observation, as indeed the journey of the sun throughout the year is depicted on the ceiling of the Dendera temple, which is divided into two halves, with 180 days allocated to each.

In his account of Heliopolis, Al-Maqrizi quoted Al-Quḍaᶜi, who said that the two obelisks there were connected to the solar calendar:

> When the sun enters a minute of Capricorn which is the shortest day of the year, it reaches the southern [obelisk] and appears on its top. Then when it [the sun] enters a minute of Cancer, which is the longest day of the year, it reaches the northern [obelisk] and appears on its top; and these are the end declination (*wa humma muntaha al-milayn*), and the Equator is between them. (Al-Maqrizi *Khiṭaṭ* 1: 622)

This idea that Egyptian monuments were built with astronomical orientations and functions in mind is indeed supported by modern research (Žába 1953; Belmonte 2001). Hawkins (1971–72: 175) noted that the obelisks in the chapel of Re-Horakhti at Abu Simbel, together with other elements, pointed towards the rising of the midwinter sun (on this obelisk, now in Cairo Museum, see Habachi 1984: 7, 98f). In recent experimental work, the use of the Egyptian obelisk as a gnomon was shown to work in practice (Isler 2001: 13ff, 135ff).

Furthermore, the medieval Arabic idea that monuments, in particular the pyramids, not only had surviving astronomical functions but could also be used as tools for working out chronologies, is now being taken seriously by Egyptologists (Spence 2000). Medieval Arab works on astronomy display a direct knowledge and use of ancient Egyptian sources, as can be seen, for example, in the Arabic names for many astronomical bodies, which on closer investigation have been shown to be of Egyptian origin (Casanova 1902; Goebs 1995). The pioneering work of Ursula Sezgin (1994–) has shown that most of the Arab knowledge of ancient Egyptian scientific inventions is in fact based on actual sources from pre-Islamic Egypt, sometimes Hellenistic but some also pharaonic.

CHAPTER 9

EGYPTIAN KINGSHIP AND STATE ADMINISTRATION

INTRODUCTION

Arab sources show a varied and rich representation of images of Egyptian kingship, or what may be called the concept of pharaonic divine rule. Their understanding went beyond the image of the oppressive pharaoh, which was a facet of one particular pharaoh and could by no means be applied to all. The sources also describe Egyptian monarchs as leading their nation in a prosperous and well-managed system of government. Some of the interest of the writers was perhaps in showing their current ruler as an even better exemplar in a line of just and efficient rulers.

Royal chronicles (*akhbar al-muluk*) were a popular genre in Arabic sources, and issues relating to Egyptian kingship were part of these writings. Ancient Egyptian kings received wide coverage in the Arab sources for three main reasons:

- The Qur'an refers to Egyptian royal deeds, in particular those of the Pharaoh of Moses.
- Moslem rulers who instigated writings on the histories of pre-Islamic nations were deeply interested in the deeds of ancient kings.
- Arab historians were fulfilling their patrons' wishes by focusing on royal chronicles.

A good example is Al-Aṣmaᶜi, who makes clear in the introduction to his book on the history of Arabs before Islam that his patron Harun Al-Rashid asked him to write a book on 'Chronicles of the Kings of the Most Ancient Arabs' (*Akhbar Muluk Al-ᶜArab Al-Ba'idah Al-Awaliyah*) (Al-Aṣmaᶜi *Tarikh*: 3). Surviving stories of royal deeds from Late Period Egypt were still current among native Egyptians, and served as an endless source for early Arab historians writing on ancient Egyptian kings and queens. These stories were also woven into the oral epic traditions of pre-Islamic kings and queens, which were written down after the advent of Islam.

Memories of ancient Egyptian monarchs survived, with their deeds interwoven with those of current monarchs. Knowledge of many ancient monarchs survived into medieval times with their correct names, for example Zoser, and others, particularly from the Late Period, such as Inaros. Arab sources were enamoured of the personality and deeds attributed to Alexander the Great and to Cleopatra. The latter was depicted by Arab writers as an able monarch and scholar who was comfortable among philosophers and scientists; she was regarded as an accomplished mathematician, alchemist and medical doctor as well as a great builder. The Arab Romance of Cleopatra is just as rich as the Alexander Romance and should be seen within the context of both Egyptian and Arab cultural environments, which viewed as normal the fact that women could hold power.

IMAGES OF THE PHARAOH

There are many extant materials, often with very favourable views of Egyptian pharaohs, but in spite of this Haarmann (1980: 56) noted as a serious obstacle facing Moslems who wanted to develop a deeper interest in the history of ancient Egypt, 'the undeniably sombre image of pharaonic Egypt in the Qur'an and in Islamic tradition'. It is true that some Moslem exegeses of Qur'anic references to a particular pharaoh portray the word as synonymous with tyranny and arrogance (Wensinck (Vajda) 1965: 917; Wood 1998: 186f).

But this may be a result of a one-sided personal interpretation of the Qur'an, since the Islamic tradition is too varied to be summarised so simply. Haarmann and others are in fact referring to the limited Qur'anic portrayal of a certain pharaoh who is depicted as having oppressed an Israelite community, as the Qur'an uses the word *firʿun* only for this particular king. In spite of the common perception of this pharaoh's image, there are also Qur'anic verses referring to his dialogue with Moses that give an impression of the Egyptian king's willingness to resolve his dispute with Moses by non-violent means (Q26: 23–35). This pharaoh is also shown seeking the opinion of his people as to what to do about Moses (Q7: 109–12) and even giving Moses the choice of date for the showdown between himself and the pharaoh's magicians (Q20: 58–59). On the appointed day, Moses was given the option to begin if he so chose (Q7: 115).

In his dialogue with Moses, the pharaoh comes across as an eloquent speaker who consults his people and, even when tired of Moses, he asks the people around for permission to kill him (Q40: 26), something a pharaoh did not have to do. The pharaoh originally threatened Moses with imprisonment if he insisted on worshipping a god other than himself (Q26: 29), hoping that the threat would persuade Moses to change his mind. Finally, as Pharaoh, in pursuit of the Israelites, was drowning in the sea, he decided to give in to Moses and to accept his God:

> We took the Israelites across the sea: Pharaoh and his soldiers in pursuit, in insolence and spite. When overwhelmed by the water, he said: I believe that there is no god but the One in whom the Israelites believe and I am one of the Moslems. (Q10: 90)

This verse became the subject of endless debate amongst the Qur'anic commentators as to whether the pharaoh should or should not be regarded as a Moslem, having so professed when he was drowning. The debate did not change the perception among lay Moslems of this pharaoh as a model of tyranny. The medieval Arab sources on the whole interpret this image in the Qur'an as representing only one particular king of Egypt; and even this pharaoh, according to some, became a Moslem, a view widely held and appreciated in some Ṣufi circles (Wensinck (Vajda) 1965: 918; Gril 1978). Some Ṣufi masters went even further, claming that this pharaoh was more perfect than Moses and that his drowning in the sea was a 'rite of baptism': such views must have been popular enough to earn the wrath of no less a figure than the eminent Moslem theologian Ibn Taimiya (d 1328) (Memon 1976: 34, 375f n 490).

Other writers tried to reconcile the image of this pharaoh as depicted in the Qur'an with their views of ancient Egyptians as believers in God. One example of this is Al-Shahrastani (d 1188), who says that the Egyptian pharaoh of Moses was:

> formerly of the Ṣabaean Sect [of Ḥarran] but left it and claimed he was the Great God. (Al-Shahrastani *Al-Milal* part 2: 329)

Once again a clear connection is made between Ancient Egyptians and the Ṣabaean. The pharaoh's claim to being a god, regardless of his actual identity, is known from ancient Egyptian sources, for example King Ramesses II, who is shown on his monuments deified while still alive (Habachi 1969; Kitchen 1982: 225f).

As part of the Arab rehabilitation process of the image of the Pharaoh of Moses, the historian Abu Al-Fida (d 1331) (*Al-Mukhtaṣar* 1: 80) cited a dialogue between God and Moses in which the latter complained that the 'infidel pharaoh' was treated favourably by God and granted a long life, and God had replied: 'I did so because he [the pharaoh] has two characteristics typical of piety: generosity and modesty' (*li-an fihi khiṣlatin min khilal al-iman; al-jud wa al-ḥaya'*). With tales like these, it is clear that for many Moslems, the pharaoh of Moses was not representative of all rulers of Egypt, and that even he could somehow be rehabilitated into the fold of Islam. This was not a unique case, as many medieval Arab writers sought to bring other pharaohs into the fold of Islam; for example, the author of the book *Akhbar Al-Zaman* (190) suggested that another pharaoh was 'indeed a monotheist'.

Attempts to understand the nature of ancient Egyptian kingship went far beyond the stereotype of the pharaoh as tyrant, as is clear in the writings of native Egyptian historians such as Ibn Ẓahirah (*Maḥasin*: 121f) and Al-Suyuṭi (*Ḥusn* 1: 44f), who portray the kings of pharaonic Egypt as models of efficiency and kindness, dedicated to the well-being of their people. This Arab image of the pharaohs is supported by ancient Egyptian sources (Badawy 1967). So the perceived image of the pharaoh as the archetype of tyranny is founded not on a Qur'anic portrayal of Egyptian kingship or on a common medieval Moslem view, but on a narrow interpretation of the Qur'anic story of a single king. The issue is further complicated by the continued willingness on the part of some researchers to yield to old prejudices whereby Egyptian kings are seen through the prism of *oriental despotism*. If such tyranny had been the norm in Ancient Egypt, then the pharaohs would not have stressed continually that their kingship was based on Ma^{c}t, the goddess of Justice, or that the king's mouth was indeed her temple (El-Saaddy 1999: 136). Nor would a king such as Horemheb have said that he was awake at all times, working for the good of Egypt and studying cases of injustice throughout the land (Labib and Abu Talib 1972: 40; Kruchten 1981: 21).

The Arab fascination with the pharaohs of Ancient Egypt is also displayed in various Arabic stories relating to pharaohs, illustrating their private as well as their public lives. This fascination led to the assimilation of narratives of Arab epics, such as that of the pre-Islamic Yemeni king Saif Ibn Dhi Yazan, which encompassed most of the motifs known in Arab epics (Yaqṭin 1994: 8–9). This ancient Yemeni king travelled throughout pharaonic Egypt observing the styles of its architecture and religious rituals, and throughout the tale we find descriptions of ancient Egyptian motifs such as searching for the Book of the Nile (Lyons 1995 1: 11; 2: 241f), and words and names such as that of the sky goddess Nut (*Sirat Saif Ibn Dhi Yazan* eg 3: 117ff, 153ff, 207ff, 319ff; 4: 4f, 96f, 276).

In the sources, the most common epithet for an Egyptian pharaoh is 'Lord of the Pillars' (*Dhu Al-Awtad*), following the Qur'anic use of this epithet for the pharaoh of Moses (Q38: 12; Q89: 10). This recalls the ancient Egyptian epithet of some pharaohs, for example Amenhotep II, Tutankhamun and Ramesses III as *hq3 iwnw*, the Lord of Iwnw, the city of Heliopolis, which is written with the sign for pillar, also called *iwnw*, in plural (Faulkner 1962: 13). The wife of the pharaoh of Moses was held in high regard in Arab sources and was named 'Asia' (likely to be the ancient Egyptian *3st/3sa* ie Isis). Her tomb was said to be near the Ibn Ṭulun Mosque in Cairo and was one of the holy sites sought out by visitors to Cairo (Al-Sakhawi *Tuḥfat*: 115). This district has been a rich source for the study of reused pharaonic antiquities, including the sarcophagus of Hepmin now in the British Museum (EA 23) (cf Jakeman 1993 2: 165). An ancient building, known locally as Mastabat Fir^{c}un, has not survived, but is described as being built of massive mud brick walls almost identical to ancient Egyptian temple precinct walls (eg at Dendera), and may have been the remains of pharaonic buildings (for this building and other pharaonic remains in the area see Salmon 1902: 70–95 and pls II: 1, 2 there; Sayyid 1988: 307f). It is worth noting that the local name for this whole area, *Qal^{c}at Al-Kabsh*, meaning 'Fort/House of the Ram', was thought to originate in a medieval Arab tradition according to which an ancient Egyptian priestess had a statue of a ram erected on top of a pillar in the area in order to protect Egypt (Salmon 1902: 78). This may indicate either that the area had in pharaonic times been a part of an avenue of rams leading to Heliopolis, the main cult centre of the sun god whose symbol was the ram, or that there was a local chapel for his worship in this area which ensured its continued sanctity down the ages. Al-Maqrizi (*Khiṭaṭ* 2: 89–90) gives an account of a building in this area erected by Khumarawayh, who ruled Egypt between 884 and 896 after the death of his father Ahmad Ibn Ṭulun. Al-Maqrizi recounts that Khumarawayh built in his residence a court named the 'House of Gold', painted in gold and lapis lazuli and decorated with images in high relief, taller than life-size, both of himself and of his favourite women and singers, adorned with crowns of real gold and the finest jewellery with fine heavy ear-rings all attached to the wall, while their bodies were painted to represent the wearing of fine linen. This is clearly a description of the bas relief art of the time, commonly seen on pharaonic walls. Was this an imitation of local ancient Egyptian buildings found in the area? Or was it a result of the ruler's interest in ancient Egyptian antiquities like his father before? Whatever the truth, it is still remarkable since it is a common misconception even among some Moslem scholars (eg Al-Qaradawi 1999: 100ff) that Islam and Moslems prohibited the representation of human images, this in spite of the fact that such representations are widespread in Islamic art (Marzuq 1974: 209). Another example cited by Al-Maqrizi (*Itᶜaẓ* 3: 71; cf Ṣayyid 1992: 165) is of the Fatimid viẓier Al-Afḍal Ibn Badr Al-Jamali (d 1094) who had in his court 'eight images of maids', four on each side, dressed in the most luxurious clothes and jewellery, who would bow down to him upon his entry until he sat down.

Medieval Arab stories of pharaohs in Persia and elsewhere are also common and may have some historical foundation, as the writers may well have seen Persian royal figures with Egyptian designs, such as that of King Darius I standing on a typical Egyptian pedestal inscribed with hieroglyphs (**Figures 9, 10**). This Persian reverence for Egyptian tradition (Myśliwiec 2000: 154) must have spread the fame of the pharaohs throughout the Persian Empire.

One of the most important roles of the pharaoh in medieval Arab sources is that of magician who employs the science of magic for the well-being of his people as well as for the destruction of his enemies. There are various sources for such imagery in Demotic/Coptic and Greco-Roman literature, where memories of Egyptian kings of older times survived (Depauw and Clarysse 2002).

Demotic romances of ancient Egyptian rulers such as Zoser, Inaros (on the latter see Lichtheim 1980: 151ff; Kitchen 1986: 455ff; Ryholt 1998) and Nectanebo (Perry 1966) also became popular in the medieval Arabic sources, which show them as heroes, with their names and deeds well recognised by the writers. Other pharaohs are perceived in Arabic sources not only as guardians of their own people but also as protectors of foreigners fleeing atrocities. One example is found in Ibn ᶜAbd Al-Ḥakam (*Futuḥ*: 31) who gives an account of a pharaoh whom he called Qumis Ibn Luqlis, a contemporary of the Babylonian king Nebuchadnezzar (II). After the latter had destroyed Bayt Al-Maqds (Jerusalem) in March 597 BCE, many of its inhabitants were said to have escaped to Egypt, where they were welcomed by the pharaoh Qumis, who refused to return them to the Babylonian king, this in spite of the latter's threats and his eventual conquest and destruction of Egypt and enslavement of its people for 40 years according, for example, to Ibn ᶜAbd Al-Ḥakam. The available ancient sources have not as yet provided references to events such as these (cf Kitchen 1986: 407 §369 with n 969).

The image of a deeply spiritual pharaoh was also portrayed in medieval Arabic sources. For example, the writer of *Akhbar Al-Zaman* describes an Egyptian king whom he called Budshir:

> It was found in some of their symbols and holy books of their priests that King Budshir bin Qfiṭwim exhausted himself in the worship of the Supreme Luminous [bodies] and realised that their spirits entered him. He became infatuated with them, and starved himself; his body gave up food and drink. When he became ecstatic, the Supreme Luminous desired him as he desired them, so they raised him up to their place and purified him of all the painful evils of earth and made him a Luminous, floating within their luminosity and he could do as they could. (*Akhbar Al-Zaman*: 166)

So fascinated were medieval Arab epic narrators and writers by the ancient Egyptian rulers that the latters' deeds were incorporated into new epics of the heroic deeds of contemporary rulers, as illustrated by the Sirat Al-Sulṭan Baybars I, which was and still is one of the most popular epics (Lyons 1995).

STATE ADMINISTRATION

Some of the medieval Arab writers I have used as sources were themselves senior officials in various government departments, for example Ibn Faḍl Allah, Al-Qalqashandi and Al-Maqrizi, and it was only natural that they would devote some of their writings to the subject of state administration under the pharaohs.

But earlier than these, writers such as the author of *Akhbar Al-Zaman* (125) attribute to one Egyptian king the organisation of the state into seven classes, indicating the high status of the priests in the Egyptian hierarchy. At the top of this social system was:

> the king, his son, the one in charge of Justice, the High Priest, the Grand Vizier, the Seal Bearer of the king and his Treasurer.

The account which best sums up medieval Arabic knowledge of ancient Egyptian administration is that of Ibn Ẓahirah (*Maḥasin*: 121–25). He quoted Ibn Zulaq and Al-Maqrizi and unnamed others in saying that the pharaoh collected taxes which amounted to 90 [*sic*] million dinars. This revenue was divided four ways, as follows:

- 10 million for the upkeep of the people;
- 10 million for governors, soldiers and scribes;
- 10 million for the upkeep of the royal household;
- 50 million reserved for pharaoh.

This amount of some 80 million dinars was calculated by Toussoun (1931: 8) as equivalent to 162 million LE (ie Egyptian pounds) in his own time. When the pharaoh wished to increase the revenue, he ordered the construction of housing, the repair of dykes and increased land reclamation.

Ibn Ẓahirah (*Maḥasin*: 122), quoting unnamed sources (see Ibn Zulaq *Faḍail*: 86), reported a slightly different division of revenue:

- a quarter for the royal household;
- a quarter for the government, viziers, noblemen, soldiers and scribes;
- a quarter saved for future needs of people;
- a quarter for digging canals and building dykes and whatever else the land needed.

Revenue savings became vital for the years of famine. In one famine, said by Ibn Ẓahirah (*ibid*; Ibn Zulaq *Faḍail*: 89) to have lasted for three years, the king was able to waive all taxes and use the savings to maintain the government. He made up for this later by collecting double taxes when the famine ended and life had returned to normal. This was the custom of the pharaohs, who according to Ibn Ẓahirah 'filled the land and built it with justice and generosity'.

The pharaoh was also said by Ibn Ẓahirah to send every year two of his administrators, one to Upper Egypt and the other to Lower Egypt, carrying grain seeds. They were to inspect the agricultural land, and if any was found lying fallow, the king would order the local official in charge to be executed and his wealth and that of his family to be confiscated.

Another thing admired by Ibn Ẓahirah was that the pharaohs left estates in the hands of their owners for a set rent which was reviewed only every four years, taking into account the state of the land, so some who had problems would pay less and others would pay more, without there being an undue burden on anyone.

This picture portraying the kings of Egypt in charge of an overall administrative system and working tirelessly for a fair distribution of the country's wealth may be based on folktales current among contemporary Egyptians, but it seems to reflect some ancient Egyptian reality as detected in royal decrees such as that of Horemheb cited above. The contemporary view may also have originated in some of the classical writings, such as that of Diodorus (I: 64; Murphy 1990: 81), in which a pharaoh 'aspired to a life free from blame and dedicated to the good of his people'.

It should be noted that the ancient Egyptian expression *ḥm.f*, translated as 'His Majesty', could also be used for 'slave/servant' (Hornung 1990b: 286), which suggests an understanding of the role of the king within society as being to give service, reflecting a well known Arabic proverb *'Sayd Al-Qawm Khadimahum'* meaning 'The master of a community is [also] its servant'. The designation *ḥm.f* also came sometimes to be used by non-royals from the time of the transition period between the Old and Middle Kingdoms, and thereafter (Hofmann 2001).

It may also be the case that, in view of some tyrannical contemporary rulers, medieval writers sought to inflate the good qualities of the ancient pharaohs by way of drawing these to the attention of their own rulers, to encourage them to aspire to emulate the model rulers of the past.

EDUCATION AND THE 'CHILDREN OF THE ROOM'

Arabic sources do not display direct knowledge on the subject of ancient Egyptian education. However, there are scattered references to kings instructing priests to make knowledge in the general sense available to people in vernacular accessible forms.

For example, the writer of the book *Akhbar Al-Zaman* said of an Egyptian king:

> He designated for every group of people (a specific) type of priest to teach them religion, which was at that time the religion of the First Ṣabaean. Each group was to send a detailed report to the king every Day. (*Akhbar Al-Zaman*: 126)

Many medieval Arab writers believed that the pharaohs and their priests were concerned with education as part of the well-being of their subjects. According to the information cited in *Akhbar Al-Zaman*, a royal interest in the teaching of their subjects is attributed to various kings. King 'Minqawis', yet to be identified, ordered the holy books of wisdom to be studied and commanded that books of wisdom be written:

> He produced the Scriptures of Wisdom and commanded that they are studied and written in the script of the common people so that they could understand them, and (he also) restored the priests to their ranks.

This function of the priests is known from various studies. Van der Horst noted that among the many functions of the hierogrammatus priests, the scholarly class of priests in Egyptian temple service, was the cultivation of knowledge of the ancient Egyptian script (van der Horst 1982: 63, 70 n 79).

One very important ancient Egyptian educational institution which appears to have survived across the ages well into the medieval period is *'k3p'*, which is still a subject of conjecture among scholars who have tried to identify the exact nature of the institution often referred to in ancient Egyptian biographies. It is believed to be an educational establishment with close links to the royal palace, and its graduates were called *'hrdw n k3p'* with the meaning 'Children of the Room' (Feucht 1995: 266–304).

But we have in medieval Arab sources a number of references by Egyptian writers (eg Ibn Al-Ṭuwayr (d 1220) *Nuzhat*: 57f; Ibn ᶜAbd Al-Ẓahir (d 1293) *Al-Rawḍa*: 51; Al-Qalqashandi (d 1418) *Ṣubḥ* 3: 477; Al-Maqrizi (d 1440) *Khiṭaṭ* 2: 453–55) to a contemporary establishment with the same name and apparently the same associations. They called it *'Al-Ṣibyan Al-Ḥujaryah'*, 'Children of the Room', in which, from their descriptions, it would seem that an ancient Egyptian institution had survived almost unchanged to medieval times.

The medieval Arabic sources describe a building, close to the royal palace of Cairo, next to Bab Al-Nasr (Victory Gate), one of the main entrances into the city, and say that this building as well as others was dedicated to young people. These were youths (*shabab*) who were selected from among the sons of *'Wujaha' Al-Nass'* 'Notables', and, according to Ibn ᶜAbd Al-Ẓahir, also supported by Al-Maqrizi, numbered about 5,000. They received special education and military training within the school, and students distinguished by either intellect or bravery went on to become leaders and even princes. Each had his own room with its own distinguishing name, such as *'Al-Manṣurah'* meaning 'Victorious', *'Al-Fatḥ'* meaning 'Annexation/Conquest', and *'Al-Jadidah'* meaning 'The New'. Each had his own weapons and his own servants. They were kept under supervision so that their time was spent positively in acquiring skills. They were always at the ready to answer the call to battle. According to Ibn Al-Ṭuwayr, they were also taught different crafts and sciences. They had their own stable situated next to their dwellings.

Both Ibn Al-Ṭuwayr and Al-Maqrizi describe how this institution was run. The King Al-Afḍal (ruled 1186–96) built seven 'Rooms' and selected from the children of the soldiery some 3,000 young men. All were under the command of a prince, and each hundred was under the supervision of two senior officials.

Al-Maqrizi, quoting Ibn Abi Ṭay, described the situation under the Fatimid Caliph Al-Muᶜizz li-Din Allah (reigned 953–75), who provided a special 'Room' for those who excelled in crafts, including scribes, and had announcements made around the country that local governors were to look out for talented youths and send them to Cairo, where they were accommodated in the 'Rooms' which, according to Al-Maqrizi, were several storeys high.

This medieval description certainly seems to mirror the ancient Egyptian *k3p* which, in the light of our current knowledge, would seem to have been established on much the same basis. It had certainly been an unusual institution with a special relationship to the royal palace. Those brought up in it achieved higher status, and had been carefully selected by the most senior officials, in some cases by the king himself.

The establishment which flourished under the Fatimids (909–1171) underwent changes after their demise and the quarters were abandoned, but the idea itself survived into the Mamluk period, according to Al-Maqrizi (*Khiṭaṭ* 2: 453), who noted the similarity between the Fatimid establishment and what was known in his day as *'Al-Mamalik Al-Sulṭaniyah'* meaning 'Mamluks of the Sulṭan', who were usually foreign-born youths bought by the Sulṭan and given strict military training and education, so that as adults they formed the upper echelons of Egyptian society. Again this recalls cases in ancient Egypt where those selected for the *k3p* included youths from foreign lands (Saleh 1966: 210).

It seems clear that this establishment had survived from Ancient Egypt through its different historical phases until the medieval period. The Arabic sources have furnished us with details which have until now been missing from the archaeological record, thus giving us a better understanding of the probable nature and extent of the establishment during the pharaonic period where such palace schools certainly flourished from the Fourth Dynasty onwards (Berlev 1990: 98).

KINGS AND QUEENS

Ancient Egyptian rulers with various stories relating to them were cited in classical sources such as Herodotus (II: 99–182), who referred to 20 different Egyptian rulers, and Diodorus (I), who referred to 29, of whom 23 have been certainly identified (Burstein 1992: 47). The works of Josephus were also known and widely used by medieval Arab scholars (Pines 1971) and would no doubt have included his version of Manetho's *History of Egypt*.

The writings of the Egyptian historian Manetho (3rd century BCE) were certainly known to medieval Arab scholars (Altheim and Stiehl 1966 3: 11ff). He is cited by Agapius (ca 940 CE) who referred to him as 'The Egyptian Sage, the Astrologer' (Agapius *Al-ᶜUnwan*: 16) and cited his book *On The Stars*. Agapius also noted that the Ṣarraneans, who worshipped sacred images, cherished Manetho's work. Manetho's work was used also by Al-Biruni (*Al-Athar*: 90ff) to compose a king list of the Egyptian dynasties from the Twenty-first Dynasty until the time of the last native pharaoh Nectanebo II of the Thirtieth Dynasty, giving a total period of 894 years for 34 native Egyptian kings, in addition to the Persian rulers of Egypt whom he did not name. This figure is almost in agreement with present-day chronology, if we take the starting point of the Twenty-first Dynasty to be 1069 BCE (Kitchen 1986: 465). This was followed by accurate recording of the reigns of the Ptolemaic Dynasty up to the death of Cleopatra, who ruled for 19 years according to Al-Biruni (*Al-Athar*: 92; Hölbl 2001: 231). Al-Biruni does not give reasons why he chose to start his Egyptian king list with the name of Diospalta, attributing to him a reign of 26 years which raises the question as to whether he was in fact King Pedubastis I, founder of the Twenty-third Dynasty and who, according to Kitchen (1986: 97f), reigned for 25 years. But Pedubastis is actually cited by Al-Biruni in the correct place in the list. It may be that Al-Biruni misread the name of the city Diospolis where, according to Manetho, the kings of the Twentieth Dynasty originated (Manetho Fr 57). All the succeeding names on Al-Biruni's list follow the same order for Dynasties 21–30 as Manetho. Al-Biruni made only a brief reference to Persian rule by referring to 'Persians until Darius [II]', giving them a total period of 111 years as against the known 120 years of their rule. It is thanks to Al-Biruni's 'Chronology' that such knowledge was kept alive among Moslem scholars (Neugebauer 1962: 210).

Events of this later period of Egyptian history must have remained vivid in the collective memory of Egyptians, to the extent that they influenced Al-Biruni into thinking that it was all the history of Egypt that was known. These memories may be evidenced by the survival of epics depicting the lives of some notable figures of this period: Psammetichus, Amasis, Inaros, and Nectanebo, as well as Cambyses, Alexander the Great and Cleopatra.

Kamal (1903) collected and studied the names of ancient Egyptian rulers as cited in medieval Arab sources. These were divided into two groups: 19 kings who reigned before the Flood and 106 kings and queens who reigned after the Flood, ending with King Nectanebo. Most of the Egyptian names used in the Arabic sources can be traced back to the list in Manetho. The name of the well-known king Ramesses does not appear in Kamal's list, but it was cited by Al-Idrisi (*Anwar*: 80) as the name of the city of Heliopolis, which according to him is cited in the Old Testament (Genesis 47: 11) and is also the name of a Delta town called by the Arab authors '*Kurat Ramesses*' in present day Menufiyah (eg Yaqut *Mu^{c}jam* 5: 216; Al-Qalqashandi *Ṣubḥ* 3: 462).

Certain kings and queens were singled out in Arabic sources for lengthy accounts, for example those who built the pyramids (A Fodor 1970; S Fodor 1970). This is also true of the queens who fought for Egypt or built walls to protect the country, such as Daluka and Qarupa (see below). But the most detailed accounts are those of Alexander the Great, as medieval Arab sources had a special regard for him as well as for Queen Cleopatra. Many speak with passionate admiration of Alexander (Christides 2000; Mazzaoui 1991; Wheeler 1998), and a great many volumes were produced in what could be termed 'Alexanderomania Arabica', no doubt continuing the older Egyptian and Greek traditions of the Alexander Romance (EI^2 4: 127ff; Jasnow 1997). Christides (2000: 166) ascribes the idea that Alexander was buried under a pyramid to 'certain absurd figments of the imagination of Arab authors like Al-Idrisi, who states that Alexander was buried under a pyramid'. In fact, Al-Idrisi in the reference given (*Anwar*: 89) was merely retelling earlier accounts by other authors and, in this particular case, was quoting Ibn Krion whose account ends with this sentence: 'Aristotle was buried in one of them [the two pyramids in Giza] and Alexander was not buried in the other.' Such misunderstandings and mistranslations of Arabic texts are unfortunately very common in current literature.

Pre-Islamic Arab history also saw several strong queens exercising power in different kingdoms that flourished in Arabia (cf the royal name list in Kitchen 2000: 741ff) as well as women occupying the highest religious offices as High Priestesses (Al-Aṣmaᶜi *Tarikh*: 124f; ᶜAjinah 1994 2: 293ff).

CLEOPATRA: 'THE VIRTUOUS SCHOLAR'

Medieval Arab historians were just as fascinated by the personality of Cleopatra as many others have been since. The image of the queen in medieval Arab sources is that of a strong and able monarch who was very protective of Egypt. These sources focus on her many talents but make not one reference to sexuality or seductive power; they admire her scientific knowledge as a scholar, and her administrative ability. The most interesting aspect of her image is that of a scholar who made significant contributions in the fields of alchemy, medicine and mathematics (Ullmann 1972a). She is shown conducting courtly seminars attended by scientists from different fields, at which she contributed to the discussions as a polymathic scientist.

Arabic sources often refer to Cleopatra as 'The Virtuous Scholar' and cite scientific books written by her as the definitive works in their field. One of the sources drawn on by the Arabs was the 'Dialogue of the Philosophers' from Greek sources, which were allegedly translations from ancient Egyptian texts. This Arabic image of Cleopatra is in contrast to her more familiar image in Greco-Roman sources and later, which presented the queen as a hedonist, a seductive woman and a deceiving and over-ambitious queen (Ertman 1990: 4ff English summary).

Arabic names of Cleopatra

It must be admitted that in the Arabic sources, as in the Greek alchemical texts, it is sometimes unclear just who is the Cleopatra being referred to, but in general Arab writers knew that this Cleopatra was the last ruler of the Ptolemaic Dynasty of Egypt. Some of the confusion lies in the names. Her original Greek/Egyptian names and titles most commonly used on contemporary monuments were:

- Cleopatra.
- Thea (eg *nṯr t*) = The Divine (also the Sage).
- Philopator (eg *mr it .s*) = She who loves her father/Beloved of her father.
- *S3t Geb* = Daughter of the God Geb (for this name see Troy 1986: 179).

Some of these had undergone phonetic changes by the time they reached the medieval Arabic writers, with the result that there seem to be a number of very different names for the same queen. Cleopatra appears in the Arabic sources under the following names:

- Qilopaṭra قلوباطرا
- Qilpaṭra قلبطرة
- Qalupaṭri قالوبطرى
- Qilawfaṭra قلاوفطرة
- Qulfidar قلفدار
- Qarupa قروبة
- Kilapaṭra كلابطرة
- Elawpaṭra ايلاوبطرة
- Elawaṭra ايلاويطرة
- Aklaupaṭr أكلاوبطر

In addition to these, there are various forms or modifications of the above names. Often the P in the name changes to F or N. Medieval Arab writers were interested in the meaning of names, so they explained the name of Cleopatra as meaning 'The Weeping Rock' or 'The Weeping Woman' (Sayyid 1985: 30). The oldest Arabic source to suggest this meaning is Agapius in the early 10th century CE in his book *Al-^{c}Unwan* (128), and the same meaning was adopted by later writers such as Al-Makeen (Sayyid *ibid*).

Cleopatra, the great builder

The Egyptian bishop, John of Nikiou, who was contemporary with the Moslem annexation of Egypt in the 7th century CE and who wrote a history of Egypt, included a section on Cleopatra which became the basis for study and interest among Arab writers. According to a new study by ^{c}Abd Al-Galil (2000: 260–62), the bishop's book, now lost and known only from an Ethiopian translation, was written in Arabic and not in Coptic or Greek. If this is so, it is the oldest book in Arabic to mention Cleopatra. The book has been translated into French (Zotenberg 1883) and into English (Charles 1916).

Bishop John of Nikiou (Charles 1916: 48–50) gives an account of Cleopatra that starts with the meeting between her, 'a pretty young virgin', and Caesar, who fell in love with her, married her and had a son with her. Caesar then gave her the throne of Egypt. The bishop goes on to describe her building projects in Alexandria, 'the like of which had never been seen before'. Among these projects was the digging of a canal to supply the city with Nile water. They included a great royal palace on an island (Pharos) to the north-west of the city, and a causeway (the Heptastadeion) across the water (Hughes-Hallett 1990: 100). All these projects were commented upon by later Arab writers such as Ibn cAbd Al-Ḥakam (*Futuḥ*: 40–41), Agapius (*Al-'Unwan*: 128) and Yaqut (*Mucjam* 1: 187).

The first known reference to Cleopatra by an Arab historian is found in Ibn cAbd Al-Ḥakam (*Futuḥ*: 40–41), who wrote his history of the Moslem annexation of Egypt in the early 9th century CE. There he refers to the Lighthouse of Alexandria, saying that:

> It was built by Daluka ... It is also said that the builder of the Lighthouse of Alexandria was Qulpatra, the queen who dug the canal/gulf into Alexandria and paved its bottom.

In these words we encounter an early possible confusion between two queens: Daluka (also called Zulaikha) and Cleopatra. We do not know the historicity of Queen Daluka, but her name is almost always used synonymously with that of Cleopatra. Both are said to have built the Alexandrian Lighthouse and a massive wall around all of Egypt to protect it against invasion, and Daluka was said to have built a Nilometer at Memphis. Though Cleopatra did not build the Lighthouse, her fame as a builder of great monuments gave rise to such claims in the medieval Arabic sources.

Among Cleopatra's buildings in Alexandria, there is a great temple described by Philo of Alexandria as 'a piece incomparably above all others' (Butler 1978: 371–72). This great temple was later converted into a Christian church by Emperor Constantine the Great (Butler 1978: 374 n 1). All the medieval Arab writers who spoke of Cleopatra were most impressed by her great building projects; amongst them were Al-Bakri, Yaqut, Ibn Al-cIbri, Ibn Duqmaq, and Al-Maqrizi.

But the most admired quality in the Queen was her political skill and courage (Hughes-Hallett 1990: 103; Hazzard 2000: 149), and she was also depicted as a very able administrator (Agapius *Al-cUnwan*: 129).

Cleopatra, the alchemist, scholar and philosopher

The traveller and historian Al-Mascudi (d 956) was the first Arab writer to give any details of the Queen's interests in science and scientists. In his book (*Muruj* 1: 304) he says of Cleopatra:

> She was a sage, a philosopher who elevated the ranks of scholars and enjoyed their company. She also wrote books on medicine, charms and cosmetics in addition to many other books ascribed to her which are known to those who practice medicine. (Cf Hughes-Hallett 1990: 99; Fraser 1972 1: 312)

Al-Mascudi also counted her among the great alchemists, together with Maria (*Muruj* 4: 257; cf Lunde and Stone 1989: 358). Al-Nadim (*Al-Fihrist*: 420) credited Queen Cleopatra with a book on alchemy named after herself, 'The Book of Queen Cleopatra'. This is also known as *Risalah*, 'Epistle of Cleopatra', and is presented in the form of a dialogue between a group of scholars and Cleopatra (Holmyard 1937: 50; Ullmann 1972b: 366; Anawati 1996: 861).

Al-Nadim (*Al-Fihrist*: 420) also refers to Maria and her book on alchemy, now lost, ascribing the Dialogue of Philosophers to Maria. This might suggest that some confusion between these two women alchemists already existed in the 10th century. In fact this confusion seems to have continued, compounded by the presence of another woman whom the same sources call 'Maria the Copt' (ie the Egyptian), sometimes called Maria the Jewess (Anawati 1996: 861). As though this alchemical mix up between Cleopatra and these two Marias were not enough, we have yet another Maria of popular legend, St Mary the Egyptian (Stevenson 1996: 21 and 80ff), who was thought to have appeared in Palestine in the 6th century CE, where we again find the two main associations of Maria the Alchemist: Master Teacher Zosimos, and the Divine Vision (Patai 1994: 74ff). Zosimos was the 3rd century CE grand master of alchemy who taught and corresponded with his student disciples Cleopatra/Maria/Theosebia/Euthasia. The Divine Vision is claimed by every alchemist to have led them to sacred knowledge and to god.

In the Greek and Arabic alchemical texts, we see a queen addressed as one of the alchemists with the name 'Theosebia' (Vereno 1992: 246ff; Fowden 1986: index; Patai 1994: index). Vereno (*ibid*) associates this name, Theosebia, with the Goddess Isis. Cleopatra regarded herself as, and assumed the character of, Isis (Witt 1997: 19, 222; Hazzard 2000: 153–54) to legitimise and cement her claim to the throne of Egypt.

From the variations of these names, I believe that the name Theosebia, written also as Euthasia, is more likely to be an Arabic rendering of parts of Cleopatra's titles, *Thea* and *Sat Geb*. Theosebia is also a perfectly good Greek name, which means 'Scribe of the God' and implies piety.

Other books credited to Queen Cleopatra include one on toxicology attributed to her by Ibn Waḥshiyah (Levey 1966: 12, 22) and one on mathematics, possibly written by an Alexandrian mathematician called Cato who dedicated his books to her. This book was said to be widely known as 'Katon's Book to Cleopatra'. Another book also dedicated to the Queen by Cato but which she is usually credited with having written, is 'The Abridged Law of Cleopatra', described as 'a simple law that is easy to understand' by Ibn Juljul in the 10th century CE (Sayyid 1985: 38), a description repeated by Ibn Al-ᶜIbri (63) in the 13th century.

Also attributed to Queen Cleopatra was the invention of certain devices and symbols used in alchemical works (Anawati 1996: 861; Berthelot 1888: 132 fig 11; Taylor 1949: 51ff).

Cleopatra, the physician

Cleopatra was apparently interested in and wrote on drugs, cosmetics and metrology (Fraser 1972 1: 372; 2: 548 n 306). It may have been as a result of her fame and interest in drugs that medieval Arabic biographies of Galen (2nd century CE) mention a female medical doctor called Cleopatra as one of his teachers, but no link to our queen can be proved. Moreover, there is no mention of a woman of this name among Galen's teachers in his biography by Sarton (1954 esp appendix 1).

In medieval Arabic sources, Galen's teacher was a female gynaecologist who was credited with teaching him all he knew of medicine and the treatment of women. Among these sources are Ibn Hunain in the 9th century (Sayyid 1985: 163), Ibn Fatik in the 10/11th century (*Mukhtar*: 289; Rosenthal 1975: 34) and Ibn Uṣaybiᶜah in the 13th century (*Ṭabaqat*: 109).

It may have been the fame of Queen Cleopatra, either as an author of medical books or due to her patronage of such works which Galen consulted, that gave rise to this claim in Arab sources of a connection between him and Cleopatra as his teacher, though Galen himself referred to the 'Cosmetics' of Cleopatra and her recipe for hair-loss treatment (cited in Rowlandson 1998: 41). There may have been a Greek healer called Cleopatra, a gynaecologist, whose work on obstetrics had long been consulted by medical practitioners. This notion is supported by Talmudic writings, where there are references to Queen Cleopatra being involved in medical experiments to determine the stages of development of the foetus (Rosner 1994: 41).

Cleopatra's Dialogue with the Philosophers

The Dialogue is known from Greek texts (Berthelot 1888: 289ff; Luck 1985: 372ff; Stavenhagen 1974: 61). It was also known in Arabic documents; for example, the 14th century alchemist Al-Jildaki quoted it in his book *Kitab Al-Shams Al-Akbar* 'The Great Book of the Sun' (Anawati 1996: 861). In this text, a dialogue takes place between Cleopatra and fellow philosophers and alchemists in which they invite her to illuminate them with her knowledge on alchemical matters.

In his study of the two Arabic alchemical texts cited above, Vereno (1992: 246ff) notes their links with ancient Egyptian ideas, a view shared by Roberts (2000: 68), who traced the main ideas of resurrection, rebirth and renewal of life through divine water back to ancient Egyptian beliefs and ideas of the hereafter as seen in the Osirian mysteries.

Another of Queen Cleopatra's many talents was that she apparently knew and spoke several languages fluently, and was the first Ptolemaic monarch to speak Egyptian and officiate at Egyptian religious ceremonies (Hazzard 2000: 148). Such active participation must have required at least a working knowledge of Egyptian religion. This may explain the presence of ancient Egyptian thought in the Dialogue of Cleopatra.

Arab romance of Cleopatra

Cleopatra appears in almost all medieval Arab sources on Ancient Egypt, often occupying a long chapter, for example in Al-Murtaḍi (French trans: 130ff). As discussed above, a major problem is the corruption of the name of the Queen. Another difficulty is that we are unable to associate Cleopatra with any Islamic story, as we can with Alexander the Great, who was assimilated into medieval

Arabic sources as the Qur'anic figure of Dhu Al-Qarneen, Alexander as an incarnation of Amun with the ram's horns.

Yet the Cleopatra of the Romance is a shrewd, cool-headed woman with great political ambitions. The central figure of the Romance is a queen called Qaruba (Charupet), the daughter of a tyrant who ruled with an iron fist and was hated by his people. Qaruba, a young woman of mild manner and disposition but also of great wit, poisoned her father. In the disputes that followed, an Ibrahimi (son of Ibrahim, meaning a Jew) was aspiring to become the next king, but the Vizier made a speech to the populace asking them to support Qaruba, which they agreed to do. After she was installed on the throne she doubled the salaries of soldiers and elevated the ranks of priests, scholars, nobles and magicians. She restored and enlarged the temples.

A foreign general called 'Gabirus' or 'Gabinius' came to Egypt on the advice of his doctor to recover from some illness. He wished to pay the Queen a visit, having it in mind to marry her and thus become King of Egypt. When the Queen heard of this she sent her trusted lady-in-waiting to report on him. It was clear that he was too strong to enter into battle with. The lady-in-waiting took valuable gifts to Gabinus and told him that her mistress was indeed in love with him and desired to marry him, but that she wished that first he build for her a great city on the coast of the Mediterranean Sea. His soldiers spent great effort on the project, but no sooner did a wall go up than mysterious creatures came out of the sea during the night and demolished the work. The Queen's aim was to exhaust the resources of Gabinus and his troops. Eventually, Gabinus built the town, but rather than giving him his reward of marriage, the Queen trod on a serpent and died.

As can be seen from this story, we have the principal known elements of the life and death of Cleopatra. The story was popular enough to have it repeated with slight variations in Al-Nuwairi (*Nihayat* 15: 254f). Interestingly, the name in this story, Qaruba or Charupet, is very similar to the name of Queen Serpot of the Demotic story-cycle of King Petubastis (Lichtheim 1980: 151ff).

The memory of this brave Queen Cleopatra may have been behind the attempts of some Arabic sources to associate her with other famous Arab queens like Al-Zaba' (Zenobia) of Tadmur, Syria who died in 285 CE and who was regarded as a descendant of Cleopatra (Al-Zerekly 1999 3: 41). Zenobia too preferred to kill herself rather than be taken prisoner by her enemy, King ᶜAmr. She took poison, saying *'bi-yadi la bi-yad ᶜAmr'* ([die] by my own hand, not that of ᶜAmr), which became a widely quoted Arab proverb.

One remarkable omission from all the medieval Arabic sources that I have studied is any reference to Cleopatra's seductive physical beauty. This absence perhaps emphasises that the fascination on the part of the Arab writers was with the conduct and achievements of the Queen rather than with her appearance. To judge from her appearance on her coins, she was not a beautiful woman in any conventional sense.

What was left of Cleopatra?

Cleopatra's fame and reputation three centuries after her death were such that Queen Zenobia styled herself as Cleopatra the New in 270 CE, when she brought Egypt under her control (Hölbl 2001: 310).

The Cleopatra cult continued to flourish well into the 4th century CE (Al-Zerekly 1999 3: 41). A place which was perhaps one of her cult centres in Alexandria survives to this day and is known locally as Ḥamamat Cleopatra – 'Cleopatra's Baths'. A similar case can be made for a place in Al-Ashmunein in Middle Egypt called Cleopatra, according to the history by Abu Al-Makarim (*Tarikh*: 221; Kramers 1954: 171). Various places in different parts of Egypt are still named after Cleopatra (see index of the Blue Guide, Egypt).

CHAPTER 10

CONCLUSIONS

It is clear from the Arabic sources that the study of ancient cultures was genuinely valued for knowledge and guidance, believing that all human history was one, albeit of different peoples living in different places, essentially sharing a common origin and common destiny. The medieval Arab study of Egyptian culture is part of this universal historical approach rather than a narrow attempt to validate holy scriptures.

Close ties between pre-Islamic Arabs and ancient Egyptians ensured a sense of identity and continuity with this ancient culture, among the newcomers under Islam from the 7th century onwards.

Arab writers drew on rich and varied sources, both pre-Islamic and contemporary. Their approach to their written sources is at times critical, but not always so. The mere fact that many writers repeated accounts of their predecessors verbatim suggests a continuous interest in their subject matter. Visiting sites and talking to local people also featured as a major source of information. But even previous eyewitness accounts were not always accepted uncritically, as Al-Baghdadi's writings in particular have shown.

The exploitation of Egyptian sites for treasure continued from Ancient Egypt, sadly some of it still being in evidence today. But this exploitation became an established profession in medieval Egypt, organised by the state. Treasure hunting manuals, produced to meet public demand, were often forgeries with fantastic claims, but some may prove to be useful for current archaeological work and, as I have shown, have contributed some of the earliest known drawings of archaeological sites. The extant copies of these manuals in manuscript collections are a testimony to their popularity among different classes of medieval society, which was encouraged by folklore depicting Egypt as the land of treasure.

For more scholarly writers, ancient sites and materials provided opportunities to study the past and bring its people back to life. Many writers had an approach to and appreciation of archaeological processes which are almost identical to the most recent approaches in the field (eg Al-Hamadani in Yemen, and Al-Idrisi in Egypt).

Serious Arab works on local archaeology and culture have been shown to contain accurate accounts of antiquities and a scholarly approach to understanding their function as well as their symbolism.

Egyptian scripts intrigued Arab writers, and were for many the key to profound knowledge and wisdom. The fact that spoken Egyptian was still alive in its Coptic phase made it possible, in conjunction with knowledge of other languages and scripts, to reach a correct understanding of the nature of ancient

Egyptian language. Whatever the motives for medieval Arabics' interest in Egyptian scripts, they undoubtedly succeeded in realising that ancient Egyptian was linked to Coptic, that Egyptian signs had phonetic values and that some were grouped as an alphabet. In addition, a few writers were able to distinguish between signs used alphabetically and those used as determinatives. The whole process of decipherment of ancient Egyptian hieroglyphics was undoubtedly assisted by the view that the ancient Egyptian and Arabic languages had so many features in common as to indicate a common origin.

There remains a large corpus of material for a future survey and study of ancient scripts in the medieval Arabic sources, as hundreds of scripts were included in their studies. It is clear that in the case of Egyptian scripts, those medieval Arab writers who concerned themselves with decipherment were mainly alchemists and often Ṣufis as well. This suggests that a detailed study is required to establish the connection between ancient Egyptian alchemy and religious philosophy, and Moslem alchemists and Ṣufis. Studies of the sources of Moslem Sufism tend to focus on its Indian and Persian roots, with an almost total absence of any consideration of an Egyptian source or input (among exceptions are Witteveen 1997: 1–4; Roberts 2000: 201–25; DuQuesne 2001b). A rich reward awaits any researcher who compares the sun hymns of Akhenaton to the Moslem Sufism of *Ishraq*, Illumination, as represented by its famous master Suhravardi (cf Corbin eg 1976, 1983, 1986). Any proficient Egyptologist will see clear parallels. Concepts such as the 'Perfect Being/God', 'Transfiguration/Transformation of the Body/Soul', 'Luminous Ones', amongst others, are common to both ancient Egyptian religion and Moslem Sufism, and any serious student of Egyptian religion will benefit from reading studies such as those of Corbin and others. Further, a detailed study of current religious practices of the Mandaeans/Ṣabaeans of Iraq and Iran and beyond might shed further light on Egyptian religion, based not only on their claim to be descended from Egyptians, but, more importantly, on the many similarities between their rituals and beliefs (eg celestial bodies, water rituals, the tree mother who suckles children, divine birth, the sun barque, the five divine epagomenal days that are counted at the end of the 360 days of the year but not regarded as part of the year, the Book of the Two Ways, the unification of the deceased with his likeness . . . and so on).

It was probably access to ancient Egyptian texts written in Demotic and Coptic, often with Greek translation, which helped Arab scholars to gain a better understanding of the complexities of Egyptian religion. But in seeking to comprehend the religious practices of the ancient Egyptians, many Arab writers resorted to contemporary observation as well as to information from earlier accounts, in particular the Greek sources. In this process, attempts were made to accommodate ancient Egyptian religion within the rich mosaic of Islamic teachings, and even to bring some eminent figures from the past, for example Thoth/Hermes, into the fold of Islam.

This approach was greatly helped by the fact that the fabric of many of the ancient Egyptian temples was still almost intact in medieval times, displaying their rich iconography, with scenes of prayers, offerings and other rituals, many of which were correctly interpreted. The temples were perceived by Arab writers as institutions of wisdom and learning, where magic played an important part in religious practice. Egyptian magic for Arab writers was a science practised by kings, queens and priests, as part of the formal structure of Egyptian religion.

The medieval writers also recognised the sanctity of Egyptian religious sites, particularly the pyramid area. Not only did they describe the survival of some ancient Egyptian practices among medieval Egyptians, but many tried to find common ground between Islamic teachings and ancient Egyptian religion, in common with some modern scholars (eg Kamal 1909: 51ff; Al-Sayyar 1995: 153ff). Many place names in Egypt still show their ancient origin, and modern Egyptians, like their medieval forebears, Moslems and Christians alike, regard as holy, places which their ancient ancestors sanctified. Colleagues in the field of Egyptology should build bridges with scholars of medieval Arab philosophy who have studied the history and origins of philosophical thought (Indian, Persian, Greek, Arabic . . .), because their insights may help to shed light on ancient Egyptian philosophical issues which are still regarded by Egyptologists as obscure. I believe that many ancient Egyptian philosophical ideas regarding the creator and the created, the sun and celestial spheres, astronomy and astrology, cyclical time, the nature and fate of the soul, to name but a few, formed the basis of later Greek and Arabic philosophy, and scholars working in the latter field have already developed methods to understand such ideas. Conversely, we can draw on ancient Egyptian texts in order to understand some of the ambiguities that still baffle those working on Greek and Arabic philosophy. Some of these ambiguities may have been an understandable result of translating a concept from ancient Egyptian into Greek or Persian, and then into Arabic.

Another subject which might benefit from further study of the medieval sources is the cult practices of the earlier Egyptian kings. Many popular practices involving royal cults are considered in some detail by the medieval sources, and certainly merit further study: this might help Egyptologists to understand the effects of cult practices on the general populace, and the folk traditions which arose from them.

The same may be said of Arabic appreciation and study of animal cults and oracles, which are valuable for their sympathetic treatment and provide an indication of the survival of some of these practices well into the medieval period.

Popular and scholarly interest in the subject of *mummia* and mummification, of both humans and animals, and the medicinal uses of the former, is common in medieval Arabic sources, and some scholars actually studied Egyptian mummies to settle anatomical problems. Questions were raised about burial contexts, and about the types of animals mummified, with reasons for the choice, and there are some accurate insights based on direct observation. It is also clear that the trade in Egyptian *mummia* and its export to the West was rampant much earlier than was previously thought.

Like their classical predecessors, Arab writers believed that Egypt was the land of science and wisdom originating with Hermes the Egyptian, to whom they attributed the invention of writing as well as the sciences of alchemy and medicine, among other disciplines. This created a corpus of writings in which accounts of Egyptian scientific mirabilia became very popular, and these should not be dismissed out of hand by modern scholars on the ground that they appear fantastic. In fact, evidence is still buried in the land of Egypt, and also in our museums, awaiting serious investigation, and it is quite possible that evidence for some of the scientific inventions described will be uncovered.

Many Arab writers believed that the Egyptian kings had been greatly concerned with the well-being of their subjects and had utilised all available sources, including magic, to achieve this. They knew that the pharaoh of Moses, as portrayed in the traditions, was a single monarch who was not a typical representative of Egyptian kingship. They depict Egyptian rulers as very learned and often pious figures, as well as efficient administrators, who were mainly concerned with the well-being of their nation. Medieval Arab sources also describe institutions which appear to have survived without interruption from pharaonic Egypt and which continued to function, offering potential to augment the evidence of the ancient Egyptian records. The example shown here, that of the 'Children of the Room', could serve as a model for further research.

The medieval Arab epics kept alive the memory of long departed pharaohs of Egypt, sometimes reproducing their Romances interwoven with those of known Arabian figures such as Saif Ibn Dhi Yazan, the pre-Islamic king of Yemen, or current monarchs such as Sultan Baybars I. Some ancient Egyptian rulers still appear under the names known to us from the archaeological record, for example Zoser, Amasis, Inaros, Nectanebo and Cleopatra. Some of the reasons for this survival, as well as being found in Coptic and Greek sources, must surely lie in the Demotic sources, many of which lie unstudied in museum cupboards.

Cleopatra was chosen as a case study, not because there is insufficient material in the Arabic sources about others, but to show how very differently her image appears in the Arabic sources from her more usual portrayal in some classical as well as modern sources. She is represented in medieval Arab sources as a philosopher and scholar without reference to her physical attributes. But this may also be seen as a reflection of the medieval Arab cultural environment which viewed powerful, intellectual women as normal, based on the well recorded history of such women from pre-Islamic Arabia and Egypt until the medieval period when many of these writers worked.

The brief background of many of the writers which I give in Appendix 1 is intended to give the reader a cursory glimpse of the seriousness of their knowledge and modes of enquiry, which are characteristic of most medieval Moslem scholarship. It is also important to note the range of backgrounds of these scholars, who treated Egypt's past and present with utmost respect and appreciation. They range from scholars of tradition such as Ibn ᶜAbd Al-Ḥakam, historians such as Al-Idrisi, Ṣufi masters such as Dhu Al-Nun Al-Miṣri, and scientists such as Al-Biruni, to alchemists such as Ibn Umail and Abu Al-Qasim Al-ᶜIraqi. Also interesting is the wide range of their countries of origin. In addition to native Egyptians, Moslem and non-Moslem, they came from places as far apart as Spain in the West and Iran and beyond in the East. Almost all spoke and wrote in Arabic, the *lingua franca* of their day.

I would like to end this conclusion on a personal note. I started this journey as an Egyptologist in search of a missing link in the history of our discipline, but of no less importance to me as an Egyptian is the light which this study has shed on the continuous links which the Egyptians maintained with their ancient heritage throughout the medieval period. It has highlighted for me the need for Egyptians as a nation to revive this collective interest and to take a more active role in the study and preservation of our heritage. This may not be easy after two and a half centuries in which the study of Egyptology has been dominated by a Eurocentric view which has virtually ignored more than a thousand years of Arabic scholarship and exploration.

Archaeologists working in other parts of the Near East are, as a result of local concerns, becoming aware of and addressing this problem of Western dominance and interpretation of their fields (Matthews 2003: 200), something which their colleagues in Egyptian archaeology are yet to address seriously. But at the same time, we must acknowledge our immense debt to our Western colleagues for their invaluable contribution.

I hope that by affording a glimpse of the richness of medieval Arabic sources and the breadth and depth of their interest in Ancient Egypt, a gap in the history of the study of Ancient Egypt is at least narrowed, though certainly not filled completely.

I have shown the long kinship between Egypt and her Arabic neighbours, and to this I must add some extracts from an eminent recent scholar, Gamal Hamdan, from his groundbreaking study, *Character of Egypt*:

> Egypt's four dimensions African, Asiatic, Nilotic and Mediterranean – each aspect has played its role in certain periods of its long history. (1: 42–45)
>
> It was impossible for Egypt to live in isolation; it was at the centre of the world. The isolation brought about by its deserts was one-sided and it was always a magnet for people. Indeed, everyone and everything came to Egypt and seldom did Egypt have to go out: trade, sailors, immigrants, conquests, colonialists, even the Nile and the winds came to it. (1: 43)
>
> Egypt is Pharaonic through its grandfather, but Arabic through its father. Yet both father and grandfather have common origins and descend from the same great grandfather. Family relationships are well established from prehistory, Islam and Arabization were merely a reaffirmation of these ties. There is no contradiction between Egyptianism and Arabism for both are the warp and the weft in a single national fabric. (1: 45)

I end as I began: with a quotation from a medieval Arabic scholar:

> We have dealt – as we think, adequately – with the problems connected with that (subject). Perhaps some later (scholar), aided by the divine gifts of a sound mind and of solid scholarship, will penetrate into these problems in greater detail than we did here. A person who creates a new discipline does not have the task of enumerating (all) the (individual) problems connected with it. His task is to specify the subject of the discipline and its various branches and the discussions connected with it. His successors, then, may gradually add more problems, until the (discipline) is completely (presented). (Ibn Khaldun *Muqaddimah* 3: 481)

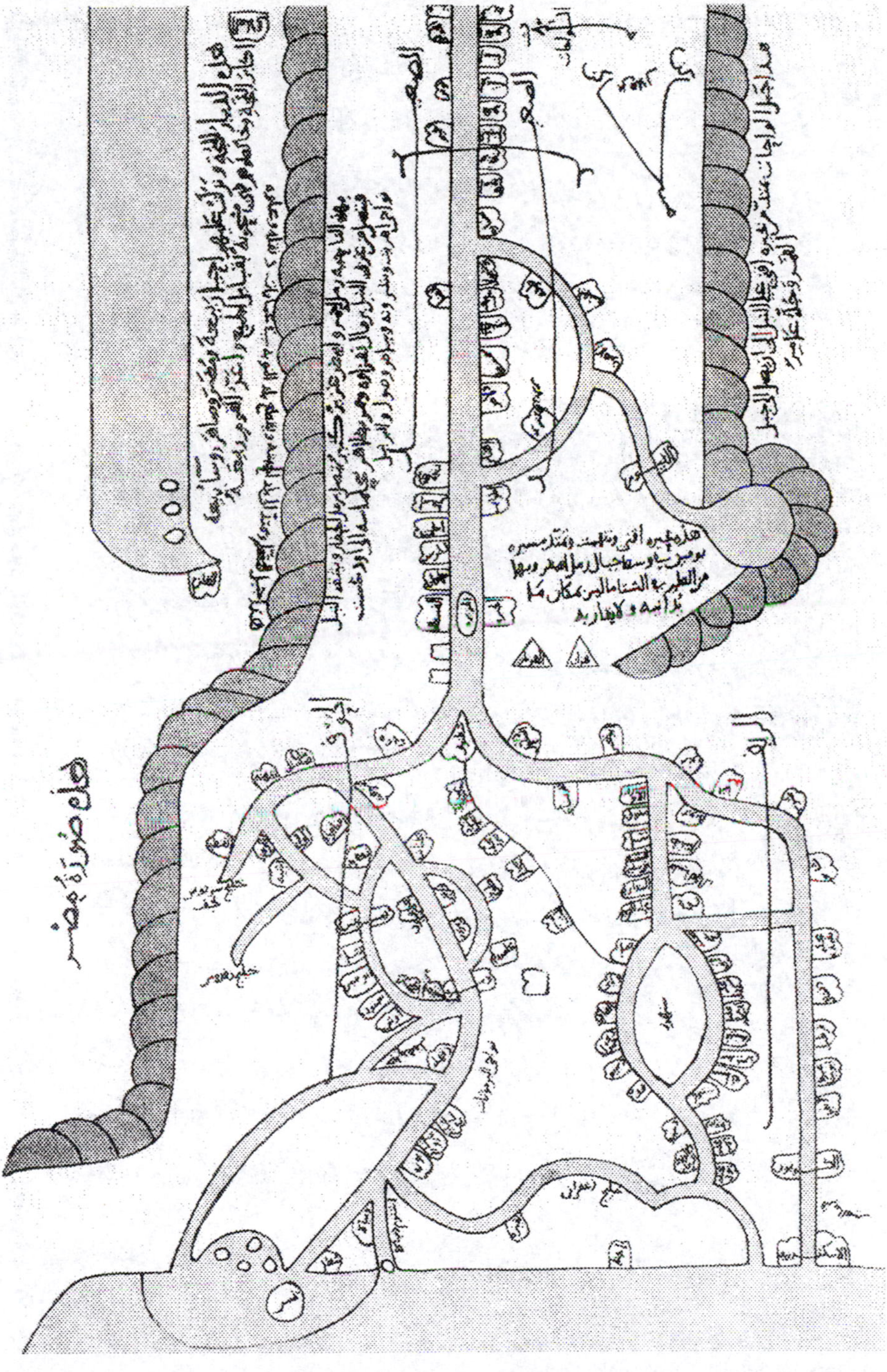

Figure 2 Map of Egypt in Ibn Ḥawqal (*Ṣurat*: facing page 128).

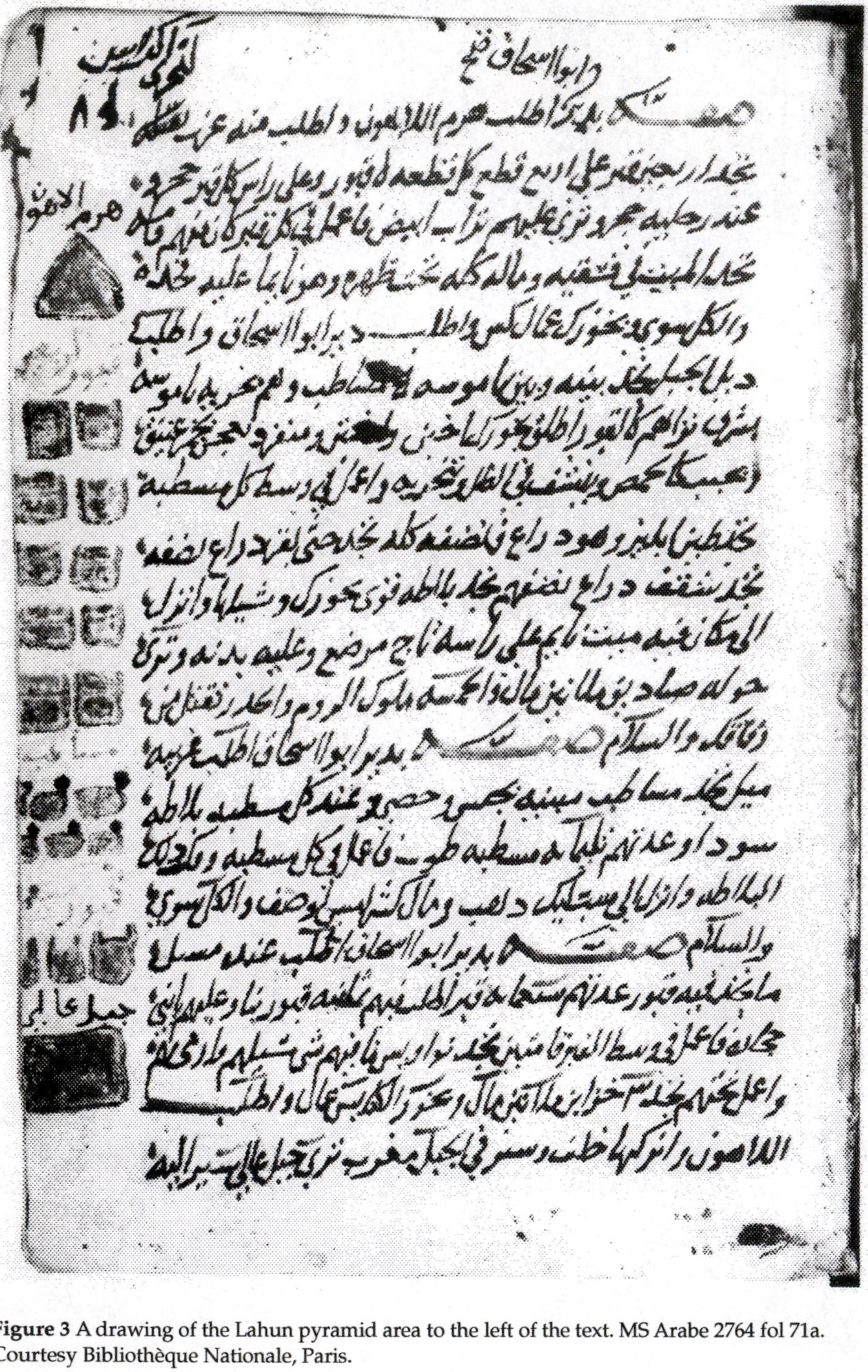

Figure 3 A drawing of the Lahun pyramid area to the left of the text. MS Arabe 2764 fol 71a. Courtesy Bibliothèque Nationale, Paris.

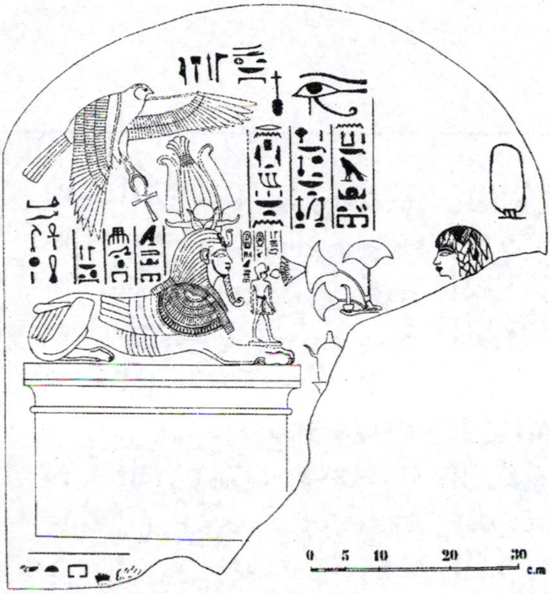

Figure 4 A New Kingdom stela showing the Sphinx with the small royal figure below his head. After Hassan 1951: fig 39.

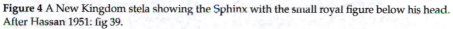

Figure 6 The Lighthouse of Alexandria in Al-Gharnaṭi, early 12th century. After Ferrand 1925: pl II.

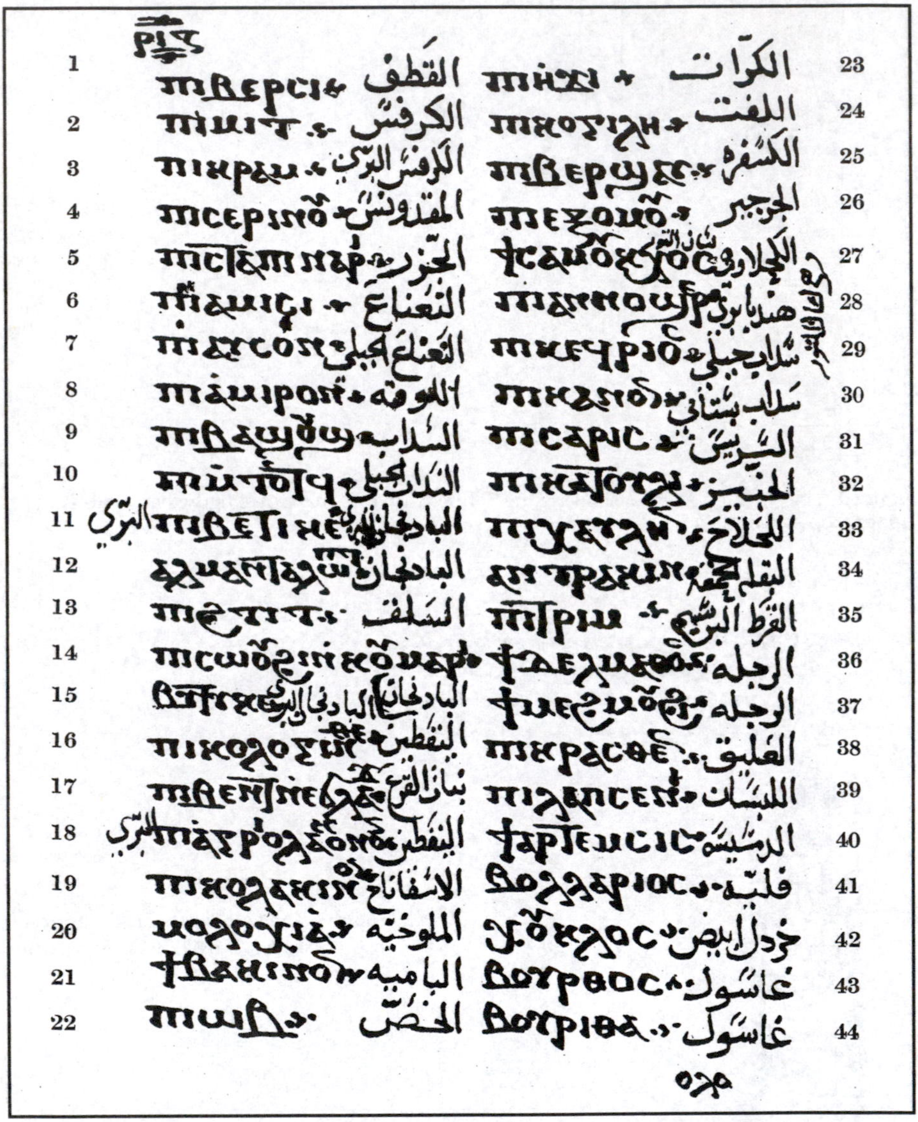

Figure 7 From the Scala Magna of Ibn Kabr. A list of vegetables in Coptic-Arabic (MS Or 1325 fol 117a British Library). After Budge 1928: 81.

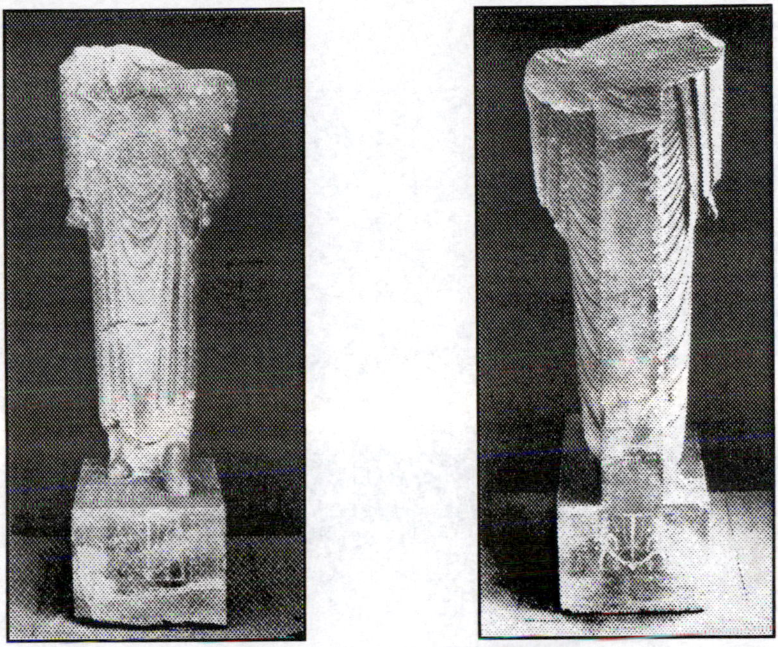

Figure 9 A statue of Darius I (522–486 BC) from Susa. After *Cahiers de la délégation archéologique Française en Iran* 4: 204 fig 20 (cf Myśliwiec 2000: 147 fig 41).

Figure 10 Egyptian inscriptions on the base of the statue of Darius I. After *Cahiers de la délégation archéologique Française en Iran* 4: 205 fig 21 (cf Roaf 1974; Myśliwiec 2000: 150–51 figs 44–45).

Figure 11 Detail of the same statue of Darius I showing the titles and names of Darius I in Egyptian hieroglyphs. After *Cahiers de la délégation archéologique Française en Iran* 4: 208 fig 24 (cf Myśliwiec 2000: 149 fig 43).

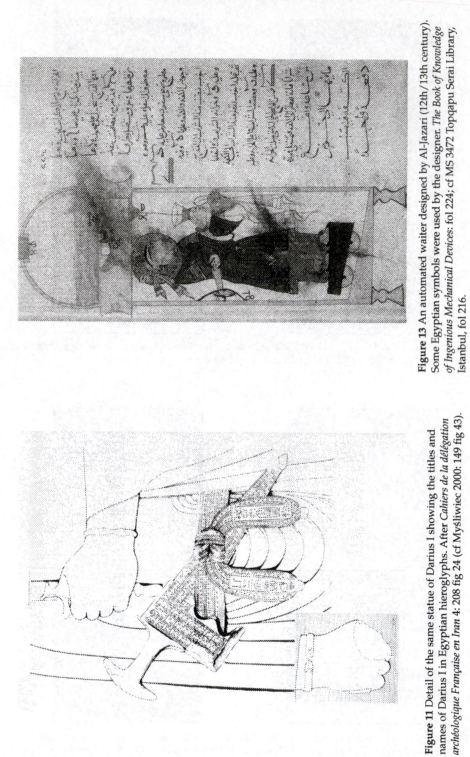

Figure 13 An automated waiter designed by Al-Jazari (12th/13th century). Some Egyptian symbols were used by the designer. *The Book of Knowledge of Ingenious Mechanical Devices*: fol 224; cf MS 3472 Topqapu Serai Library, Istanbul, fol 216.

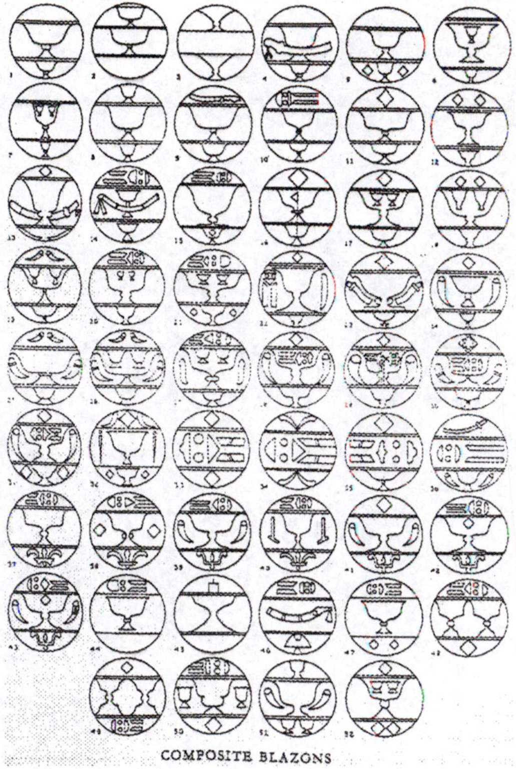

Figure 14 Use of hieroglyphs for *Nb*, *M3ᶜt*, *Rᶜ* (and perhaps *T3wy*) in Islamic Art for Mamluk emblems. These denote Lord of Justice, The Sun, of the Two Lands. After Mayer 1933: 30. By permission of Oxford University Press.

Figure 15 The Coptic alphabet with its phonetic values and order correctly identified. Dhu Al-Nun Al-Miṣri (*?all*, MS Muallim Cevdet K 290 fol 12a, top and 12b below).

Figure 16 Egyptian alphabet according to Ibn Waḥshiyah (*Shauq*, MS Arabe 6805 fol 92b on the right and 93a on the left). Courtesy Bibliothèque Nationale, Paris.

Figure 17 Ibn Waḥshiyah *Shauq*: fol 93b to the right and 94a to the left.

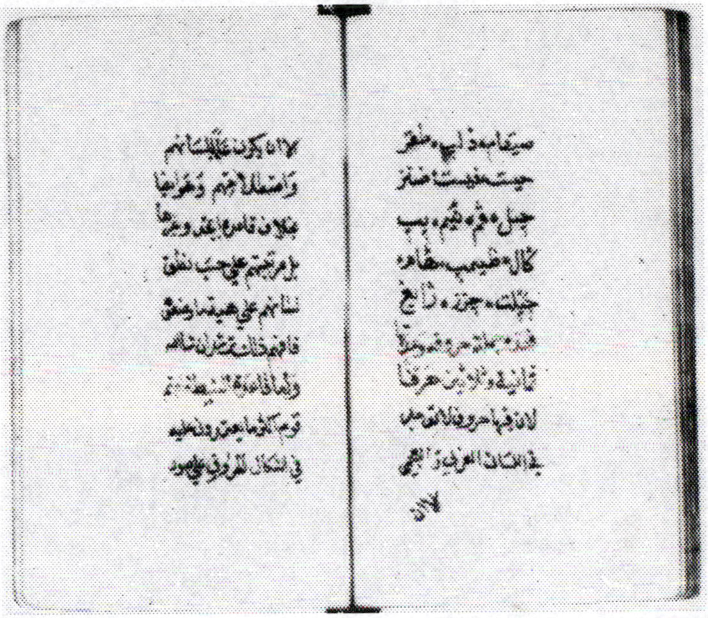

Figure 18 Ibn Waḥshiyah *Shauq*: fol 94b to the right.

Figure 19 Ibn Waḥshiyah *Shauq*: fol 56a to the left.

Figure 20 Ibn Waḥshiyah *Shauq*: fol 56b to the right.

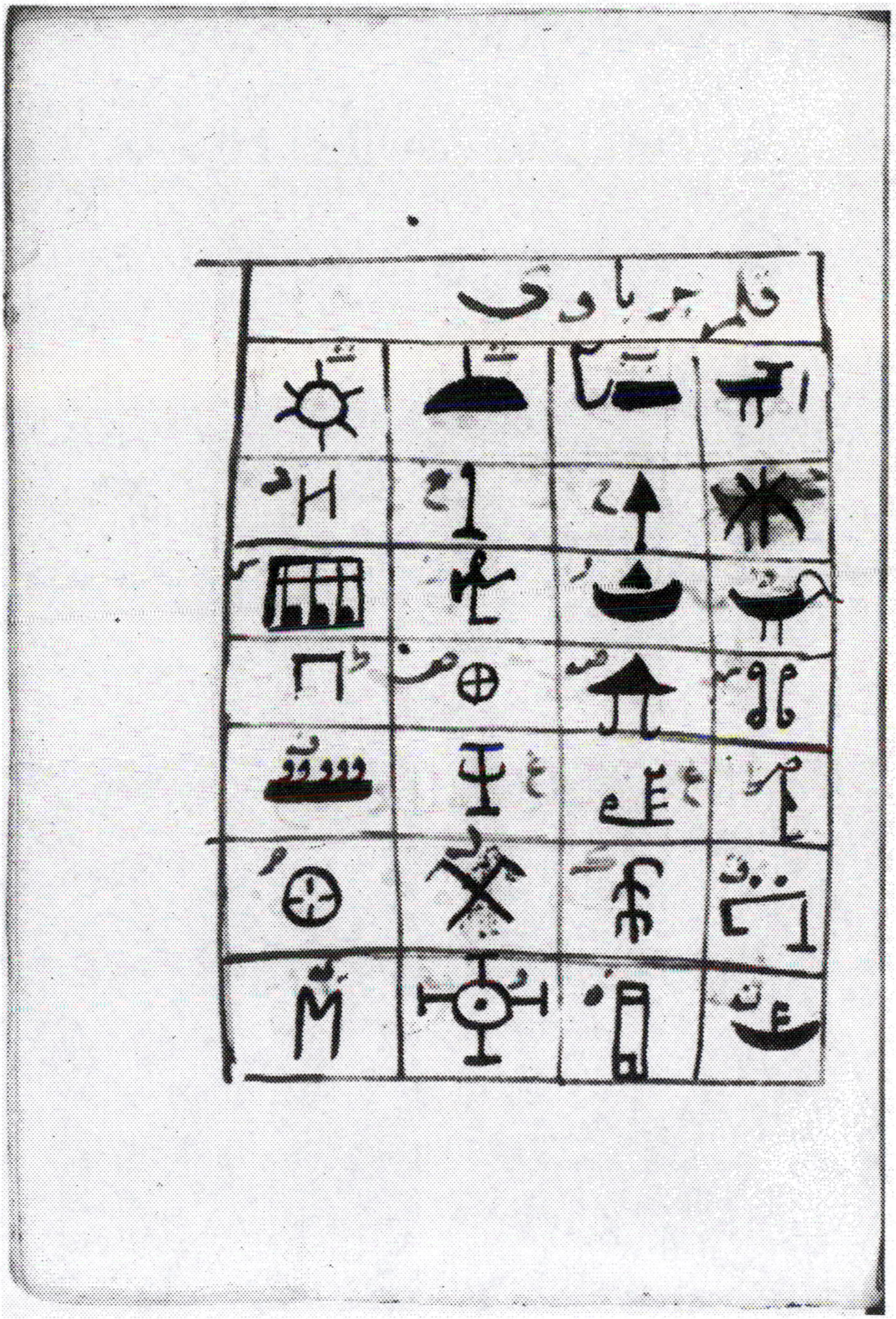

Figure 23 Egyptian alphabet deciphered in Abu Al-Qasim Al-ᶜIraqi MS Arabe 2676 fol 18a. Courtesy Bibliothèque Nationale, Paris.

Figure 25 A script named after the Ṣufi/alchemist Jabir Ibn Ḥayan in Dhu Al-Nun (*Ḥall* fol 36b top). Many letters resemble Egyptian Demotic.

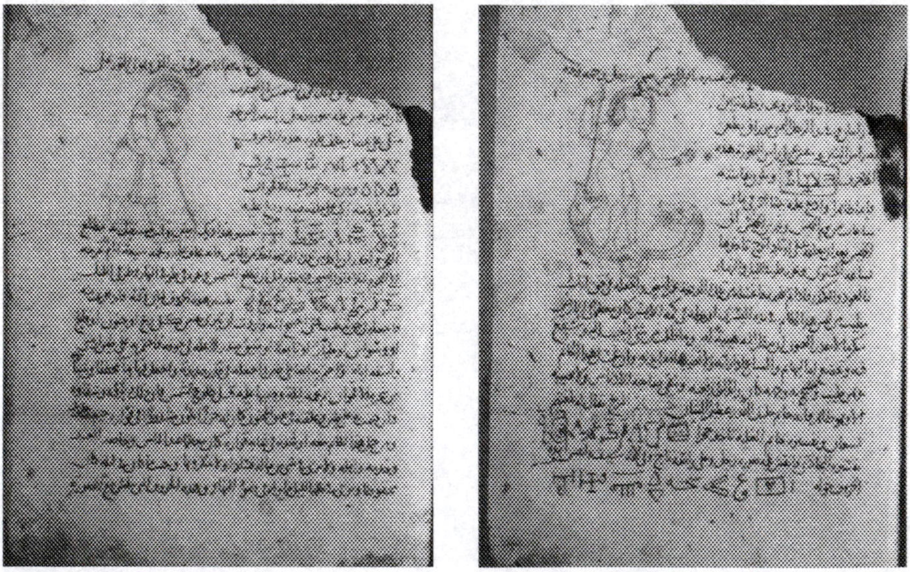

Figure 26 The Egyptian god Horus copied in a medieval Arabic book of magic, *Kitab Al-Mala?is* (MS Bodleian Arabe d 221 fol 49a to the left and 51a to the right). Courtesy Bodleian Library (cf Beeston 1962: pl II).

Figure 1 ***(colour)*** A watercolour by Petrie of a medieval Moslem tomb at Bab Al-Wazir, Mamluk cemetery, Cairo. © Petrie Museum of Egyptian Archaeology, University College London. W 13.8 cm, H 22.7 cm.

Figure 5 ***(colour)*** A medieval astrologer offering incense at the Temple of Akhmim (*Kitab Al-Bulhan* MS Bodleian Or 133 fol 29a). After Carboni 1988: pl 18 and pp 71f.

Figure 8 ***(colour)*** An example of Arabic texts on Fatimid textiles emulating Egyptian hieroglyphs. Two Arabic words that are repeated (*Al-Yomn wa Al-Iqbal*) mean 'Prosperity and Good Fortune'. Cairo, Museum of Islamic Art No 596. Courtesy of the Museum of Islamic Art, Cairo. My thanks to Mohamed Abbas Selim (cf Stillman 1997: 49 fig 15).

Figure 12 ***(colour)*** Egyptian hieroglyphs/symbols inspired tool designs in medieval Arabic alchemy. Abu Al-Qasim Al-^{c}Iraqi (*Kitab Al-Aqalim Al-Sab^{c}ah* MS Add 25724 fol 11a British Library).

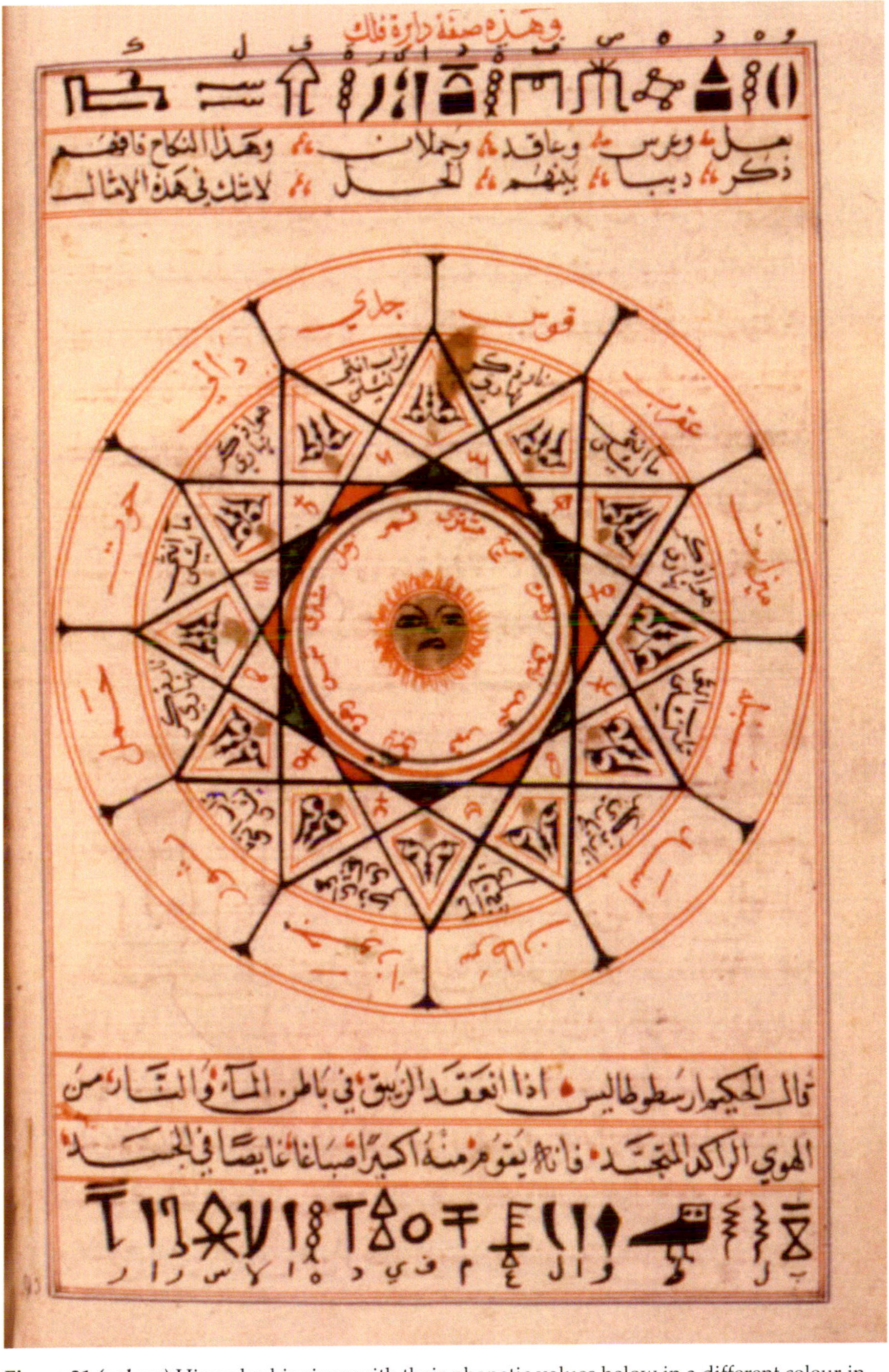

Figure 21 ***(colour)*** Hieroglyphic signs with their phonetic values below in a different colour in Abu Al-Qasim Al-ᶜIraqi (*Al-Aqalim* MS Add 25724 British Library), fol 21b.

Figure 22 ***(colour)*** Abu Al-Qasim Al-ᶜIraqi *Al-Aqalim*: fol 22a.

Figure 24 ***(colour)*** A stela of King Amenemhat II (ca 1928–1895 BCE) of the Twelfth Dynasty, as copied in Abu Al-Qasim Al-ʿIraqi (*Al-Aqalim* MS Add 25724 British Library), fol 50a.

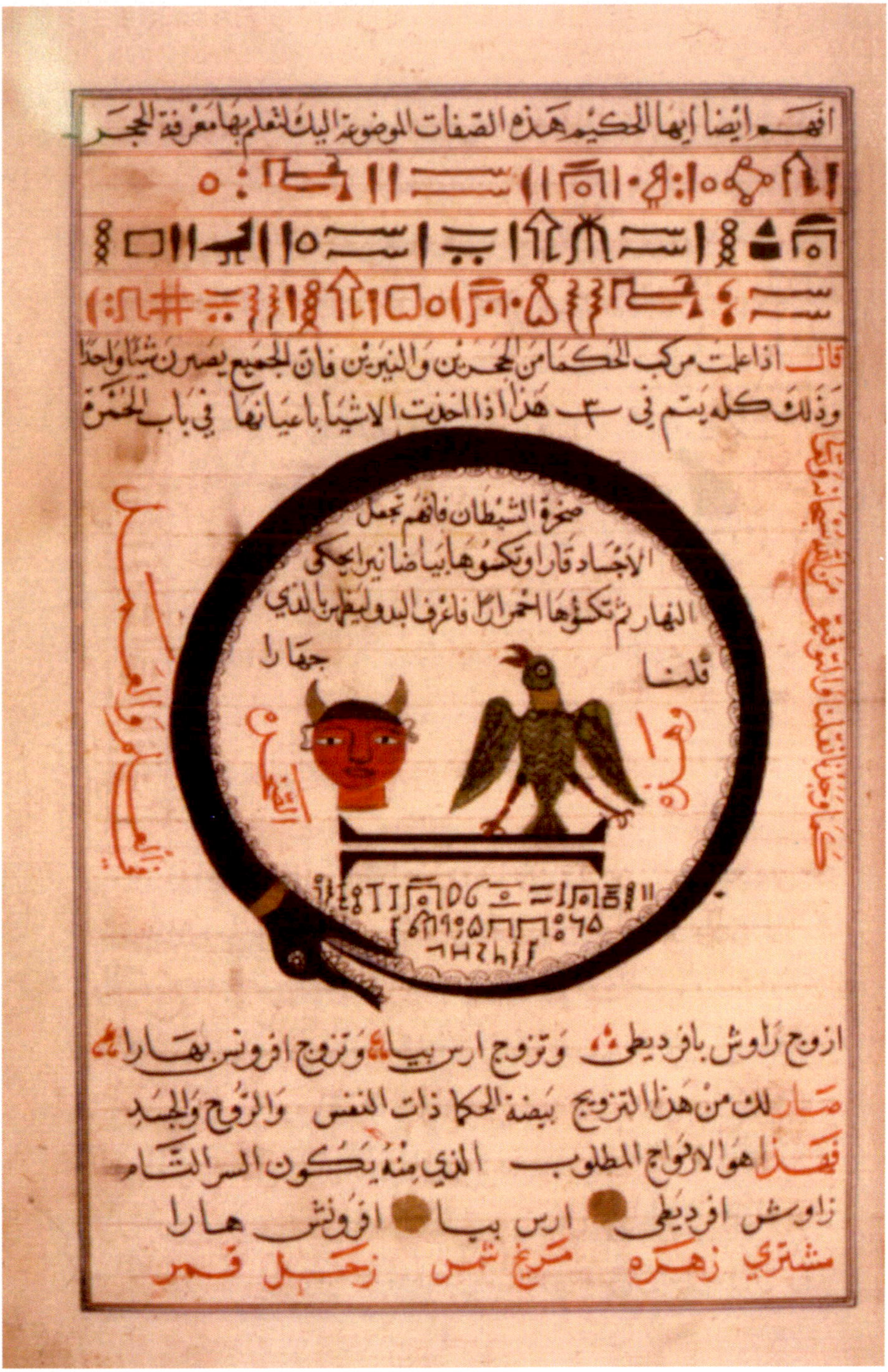

Figure 29 ***(colour)*** The Egyptian Ouroboros copied with hieroglyphs in the alchemical book of Abu Al-Qasim Al-ᶜIraqi (*Kitab Al-Aqalim Al-Sabᶜah* MS Add 25724 fol 4a British Library).

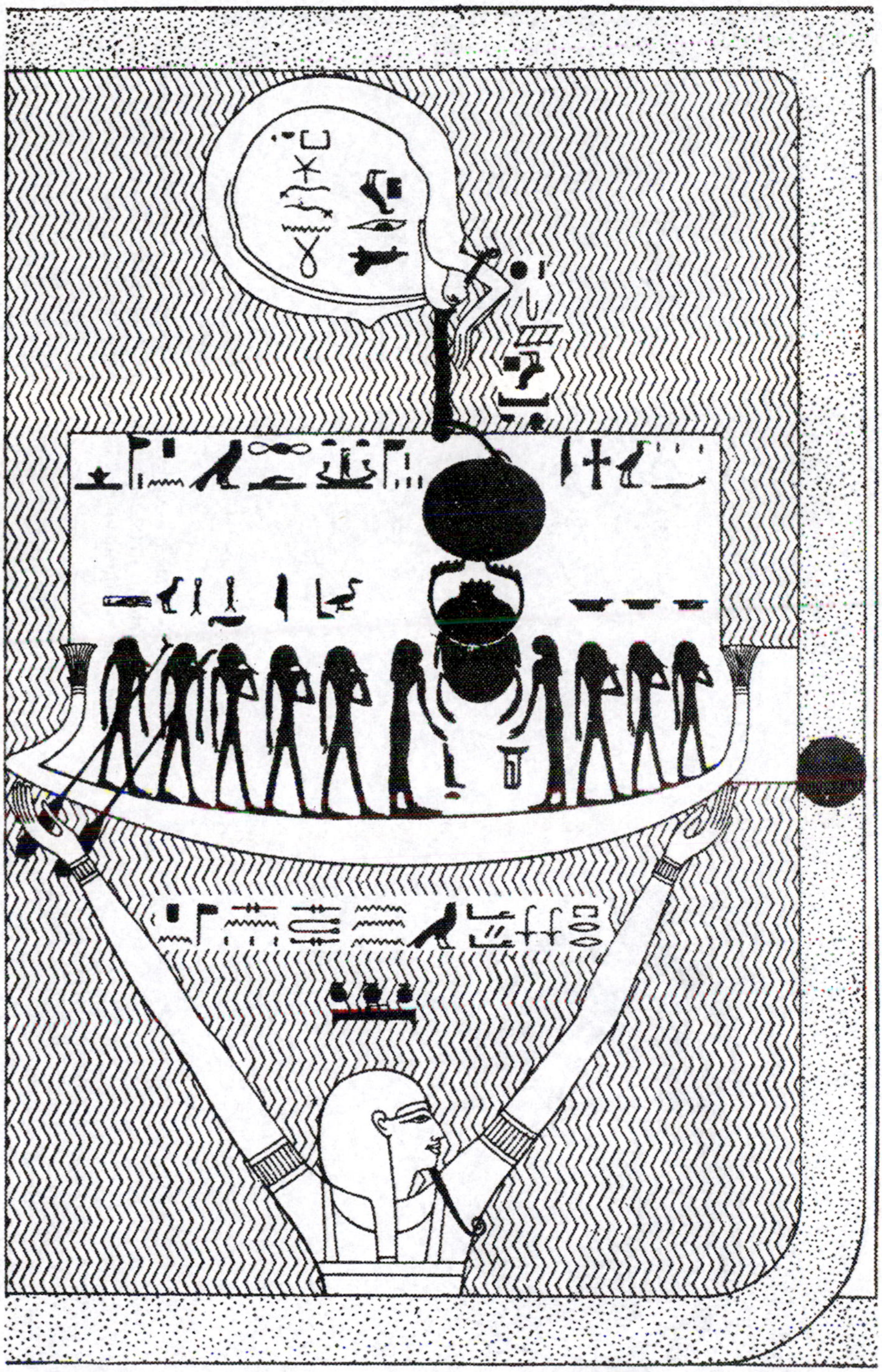

Figure 27 The primordial god Nu emerges from chaos, lifting up the Sun's Barge. From the Book of Gates on the alabaster sarcophagus of King Seti I presently at Sir John Soane Museum, London. After Budge 1908: 25 (cf Hornung 1992: 108).

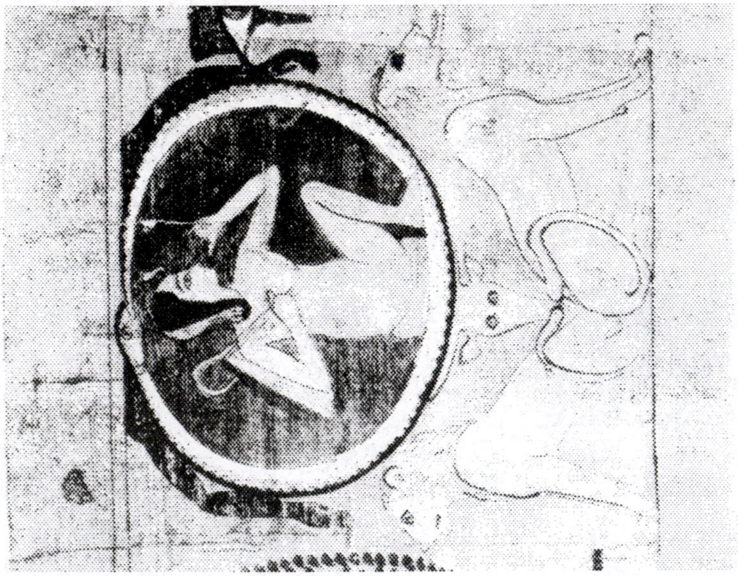

Figure 28 The Ouroboros serpent protects the sun god. Papyrus of ?r Wbn, Egyptian Museum, Cairo (Piankoff and Rambova 1957: 2, pl 1; cf Hornung 1990a: 107).

Figure 30 *Mummia* listed as medicine written in Egyptian script according to Ibn Waḥshiyah (*Shauq* MS Arabe 6805 fol 77a to the left). The word for *mummia* is written on third line from the top, with a human head.

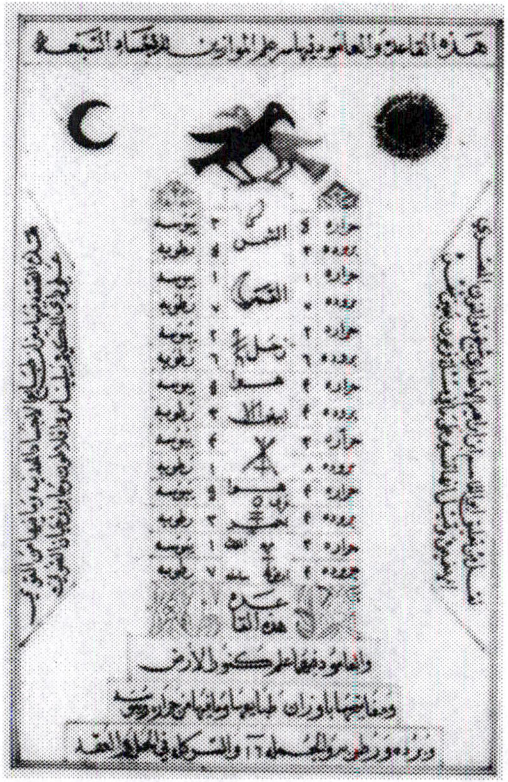

Figure 31 The 'Obelisk of Pharaoh' from Heliopolis, as copied and used in a book on alchemy by Abu Al-Qasim Al-ᶜIraqi (*Kitab Al-Aqalim Al-Sabᶜah* MS Add 25724 fol 15a British Library).

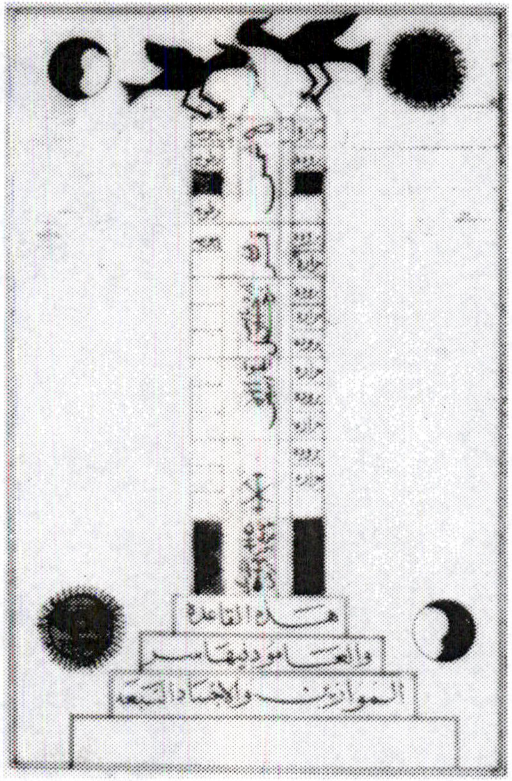

Figure 32 An Egyptian obelisk in Abu Al-Qasim Al-ᶜIraqi (*Kitab Al-Aqalim Al-Sabᶜah* MS Add 25724 fol 2a British Library). Here the body of the obelisk is standing on a step base, displaying alchemical elements.

Figure 33 Names of the archangels Michael and Gabriel correctly written in Coptic in Abu Al-Qasim Al-ᶜIraqi (*Kitab Al-Aqalim Al-Sabᶜah* MS Add 25724 fol 21b British Library).

APPENDIX 1

BIOGRAPHIES OF ARAB WRITERS

INTRODUCTION

> I commend you not to learn your sciences from books unaided, even though you may trust your ability to understand. Resort to professors for each science you seek to acquire; and should your professor be limited in his knowledge, take all that he can offer until you find another more accomplished than he. You must venerate and respect him; and if you can render him assistance from your worldly goods, do so; if not, then do so by word of mouth, singing his praises. ... You should read histories, study biographies and the experiences of nations. By doing this, it will be as though, in his short life span, he (the student of history) lived contemporaneously with peoples of the past, was on intimate terms with them, and knew the good and the bad among them.

This was Al-Baghdadi's advice to students as quoted in Ibn Abi Uṣaybiᶜah's *Ṭabaqat*: 643 and translated by Makdisi (1981: 89).

For several centuries, between the break-up of the Holy Roman Empire and the start of the European Renaissance, the Arab sciences were the most advanced in the world (Huff 1993: 52) and were truly universal, having inherited many of their theories from pre-existing traditions, Egyptian and Hellenistic as well as Syriac, Indian, Chinese and Persian (Nasr 1968: 25; Rashid 2002: 303). In the cultural milieu of the Arab period scholars from different ethnic, religious and linguistic backgrounds travelled freely and mingled with fellow scholars in other areas where they were sometimes even offered residencies and teaching jobs with generous stipends. Such an atmosphere could only have encouraged open exchange and debate among scholars, without fear of prosecution or poverty, except in very exceptional circumstances.

This was helped by free accommodation available to travellers, who often made use of hospitality provided by Ṣufi institutions (*Khanqah* and *Zawiya*), so with free board and lodging provided the cost of travel would not have been a major problem (Hillenbrand 1994: 219f).

Since Arabic soon became the *lingua franca* of the Moslem world, travellers were generally able to converse with local people without the distortions of translation. Even in periods when the political and military power of the Moslem states was in decline or being demolished, for example during the Mongol invasion, scholars seem to have been able to continue to travel, study and write.

Arab scholars knew of and learned from pre-Islamic sources. Many actually were familiar with several other languages such as Hebrew, Coptic and Greek, in addition to their native tongue, which may have been, for example, Arabic, Syriac or Persian. In the writings I have studied, most seem to have been meticulous in quoting their sources. Of course some of the sources may have been unreliable, or misinterpreted, or overtaken by later developments, making unreliable any work not based on direct observation. There is also a close link between history and religious studies in some of the writings, but this is not a problem limited to the Arabic histories; it is a problem in medieval historical writings in both East and West.

For the study of literature and grammar, pre-Islamic poetry provided a rich source of examples and materials. The subject matter of this poetry covered diverse aspects of life: religious, social, erotic, archaeological and historical. Most rulers were interested in pre-Islamic history and many invited historians of the day to narrate historical events during evening sessions: Al-Mas^cudi (*Muruj* 3: 40–41) tells us of the Umayyad Caliph Mu'awiyah Ibn Abi Sufyan (ruled 661–80) spending his evenings listening to the ancient histories of Arabs and non-Arabs alike and having this narrative recorded in writing. Al-Aṣma^ci (d 832) says in the introduction to his 'History of the Arabs before Islam' (*Tarikh*: 3) that the Abbasid Caliph Harun Al-Rashid (ruled 786–809) ordered the collection of this ancient history. A similar attitude to ancient history was shown by Ibn Ṭulun in Egypt, as reported by Al-Mas^cudi (*Muruj* 1: 347ff). This royal patronage played a significant role in encouraging a non-religious interest in historical writings.

There can be no doubt that medieval Arab scholars and writers have transmitted much from their own observation, enquiry and interpretation, and that they were in many cases aware of and had studied in depth the works of previous scholars, both classical and later. There is much repetition in many of these medieval writings, as scholars drew from the same sources, but this is not entirely negative as it has often led to the preservation of otherwise lost sources.

It is also clear that the medieval Islamic world had no internal frontiers creating barriers to travel and settlement, notwithstanding customs and excise, and that in many cases the reputations of scholars had gone before them so that they were offered hospitality and work in many of the places to which they travelled.

In this Appendix, where possible, I have tried to give a balanced account of my sources, against which their interest, scholarship and interpretation might be judged.

The writers I have selected for discussion here are chosen because their works reflect a wide interest in Ancient Egypt, but more specifically an interest in those areas I cover in this work. Some were native Egyptians; others were visitors who came for various purposes such as trade, study, or en route to the pilgrimage in Arabia. Many visited Egypt specifically to seek knowledge in Egyptian centres of learning such as Alexandria, Cairo and Quṣ. Some visited Egypt as part of a world tour. Some writers, particularly geographers such as Al-Iṣṭakhari, Ibn Ḥawqal and Al-Muqadasi (*Aḥsan*), furbished their accounts, including Egypt, with geographical maps with details of the landscape.

Many of these writers seem to have had a sense of the continuity between contemporary Egyptians and their ancestors in pharaonic Egypt, often expressing this as natural and to be expected. Al-Sakhawi (d 1482) wrote a guide-book to Cairo's funerary landmarks, tombs of the saints and holy places, and started his book with a visit to Heliopolis and the pyramids of Giza. He gave a clear message connecting the past and present and assuming continuity in the Egyptian heritage from ancient Egyptian to contemporary Moslem sites (Al-Sakhawi *Tuḥfat*: 16–20).

BIOGRAPHIES OF THE WRITERS

I cover here the writers who are my main sources, in chronological order, but in some cases there is a total absence of biographical detail. All dates cited are in CE (common era).

(1) Ayub Ibn Maslama (9th century)
An early writer whose main interest was in ancient scripts. He is later described by Al-Idrisi (*Anwar*: 61) as an Egyptian scholar with great knowledge of ancient Egyptian scripts, who was said to have deciphered various texts inscribed on the pyramids and other places for the Caliph Al-Ma'moun during his visit to Egypt in the year 831.

Al-Idrisi also describes an old, badly damaged book by Ayub Ibn Maslama entitled *Al-Ṭalismat Al-Kahinya* (Priestly Talismans) which he said contained translations of many ancient Egyptian inscriptions. The book itself has not been traced. There is, in the manuscript collection in Damascus, in the Al-Asad Library (formerly known as Al-Ẓahiriyah), a book attributed to him by Sezgin (1967 1: 934), but I believe that this is not his work (see Chapter 5 above).

There is no other known bibliographical information for Ayub Ibn Maslama.

(2) Dhu Al-Nun Al-Miṣri (d 861)
Born in 796 in Akhmim in Upper Egypt, the son of a Nubian slave. He lived much of his life either in, or next to, one of the famous temples of Akhmim. This city was the capital of the Ninth Nome in Upper Egypt and was known in the Greco-Roman period as Panopolis. It was a major centre for the cult of Min, the god of fertility and protector of the deserts. Akhmim was also known during that period as a centre for the study of alchemy, producing such famous practitioners as Zosimos of Panopolis. The city of Akhmim maintained its fame for the study of alchemy well into the medieval period. Egyptian temples had been centres of alchemy and were perceived as such by Arab writers.

The connection between Dhu Al-Nun and the town of Akhmim is interesting as Hermes is also said to have lived there, teaching the science of alchemy in its temple (Plessner 1954: 50–51). In later times the temple was believed to have two of Christ's disciples buried there, though according to Al-Ya^{c}qubi they were buried in the monastery of Abu Shenuda nearby (Al-Ya^{c}qubi *Al-Buldan*: 332).

Al-Bakri (d 1094) said of Dhu Al-Nun:

> It is said that Dhu Al-Nun of Akhmim was able to comprehend as much as he could of the sciences of the *birba* (temple), so much so that he mastered the craft, made

> diamonds, and was carried to Iraq in one night; he mastered other sciences as well, because in his youth he served a monk called Ṣaṣ who was at Akhmim, who taught him the script and showed him (how to make) the offering, the incense, and the name of the Spirit and commended him to keep that (to himself). When Dhu Al-Nun learnt what he learnt, he plastered the 'House of Wisdom' with the clay of wisdom which cannot be removed unless the stone is removed with it, and if removed (this) will damage the script used for the symbols. (Al-Bakri *Al-Masalik* 2: § 901)

The study (Chapter 5 above) of the manuscripts ascribed to Dhu Al-Nun shows his interest in and knowledge of ancient Egyptian as well as other scripts.

He was certainly a key figure in the lineage of transmission of alchemy. He was widely believed to have acquired the secrets of ancient Egyptian knowledge and wisdom from the inscriptions and reliefs of the temple where he lived (Al-Mas^cudi *Muruj* 1: 360; Al-Qifṭi *Ikhbar*: 185; ^cAbdeen 1964: 164). He is also credited with introducing into Islam the idea of Gnosis (*Ma^crifa*), which is inner knowledge received as revelation while in ecstasy, and which differs from intellectual and traditional knowledge obtained through study and reason. Dhu Al-Nun said of this Gnosis:

> Everything which the eyes see is related to knowledge, and that which the heart knows is related to certainty. (Al-Kalabadhi *Al-Ta^caruf*: 73)

It would appear that Dhu Al-Nun tried to use his knowledge to bridge the gap between ancient Egyptian wisdom and Islamic Sufism. Ṣufi masters of Islam acknowledged his influence, for example Ibn Al-^cArabi (d 1240), who wrote a book on the virtues of Dhu Al-Nun Al-Miṣri (*Al-Kawkab*), and Al-Rumi (d 1273), who counted Dhu Al-Nun among his masters (Nasr 1987: 136). A disciple of Dhu Al-Nun named ^cUthman Ibn Suwaid Al-Akhmimi, also a noted alchemist, wrote a book about his master under the title *'Kitab Ṣarf Al-Tawhum ^can Dhi Al-Nun Al-Miṣri'* (Dispersion of Illusion about Dhu Al-Nun Al-Miṣri) (Al-Nadim *Al-Fihrist*: 424). Some centuries later, Al-Suyuṭi wrote a treatise on Dhu Al-Nun: *'Al-Maknun fi Manaqib Dhi Al-Nun'*.

Dhu Al-Nun was also a noted poet. Among the works ascribed to him is a long poem of 151 verses, known as *Al-Qasida fi Al-Ṣan^cah Al-Karimah* (Poem on the Noble Craft). This is still unpublished (MS Add 7590 British Library *'Shadhrat Al-Dhahab'*, fols 85–90). In several verses he shows that he clearly understands the value of the knowledge and the sciences inherited from the Egyptian priests which are still visible on the stone walls of the temples (Verse 39). He states moreover that he was their student (*wa kanu min qabl ashiyakhia*) (Verse 45).

In addition to these ancient Egyptian teachings, Dhu Al-Nun had several contemporary teachers who influenced him, including several women, but he singled out a woman scholar of the Qur'an and a Ṣufi called Fatima Al-Nisabouriyah (d 838) whom he described as 'my teacher' (*wa hiya ustadhi*) (Al-Sulami *Dhkr*: 62).

At Akhmim a Ṣufi *Zawiya* (a place where Ṣufis live and travellers are given free accommodation) was named after Dhu Al-Nun (El-Hagagy 1968: 108), and this may be the one described and praised by Ibn Jubayr (*Riḥlah*: 67) in the 12th century as the Mosque of Dhu Al-Nun, which he said was a place full of grace (*barakah*). He was also regarded as the patron saint of physicians (Behrens-Abouseif 1998: 209).

When he died, it was said that his funeral procession was accompanied by green birds, and his tomb below the Muqatam Hills in Cairo became a popular destination for visitors, where their prayers would be answered (Al-Sakhawi *Tuḥfat*: 366f).

Bibliography of Dhu Al-Nun Al-Miṣri:

Ibn Khalikan *Wafiyat*: 1: 291–94

Ibn Al-ᶜArabi *Al-Kawkab*

Al-Suyuṭi *Al-Maknun*

Smith (1965)

Nurbakhsh (1999)

Al-Ṭayb (2002)

Kingsley (1995: 388ff)

(3) Ibn ᶜAbd Al-Ḥakam, ᶜAbd Al-Raḥman Ibn ᶜAbd Allah (d 871)

An Egyptian historian born in the year 803 at Fusṭaṭ (Old Cairo) to a distinguished family of scholars of Islamic religious studies. As he was born less than a century and half after the Moslem annexation of Egypt, he was able to collect many of the oral traditions of that event, which were still alive and therefore easier to authenticate, using the same methods other Moslem historians (Khalidi 1994: 17) had used for the authentication of the Ḥadith of the Prophet Mohammad. The sources of Ibn ᶜAbd Al-Ḥakam were mainly a group of distinguished Egyptian scholars such as Al-Layth Ibn Saᶜd and Ibn Lahiᶜah who had established a native school of Islamic studies. His own work was first orally transmitted and later written down under the title *Futuḥ Miṣr*, which was edited by Torrey and published in 1921 as *Conquest of Egypt*. This book, the first written by a native Egyptian, shows him as a nationalist historian, which may be a reaction to the harsh treatment of his family at the hands of the Abbasid Caliph Al-Mutawakil in Baghdad, but it can also be seen within the context of the struggle between proud native Egyptians and the central Abbasid caliphate in Iraq (Khalidi 1994: 65). This may partly explain why Ibn ᶜAbd Al-Ḥakam started his book with a chapter on the commendations of the Prophet Muhammad of the Copts and the virtues of Egypt, which, like the rest of his book, became the standard to be followed by almost all later writers on Egypt. His book displays a good knowledge of native traditions and of the ancient history and monuments of Egypt.

Bibliography of Ibn ᶜAbd Al-Ḥakam:

Torrey (1921), the English introduction

Rosenthal (1971)

Enan (1991: 8–20)

ᶜAṣi (1992a)

(4) Al-Ya^{c}qubi, Ahmad Ibn Abi Ya^{c}qub Isḥaq Ibn Ja^{c}far Ibn Wahb Ibn Waḍiḥ (d ca 905)

Born in Baghdad to a noble family with close ties to the Abbasid Caliphs. His great grandfather Waḍiḥ was the ruler of Egypt for a short while during the reign of Caliph Al-Mahdi. Al-Ya^{c}qubi left Baghdad at a young age and travelled widely, acquiring new titles reflecting both his knowledge and his long stay in certain places. He was known variously as Al-Ikhbari (the historian), Al-Iṣfahani (the one from Iṣfahan), and Al-Miṣri (the Egyptian). He wrote several books, two of which I have used here. These are a two-volume study of universal history, *Tarikh Al-Ya^{c}qubi*, which starts with Adam, and displays a deep knowledge of and interest in the various religions of nations and peoples, making him perhaps the first historian of world culture in the Islamic period (Khalidi 1994: 2, 115ff). The second book is a work of geography entitled *Al-Buldan* 'The Countries'. This is a study of the countries he visited, both in and beyond the Moslem world, in which he covered natural, human and economic geography as well as giving cultural, historical and topographic information. His method is primarily personal observation, or interviews with trusted acquaintances for what he could not see for himself. He also quotes earlier writers and uses official documents such as tax records.

Bibliography of Al-Ya^{c}qubi:

^{c}Aṣi (1992b)

Khalidi (1994: 115ff)

Al-Zerekly (1999 1: 95)

Zaman (2002)

(5) Ibn Al-Faqih Al-Hamadhani, Ahmad Ibn Muhammad (9th/10th century)

Little is known of his life but he may have been born in Hamadhan, Iran, as his surname suggests. His *Kitab Al-Buldan* is more of a literary work than a detailed geographic description, but it gives some idea of the literary interests common in the Arabic culture of his time. He clearly used the works of earlier geographers, often without giving their names. His book includes a chapter on Egypt and its Nile, starting with the reason for it being called Miṣr, and gives its name in Greek as Macedon (*maqduniya*). In this book (*Al-Buldan*: 130) he gives the names of the god worshipped by the Beja of Nubia in several local languages: *baḥir* in Beja; *lamkaluglu* in Zinjiya (Negroit); *abunuda* in Coptic; and *mazikish* in Berber.

Bibliography of Ibn Al-Faqih:

Massé (1971)

Al-Hadi (1996: 9–43)

(6) Ibn Khurdadhiba, Abu Al-Qasim ^{c}Ubayd Allah (d ca 912)

Born in Khurasan, Persia about 820 to a rich and highly educated family. His father was a local governor who sent his son to study music and literature. Ibn Khurdadhiba then entered the inner circle of the Abbasid Caliph Al-Mu^{c}tamid (ruled 870–92 CE) and became the head of the department of post and intelligence in another Persian province. He wrote many books on literary themes, the pleasures of life, the genealogy of the Persians, and a history of pre-Islamic nations which was regarded by Al-Mas^cudi as the most comprehensive book on its subject. His job entailed a great deal of travel and his book on geography, *Al-Masalik wa Al-Mamalik,* reads like a road guide book for travellers, with detailed notes of distances and observations on economies. It is regarded as the first book of descriptive geography in Arabic. He used the book of the Alexandrian astronomer/geographer Ptolemy, either from a Greek text or from a Syriac translation. His descriptions of monuments are realistic and detailed, often noting inscriptions on ancient buildings. His work became the foundation for almost all later Arab geographers. He called the Mediterranean Sea the Green Sea *'Al-Baḥr Al-Akhḍar'*, which might be of interest to Egyptologists who are still trying to identify what ancient Egyptians called *w3ḏ wr,* but this name was also sometimes used to mean the Atlantic Ocean. The Mediterranean Sea is normally known in Arab sources as Baḥr Al-Rom, the Roman Sea, where Roman means Byzantine/Greek.

Bibliography of Ibn Khurdadhiba:

Krachkovski (1957: 147–50 [Arabic 167–71])

Hadj-Ṣadok (1971)

(7) Al-Razi, Abu Bakr Muhammad Ibn Zakariya (d 925)
Born in Rayy, Iran about 854 but spent most of his life in Baghdad, where he headed its medical school and hospital. He was well versed in several languages including Greek, and he distinguished himself as a physician, philosopher and alchemist. He wrote more than 200 works on these subjects, in addition to others, including logic. He is also known as an independent free-thinker who advocated a rational empirical methodology. More than 80 of his works are on philosophy, including debates on the nature of theology which in some fundamentalist circles earned him the reputation of heretic, though what he in fact opposed was the ritualisation of religion and its obsession with and mystification of its founders. His fame rests mainly on his medical writings, which were widely translated into Latin and regarded as standard textbooks of medicine.

Bibliography of Al-Razi:

Goodman (1995)

Stroumsa (1999: 87–120)

Al-Azmeh (2001b)

(8) Al-Iṣṭakhari, Abu Isḥaq Ibrahim Ibn Muhammad (d ca 934)
Perhaps a native of Iran born about 850. He was one of the earliest Moslem geographers to use maps as a basic element of geography and illustrated his text with carefully prepared national maps, thus creating a descriptive atlas of each country he visited. His book *Al-Masalik wa Al-Mamalik* bears the standard title of many of the Arab geographies, conveying the idea of a guide to the roads to countries and kingdoms, but because of his new approach to the detail and accuracy of his maps, his work was widely quoted by his successors, and, in the case of his student Ibn Ḥawqal, imitated faithfully.

His map of Egypt shows two pyramids at Giza as the only historical landmark and it was reproduced by his student Ibn Ḥawqal with more detail (**Figure 2**).

Bibliography of Al-Iṣṭakhari:

Krachkovski (1957: 196–98 [Arabic 214–16])

Miquel (1978)

(9) Ibn Waḥshiyah, Abu Bakr Ahmad Ibn ᶜAli Ibn Qays Al-Kasdani Al-Qusayni Al-Nabaṭi Al-Ṣufi (9th/10th century)

Little is known about this writer, though he is referred to by many others. His works were well known to his near contemporary Al-Nadim (*Al-Fihrist*: 372, 423), who said that Ibn Waḥshiyah was from Qusayn near Kufa in Iraq, and who listed many of his books on magic, statues, offerings, agriculture, alchemy, physics, and medicine that were either written, or translated from old books, by Ibn Waḥshiyah. Ibn Waḥshiyah (*Shauq* fol 87a) certainly made a long sojourn in Egypt, but we do not know the exact purpose or duration of his stay, though Al-Nadim (*Al-Fihrist*: 372, 424) hinted at the purpose when he mentioned written debates as taking place between Ibn Waḥshiyah and some Egyptian alchemists from Akhmim (cf Levey 1966: 10).

Al-Nadim (*ibid*: 423) tells us that he saw a book on the decipherment of ancient scripts in Ibn Waḥshiyah's own handwriting, commenting that these included the letters used to 'gain the ancient sciences of *Barabi* (Egyptian temples)', which must be a reference to Ibn Waḥshiyah's work *Shauq Al-Mustaham,* which covers 93 scripts (see Chapter 5). Indeed, Ibn Waḥshiyah must have been a best-selling author of his day, his popularity continuing across time and distance, as is demonstrated by medieval Spanish translations of his works (Darby 1941). In his book on Nabataean Agriculture *Al-Filaḥaa Al-Nabaṭaiya* (1: 5ff), Ibn Waḥshiyah wrote that he searched for science books of his ancient ancestors until he finally found some written in old Syriac, which had been kept hidden with descendants of the old Kasadean people. He was admonished by the Elder of this people for attempting to translate their ancient sciences, thus revealing their secret knowledge to outsiders. But Ibn Waḥshiyah argued that their ancestors prohibited the revelation of religious secrets but not universal sciences, which they should be proud to share with outsiders, even if this seemed at first sight to be against the instructions of their ancestors. He insisted that these secrets be revealed for the benefit of their fellow human beings, but also to show the great scientific achievements of his ancestors. It is tempting to see in this name Kasadean, the old Kassites of ancient Mesopotamia, first attested in Hammurabi (1792–1750 BCE) (for a recent summary of current knowledge of the Kassites see Sommerfeld 1995). The name Kasadani is usually translated as Chaldean. However, the word Kasadani is closer to Kassite than Chaldean, and we must bear in mind that the former was part of the latter. Indeed, Al-Nadim (*Al-Fihrist*: 372) himself suggested that Ibn Waḥshiyah was of the Kassadeans who were 'the ancient inhabitants of earth' and 'a descendant of [King] Sennacherib'. If this was the case, then the statement of Ibn Waḥshiyah that he merely translated the works of his ancient ancestors may shed some light on a culture from which 'not a single Kassite text, nor a quotation of a Kassite sentence or expression, has been preserved'

(Sommerfeld 1995: 917). It would suggest that much of the pre-Moslem heritage of Mesopotamia may have been preserved in medieval Arabic scholarship just as it was in the case of ancient Egypt. Ibn Waḥshiyah is mentioned among the translators (Al-Qalqashandi *Ṣubḥ* 1: 558) and is said to have been employed by the Abbasid Caliphs specifically to translate ancient Mesopotamian works (*Nabaṭaean*) into Arabic (*Ḥajji Kḥalifa* 1: 525). This may explain the statements made by Ibn Waḥshiyah that he translated his books from ancient sources. This has been the subject of intense scholarly debate since the mid-19th century, with some claiming that Ibn Waḥshiyah himself is a fictitious character or that his works are forgeries. Both claims have been strenuously refuted (for a recent comment see Hämeen-Anttila 2002/3 with further references therein).

Bibliography of Ibn Waḥshiyah:

Sezgin (GAS 4: 282–83)

Fahd (1971, 1993)

Fück (1951: 105–06)

Al-Zerekly (1999 1: 170–71)

(10) Ibn Umail, Muhammad (10th century)

Ibn Umail was an Egyptian alchemist and a regular visitor to ancient Egyptian sites, as can be seen in his account of his visits with friends to a chapel at Abu Ṣir (Stricker 1942). It was from his very full description of this site in his book *Al-Ma' Al-Waraqi* that Stricker was later able to reconstruct the details of the chapel (see Chapter 4 above).

Ibn Umail was immersed in the pharaonic milieu that shaped his knowledge of alchemy, and he compared Arabic elements of alchemy to elements in ancient Egyptian temples (Abt 2003: 9). He accumulated a wealth of knowledge of ancient Egyptian themes, particularly of deities and religious thinking, as we can see from his description of the chapel at Abu Ṣir. Another indication of such knowledge is his poetic description of a dog within an alchemical operation, which I quote here in full:

> And it is the key and it is the dog to which they (the ancients) pointed in their books, and it is the hidden with which the work should start and finish, and in it not outside it. . . .
>
> Poem:
> The dog in it is a guard for our souls.
> And the dog drives away the violence of the firs.
> The dog protects their sprits in their bodies.
> And the dog is in them, irremovable.
> And the dog overcomes them dissolving their breathing,
> Like something similar to magnesia from the universe.
> And the dog makes appear souls from what contains it.
> And the dog chases away the darkness of the fats.
> And the dog purifies them and makes appear their colour, similar as white talcum, safely.
> And the dog opens every lock that is difficult to open anytime.

And the dog is called the sheikh in their examples.
And the dog is called the lion in their texts.
And the dog is called the anger in their description, so understand its description.
And the dog is like the poison in the bodies.
And the dog is the dog.

(Translation after Abt *et al* 2003: 149.)

Bibliography of Ibn Umail:

Ruska (1935)

Strohmaier, G (1971) and the bibliography there

Sezgin (GAS 4: 283–88)

Ronca (1995)

Anawati (1996: 870–72)

Abt (2003: 8–10)

(11) Al-Mascudi, Abu Al-Ḥassan cAli Ibn Al-Ḥusain (d ca 956)
Born in Baghdad to a family that traced its origins to a well-known companion of the Prophet Muhammad named cAbd Allah Ibn Mascud. After travelling for 33 years around the world, possibly including Europe, he took up residence in Fusṭaṭ, Egypt, where he later died and was buried. In the two of his books published to date, we find descriptions of Egyptian antiquities and of contemporary practices which resulted from direct observation in addition to his use of earlier sources. He was particularly interested in comparative religion and seemed at ease debating the subject with contemporary scholars in the field.

Bibliography of Al-Mascudi:

Khalidi (1974)

Shboul (1979) see pp 305–29 for early works on Al-Mascudi

Lunde and Stone (1989: 11ff)

Pellat (1991)

Al-Azmeh (2001a)

(12) (Anon) *Akhbar Al-Zaman* (10th century?)
This book is a valuable source on Ancient Egypt entitled 'Chronicles of Time'. It describes Genesis and the countries to which Adam and his descendants travelled and so contains sections on India, China, Greece, Persia and Africa, though more than half is dedicated to Egypt. There has been much learned discussion over the years as to who might be the author of this book of some 200 pages, and whether it might be a collection of the works of several writers. Most of it was translated into French by the orientalist Baron Carra de Vaux and published in Paris in 1898. The section on Egypt was the subject of a study review by Maspero (1899). De Vaux suggests, and Maspero agrees, that the writer is an armchair scholar. Much of the script repeats whole pages of texts which are also found in Al-Mascudi,

Al-Maqrizi, and Al-Murtaḍi. Maspero suggested that they were all using the same older texts, as the writer of *Akhbar Al-Zaman* refers frequently to having taken them directly from the storage chests of the priests, and from the writings of the Egyptians/Copts. The latter source for the book may help to explain its tendency towards a nationalistic bias. Maspero thought very highly of the work and had no problem in relating it to his own knowledge of Egyptology. Ferré (1991) found the style of the book not incompatible with that of Al-Masᶜudi and thought that it might therefore be one of his works, while Khalidi (1974: 154f) reached the conclusion that *Akhbar Al-Zaman*'s style is quite different from that of Al-Masᶜudi and therefore cannot be his. This last view agrees with the one reached much earlier by Krachkovski (1957: 184 (ar tr 202)).

In spite of the lack of agreement among scholars as to the identity of the author or the date of the book, I have found it particularly useful for its descriptions of royal rituals and details of the lives of pharaohs, descriptions of magic practices and descriptions of monuments. Much of the information in the book is supported by evidence from modern Egyptological studies.

Bibliography:

Ferré (1991)

Sezgin (1994, 1997, 2002)

(13) Al-Hamadani, Ibn Al-Hai'k, Al-Ḥassan Ibn Ahmad Ibn Yaᶜqub (d 945)
Born and brought up in Ṣanᶜa', Yemen, and travelled widely around Arabia. He wrote a 10 volume work called *Al-Iklil* on the history and ancient kings of Himyar and a book on the history and description of Arabia, *Ṣifat Jazirat Al-ᶜArab*. In these books he translated texts from the ancient Himyraite script. He also wrote on alchemy, geology and zoology, and was a prolific poet. In short, he is an encyclopaedist in the best tradition of medieval Arabic scholarship.

Bibliography of Al-Hamadani:

Faris (1938)

Krachkovski (1957: 166–70 (ar 186–89))

Al-Zerekly (1999 2: 179)

(14) Al-Biruni, Abu Al-Riḥan Muhammad Ibn Ahmad (d ca 1050)
Born to an Iranian family in Khwarizm on the southern shores of the Aral Sea, he studied several sciences in his homeland, particularly mathematics. He was soon to become one of the greatest scholars of the medieval world, and was known as a distinguished mathematician, astronomer, physicist, geographer, historian, chronologist, ethnographer, linguist and translator. His works, covering these fields and others, total 180, including his translations from and to Sanskrit, for example his translations of the Elements of Euclid, and Al-Magast of Ptolemy into Sanskrit.

In spite of his fluency in different languages, including his native Persian, he wrote in Arabic. His well-known book on the chronology of nations (*Al-Athar Al-Baqiya ᶜan Al-Qurun Al-Khaliya*) has a chapter on Egypt, in which he gives the chronology of nine centuries of its later history with a king list of the Egyptian dynasties from the Twenty-first Dynasty until the last native pharaoh (see Chapter 9 above).

His knowledge of several languages, including Syriac, Greek and Turkish, makes it likely that he had read an earlier accurate account of Egyptian history, such as that of Manetho. He also wrote highly regarded scientific works on mineralogy and medicinal drugs where he often cited the name of the material in several languages.

Bibliography of Al-Biruni:

Boilot (1960)

Nasr (1978: 107–16)

Al-Ṭaba^{c} and Al-Hashimi (1993)

(15) Al-Shahrastani, Abu Al-Fatḥ Muhammad Ibn ^{c}Abd Al-Karim (d 1153)

Born in Shahrastan (currently in the Republic of Turkmenistan) in 1086 and later moved to Baghdad having studied various Islamic religious sciences. In Baghdad he taught religion at the prestigious school, Niẓamiya. He is known as a historian of religions and philosophical doctrines. His most famous work, *Al-Milal wa Al-Niḥal,* aimed to be the most authoritative history of all religious creeds from the beginning of humanity to his own time. It covers the many sects and sub-sects of Islam, but perhaps its most useful section is the one covering other religions, past and contemporary, for example those of ancient Arabia, in addition to the cults of the Ṣabaeans (of Ḥarran), Hermeticists, Mazdaeans, Mannichaeans, Hindu sects, Jews and Christians. All of these received equal, unbiased and detailed treatment with a high standard of scholarship drawn from the original sources of the various creeds. Nowhere did Al-Shahrastani intentionally misrepresent non-Islamic materials, and to make them more easily understood he almost always presented them in the form of a lively dialogue between two debaters arguing on behalf of their beliefs. This type of comparative universal study of religions, sects and philosophies was original to Islam and not known in Greco-Roman sources (Goitein 1963: 429f). As a measure of its impact, there are medieval translations of this book in Persian and Turkish, and also later in German and French.

Bibliography of Al-Shahrastani:

Monnot (1997)

Al-Zerekly (1999 6: 215)

(16) Al-Harawi, Taqi Al-Din Abu Al-Ḥassan ^{c}Ali (Al-Sa'iḥ) (d 1215)

Born in Mosul, Iraq and spent most of his life travelling before settling at Aleppo, Syria where he died. He was known as *Al-Sa'iḥ Al-Zahid*, the Ascetic Traveller, as he spent his travelling years visiting cenotaphs of saints. This puts his book with its accounts of these visits into a category that could be called spiritual geography. Al-Harawi wrote on subjects as varied as military tactics, history, ancient monuments and the occult. His account of his visit to Egypt sometime before the end of the 12th century is in his book 'Indicators/Guides to Knowledge of [Holy] Visits', *Al-Isharat ila Ma^{c}rifat Al-Ziyarat*. During his travels in Egypt he made a habit of inscribing his name and date of visit on many of the monuments. This book was written from memory since his notes were lost during his travels, yet it was considered by Yaqut as a reliable source of information and quoted extensively in his book *Mu^c^jam*.

Bibliography of Al-Harawi:

Krachkovski (1957: 318–20 [Arabic 345–47])

Sourdel-Thomine (1971)

(17) Yaqut Al-Ḥamawi Al-Rumi (d 1229)

Sold as a child-slave to a merchant from Ḥama, Syria, who resided in Baghdad, hence the name adopted by Yaqut. The merchant gave him a good education and used him as a scribe and commercial assistant who travelled with him. These travels and later those on his own account enabled Yaqut to collect the material for a work 'Dictionary of Countries' (*Muᶜjam Al-Buldan*), which is the most important of his many works. He also worked as a copyist and trader in books, a job which undoubtedly gave him access to many written sources. He illustrated many of his entries with simple drawings such as that of the Lighthouse of Alexandria, but his sketch does not have great value when compared with that of Al-Gharnaṭi. Yaqut starts his entries with the exact pronunciation of the place name according to its local population, followed by different pronunciations, often with its etymology. He then gives the exact location of other places elsewhere with the same name. Throughout, his text is dotted with biographies of notable people who belong to the place, and with historical events and poetry.

Bibliography of Yaqut:

Al-Shami (1981)

Al-Saᶜdi (1992)

Gilliot (2002)

(18) Al-Baghdadi, Muwafaq Al-Din ᶜAbd Al-Laṭif Ibn Yousuf Ibn Muhammad Ibn ᶜAli, also known as Ibn Al-Labad, Ibn Nuqṭa and Al-Muttajan but often quoted in the West as ᶜAbd Al-Laṭif (d 1231)

A physician, historian and philosopher, born in Baghdad in 1161 to a family of scholars who were well versed in different disciplines, in particular Islamic religious studies and the books of pre-Islamic scholars, particularly the Greeks. He is highly acclaimed by the biographer Ibn Abi Uṣaybiᶜah (d 1270), who dedicated to him a chapter in his famous catalogue of biographies of physicians (*Ṭabaqat*: 634–48). Many times in his youth Ibn Abi Uṣaybiᶜah had met Al-Baghdadi, a friend of his grandfather and a teacher to both his father and uncle.

Al-Baghdadi was taught first by his father and later by eminent teachers in Baghdad. He obtained certificates of approval as a scholar of the Ḥadith from several masters in Iraq, Iran, Syria and Egypt. He also excelled in the Qur'an, Fiqh (jurisprudence) and language studies as well as literature, particularly poetry and narrative assemblies (*maqamat*). In Baghdad he also studied alchemy with a distinguished scholar from Morocco. This led him to become deeply interested in the craft of alchemy and the writings of, among others, Jabir, Ibn Waḥshiyah and Ibn Sina. He later decided that alchemy was too mystical, repudiating its teachers and practitioners and calling it an abhorrent craft.

At the age of 28 (1189), he spent a year in Mosul teaching religious studies and whilst there read the works of the famous Ṣufi of Illumination, Al-Sahrourdi, though he did not agree with his mystical approach. He enjoyed academic seminars in Damascus and had a short stay in Al-Quds (Jerusalem) before going on to Cairo (1191), where he was given a house, a monthly stipend and a job by officials of Sulṭan Salahdin. His main aim in Cairo was to meet eminent scholars and in particular Moses Maimonides (d 1208), whom he found impressive as an honourable scholar '*Faḍil*' but who in his view was too obsessed with worldly ambitions. Another Egyptian scholar who left a great impression on him was Abu Al-Qasim Al-Shariᶜi, who was well versed in the 'sciences of the ancients' and introduced Al-Baghdadi to ancient Greek/Egyptian philosophy.

In 1192 he returned to Al-Quds to visit Sulṭan Saladin and was impressed with his personality, humility and generous reception of scholars in spite of being much occupied with war. Back in Damascus he devoted himself to the study of the books of the ancients (*kutub al-qudama*). On his return to Egypt he took up a teaching post at Al-Azhar Mosque and University. His daily routine as described by himself was as follows:

> I teach people at Al-Azhar from morning until four o'clock pm. Then mid-day the reading of medicine commences and at the end of the day I teach another session, perhaps on ancient sciences. At night I do my own research. (Makdisi 1981: 87)

Some nine years later, in 1200, Al-Baghdadi returned again to Al-Quds where he taught, particularly Arabic grammar, at Al-Aqṣa Mosque until the year 1207 when he returned to Damascus, excelled in medicine and wrote a number of medical books. He visited Aleppo, Turkey and Afghanistan in 1229. Forty-five years after he first left Baghdad, Al-Baghdadi returned but fell ill and died on Sunday 9 November 1231.

Books by Al-Baghdadi:

Ibn Abi Uṣaybiᶜah (*Ṭabaqat*: 645–48) listed 173 titles of works by Al-Baghdadi covering a very wide range of subjects:

- 13 on linguistics
- 2 on jurisprudence
- 4 on literary criticism
- 53 on medicine
- 10 on flora and fauna

- 48 on philosophy, logic and psychology
- 3 on the Oneness of God
- 3 on history
- 3 on mathematics and physical sciences
- 4 on education
- 2 on magic and minerals
- 23 Varia (see Badawi 1964: 17; Ghalioungui 1985: 44ff)

Sadly, few of these works have been found, but amongst those which have is his celebrated book about his journey and stay in Egypt entitled *'Al-Ifadah wa Al-I^{c}tibar fi Al-'Umour Al-Mushahada wa Al-Ḥawadith Al-Mu^{c}ayanah bi-Arḍ Miṣr'* (Observations and Reflections on Things Seen and Events Witnessed in the Land of Egypt). This book *Akhbar Miṣr* is yet to be found, but Al-Baghdadi himself abridged it in *Al-Ifadah*, which is known from a copy in the author's handwriting in the Bodleian Library, Oxford, and was studied and translated into Latin during the 18th century and later, in 1810, into French. It was only in 1964 that an English translation was produced, but unfortunately it is full of mistakes.

The longest chapter in the book, Chapter 4, and the one which has received most attention from scholars, is Al-Baghdadi's account of his visits to and studies of ancient Egyptian monuments. It is comprehensive and accurate on the whole (Rizkana 1964: 65). He described the pyramids, the Sphinx, tombs, temples, statues and the mummification of both humans and animals. He focused on special sites, for example Memphis, Abusir and Alexandria. When writing of a monument, Al-Baghdadi gave its name, location, material, measurements and its distance from other monuments. He also showed remarkable insight into the influence of Ancient Egypt on the religious practices of contemporary Egyptians, in particular their obsession with icons representing god and angels (*ibid*: 110). Al-Baghdadi put this obsession down to the influence of their ancient ancestors, but was quick to suggest that the ancient Egyptians had indeed known that god was beyond human rational understanding, let alone representation.

As a scientist himself, Al-Baghdadi admired the scientific achievements of the ancient Egyptians, disparaging those members of the public who thought that the ancient people lived to a very old age, had huge bodies and utilised magic to move stones, suggesting instead that the reason the ancient works were so excellent was because of advanced engineering knowledge and skills under good administration, with patient hard work, perfect knowledge and use of tools, and total dedication (*ibid*: 107).

Al-Baghdadi (*ibid*: 117ff) also commended contemporary architecture, engineering and the layout of houses, built under an architect's supervision, where people lived in the higher parts of the buildings with windows facing the north wind, and he singled out for special comment the air shafts of the houses. Most important of all, he said, were their drainage channels, so well built that they remained long after the house itself had gone. He also admired the markets and wide streets. He gave a detailed account of public baths, admiring their design and interior decoration, with plenty of light and colour, so that those who went to bathe liked to linger. The book also includes descriptions of produce grown and its preparation for meals.

In part two (*ibid*: 127), he sets out to examine the laws of nature governing the Nile flood, his stated aim being to produce a chart to establish a pattern to help to predict future levels.

Very important as well as interesting is Al-Baghdadi's lengthy and detailed eyewitness account of the effects of the drought of 1200–01, which included resort to cannibalism, followed by the devastation and plague caused by the major earthquake of 19 May 1202. Al-Baghdadi's opening sentence is remarkable for its drama and poetry: 'the year has arrived ravaging the means of life' ودخلت سنة سبع مفترسة أسباب الحياة *wa dakhalat sanat sab*^{c} *muftarisat asbab al-ḥayiah*. Few medieval sources refer to the calamities brought on by drought, and those which do give only a short account. His description is important, though it refers to contemporary times, as we have very little in the way of references from pharaonic times to what must have been a regular if not frequent occurrence. One very important reference is to be found in the tomb of Ankhtifi at Al-Mo^{c}alla from the First Intermediate Period (Vandier 1950: 220ff; Schenkel 1965: 45ff), and a second in the the Dialogue of Ipuwr (Parkinson 1997: 166–99. For detailed studies of the drastic effects of famine in Egypt see Vandier 1936; Hassan forthcoming).

Al-Baghdadi wrote as a scientist who was well aware of the natural laws of physics and the cycles of nature. He recorded what he had personally observed with very few references to previous books or other people's accounts. And, importantly, he had the courage to criticise, in spite of their icon status, the likes of Galen and Ibn Sina (Avicenna) when he thought that they were wrong.

Al-Baghdadi was certainly a scholar of great originality and independence of thought who strove passionately for what he believed to be right (Ullmann 1997: 48). This would suggest that his accounts of his Egyptian sojourns are as reliable and as accurate as could be expected from any scholar (Ghalioungui 1985: 153–55).

Bibliography of Al-Baghdadi:

Ibn Abi Uṣaybi^{c}ah (*Ṭabaqat*: 634–48)

De Sacy 1810

Stern (1960). EI^{2} 1: 74

Ṣadiq (1964)

Enan (1969: 130–40)

Makdisi (1981: 84–91)

Sabanu (1983)

Ghalioungui 1985

Al-Zerekly (1999 4: 61)

(19) Ibn Al-Bayṭar, Abu Muhammad ^{c}Abd Allah (d 1248)
Born in Malaga towards the end of the 12th century and studied botany and pharmacology in Seville before travelling to North Africa and beyond, collecting and studying plants. When he arrived in Egypt, he was appointed head of the Apothecaries' Garden. He later travelled to Damascus, still in pursuit of plants, and died there. His books show a vast knowledge based on personal observation as well as on his studies of the works on drugs and plants of his predecessors, in particular the works of Dioscorides.

Bibliography of Ibn Al-Bayṭar:

Vernet (1971)

(20) Al-Idrisi, Abu Ja^{c}far Muhammad Ibn ^{c}Abd Al-^{c}Aziz (d 1251)
Born in Upper Egypt of a Moroccan family residing in Egypt. He studied both literature and Islamic studies in Egypt, the latter with a famous woman scholar, Fatima bint Sa^{c}d Al Khayr, originally from Andalusia, who later lived in Iraq before settling in Egypt. One of his most useful works is a six-chapter volume on the pyramids of Giza, which took him five years to complete and which is distinguished from others, earlier and later, by its systematic and concise structure, and the author's rigorous scholarly approach. He gave detailed architectural descriptions, not only of the Giza site, but of the route there from the south of the Fatimid city, and also described contemporary activities taking place around the Pyramids. He mentioned the Sphinx only in passing, complaining that too many stories were already circulating about it.

Al-Idrisi also wrote a book on the history of Upper Egypt, and another on the general history of Egypt.

Bibliography of Al-Idrisi:

Haarmann (1982a, 1991a)

Al-Idfui *Al-Ṭali^{c}*: 534–36

Gawad (1947)

Al-Zerekly (1999 6: 208)

(21) Al-Qazwini, Zakariya Ibn Muhammad (d 1283)
Born in Qazwin about 1203. At some point in his life he served as a judge in Iraq, which suggests that he must have studied Islamic jurisprudence. Shortly after the Mongol destruction of Baghdad in 1258, he retired from public duties and devoted himself entirely to scientific pursuits. His fame and popularity among medieval readers, to judge from the extant copies and translations in Persian and Turkish, reflected perhaps the appeal of his style of writing, which simplified complex scientific questions for the public rather than describing the originality of new theories. His works were mosaics of the previous and current knowledge of his day. His book on cosmography, 'Wonders of Creatures and Marvels of the [Things] Created' (*^{c}Aajaib Al-Makhluqat wa Gharaib Al-Mawjudat*) deals first with questions of celestial phenomena and issues relating to the stars such as chronology and calendars. He then deals with natural phenomena relating to the earth, for example the elements and climate, earthquakes and other geological

questions, with some interesting observations about changes in landscape such as mountains becoming valleys or lands that disappear and reappear in some kind of geological cycle. All this had already been discussed in the works on geology by the group Ikhwan Al-Ṣafaa (Said 1950) and in several other medieval Arab geological writings (El Sokkary 1973: 18ff), but Al-Qazwini succeeded in explaining it in laypersons' language. Copies of his cosmography are usually illustrated with geometrical tables and vividly coloured pictures of plants and animals.

His other book on geography, entitled 'Monuments of the Countries and Histories of [their] Peoples', *Athar Al-Bilad wa Akhbar Al-ᶜIbad*, was also very popular and was abridged and translated into Persian and Turkish, though over half of the material was borrowed from Yaqut's *Muᶜjam*.

Al-Qazwini wrote on astronomy, geography, geology, geomorphology, mineralogy, botany, zoology and ethnography and in the process he has preserved for us some texts which would otherwise be lost. It was he who kept alive the theory that the earth was in the form of a ball revolving around its centre.

Bibliography of Al-Qazwini:

Krachkovski (1957: 358–66 [Arabic 387–97])

Lewicki (1978)

Badiee (1978)

(22) Abu Al-Qasim Al-ᶜIraqi (d 1341)

An alchemist who may have come originally from Iraq as his surname suggests, but he lived in Egypt, where he died. His books on alchemy drew on his predecessors, particularly Ibn Umail. Like other alchemists before him, believing that Egypt was the origin of alchemy, he used Egyptian antiquities to illustrate his books. In the source used here entitled *Kitab Al-Aqalim Al-Sabiᶜah*, 'The Seven Spheres' (MS Add 25, 724 British Library) he drew many Egyptian objects and signs as alchemical apparatus (eg **Figure 12**).

He was familiar with Egyptian scripts and drew an ancient Egyptian stela, its signs correctly copied and easily identified (**Figure 24**). He also used the motif of an Egyptian obelisk as a conduit of alchemical knowledge (**Figures 31, 32**). A clear reference is made on **Figure 31** to *Misalat Firᶜun*, 'Obelisk of Pharaoh' at Heliopolis, and authentic Egyptian motifs are depicted such as the bird on top, normally the falcon god Horus, and immediately below it the sun, and on the base of the obelisk is written 'This base and the pillar have the science of earth treasures, and their keys with measurements/weights [*awzan*] of their natures and what is inside them of heat, dryness, coolness and humidity and the total is 16. And the entire secret is in dissolving and binding *al-ḥal wa al-ᶜaqd*'. So the body of the obelisk is here used for transmitting knowledge of the nature of minerals, and for alchemists this was closely connected with Hermetic tradition. This connection seems to have an ancient Egyptian origin, as Kákosy (1989a) pointed out that the obelisks of King Nectanebo at the British Museum indeed have a connection with Thoth/Hermes and his wisdom and may have been known to the god's disciples.

The same precision is applied to Al-Qasim's knowledge of Coptic icons, from which he also copied correctly, in beautiful script, the names of the archangels Michael and Gabriel (**Figure 33**). All the plates in this manuscript are in vivid colours. A testimony to his popularity is the number of extant copies of his books in different manuscript collections.

Like other alchemists, he concerned himself with the question of the creation of Adam and Eve as a metaphor for all things. In *Al-Aqalim* (fol 55a) he says that they were created as a result of combining certain materials mixed together at a certain temperature and humidity, suggesting that the same process applied to all creatures and hinting at the possibility of repeating this process with the same results. This may echo some ancient Egyptian ideas, traces of which remain in the well-known myth of Shu and Tefnut and the part they played in the Egyptian myth of creation.

Bibliography of Abu Al-Qasim Al-ᶜIraqi:

Holmyard (1926)

Ullmann (1972b: 236)

Anawati (1996: 874)

(23) Al-Qalqashandi, Ahmad Ibn ᶜAli (d 1418)

Born in a village in the Delta in 1355, he studied literature and jurisprudence at Cairo and Alexandria, where he also excelled in linguistics, eulogy and composition. These skills ensured him a good job in the Chancery, the *Diwan Al-Insha'* (literally the Department of Composition), responsible, amongst many other jobs, for correspondence between the rulers of Egypt and their foreign counterparts. This Chancery was normally staffed by highly educated people with a deep knowledge of history, geography and political and diplomatic protocols. It was during his employment there that Al-Qalqashandi wrote his encyclopaedic work 'Illumination for the Dim-Sighted', *Ṣubḥ Al-Aᶜsha*. This was the age of encyclopaedic works and Al-Qalqashandi was following in the footsteps of and copying from the works of Ibn Faḍl Allah Al-ᶜUmari such as *Masalik Al-Abṣar*, amongst others. Al-Qalqashandi praised all these previous works, pointing out their individual advantages, and explained that his aim was to write a new one that would bring all those advantages together. It took him about 10 years to complete and, like other similar works of the period, he collated in it all known knowledge relevant to the work in that Diwan. This included literature, foreign languages, religious studies, economics, sociology, geography and history, in addition to some knowledge of the natural sciences such as medicine, astronomy and agriculture as well as the mechanical and physical sciences, and books on the sciences of ethics and politics, jurisprudence and genealogy.

Among his admirable achievements was his interest in studying the meanings of topographical names (onomastica), as can be seen from his chapter on world geography (*Ṣubḥ* 3: 228ff). His direct observations on the Egyptian landscape and the administrative divisions of the country are reliable and have already been studied by Wüstenfeld (1879) and Jeffreys (1985, 1999).

Al Qalqashandi's main sources are:

- Direct observations of phenomena or events where he says 'I saw or witnessed'.
- Enquiring from specialist and scholars: 'I asked so and so about . . .'.
- Direct oral transmission of knowledge: 'I was told by so and so . . .'.
- Official documents in his charge. Due to his free access to the official archives of the Egyptian government, he shed great light on some very important administrative and political documents and on Egypt's relations with other countries.
- Previous books by Arabs and non-Arabs, Moslems and non Moslems alike.

He is accurate in his sourcing of information and always cites the title and author of his source, or at least the title or the author of the book assuming they were generally known. There are a few mistakes in the authorship of books he cited which may be down to his using copies abridged by other authors and assigning the book to the abridger, for example the book of ᶜ*Ajaib Al-Makhluqat* by Al-Qazwini which is cited by Al-Qalqashandi as authored by Ibn Al-Athir (eg *Ṣubḥ* 3: 309, 310).

Bibliography of Al-Qalqashandi:

Wüstenfeld (1879)

Bosworth (1978)

Enan (1991: 76–84)

ᶜIz Al-Din (1990)

(24) Al-Maqrizi, Taqi Al-Din Ahmad Ibn ᶜAli Ibn ᶜAbd Al-Qadir (d 1440)
Born in Cairo in 1364, where his father had moved from Syria to take up a number of senior jobs as a Mufti, a judge and teacher. So Al-Maqrizi was brought up in a highly learned environment, in which his teachers were said to number 600. The most important of these teachers was the renowned scholar Ibn Khaldun. He also travelled outside Egypt, spending 10 years in Damascus and five years in Mecca where he taught religious studies.

Al-Maqrizi was a prolific writer, his works exceeding 200, varying in length from a few pages to multi-volume works. His main interest was in the history of Egypt and in the biographies of its distinguished people. As he grew older, he revised his books, rewriting, amending or adding to many of them. He used extensive sources for his writing. The principal book of Al-Maqrizi that I have used for this work is *Khiṭaṭ*, on the history and topography of Cairo in particular and Egypt in general, which quotes 140 sources from 128 authors. He has been accused of being careless in his citations of sources, an accusation which has been thoroughly investigated by Enan (1991: 97–104) and considered groundless. There are indeed a few cases in Al-Maqrizi's works where he quotes someone without giving the source, but in works of this nature, one of them of 100 volumes, such errors may be forgiven. It is also worth noting that his most widely quoted book *Khiṭaṭ* has been published in partial editions and translations which use an unrevised draft of Al-Maqrizi, and it is only very recently that an accurate edition of this work by AF Sayyid (2002–) has been published.

Al-Maqrizi, in spite of his family's non-Egyptian origin, spoke passionately of the country and sought every opportunity to show his love of study of its history, as explained in his introduction to *Khiṭaṭ*. He was fascinated by its people across the ages, its pharaonic as well as its Coptic pre-Islamic heritage, dedicating eight chapters of his book to the history of the Coptic church and its patriarchs (Diab 1998). He wrote on geology, observing seashells on top of mountains and suggesting that Egypt was originally under water, which gradually receded from south to north. In making this observation, he was perhaps following, in addition to his personal observations, the classical writers, such as Herodotus (II: 5, 10, 12) and medieval Arabic ones such as Ibn Sina (El-Sokkary 1973: 48). He also used Orosius' *History*, which was widely available in Arabic then (Penelas 2001). He said that he spent many years collecting material for the book, from which he distilled the history of Egypt's remaining antiquities. His book also gives a detailed picture of urban, social and artistic developments in medieval Egypt, with detailed accounts of the affairs of ordinary people, and their interaction with natural processes and with the authorities, showing the active role played by the common people, and demonstrating that history was not just the result of the actions of rulers and the elite. This book can be summed up as a political, economic, cultural and social history of Egypt and its people. Al-Maqrizi had the courage to speak out about the effects of official corruption, especially during times of famine, in his short but valuable book *Ighathat*, in which he deals with the attitudes that led to the suffering and poverty that he himself witnessed. His material on the population of Egypt has been a very useful source (Hassan 1993).

He may not be known as a critical writer of history, but Al-Maqrizi has preserved for us some valuable sources which would otherwise have been lost and, more importantly, has painted for us a vivid picture of the people of Egypt, their manners, customs, and their different creeds and religious practices.

Bibliography of Al-Maqrizi:

Rosenthal (1991) and references on p 194

Sayyid (1995: 35ff, 2002)

(25) Ibn Al-Wardi, Siraj Al-Din Abu Hafṣ ᶜUmar (d 1457)

Perhaps born in Egypt but often confused with another Ibn Al-Wardi, a Syrian historian who died a century earlier. He wrote *Kharidat Al-ᶜAjaib wa Faridat Al-Gharaib* in response to a request by the local governor (of Aleppo?), who asked him also to make a globe of the world showing longitudes, latitudes, heights and depressions. At the outset, the author expressed his fear that he was not up to the task, and so started by consulting renowned books in the field, such as those of the astronomers Ptolemy and Naṣr Al-Din Al-Ṭusi, as well as Al-Masᶜudi and others.

The title of his book immediately draws attention to it – 'Wonders and Marvels' – though it is primarily a work of cosmography and eschatology, but written in a popular style to entertain the reader. It is clear that Ibn Al-Wardi was very well read and familiar with many sources, as he himself claimed in his introduction. This work was so popular that it was translated into Persian and

Turkish, its Turkish copies being extant in many manuscript collections. The section on Egypt received the attention of Fraehn (1804), who translated and commented on it.

Bibliography of Ibn Al-Wardi:

Krachkovski (1957: 490–96 [Arabic 539–46])

Al-Zerekly (1999 5: 67, col 3 n 1)

(26) Al-Suyuṭi, Jalal Al-Din ᶜAbd Al-Raḥman Ibn Abi Bakr (d 1505)
Born in Cairo in 1445 to a highly learned family. Before the age of eight he had memorised and was able to recite the entire Qur'an. He learned various Islamic religious disciplines, particularly the Ḥadith, at the feet of hundreds of teachers, whom he listed in one of his books. Among them were a dozen or so well known women scholars specialising in the science of the Ḥadith. In spite of being a contemporary of no less than 11 Sulṭans/rulers of Egypt, he declined not only their offers of employment but even their company, devoting his life to study, teaching and writing, producing about 600 works in seven main areas of knowledge: the Qur'an, the Ḥadith, Fiqh (jurisprudence), Arabic linguistics, history, biographies and literature, and in addition a score or so on such diverse subjects as Sufism, medicine, food, flora and sexology.

Before he was 30 years old, Al-Suyuṭi's works were being sought after throughout the Near East. He was also consulted on religious matters by Moslems from as far afield as Takrur (in modern day Chad), perhaps as a result of his travels to that country, as well as by others from Arabia, the Levant, India and North Africa (*Ḥusn* 1: 291). The last 40 years of his life were spent in near total isolation from public life, perhaps as a reaction to the widespread corruption in academic life, where there was collusion with the corrupt rulers of the country. This was towards the end of the Mamluk reign in Egypt, a period of general cultural decline and political instability.

Though known mainly for his religious and linguistic works, Al-Suyuṭi was also a historian who produced over 50 such works including several on Egypt. The most important for my purposes is *Ḥusn Al-Muḥaḍarah,* which he introduced by describing the 'Virtues of Egypt' before and after Islam, covering monuments, particularly the pyramids of Giza, and the Nile, citing much poetry in their praise and description. It is true that he reproduced many contemporary myths about the pharaonic past of Egypt, but he is also precise in quoting and naming his sources, an act which in itself saved many texts from oblivion, and he did so with an open but critical mind, which makes it one of his most important works.

Bibliography of Al-Suyuṭi:

Al-Suyuṭi (*Ḥusn* 1: 289–97)

Nemoy (1939)

Enan (1991: 142–51)

Al-Shakᶜah (1994)

Geoffroy (1997)

APPENDIX 2

BOOKS ON ANCIENT EGYPT USED BY AL-IDRISI

A list of books on Ancient Egypt cited by Al-Idrisi (d 1251) in his book on the pyramids (*Anwar*: 251–53).

1 المسعودى أخبار الزمان
2 --- الاستذكار لما مر فى سالف الأعمار
3 --- التنبيه والاشراف
4 --- ذخائر العلوم فى ما كان فى سالف الدهور
5 --- مروج الذهب ومعادن الجوهر
6 أبو زيد البلخى التاريخ المختص بأخبار مصر وعجائبها ودفائنها وفراعنتها
7 --- صفة الأرض والأقاليم
8 أبو جعفر الادريسى الأدوار والفترات
9 --- الجوهرة اليتيمة فى أخبار مصر القديمة
10 --- مطلع الطالع السعيد فى أخبار الصعيد
11 الوصيفى اسرار البرابى وعلوم الأولين من حكماء المصريين
12 البغدادى الافادة والاعتبار
13 أبو معشر البلخى الألوف فى بيوت العبادات
14 الجاحظ البلدان
15 قسطنطين السريانى تاريخ قسطنطين "العنوان"
16 يوسف ابن كريون الاسرائيلى تاريخ يوسف ابن كريون
17 التوراة
18 القضاعى الخطط
19 الكندى الخطط
20 أبو الصلت الرسالة
21 ثابت ابن قرة رسالة فى ديانة الحرانيين
22 ابن الفرات رسالة فى فضائل مصر
23 ابن وحشية سحر النبط
24 ابن جلجل طبقات الفلاسفة والأطباء
25 صاعد الأندلسى طبقات الفلاسفة والحكماء
26 أيوب ابن مسلمة الطلسمات الكاهنية
27 كتاب العلم المخزون فى علم الطلسمات وغيرها من أسرار علومهم الخفيات
28 كتاب فى علوم المطالب
29 كتاب المختار من معرفة...والأثار
30 كتاب مسيسون الراهب

31 أبو عبيد البكرى المسالك والممالك

32 --- معارف الجن

33 --- معجم ما استعجم

34 المهلبى المسالك والممالك

APPENDIX 3

PRIMARY ARABIC SOURCES

- Surnames of medieval Arab writers are in bold and are listed regardless of the definite article Al and the prefixes Abi, Abu and Ibn.
- All dates cited here follow the Common Era = CE.
- Anonymous books are listed under their titles in ***<u>bold underlined italic</u>***.
- If there is more than one edition or translation of the same book, the one used in this work is followed by the words (used here).
- English translations of texts from the Qur'an are broadly those of *The Holy Qur'an: English Translation of the Meanings and Commentary* published by King Fahd Holy Qur'an Printing Complex, Al-Medina, Saudi Arabia 1410 H (1989).
- Anonymous manuscripts are cited in full detail in the text and are not listed here.

Agapius, Ibn Qusṭanṭin (Agapius Episcopus Mabbugensis) (d ca 940). *Kitab Al-^{c}Unwan*. Ed L Cheikho. Louvain: Imprimerie Orientaliste 1954 (CSCO 65).

<u>Akhbar Al-Zaman</u> (Anonymous author 10th–12th century?). Ed A Al-Ṣawi. Cairo: ^{c}Abd Al-Ḥamid Ḥanafi 1938 (used here). A French translation and study Carra de Vaux, *L'Abrégé des merveilles*. Paris: C Klincksieck 1898. (Cf Maspero 1899, Ferré 1991 and U Sezgin 1994, 1997.)

Ibn Al-^{c}Arabi, Muḥy Al-Din (d 1240). *Kitab Al-Kawkab Al-Duri fi Manaqib Dhi Al-Nun Al-Miṣri*. French translation and study R Deladrière, *La vie merveilleuse de Dhû-l-Nûn l'Égyptien*. Paris: Sindbad 1988 (used here).

Al-Aṣma^{c}i, ^{c}Abd Al-Malik Ibn Qurayb (d 828). *Tarikh Al-^{c}Arab Qabl Al-Islam*. Ed M Al-Yasin. Baghdad: Al-Maktabah Al-^{c}Ilmiyah 1959.

Ayub Ibn Maslama (Attributed) (first half of the 9th century). *Kitab Aqlam Al-Mutaqadimeen*. MS 10244 Al-Assad Library (formerly known as Al-Ẓahiriyah), Damascus.

Al-Baghdadi, ^{c}Abd Al-Laṭif (d 1232). *Kitab Al-Ifadah wa Al-I^{c}tibar fi Al-'Umour Al-Mushahadah wa Al-Ḥawadith Al-Mu^{c}ayanah bi-Arḍ Miṣr*. Ed with commentary P Ghalioungui. Cairo: Al-Hay'ah Al-Miṣriyah Al-^{c}Amah li-Al- Kitab, 2nd edn 1985 (used here). French translation and study S de Sacy, *Relation de l'Egypte par Abdallatif*. Paris 1810. English translation K Z and J and I Videan, *The*

Eastern Key. London 1964 (This translation is not always accurate but is published with the Arabic text and has some explanatory notes.)

Al-Bakri, Abu ^{c}Ubayd ^{c}Abd-Allah Ibn ^{c}Abd Al-^{c}Aziz (d 1094). *Kitab Al-Masalik wa Al-Mamalik*. Ed AP Van Leeuwen and A Ferre. 2 vols, Tunis: Al Dar Al-^{c}Arabiyah li-Al-Kitab 1992.

Al-Bakwi, ^{c}Abd Al-Rashid Ṣaleḥ Ibn Nuri (15th century). *Kitab Talkhiṣ Al-Athar wa ^{c}Ajaib Al-Malik Al-Qahar*. Facsimile of the Arabic text with Russian translation and commentary 3. М. БУНИЯТОВА, Moscow: НАУКА 1971.

Al-Baladhuri, Abu Al-Ḥassan Ahmad Ibn Yaḥiya (d 892). *Futuḥ Al-Buldan*. Ed R Radwan. Reprinted 1983, Beirut: Dar Al-Kutub Al-^{c}Ilmiyah (used here). Translated into English with a study in 2 vols, *The Origins of the Islamic State* New York: Columbia University. Vol I by by P Hitti in 1916 and vol II by F Murgotten in 1924. Reprint New Jersey: Gorgias Press 2003.

– *Ansab Al-Ashraf*. Ed I ^{c}Abbas. Beirut: Catholic Press 1978.

Al-Balawi, Abu Muhammad ^{c}Abd Allah (10th century). *Sirat Ahmad Ibn Ṭulun*. Ed MK ^{c}Ali. Damascus: Al-Maktabah Al-^{c}Arabiyah 1939.

Ibn Basam, Muhammad Ibn Ahmad Al-Muḥtasib (d ca 1225). *Anis Al-Jalis fi Akhbar Tinnis*. Ed G El-Shayyal, Majalat Al-Majma^{c} Al-^{c}Ilmi Al-^{c}Iraqi (*Journal of the Academy of Science*), Baghdad: 14 (1967) 151–89.

Ibn Al-Baytar, Ḍiau Al-Din Abi Muhammad ^{c}Abd Allah Ibn Ahmad Al-Andalusi (d 1248). *Al-Jami^{c} li-Mufradat Al-Adwiya wa Al-Aghdhiya*. 2 vols, Beirut 1992 (used here). French translation L Leclerc, *Traité des simples par Ibn el-Beitar*. 3 vols, Paris 1883–87. German study by A Dietrich, *Die Dioskurides-Erklärung des Ibn al-Baitar*. Göttingen: Vandenhoeck & Ruprecht 1991.

Al-Biruni, Abu Al-Riḥan Muhammad Ibn Ahmad (d 1048). *Al-Athar Al-Baqiya ^{c}an Al-Qurun Al-Khaliya*. Ed E Sachau. Leipzig: Otto Harrassowitz 1923. English translation by E Sachau, *The Chronology of the Ancient Nations*. London: William Allen (for the Oriental Translation Fund of Great Britain and Ireland 1879). Reprinted in Frankfurt: Minerva 1969.

– *Kitab Al-Ṣaydanah*. Ed and translated into English S Ḥamarneh, *Al-Biruni's Book on Pharmacy and Materia Medica*. 2 vols, Karachi 1973.

– *Kitab Al-Jamahir fi Ma^{c}rifat Al-Jawahir*. Ed Y Al-Hadi. Iran: Elmi va Farhangi 1995.

Al-Bukhari, Mohammad Ibn Isma^{c}il (d 870). *Ṣaḥiḥ Al-Bukhari*. Ed T Sa^{c}d. 4 vols, Mansurah: Maktabat Al-Iman 1998.

Al-Buni, Ahmad Ibn ^{c}Ali (d 1225). *Shams Al-Ma^{c}arif Al-Kubra*. Beirut: Al-Maktabah Al-Thaqafiyah (nd).

Cohen Al-Haroni (Al-^{c}Aṭar) (da 1260). *Minhaj Al-Dukan wa Dustur Al-A^{c}iyan fi A^{c}mal wa Trakib Al-Adwiyah Al-Nafi^{c}ah li-Al-Abdan*. Cairo: Al-Ḥalabi 1971 (used here).

Ibn Al-Dawadari, Abu Bakr Ibn ^{c}Abd Allah *Kanz Al-Durar wa Jami^{c} Al-Ghurar* Vol 3. Ed MA Gamal Ad-Din. Cairo and Wiesbaden: Steiner 1981.

Al-Dimishqi, Shams Al-Din Abu ^{c}Abd Allah Muhammad Ibn Shaikh Al-Ribwah (d 1328). *Nukhbat Al-Dahr fi ^{c}Ajaib Al-Bar wa Al-Baḥr*. French translation by A Mehren, *Manuel de la cosmographie du moyen age*. 1874. Reprint Amsterdam: Meridian 1964 (used here).

Ibn Duqmaq, Ṣarm Al-Din Ibrahim Ibn Muhammad Al-Miṣri (d 1406). *Al-Intiṣar li-Wasiṭat ^{c}Aqd Al-Amṣar*. Only vols 4 and 5. Ed C Vollers, *Description de l'Egypte*. Cairo 1893.

Ibn Faḍl Allah, Shihab Al-Din Ahmad Al-^{c}Umari (d 1349). *Masalik Al-Abṣar fi Mamalik Al-Amṣar*. Ed A Sayyid (sections on Miṣr, Al-Sham, Al-Hijaz and Al-Yemen). Cairo: Institut Français d'Archéologie Orientale 1985.

Al-Fakhri, ^{c}Ali Ibn Muhammad Ibn ^{c}Abd-Allah (15th century). *Talkhiṣ Al-Bayan fi Dhikr Firaq Ahl Al-Adyan*. Ed R Al-Bandar. London: Dar Al-Ḥikma 1994.

Ibn Al-Faqih Al-Hamadhani, Abu Bakr Ahmed Ibn Muhammad Ibn Isḥaq (9th/10th century). *Kitab Al-Buldan*. An abridged copy ed by M de Goeje. Leiden: BGA 5, 1885. The complete text was found and ed by Y Al-Hadi, Beirut: ^{c}Alam Al-Kutub 1996 (used here).

Ibn Fatik, Abu Al-Wafa' Al-Mubashir (10th/11th century). *Kitab Mukhtar Al-Ḥikam wa Maḥasin Al-Kalim*. Ed ^{c}A Badawi. Madrid: Instituto Egipcio de Estudios Islamicos 1958.

Al-Fayruzabadi, Muhammad Murtaḍa Al-Ḥusayni Al-Zabidi (14th century). *Taj Al-^{c}Arus min Jawahir Al-Qamus*. Ed ^{c}A Shiri. 18 vols, Beirut: Dar Al-Fikr 1994.

Abu Al-Fida, ^{c}Imad Al-Din Isma^{c}il (d 1331). *Al-Mukhtaṣar fi Akhbar Al-Bashar*. Ed M ^{c}Azab *et al*. 4 vols, Cairo: Dar Al-Ma^{c}arif 1998.

Al-Ghalani, Muhammad Al-Kashnawi (d 1741). *Al-Dur Al-Manẓum wa Khilaṣat Al-Sir Al-Maktum fi Al-Siḥr wa Al-Ṭalaṣim wa Al-Nujum*. 2 vols, Cairo: Al-Ḥalabi 1961.

Al-Gharnaṭi, Abu Ḥamid ^{c}Abd Al-Raḥim Ibn Soliman (d 1169). *Tuḥfat Al-Albab wa Nukhbat Al-I^{c}jab*. Ed I Al-^{c}Arabi. Casablanca: Dar Al-Afaq Al-Jadidah 1993 (used here). This edn does not include the illustrations, for which see Ferrand's edn in the *Journal Asiatique* 207 (1925) 1–148 and 199–303. Also the Spanish translation by Ana Ramos, *Tuḥafa Al-Albab*. Madrid: Insituto de Cooperación con El Mundo Árabe 1990.

Al-Ghazali, Abu Hamid (d 1111). *Iḥya ^{c}Ulum Al-Din*. Beirut: Dar Al-Ma^{c}rifah (nd). English translation (used here) Maulana Fazul Karim, *Imam Ghazali's Iḥya ^{c}Ulum-id-din*. 4 vols, New Delhi: Kitab Bhavan 1982.

Ibn Al-Haj, Abu ^{c}Abd Allah Muhammad Ibn Muhammad Al-^{c}Abdari (d 1337). *Al-Madkhal*. 4 vols, Cairo: Maktabat Dar Al-Turath (nd).

Ibn ^{c}Abd Al-Ḥakam, Abu Al-Qasim ^{c}Abd Al-Raḥman (d 871). *Futuḥ Miṣr*. Ed Ch Torrey. New Haven: Yale Oriental Research Series III, 1922.

Al-Hamadani, Al-Ḥasan Ibn Ahmad Ibn Ya^{c}qub, Ibn Al-Ḥai'k (d 945). *Kitab Al-Iklil*. Vol 1 ed M Al-Akwa^{c} Al-Ḥawali. Cairo: Maṭba^{c}at Al-Sunna Al-Muḥammadiyah 1963. Vol 8 ed A Al-Karmali. Baghdad: Syrian-Catholic Press 1931 and see Faris 1938.

– *Ṣifat Jazirat Al-^{c}Arab*. Ed MA Al-Akwa^{c} Al-Ḥawali and supervised by H Al-Jasir. Riyadh 1974.

Al-Harawi, Abu Al-Ḥasan ^{c}Ali Ibn Abi Bakr (d 1214). *Kitab Al-Isharat ila Ma^{c}rifat Al-Ziyarat*. Ed J Sourdel-Thomine. Beirut: Catholic Press 1953 (used here). French translation by the editor, *Guide des lieux de pélerinage*. Damascus 1957.

Ibn Ḥawqal, Abu Al-Qasim Muhammad Ibn ^{c}Ali (d 988). *Ṣurat Al-Araḍ*. Ed J Kramers, Leiden 1938–39. Reprint, Cairo: Dar Al-Kitab Al-Islami (used here), (nd). French translation J Kramers and G Wiet, *La Configuration de la Terre*. Paris/Beirut: UNESCO 1965.

Abu Hilal Al-^{c}Askari, Al-Ḥasan Ibn ^{c}Abd Allah Ibn Sahl (d 1009). *Al-Ḥath ^{c}ala Ṭalab Al-^{c}Ilm*. Ed ^{c}A Diab. Cairo: Dar Al-Faḍilah 1998.

Al-Ḥikayat Al-^{c}Ajiba wa Al-Akhbar Al-Ghariba (14th century). Ed H Wehr, Beirut 1956. Reprint Köln: Al-Kamel 1997.

Ibn Al-^{c}Ibri, Abu Al-Faraj Yuḥana Al-Malṭi [Bar Hebraeus] (d 1286). *Tarikh Mukhtaṣar Al-Duwal*. Ed A Ṣaliḥani. Beirut: Catholic Press 1890.

Al-Idfui, Abu Al-Faḍl Kamal Al-Din (d 1347). *Al-Ṭali^{c} Al-Sa^{c}id Al-Jam^{c} Asma' Nujaba' Al-Ṣa^{c}id*. Ed SM Ḥassan and T Al-Hajiri. Cairo: Al-Dar Al-Miṣriyah li Al-Talif wa Al-Tarjamah 1966.

Al-Idrisi, Abu ^{c}Abd Allah Muhammad Ibn Muhammad (d 1165). *Nuzhat Al-Mushtaq fi Ikhtraq Al-Afaq*. Ed E Cerulli, F Gabrieli, G Levi Della Vida, L Petech, G Tucci, A Bombaci, U Rizzitano, R Rubinacci and L Veccia Vaglieri. 2 vols, Naples/Rome: Istituto Universitario Orientale de Napoli 1970–71 (used here). French translation by PA Jaubert, *Géographie d`Edrisi*. 2 vols, Paris 1836–40.

Al-Idrisi, Abu Ja^{c}far Muhammad Ibn ^{c}Abd Al-^{c}Aziz (d 1251). *Anwar ^{c}Ulwiyy Al-Ajram fi Al-Kashf ^{c}an Asrar Al-Ahram*. First published as a facsimile edn by U Sezgin, *Light on the Voluminous Bodies to Reveal the Secrets of the Pyramids*. Institute for the History of Arabic-Islamic Science, the Johann Wolfgang Goethe University, Frankfurt am Main 1988. New edn with an introduction in German U Haarmann in Beiruter Texte and Studen, Bd 38, Beirut and Stuttgart: Steiner 1991 (used here).

Al-Iṣfahani, El-^{c}Imad Al-Katib (d 1201). *Sana Al-Barq Al-Shami*. Abridged by Al-Fatḥ Al-Bendari in 1224. Ed F Al-Nabarawi, Cairo: Al-Khangi 1979.

Al-Iṣtakhari, Ibn Isḥaq Ibrahim Ibn Muhammad (d ca 934). *Al-Masalik wa Al-Mamalik*. Ed M Al-Ḥusaini and M Ghurbal. Cairo: Wizarat Al-Thaqafah 1961.

Al-Istibṣar fi ^{c}Ajaib Al-Amṣar (Anonymous author 12th century). Ed with French translation of the parts on Egypt by S ^{c}Abd Al-Ḥamid. Alexandria 1958, 2nd rev edn Casablanca: Dar Al-Nashr Al-Maghribyah 1985 (used here). Cf Levtzion 1979.

Ibn Iyas, Abu Al-Barakat Muhammad Ibn Ahmad (d 1542). *Badai^{c} Al-Zuhur fi Waqai^{c} Al-Duhur*. Ed Muhammad Muṣṭafa. 5 vols, reprint of 2nd rev edn 1982–84. Cairo: Al-Hay'ah Al-Miṣriyah Al-^{c}Amah li-Al-Kitab.

Jabir Ibn Ḥayan (d ca 815). *Tadbir Al-Iksir Al-A^{c}ẓam*. Ed P Lory with an introduction, Damascus: Institut Français de Damas 1988.

Al-Jaḥiẓ, ^{c}Amr Ibn Baḥr (d 771). *Kitab Al-Ḥaywan*. Ed ^{c}A Harun. 7 vols, Cairo: Al-Khangi 1969. First published by Al-Ḥalabi 1947.

– *Rasail Al-Jaḥiẓ*. Ed ^{c}A Harun. 4 vols, Cairo. Reprint Beirut: Dar Al-Jil 1991.

Al-Jazari, Badi^{c} Al-Zaman Abu Al-^{c}Iz Isma^{c}il Ibn Al-Razaz (12th/13th century). *Kitab fi Ma^{c}rifat Al-Ḥayl Al-Handasiyah*. Fascimile publication of the Arabic text in Topqapu Serai Library in Istanbul, No 3472. Ankara: Kültür Bakanliği 1990. English translation by D Hill, *The Book of Knowledge of the Ingenious Mechanical Devices*. Boston: Reidel 1974. (Cf Coomaraswamy 1924.)

Al-Jildaki, Aidamur (14th century). *Kitab Al-Durr Al-Maknun fi Sharḥ Qasidat Dhi Al-Nun Al-Miṣri*. MS 4025, fols 30R ff. Chester Beatty Library, Dublin.

Al-Jobri, ^{c}Abd Al-Raḥim (da 1264). *Al-Mukhtar fi Kashf Al-Asrar wa Hatk Al-Astar*. Ed ^{c}Iṣam Shaparo. Beirut: Dar Al-Taḍamun 1992 (used here). French translation R Khawam, *Le Voile arraché: L'Autre Visage de l'Islam*. Paris: Phébus 1979.

Ibn Jubayr, Abu Al-Ḥasan Muhammad Ibn Ahmad (d 1217). *Rihlat Ibn Jubayr*. Ed M Zainhom. Cairo: Dar Al-Ma^{c}arif 2000 (used here). Earlier edn by W Wright revised by M de Goeje, Leiden: Brill 1907, reprinted Warminster: Aris & Phillips for the EJW Memorial Trust 2001. English translation R Broadhurst, *The Travels of Ibn Jubayr*. London: Jonathan Cape 1952.

Ibn Juljul (da 994). *Ṭabaqat Al-Aṭiba' wa Al-Ḥukama'*. Ed F Sayyid. Cairo 1955. Reprint 1985, Beirut in the same vol, Ibn Ḥunien, *Tarikh Al-Aṭiba' wa Al-Falasifah*.

Al-Kalabadhi, Abu Bakr Muhammad Ibn Isḥaq (d 994). *Kitab Al-Ta^{c}arruf li-Madhhab Ahl Al-Taṣawuf*. Ed A Arberry, Cairo 1933, rep 1994 (used here). English translation A Arberry, *The Doctrine of the Sufis*. Cambridge: CUP 1978.

Ibn Al-Kalbi, Hisham Ibn Muhammad (d 820). *Kitab Al-Aṣnam*. Ed A Zaki. Cairo: Dar Al-Kutub 1924. 3rd reprint 1995 (used here).

Ibn Khaldun, ^{c}Abd Al-Raḥman Ibn Muhammad (d 1406). *Al-Muqaddimah*. Ed ^{c}A Wafi, 4 vols, Cairo: Lajnat Al-Bayan Al-^{c}Arabi 1960–67. English translation F Rosenthal, *The Muqaddimah: An Introduction to History*. 3 vols, Princeton: Princeton University Press. 2nd edn 1967 (used here). First published London: Routledge and Kegan Paul 1958.

Ibn Khalikan, Ahmad Ibn Muhammad Ibn Ibrahim (d 1281). *Wafiyat Al-A^{c}yan wa Anba' Al-Zaman*. Ed I ^{c}Abbas. 6 vols Beirut: Dar Sader. English translation De Slane, *Ibn Khallkan's Biographical Dictionary*. 4 vols, London and Paris 1842–43. Reprinted Beirut: Libraire du Liban 1970 (used here).

Ibn Al-Khaṭib, Lisan Al-Din Muhammad Ibn ^{c}Abd Allah (d 1374). *Kitab ^{c}Amal man Ṭaba li-man Ḥaba*. Ed M Vázquez de Benito. Salamanca: University of Salamanca 1972.

Ibn Khurdadhiba, Abu Al-Qasim ^{c}Ubayd Allah Ibn ^{c}Ali (d ca 912). *Al-Masalik wa Al-Mamalik*. Ed M de Goeje, Leiden: BGA 6, 1889 (used here). French translation C Barbier de Menyard, *La Livre des routes et des provinces*, Paris 1865.

Al-Kindi, Abu Yosuf Ya^{c}qub Ibn Isḥaq (d 867). *Kitab Al-Aqrabadhin*. English translation with a study M Levey, *The Medical Formulary or Aqrābādhin of Al-Kindi*. Milwaukee and London: University of Wisconsin Press 1966 (used here).

Ibn Al-Kindi, ^{c}Umar Ibn Muhammad Ibn Yosuf (10th century). *Faḍail Miṣr Al-Maḥrousah*. Ed ^{c}A ^{c}Umar. Cairo: Al-Hay'ah Al-Miṣriyah Al-^{c}Amah li-Al-Kitab, new edn 1997.

Abu Ma^{c}shar Al-Balkhi, Ja^{c}far Ibn Muhammad Ibn ^{c}Umar (d 886). *Kitab al-Milal wa al-Duwal*. Ed with English translation K Yamamoto and C Burnett, *Abu Ma^{c}šar on Historical Astrology*. 2 vols, Leiden: Brill 2000.

Al-Maghrabi, Ibn Al-Ḥaj Al-Tilmsani (d 1337). *Shumus Al-Anwar wa Kunuz Al-Asrar*. Unedited, Cairo: Al-Ḥalabi 1938.

Al-Magriṭi, Abu Al-Qasim Muslamah Ibn Ahmad [attributed] (d ca 1007). *Kitab Ghayat Al-Ḥakim wa Aḥaq Al-Natijatin bi-Al-Taqdim*. Ed H Ritter Leipzig/ Berlin: Teubner 1933. German translation H Ritter and M Plessner "Picatrix" Das Ziel des Weisen von Pseudo-Mağriti. London: The Warburg Institute, University of London 1962.

Maimonides (Musa Ibn Maimun) (d 1204). *Sharḥ Asma' Al-^{c}Aqaqir*. French translation M Meyerhof, Cairo 1940. English translation from French by F Rosner, *Moses Maimonides' Glossary of Drug Names*. Haifa: The Maimonides Research Institute 1995 (used here).

Abu Al-Makarim, Sa^{c}d Allah (12th century). *Tarikh Al-Kanais wa Al-Adyrah*. Ed Fr Samuel Al-Suryani, 2 vols Cairo 1984. First attributed to Abu Salih Al-Armani and edited with English translation by B Evetts, *The Churches and Monasteries of Egypt*. Oxford: Clarendon 1895 (used here). (This translation should be used with caution because of its many mistakes.)

Al-Maqrizi, Abu Al-^{c}Abbas Ahmed Ibn ^{c}Abd Allah (d 1440). *Kitab Al-Mawa^{c}iz wa Al-I^{c}tbar fi Dhikr Al-Khiṭaṭ wa Al-Athar* [*Khiṭaṭ*]. New critical edn by AF Sayyid, 5 vols (6 parts). London: Al-Furqan 2002–04.

– *Al-Bayan wa Al-I^{c}rab ^{c}Ama bi-Arḍ Miṣr mn Al-A^{c}rab*. Ed with extensive study ^{c}A ^{c}Abdeen, Alexandria: Dar Al-Ma^{c}rifah Al-Jami^{c}iyah 1989.

– *It^{c}az Al-Ḥunafa bi-Akhbar Al-A'ima Al-Faṭimeen Al-Khulafa*. 3 vols: Vol 1 ed by G El-Shayyal, 1st edn Cairo 1967. Vols 2 and 3 ed by M Ahmad, 1st edn Cairo 1971–73. 2nd edn 3 vols Cairo: Al-Majils Al-A^{c}laa li-Al-Shu'un Al-Islamiyah 1996.

– *Ighathat Al-Umah bi-Kashf Al-Ghamah*. Ed M Ziadah and G El-Shayyal, Cairo 1957; Ed B Al-Siba^{c}i, Himṣ 1957 (used here). English translation and study by A Allouche, *Mamluk Economics: A Study and Translation of Al-Maqrizi's Ighathah*. Salt Lake City: University of Utah Press 1994.

Al-Mas^{c}udi, Abu Al-Ḥasan ^{c}Ali Ibn Al-Ḥusain (d ca 956). *Al-Tanbih wa Al-Ishraf*. Ed M de Goeje, Leiden: Brill (used here). French translation C de Vaux, *Le Livre de l'avertissement et de la revision*. Paris 1938.

– *Muruj Al-Dhahab wa Ma^{c}adin Al-Jawhar*. Ed M ^{c}Abd Al-Ḥamid, Cairo. Reprint, Beirut: Al-Maktabah Al-^{c}Aṣriyah 1988 (used here). French translation by C Barbier de Meynard and P de Courteille, *Les prairies d'or*. Paris: Société Asiatique 1861–77. Critical Arabic edn C Pellat. 7 vols, Beirut: University of Lebanon 1965–79.

Al-Minufi, Ahmad Ibn ^{c}Abd Al-Salam (d 1524). *Al-Fayḍ Al-Madid bi-Akhbar Al-Nil Al-Sa^{c}eed*. MS 1639–48076 Marseille, Bibliothèque Municipale (used here). For a partly edited text and French translation of the first 3 sections of Chapter 1, see l'Abbé Bargès in *Journal Asiatique*, 3rd series, vol III, 1837: 97–164; vol IX, 1840: 101–31; vol XVI, 1846: 485–521.

Miskawaih, Abu ^{c}Ali Ahmad Ibn Muhammad (d 1030). *Tahdhib Al-Akhlaq*. Ed Constantine K Zurayk. Beirut: The American University Press 1966.

Al-Mu^{c}jam Al-Waseeṭ 2 vols, Cairo: Majma^{c} Al-Lughah Al-^{c}Arabiyah 1985.

Al-Muqadasi, Muṭahar Ibn Ṭahir (ca 950). *Kitab Al-Bad' wa Al-Tarikh*. Ed and translated into French by C Huart (attributed there to Abu Zaid Al-Balkhi). 3 vols, Paris 1899–1903.

Al-Muqadasi, Shams Al-Din (d 985). *Aḥsan Al-Taqasim fi Maᶜrifat Al-Aqalim*. Ed M de Goeje, Leiden. 2nd edn 1906 (used here). English translation B Collins and reviewed by MH Al-Taj, *The Best Divisions for the Knowledge of the Regions*. London: Centre for Muslim Contributions to Civilization 1994.

Al-Murtaḍi. French translation (of the Arabic text now lost) P Vattier *L'Egypte de Murtadi fils du Gaphiphe*. Paris: 1666. Reprinted with a study by G Wiet. Paris: L'Ecole des langues orientales 1953. English translation from French J Davies of Kidwolly, *The Egyptian History Treating of the Pyramids, the Inundation of the Nile, and other Prodigies of Egypt According to the Opinions and Traditions of the Arabians*. London: Printed by RB for Thomas Basset, at the George near Cliffords Inn, Fleet Street 1672.

Al-Nabulsi, Abu ᶜUthman Ibn Ibrahim (13th century). *Tarikh Al-Fayum wa Biladih*. Ed B Moritz, Cairo: Bibliothèque Khèdiviale 1898. Reprint Beirut: Dar Al-Jil 1974. Recently studied by I König, Die Oase Al-Fayyūm nach ᶜUthmān Ibn Ibrāhīm An-Nābulsī, *Zeitschrift für Geschichte der Arabisch-Islamischen Wissenschaften* 10 (1995/96): 190–253.

Al-Nadim, Abu Al-Faraj Muhammad Ibn Abi Yaᶜqub Isḥaq (d 920). *Al-Fihrist*. Ed Riḍa Tajaddud, 3rd edn Tehran: Dar Al-Masirah 1988 (used here). English translation B Dodge, *The Fihrist of al-Nadim*. 2 vols, New York and London: Columbia University Press 1970.

Naṣir-e Khisraw (da 1087). *Sefernama*. Arabic translation by Y Al-Khashab, Cairo 1943 (used here). Translated from Persian into English W Thackston Jr, *Book of Travels (Safarnama)*. New York: The Persian Heritage Foundation 1986.

Dhu Al-Nun Al-Miṣri, Abu Al-Fayḍ Thuban Ibn Ibrahim (d ca 860). *Ḥall Al-Rumuz wa Bar' Al-Asqam fi Kashf ᶜUlum Uṣul Lughat Al-Aqlam*. MS Muallim Cevdet K 290 Ataturk Kitapligi, Istanbul.

– *Al-Qaṣidah fi Al-Ṣanᶜah Al-Karimah*. MS Add 7590, *Shuzur Al- Dhahab* fols 85–90. British Library, London.

Al-Nuwairi, Shihab Al-Din Ahmad Ibn ᶜAbd Al-Wahab (d 1331). *Nihayat Al-Arb fi Funun Al-Adab*. 31 vols, Cairo: Markaz Taḥiqiq Al-Turath 1923–92.

Ibn Qadi Shuhba (d 1448). *Tarikh Ibn Qadi Shuhba*. Ed A Darwich, 4 vols, Damascus: Institut Français de Damas 1977–97.

Al-Qalqashandi, Shihab Al-Din Abu Al-ᶜAbbas Ahmed Ibn ᶜAli Al-Miṣri (d 1418). *Kitab Ṣubḥ Al-Aᶜsha fi Ṣinaᶜat Al-Insha*. [*Ṣubḥ*] 14 vols, Cairo 1913–20. Ed M Shams Al-Din, 15 vols, Beirut: Dar Al-Fikr (used here). German study of the chapters on Egypt, F Wüstenfeld, *Die Geographie und Verwaltung von Ägypten nach dem Arabischen des Abul ᶜAbbas Ahmed ben ᶜAli el-Calcaschandi*. Göttingen: Abhandlungen der Königlichen Akademie der Wissenschften 1879.

Abu Al-Qasim Al-ᶜIraqi (d 1341). *Kitab Al-Aqalim Al-Sabᶜah*. MS Add 25724. British Library, London.

– *Kitab Ḥall Al-Rumuz wa Fak Al-Aqlam* [?] MS Arabe 2676. Bibliothèque Nationale, Paris (cf MSS Arabe 2657 and Arabe 2703 in the same library; MS Add 23420 British Library, London; MS 10244 Al-Assad Library, Damascus. They may all be by the same author and indeed even the same book).

Al-Qazwini, Zakaria Ibn Muhammad Ibn Yaḥya (d 1274). *Kitab Athar Al-Bilad wa Akhbar Al-ᶜIbad*. Beirut: Dar Sader 1960.

– *Kitab ᶜAjaib Al-Makhluqat wa Gharaib Al-Mawjudat*. Cairo: Al-Ḥalabi (nd). Cf Badiee 1978.

Al-Qifṭi, Jamal Al-Din Abu Al-Maḥasin ᶜAli Ibn Yosuf (d 1248). *Ikhbar Al-ᶜUlma' bi-Akhbar Al-Ḥukama'*. Cairo: Al-Mutanabi (nd) (used here). An abridged copy by Al-Zuzini was edited by J Lippert, Leipzig 1903 under the title *Ta'rikh Al-Ḥukama'*. New edn Ed ᶜA Diab, Kuwait, 2 vols, 1998.

Ibn Al-Quff, Amin Al-Daulah Abu Al-Faraj (d 1286). *Jamiᶜ Al-Gharaḍ fi Ḥifẓ Al-Ṣiḥah wa Dafᶜ Al-Maraḍ*. Ed S Al-Ḥamarneh. Amman: University of Jordan Press 1989.

Al-Razi, Abu Bakr Muhammad Ibn Zakaria (d 925). *Kitab Al-Ḥawi fi Al-Ṭib*. 22 vols, Hyderabad-Deccan: The Dairat'l-Maᶜarif-il-Osmania (Osmania Oriental Publications Bureau), 1955–.

– *Ṭabib man la-Ṭabib Lahu*. Ed M Al-Rashidi. Cairo: Dar Rikabi 1998.

Ibn Rusta, Abu ᶜAli Ahmed Ibn ᶜUmar (da 913). *Al-Aᶜlaq Al-Nafeesah*. Ed M de Goeje. Leiden: Brill, BGA 7, 1892. Reprint 1967 (used here). French translation G Wiet, *Les Atours précieux*. Cairo: Institut Français d'Archéologie Orientale 1955.

Ibn Saᶜid Al-Maghrabi, Abu Al-Ḥassan ᶜAli Ibn Musa (d 1286). *Al-Nujum Al-Zahirah fi Ḥuli Ḥaḍrat Al-Qahirah*. Ed Naṣar. Cairo: Dar Al-Kutub, 2nd edn 2000. First published 1970.

– *Kitab Al-Jughrafiyah*. Ed I Al-ᶜArabi. Beirut: Al-Maktab Al-Tujari li-Al-Ṭibaᶜah wa Al-Nashr wa Al-Tawziᶜ 1970.

Ṣaᶜid Al-Andalusi, Abu Al-Qasim Ṣaᶜid Ibn Ahmad (also known as Qadi Ṣaᶜid) (d 1170). *Ṭabaqat Al-Umam*. Ed H Mou'nes, Cairo: Dar Al-Maᶜarif 1998. English translation S Salem and A Kumar, *Science in the Medieval World: 'Book of the Categories of Nations'*. Austin: University of Texas Press 1991 (used here).

Al-Sakhawi, Abu Al-Ḥassan Nur Al-Din ᶜAli Ibn Ahmad (d 1482). *Tuḥfat Al-Aḥbab wa Bughyat Al-Ṭulab fi Al-Khiṭaṭ wa Al-Mazarat wa Al-Tarajim wa Al-Biqaᶜ Al-Mubarakat*. Cairo: Maktabat Al-Kulyiat Al-Azharyah, 2nd edn 1986.

Abu Al-Ṣalat, 'Umyah Ibn ᶜAbd Al-ᶜAziz Al-Andalusi (d 1134). *Al-Risalah Al-Miṣriyah*. Ed ᶜA Harun in *Nawadir Al-Makhṭuṭat* Vol 1: 5–56. Cairo: Al Ḥalabi, 2nd edn 1972.

Al-Shahrastani, Abu Al-Fatα Muhammad Ibn ᶜAbd Al-Kareem (d 1153). *Kitab Al-Milal wa Al-Niḥal*. Ed A Muhammad. 3 vols, Beirut: Dar Al-Surur 1948–49. New edn of three parts in one vol (used here), Beirut: Dar Al-Kutub Al-ᶜIlmiyah. Most recent edn by W Cureton, New Jersey: Gorgias Press 2003.

Ibn Sina, (Avicenna) Abu ᶜAli Ḥusain Ibn ᶜAbd Allah (d 1037). *Al-Qanun fi Al-Ṭib*. 4 vols, Cairo (nd).

Sirat Saif Ibn Dhi Yazan Unedited, Cairo: Al-Mashhad Al-Ḥusayni 1972.

Al-Sulami, Abu ᶜAbd Al-Raḥman Muhammad Ibn Al-Ḥusain (d 1021). *Dhkr Al-Nuswah Al-Mutᶜabidat Al-Ṣufiyat*. Ed M Al-Ṭanaḥi, Cairo: Al-Hay'ah Al Miṣriyah Al-ᶜAmah li-Al-Kitab and Al-Khangi 1999.

Al-Suyuṭi, Jalal Al-Din ᶜAbd Al-Raḥman Ibn Al-Kamal (d 1505). *Kitab Ḥusn Al-Muḥaḍarah fi Tarikh Miṣr wa Al-Qahirah*. [*Ḥusn*] Ed M Ibrahim. 2 vols, Cairo: Al-Ḥalabi 1967–68. Reprinted Cairo: Dar Al-Fikr 1998.

– *Kitab Al-Maknun fi Manaqib Dhi Al-Nun*. Ed AH Mahmoud, Cairo: Maktabat Al-Adab 1992.

– *Kitab Al-Kanz Al-Madfoun wa Al-Fulk Al-Mashḥoun* (attributed) Unedited reprint, Cairo: Al-Ḥalabi 1970.

Al-Tahanawi, Mohammad ^{c}Ali (da 1745). *Kashaf Iṣṭlaḥat Al-Funun*. Ed A Basaj. 4 vols, Beirut: Dar Al-Kutub Al-^{c}Ilmiyah 1998.

Al-Tha^{c}labi, Abu Isḥaq Ahmad Ibn Muhammad Al-Nisabouri (d 1036). *Qiṣaṣ Al-Anbiya' Al-Musama ^{c}Rais Al-Majalis*. Beirut: Dar Al-Kutub Al-^{c}Ilmiyah 1994.

Al-Tujibi, Al-Qasim Ibn Yosuf (d 1329). *Mustafad Al-Riḥlah wa Al-Ightrab*. Ed ^{c}A Manṣour, Tunis: Al-Dar Al-^{c}Arabiyah li-Al-Kitab 1975.

Ibn Al-Ṭuwayr, Abu Muhammad Al-Murtaḍai (d 1220). *Nuzhat Al-Muqlatayn fi Akhbar Al-Daulatayn*. Ed AF Sayyid. Beiruter Texte and Studen, Bd 39, Beirut and Stuttgart: Steiner 1992.

Ibn Umail, Muhammad (10th century). *Sharḥ Al-Ṣiwar wa Al-Ashkal*. MS Arabe 2609 Bibliotheque Nationale, Paris (cf Stapelton *et al* 1933; Abt and Madelung 2003).

Ibn Abi Uṣaybi^{c}ah, Muwafaq Al-Din Abi Al-^{c}Abbas Ahmad Ibn Al-Qasim (d 1270). *Kitab ^{c}Uyun Al-Anba' fi Ṭabaqat Al-Aṭiba'*. [*Ṭabaqat*]. Beirut: Dar Al-Kutub Al-^{c}Ilmiyah 1998.

Wahb Ibn Munabbih (d 732). *Al-Tijan fi Muluk Ḥimiyar*. Cairo: Quṣur Al-Thaqafah 1996. First published in Ṣan^{c}a': Markaz Al-Dirasat wa Al-Abḥath Al-Yamaniyah 1979.

Al-Wahrani, Al-Sheikh Rukn Al-Din Mohammad (d 1575). *Manamat Al-Wahrani wa Maqamatih wa Rasailih*. Ed I Sha^{c}lan and M Naghsh. Cairo 1968. Reprint Köln: Al-Kamel 1998.

Ibn Waḥshiyah, Abu Bakr Ahmad Ibn ^{c}Ali Ibn Qys Al-Kasadani (10th century). *Kitab Shauq Al-Mustaham fi Ma^{c}irfat Rumuz Al-Aqlam*. MS Arabe 6805 Bibliothèque Nationale, Paris (used here). English translation of another version J Hammer, *Ancient Alphabets and Hieroglyphic Characters Explained; with an Account of the Egyptian Priests, their Classes, Initiation, and Sacrifices in the Arabic Language by Ahmad Bin Abubekr Bin Wahshih*. London: Bulmer 1806.

Al-Waqidi, Abu ^{c}Abd Allah Mohammad Ibn ^{c}Umar (attributed) (d 919). *Futuḥ Al-Bahnasa Al-Ghara'*. Cairo: Muṣtafa Al-Ḥalabi.

Ibn Al-Wardi, Siraj Al-Din Abi Ḥafṣ ^{c}Umar (d 1457). *Kharidat Al-^{c}Ajaib wa Faridat Al-Gharaib*. Unedited edn, Cairo: Al-Ḥalabi 1939. The Egyptian materials in this book were studied and translated into Latin by C Fraehn, *Aegyptus auctore Ibn al-Vardi*. Halle 1804.

Al-Ya^{c}qubi, Abu Al-^{c}Abbas Ahmad Ibn Abi Ya^{c}qub (d ca 905). *Tarikh Al-Ya^{c}qubi*. Ed M Houtsma. 2 vols, Leiden 1883. Reprinted Beirut: Dar Sader 1960.

– *Kitab Al-Buldan*. Ed M de Goeje. Leiden 1892 (used here). French translation G Wiet, *Les pays*, Cairo: Institut Français d'Archéologie Orientale 1937.

Yaqut, Ibn ^{c}Abd Allah Al-Ḥamawi Al-Rumi (d 1229). *Mu^{c}jam Al-Buldan*. Ed F Wüstenfeld. Leipzig 1866–73. Reprinted Beirut: Dar Sader 1995.

– *Al-Moshttarik Waḍ^{c}a wa Al-Muftariq Ṣuq^{c}a*. Ed F Wüstenfeld. Göttingen 1846. Reprinted Beirut: ^{c}Alam Al-Kutub 1986.

Ibn cAbd Al-Ẓahir (d 1293). *Al-Rawḍa Al-Bahiyya Al-Ẓahirah fi Ḫiṭaṭ Al-Muczziyyah Al-Qahira*. Ed AF Sayyid, Cairo: Arabian House Bookshop.

Ibn Ẓahirah (15th century?). *Al-Faḍail Al-Bahirah fi Maḥasin Miṣr wa Al-Qahirah*. Ed M Al-Saqqa and K Al-Muhandis, Cairo: National Library Press 1969.

Ibn Zohr, (Avezoar) Abu Marawan cAbd Al-Malik (d 1162). *Kitab Al-Taisir fi Al-*Mudawat wa Al-Tadbir. Ed M Al-Khuri. Al-Munaẓamah Al-cArabiyah li-Al-Tarbiyah wa Al-Thaqafah wa Al-cUlum (nd).

Al-Zohri, Abu cAbd Allah Muhammad Ibn Abi Bakr (db 1161). *Kitab Al-Jughrafiyah*. Ed MH Ṣadiq, Beirut 1968. Reprint Cairo: Maktabat Al-Thaqafah Al-Diniyah (nd).

Ibn Zulaq, Al-Ḥassan Ibn Ibrahim (d 997). *Faḍail Miṣr wa Akhbariha wa Khawaṣiha*. Ed cA M cUmar, Cairo: Al-Hay'ah Al-Miṣriyah Al-cAmah li-Al-Kitab 1999.

BIBLIOGRAPHY

Abada, A (2003) *Manda'iaw Al-ṣaba'a Al-Aqdamoun*. Ed R Al-Khayoun. London: Dar Al-Hikma.

^{c}Abbas, J (1992) *Athar Miṣr Al-Qadeemah fi Kitabat Al-Raḥalah Al-^{c}Arab wa Al-Ajanib*. Cairo: Al-Dar Al-Maṣriyah Al-Lubnaniyah.

^{c}Abd Allah, ^{c}A (1979) Al-Uṣul Al-^{c}Arabiyah-Al-Samiyah fi Ḥaḍarat Al-Hyksos wa Tarikhihm. *Majalat Kuliat Al-Adab (Bulletin of the College of Arts, University of Baghdad)* 25: 71–114.

^{c}Abd Allah, ^{c}A (1995) *Al-Kitabah Al-Abjadiyah fi Miṣr Al-Qadeemah*. Riyadh: University of King Saud.

^{c}Abd Allah, Y (1991) *Mu^{c}jam Al-Mu'arkhin Al-Moslemin ḥata Al-Qarn 12 H*. Beirut: Dar Al-Kutub Al-^{c}Ilmiyah.

^{c}Abd Al-Bar, I (2000) *Kashf Al-Sitar ^{c}an Fatḥ Al-Kunuz wa Istikhraj Al-Athar*. Cairo: Al-Faruq Al-Ḥadithah.

^{c}Abd Al-Galil, O (2000) *Tarikh Miṣr li-Yoḥana Al-Niqusi*. Cairo: Dar ^{c}Ain.

Abd El-Ghany, M (1989) The Arabs in Ptolemaic and Roman Egypt through Papyri and Inscriptions. In *Egitto e storia antica dall'ellenismo all'età araba*. Atti del Colloquio Internazionale, Bologna: Cooperativa Libraria Universitaria Editrice, 232–42.

^{c}Abd Al-Ḥamid, S (1954) Mulaḥaẓat ^{c}an Miṣr kama Ra'aha wa Waṣafaha Al-Jughrafyun wa Al-Raḥalah Al-Magharibah fi Al-Qarnin 6, 7 li-Al-Hijrah [12–13 AD], Naqd Al-Maṣadir. *Majalat Kulyat Adab Alexandria* 91–118.

^{c}Abd Al-Wahab, H (1994) *Tarikh Al-Masajid Al-Athariyah*. Cairo: Al-Hay'ah Al-Miṣriyah Al-^{c}Amah li-Al-Kitab. 2nd edn. First published 1946.

Abdel Tawab, A (1986) Relations of Monks and Moslems in the First Century of the Higra: A Study on the Relation between the Umayyad Rulers and the Christian Population of Egypt. In P Bridel (ed) *Le site monastique copte des Kellia: Sources historiques et explorations archéologiques. Actes du colloque de Genève, 13–15 août 1984*. Genève: Mission suisse d'archéologie copte de l'Université de Genève, 323–25.

^{c}Abdeen, ^{c}A (1964) *Lamaḥat min Tarikh Al-Ḥayah Al-Fikriyah Al-Miṣriyah qabl Al-Fatḥ Al-^{c}Arabi wa Ba^{c}dah*. Cairo: Al-Shubukshi Press.

Abdi, K (1999) Bes in the Akhaemenid Empire. *Ars Orientalis* 29: 111–40.

Abdi, K (2002a) An Egyptian Cippus of Horus in the Iran National Museum, Tehran. *Journal of Near Eastern Studies* 61: 203–10.

Abdi, K (2002b) Notes on the Iranianization of Bes in the Achaemenid Empire. *Ars Orientalis* 32: 133–62.

Abdul-Rahman, A (1986) Arabic Proverbs of 'Af^{c}al Attafḍeel'. *Arab Journal for the Humanities*. Kuwait: Kuwait University, 6: 21: 40–86.

Abi Khuzam, A (1995) *Al-Ruḥ Al-Ṣufiya fi Jamaliyat Al-Fan Al-Islami*. Beirut.

Abou-Bakr, O (1992) The Symbolic Function of Metaphor in Medieval Sufi Poetry: The Case of Shushtari. *Alif: Journal of Comparative Poetics*, American University in Cairo, 12: 40–57.

Abt, T (2003) *The Great Vision of Muḥammad Ibn Umail*. Los Angeles: CG Jung Institute.

Abt, T and W Madelung (2003) (eds) *Ibn 'Umail, Book of the Explanation of the Symbols (Kitāb Ḥall ar-Rumūz by Muḥammad Ibn Umail)*. Translated from Arabic by S Fuad and T Abt. Zurich: Human Heritage Publications (Corpus Alchemicum Arabicum 1).

Al-^{c}Adl, S (2002) *Al-Hieroghlyphiya Tufasir Al-Qur'an Al-Kareem*. Cairo: Madbouli.

Affifi, A (1951) The Influence of Hermetic Literature on Moslem Thought. *Bulletin of the School of Oriental and African Studies* 13: 840–55.

Aharoni, Y (1966) The Use of Hieratic Numerals in Hebrew Ostraca and the Shekel Weights. *Bulletin of the American School of Oriental Research* 184: 13–19.

Ahmad, M (1987) *Al-Hijrat Al-^{c}Arabiyah Al-Qadeemah min Shibih Al-Jazirah Al-^{c}Arabiyah wa Bilad Al-Rafidin wa Al-Sham ila Miṣr*. Damascus: Dar Ṭalas.

Al-Ahsan, A (1999) The Origin of Human History and the First Man. *Islamic Studies* 38: 63–86.

^{c}Ajinah, M (1994) *Mausu^{c}at Asaṭir Al-^{c}Arab*. 2 vols, Beirut: Al-Farabi.

^{c}Ali, J (1969) *Al-Mufaṣal fi Tarikh Al-^{c}Arab qabl Al-Islam*. Beirut: Dar Al-^{c}Ilm li-Al- Malayin. Vol 2.

Allam, S (1992) Observations on Civil Jurisdiction in Late Byzantine and Early Arabic Egypt. In J Johnson (ed) *Life in a Multi-Cultural Society: Egypt from Cambyses to Constantine and Beyond*. Chicago: Oriental Institute of the University of Chicago, 1–8.

Allen, J (2000) *Middle Egyptian. An Introduction to the Language and Culture of Hieroglyphs*. Cambridge: CUP.

Allen, T (1936) Types of Rubrics in the Egyptian Book of the Dead. *Journal of the American Oriental Society* 56: 145–54.

Altheim, F, R Stiehl *et al* (1964–) *Die Araber in der Alten Welt*. 5 vols, Berlin: Walter de Gruyter.

Amélineau, É (1887) *Étude sur le christianisme en Égypte au septième siècle*. Paris: Ernest Leroux.

Amélineau, É (1888) *Contes et romans de l'Égypte chrétienne*. 2 vols, Paris: Ernst Leroux.

Anawati, G (1996) Arabic alchemy. In R Rashed (ed) *Encyclopedia of the History of Arabic Science*. 3 vols, London and New York: Routledge, 3: 853–85.

Arnold, D (1991) *Building in Egypt: Pharaonic Stone Masonry*. New York and Oxford: OUP.

^{c}Aṣi, H (1992a) *^{c}Abd Al-Raḥman Ibn ^{c}Abd Al-Ḥakam*. Beirut: Dar Al-Kutub Al-^{c}Ilmiyah.

^{c}Aṣi, H (1992b) *Al-Ya^{c}qubi*. Beirut: Dar Al-Kutub Al-^{c}Ilmiyah.

Assmann, J (1997) *Moses the Egyptian. The Memory of Egypt in Western Monotheism*. Cambridge, MA: Harvard University Press.

Assmann, J (2002) *The Mind of Egypt. History and Meaning in the Time of the Pharaohs*. Translated from German by A Jenkins. New York: Metropolitan Books.

Atiya, A (1986) 'Ḳipt'. *Encyclopaedia of Islam*, 2nd edn 5: 89–95.

Aufrère, S (1984) Études de lexicologie et d'histoire naturelle IV–VI. *Bulletin de l'Institut Français d'Archéologie Orientale* 84: 1–21.

Aufrère, S and N Bosson (1998) Le Père Guillaume Bonjour (1670–1714). Un orientaliste méconnu porté sur l'étude du copte et le déchiffrement de l'égyptien. *Orientalia* 67: 497–506.

Aufrère, S and N Bosson (2000) Un dictionnaire des curiosités égyptiennes … une approche de sémantique historique. *Études coptes VII*: 1–15.

Al-Azmeh, A (2001a) *Al-Mas^{c}udi*. Beirut: Riad El-Rayyes Books.

Al-Azmeh, A (2001b) *Abu Bakr Al-Razi*. Beirut: Riad El-Rayyes Books.

Bachatly, C (1931) Legends about the Oblelisk at Maṭaria. *Man* 189: 195–96.

Badawi, ^{c}A (1964) Muwafaq Al-Din ^{c}Abd Al-Laṭif Al-Baghdadi, Ḥayatuh wa Mu'alafatuh wa Falsafatuh. In D Ṣadiq (ed) *Muwafaq Al-Din ^{c}Abd Al-Laṭif Al-Baghdadi fi Al-Dhikra Al-Mu'awiyah Al-Thaminah li-Miladih*. Cairo: Al-Dar Al-Qawmiyah, 1–29.

Badawi, A (1948) Ayam Al-Hyksos. *Al-Majalah Al-Tarikhiyah Al-Miṣriyah (Egyptian History Journal)* 1: 1+2: 41–86.

Badawi, A (1965) *Al-Athar Al-Miṣriyah fi Al-Adab Al-^{c}Arabi*. Cairo: Dar Al-Qalam.

Badawi, A and H Kees (1958) *Handwoerterbuch der Aegyptischen Sprache* [*sic*]. Cairo: ^{c}Ain Shams University.

Badawy, A (1967) The Civic Sense of Pharaoh and Urban Development in Ancient Egypt. *Journal of the American Research Center in Egypt* 6: 103–09.

Badiee, J (1978) *An Islamic Cosmography: The Illustrations of the Sarre Qazwini*. Unpublished PhD thesis, University of Michigan.

Baer, G (1968) 'Ali Mubarak's *Khiṭaṭ* as a Source for the History of Modern Egypt. In P Holt (ed) *Political and Social Change in Modern Egypt*. Oxford: OUP, 13–27.

Baines, J and J Málek (1980) *Atlas of Ancient Egypt*. London: Phaidon.

Bakar, O (1998) *Classification of Knowledge in Islam*. Cambridge: Islamic Texts Society.

Bakir, A (1978) *An Introduction to the Study of the Egyptian Language. 'A Semitic Approach'*. Cairo: General Egyptian Book Organization.

Bakr, I (2001) Ein Studienobjekt am Wegesrand. Die Pyramiden bei den arabischen Reisenden des Mittelalters. *Antike Welt. Zeitschrift für Archäologie und Kulturgeschichte* 32: 337–44.

Ball, J (1989) *The Body Snatchers*. New York: Dorset Press.

Barbulesco, L (2002) L'itinéraire hellénique de Tâhâ Ḥusayn. *Revue des mondes muslmans et de la Méditerranée* 95–98: 297–305.

Bashear, S (1997) *Arabs and Others in Early Islam*. New Jersey: Darwin Press.

Baudy, G (1986) *Adonisgärten: Studen zur antiken Samensymbolik*. Frankfurt am Main: Anton Hain (Beiträge zur Klassischen Philologie 176.)

Becker, C (1931) *Das Erbe der Antike im Orient und Okzident*. Leipzig: Quelle und Meyer.

Beeston, A (1962) An Arabic Hermetic Manuscript. In *The Bodleian Library Record* 7 (1 June 1962): 11–23.

Behlmer, H (1996) Ancient Egyptian Survival in Coptic Literature: An Overview. In A Loprieno (ed) *Ancient Egyptian Literature: History and Forms*. Leiden: Brill, 567–89.

Behrens-Abouseif, D (1998) *Beauty in Arabic Culture*. Princeton: Markus Wiener.

Bell, I (1922) Hellenic Culture in Egypt. *Journal of Egyptian Archaeology* 8: 139–55.

Bell, I (1948) *Egypt from Alexander the Great to the Arab Conquest*. Oxford: Clarendon.

Berkey, J (2001) *Popular Preaching & Religious Authority in the Medieval Islamic Near East*. Seattle and London: University of Washington Press.

Berlev, O (1990) Bureaucrats. In Donadoni (ed) *The Egyptians*. Translated by R Bianchi, A Crone, C Lambert and T Ritter. Chicago: University of Chicago Press, 87–119.

Belmonte, J (2001) On the Orientation of Old Kingdom Egyptian Pyramids. *Archaeoastronomy no 26, Supplement to Journal for the History of Astronomy* 32: 1–20.

Berthelot, M (1888) *Collection des anciens alchimistes grecs*. Paris. Reprint London: Holland Press 1963 (used here).

Betz, H (ed) (1992) *The Greek Magical Papyri in Translation*. Chicago: University of Chicago Press.

Bierbrier, M (1995) *Who Was Who in Egyptology*. London: Egypt Exploration Society. 3rd rev edn. 1st edn W Dawson 1951, 2nd edn E Uphill 1969.

Bietak, M (1996) *Avaris: The Capital of the Hyksos*. London: British Museum Press.

Bilabel, F, A Grohmann and G Graf (1934) *Griechische, koptische und arabische Texte zur Religion und religiösen Literatur in Ägypten Spätzeit*. Heidelberg: Universitätsbibliothek.

Bisson de la Rouque, F, G Contenau and F Chapouthier (1953) *Le Trésor de Tôd*. Cairo: Institut Français d'Archéologie Orientale.

Blackman, A (1916) The Pharaoh's Placenta and the Moon-God Khons. *Journal of Egyptian Archaeology* 3: 235–49.

Blackman, W (1927) *The Fellahin of Upper Egypt*. London: George Harrap.

Blanco, A (1984) Hermetism. A Bibliographical Approach. *Aufstieg und Niedergang der römischen Welt. Geschichte und Kultur Roms im Spiegel der neueren Forschung* [ANRW] II. 17. 4: 2240–81.

Blau, J (1979) Some Observations on a Middle Arabic Egyptian Text in Coptic Characters. *Jerusalem Studies in Arabic and Islam*. 1: 215–62. Reprinted in J Blau (1988) *Studies in Middle Arabic and its Judaeo-Arabic Variety*. Jerusalem. 145–93.

Blochet, E (1907) Peintures de manuscrits arabes à types byzantins. In *Revue Archéologique*. Paris. 4th Series: 9: 193–223.

Blochet, E, Études sur le gnosticisme musulman. 5 articles in *Rivista degli Studi Orientali*: (1909) 2: 717–56; (1910) 3: 177–203; (1911–12) 4: 47–79 and 267–300; (1914–15) 6: 5–67.

Boessneck, J von, A von den Driesch and A Eissa (1992) Eine Eselsbestattung der 1 Dynastie in Abusir. *Mitteilungen des Deutschen Archäologischen Instituts Abteilung Kairo* 48: 1–10 and pl 1.

Boilot, D (1960) Al-Biruni. *Encyclopaedia of Islam*, 2nd edn 1: 1236–38.

Bolman, E (2002) (ed) *Monastic Visions. Wall Paintings in the Monastery of St Anthony at the Red Sea*. Cairo: American Research Center in Egypt.

Boorn, G van den (1985) Wd^{c}-ryt and Justice at the Gate. *Journal of Near Eastern Studies* 44: 1–25.

Bosworth, C (1978) Al-Ḳalḳashandi. *Encyclopaedia of Islam*, 2nd edn 4: 509–11.

Bosworth, C (1993) Miṣr, Egypt. *Encyclopaedia of Islam*, 2nd edn 7: 146.

du Bourguet, P (1976) *Grammaire fonctionnelle et progressive de l'Égyptien Démotique*. Louvain: Peeters.

Bowman, R (1944) An Aramaic Religious Text in Demotic Script. *Journal of Near Eastern Studies* 3: 219–31.

Boylan, P (1922) *Thoth: The Hermes of Egypt*. Oxford: OUP.

Breasted, J (1927) *Ancient Records of Egypt from the Earliest Times to the Persian Conquest*. 5 vols, Chicago: University of Chicago Press. Reprinted London 1988.

Bresciani, E (1990) Foreigners. In S Donadoni (ed) *The Egyptians*. Translated by R Bianchi, A Crone, C Lambert and T Ritter. Chicago: University of Chicago Press, 221–53.

Brière, Y de la (1935–38) La mémoire de Champollion. *Mélanges G Maspero*. Cairo: Institut Français d'Archéologie Orientale, 1: 443–55.

Bringi, S (1997) *Al-Ṣabai'h Al-Mindai'yun*. Translated from Persian into Arabic by J Ahmad. Beirut: Dar Al-Kunuz Al-Adabiyah.

Broadhurst, R (1952) *The Travels of Ibn Jubayr*. London: Jonathan Cape.

Brockelmann, C. (1938) Zur Semito-Ägyptischen Etymologie. *Mélanges G Maspero* I (1935–38). Cairo: Institut Français d'Archéologie Orientale du Caire, 379–83.

Brockelmann, C (1943–49) *Geschichte der arabischen Literatur*. Vols 1–2, Leiden: Brill; Supplement vols 1–3, Leiden: Brill 1937–42.

Breyer, F von (2003) Der semitische Charakter der Altägyptischen Sprache. *Die Welt des Orients* 33: 7–30.

Budge, W (1893) *The Mummy*. Cambridge. Reprint London 1995.

Budge, W (1898) *The Egyptian Book of the Dead*. London. Reprint Dover Publications.

Budge, W (1908) *Egyptian Ideas of the Afterlife*. London. Reprint Dover Publications 1995.

Budge, W (1926) *Cleopatra's Needles and other Egyptian Obelisks*. London: Religious Tract Society. Reprint Dover Publications.

Budge, W (1928) *The Divine Origin of the Craft of the Herbalist*. London: Society of Herbalists. Reprint Dover Publications.

Budge, W (1929) *The Rosetta Stone*. London. Reprint Dover Publications 1989.

Budge, W (1930) *Amulets and Superstitions*. London: Humphrey Milford and OUP.

Burnett, C (1976) The Legend of the Three Hermes and Abu Ma^{c}shar's *Kitab Al-Uluf* in the Latin Middle Ages. *Journal of the Warburg and Courtauld Institutes* 39: 231–34.

Burnett, C (1996) Talismans: Magic as Science? Necromancy among the Seven Liberal Arts. In C Burnett, *Magic and Divination in the Middle Ages*. Hampshire: Variorum, 1–15.

Burnett, C (2003) Images of Ancient Egypt in the Latin Middle Ages. In T Champion and P Ucko (eds) *The Wisdom of Egypt: Changing Visions through the Ages*. London: UCL Press, 65–99.

Burnett, C, K Yamamoto and M Yano (1997) Al-Kindi on Finding Buried Treasure. *Arabic Science and Philosophy* 7: 57–90.

Burstein, S (1992) Hecataeus of Abdera's History of Egypt. In J Johnson (ed) *Life in a Multi-Cultural Society: Egypt from Cambyses to Constantine and Beyond*. Chicago: Oriental Institute of the University of Chicago, 45–49.

Butler, A (1978). *The Arab Conquest of Egypt and the Last Thirty Years of the Roman Dominion*. Oxford: Clarendon.

Butzer, K (1976) *Early Hydraulic Civilization in Egypt. A Study in Cultural Ecology*. Chicago: University of Chicago Press.

Cameron, A (1997) Hellenism and the Emergence of Islam. *Dialogos: Hellenic Studies Review* 4: 4–18.

Camille, M (1999) The Corpse in the Garden: *mummia* in Medieval Herbal Illustrations. *Micrologus* 7: 296–318.

Camps, G (1994) Amon-Rê et les béliers à sphéroïde de l'Atlas. *Hommages à Jean Leclant*, Vol 4. Cairo: Institut Français d'Archéologie Orientale, Bibliothèque d'Étude, 106/4: 29–44.

Carboni, S (1988) *Il Kitāb al-bulhān di Oxford*. Torino: Editrice Tirrenia Stampatori.

Carrubba, R (1981) The First Detailed Report on Persian Mummy. *Physis* 32: 459–71.

Casanova, P (1902) De quelques légendes astronomiques Arabes. Considérées dans leurs rapports avec la mythologie égyptienne. *Bulletin de l'Institut Français d'Archéologie Orientale du Caire* 2: 1–39.

Caton-Thompson, G (1944) *The Tombs and Moon Temple of Hureidha*. Oxford: OUP.

Cauville, S (1995) *Le Temple de Dendera. Guide archéologique*. 2nd edn. Cairo: Institut Français d'Archéologie Orientale.

Černý, J (1935) Questions addressés aux oracles. *Bulletin de l'Institut Français d'Archéologie Orientale du Caire* 35: 41–58 and plates 1–4.

Černý, J (1976) *A Coptic Etymological Dictionary*. Cambridge: CUP.

Charles, R (1916) *The Chronicle of John, Bishop of Nikiu*. London: William & Norgate.

Charpentier, G (1981) *Recueil de matériaux épigraphiques relatifs a la botanique de l'Égypte antique*. Paris: Trismégiste.

Chassinat, É (1955) *Le manuscrit magique copte no 42573 du Musée Égyptien du Caire*. Cairo: Institut Français d'Archéologie Orientale (Bibliothèque d'études Copte 4).

Christides, V (2000) The Tomb of Alexander the Great in Arabic Sources. In I Netton (ed) *Studies in Honour of CE Bosworth*. 2 vols, Leiden: Brill, 1: 165–73.

Clarysse, W (1978) Notes on Some Graeco-Demotic Surety Contracts. *Enchoria* 8: 2: 5–8.

Clarysse, W (1983) Literary Papyri in Documentary 'Archives'. In E Van 't Dack, P van Dessel and W van Gucht (eds) *Egypt and the Hellenistic World*. Proceedings of the International Colloquium, Leuven, 24–26 May 1982. Leuven: Lovanii, 43–61.

Coles, R (1981). A Quadrilingual Curiosity in the Bodleian Library in Oxford. In *Proceedings of the XVI International Congress of Papyrology*. Chicago: Scholars Press, 193–97.

Collombert, P (2002) Le conte de l'hirondelle et de la mer. In K Ryholt (ed) *Acts of the 7th International Conference of Demotic Studies*. Copenhagen: Museum Tusculanum Press, 59–76.

Cook, M (1983) Pharaonic History in Medieval Egypt. *Studia Islamica* 57: 67–103.

Coomaraswamy, A (1924) *The treatise of al-Jazari on automata: leaves from a manuscript of the Kitab fi ma'arifat al-hiyal al-handasiya in the Museum of Fine Arts, Boston, and elsewhere*. Boston: Museum of Fine Arts.

Corbin, H (1976) *Spiritual Body and Celestial Earth*. Translated from French by N Pearson. Princeton: Princeton University Press. Published in London: Tauris 1990.

Corbin, H (1983) *Cyclical Time and Ismaili Gnosis*. Translated from French by R Manheim and J Morris. London: Kegan Paul International and Islamic Publications.

Corbin, H (1986) *Temple and Contemplation*. Translated from French by P and L Sherrard. London: Kegan Paul International and Islamic Publications.

Cory, A (1840) *The Hieroglyphics of Horapollo Nilous*. London: William Pickering.

Coulmas, F (1999) *The Blackwell Encyclopedia of Writing Systems*. Oxford: Blackwell. First published 1996.

Crabbs Jr, A (1984) *The Writing of History in Nineteenth Century Egypt: A Study in National Transformation*. Detroit: Wayne University Press.

Creswell, K (1926) *The Works of Sultan Bibars Al-Bunduqdari in Egypt*. Cairo: Institut Français d'Archéologie Orientale du Caire.

Cromer, Earl of (1908) *Modern Egypt*. 2 vols, London: Macmillan.

Crone, P and M Cook (1977) *Haggarism: The Making of the Islamic World*. Cambridge: CUP.

Crum, W (1939) *Coptic Dictionary*. Oxford: OUP.

Crum, W (1942) An Egyptian Text in Greek Characters. *Journal of Egyptian Archaeology* 28: 20–31.

Curran, B (2003) The Renaissance Afterlife of Ancient Egypt (1400–1650). In T Champion and P Ucko (eds) *The Wisdom of Egypt: Changing Visions through the Ages*. London: UCL Press, 101–31.

El Daly, ᶜA (1983) *Al-Pardiyat Al-ᶜArabiyah*. Cairo: Al-Khangi.

El Daly, O (2000) Egyptian Deserts in Early Medieval Arabic Travel Writing. In J Starkey and O El Daly (eds) *Desert Travellers from Herodotus to TE Lawrence*. Durham: University of Durham and Association for the Study of Travel in Egypt and the Near East (Astene), 21–32.

El Daly, O (2002) Punt in the Geographical Dictionary of the Moslem Traveller Yaqut. *Discussions in Egyptology* 54: 61.

Dannenfeldt, K (1985) Egyptian Mummia: The Sixteenth Century Experience and Debate. *Sixteenth Century Journal* 16/2: 163–80.

Darby, G (1941) Ibn Waḥshīya in Medieval Spanish Literature. *Isis* 33: 433–38.

Daressy, G (1917) Indicateur topographique du 'Livre des perles enfouies et des mystères précieux'. *Bulletin de l'Institut Français d'Archéologie Orientale du Caire* 13: 175–230 and plates 1–3.

Daressy, G (1918) second part of the above 14: 1–32.

Darnell, J (2004) *The Enigmatic Netherworld Books of the Solar-Osirian Unity. Cryptographic Compositions in the Tombs of Tutankhamun, Ramesses VI and Ramesses IX*. University Press Fribourg Switzerland: Vandenhoeck & Ruprecht Göttingen (OBO 198).

Dasen, V (1993) *Dwarfs in Ancient Egypt and Greece*. Oxford: OUP.

Daumas, F (1983) L'alchimie a-t-elle une origine égyptienne? In *Das römanisch-byzantinische Ägypten*. Mainz am Rhein: Philipp von Zabern, 109–18.

D'Auria, S, P Lacovara and C Roehrig (1988) *Mummies & Magic*. Boston: Museum of Fine Arts.

David, R (2000) *The Experience of Ancient Egypt*. London: Routledge.

Davies, S and H Smith (1997) Sacred Animal Temples at Saqqara. In S Quirke (ed) *The Temple in Ancient Egypt*. London: British Museum Press, 112–31.

Dawson, W (1927) Mummy as a Drug. *Proceedings of the Royal Society of Medicine* 21/1 (November 1927), 34–39.

Dawson, W (1932) An Eighteenth-Century Discourse on Hieroglyphs. In *Studies presented to F Ll Griffith*. London: Egypt Exploration Society.

Deblauwe, F (1991) Old South Arabian Trade Routes. *Orientalia Lovaniensia Periodica* 22: 133–58.

Deladrière, R (1988) *La vie merveilleuse de Dhû-l-Nûn l'Égyptien*. Paris: Sindbad.

Derchain, P (1972) *Hathor Quadrifrons: recherches sur la syntaxe d'un mythe Égyptien*. Istanbul: Nederlands Historisch-Archaeologisch Instituut.

Derchain, P (1990) L'Atelier des orfèvres à Dendara et les origines de l'alchimie. *Chronique d'Égypte* 65: 219–42.

Derchain, P (1995) La justice à la porte d'Évergète. In D Kurth, W Waitkus and S Woodhouse (eds) *Ägyptologische Tempeltagung 3: System und Programme der ägyptischen Tempeldekoration*. Wiesbaden: Harrassowitz, 1–12.

Depauw, M (1997) *A Companion to Demotic Studies*. Brussells: Fondation Égyptologique Reine Élisabeth.

Depauw, M and W Clarysse (2002) When a Pharaoh becomes Magic. *Chronique d'Égypte* 77: 55–64.

Al-Dhahabi, M (1976) *Al-Tafsir wa Al-Mofasron*. 2 vols, 2nd edn. Cairo: Dar Al-Kutub Al-Ḥadithah.

Diab, A (1997) *Tarikh Al-Yahud of Al-Maqrizi*. Cairo: Dar Al-Faḍilah.

Diab, A (1998) *Tarikh Al-Aqbaṭ of Al-Maqrizi*. Cairo: Dar Al-Faḍilah.

Diethart, J and H Satzinger (1983) Eine Griechisch-koptische Wörterliste. In *Festschrift zum 100-jährigen Bestehen der Papyrussamlung der Österreichischen Nationalbibliothek. Papyrus Erzherzog Rainer*. 206–13 and pl 17.

Dietrich, A (1991) *Die Dioskurides-Erkärung des Ibn al-Baitar*. Göttingen: Vandenhoeck & Ruprecht.

Dijk, J van (1989) The Canaanite God Ḥauron and his Cult in Egypt. *Göttinger Miszellen* 107: 59–68.

Dimick, J (1959) The Embalming House of the Apis Bull. In R Anthes *et al*, *Mit Rahineh 1955*. Philadelphia: University Museum, University of Pennsylvania, 75–79.

Diodorus Siculus. Translated into English by C Oldfather, Cambridge, MA: Harvard University Press, Loeb Classical Library, Books I and II 1933. Reprinted 1989.

Dittmann, K (1936) The Significance of Egyptian Antiquity for the History of European Culture. *Bulletin of the Faculty of Arts of the University of Egypt [Cairo]* 4: 1–15.

Dodge, B (1970) *The Fihrist of al-Nadim: A Tenth-Century Survey of Muslim Culture*. 2 vols, New York and London: Columbia University Press.

Donner, H (1995) *Isis in Petra*. Leipzig: Leipzig University.

Donner, M (1998) *The Narratives of Islamic Origins*. New Jersey: Darwin Press.

Doresse, J (1960) *Des hiéroglyphes à la croix: ce que le passé pharaonique a légué au christianisme*. Istanbul: Nederlands Historisch-Archaeologisch Instituut.

Dornseiff, F (1925) *Das Alphabet in mystik und magie*. Leipzig and Berlin: Teubner.

Drenkhahn, R (1976) *Die Handwerker und ihre Tätigkeiten im alten Ägypten*. Wiesbaden: Harrassowitz.

Drower, E (1937) *The Mandaeans of Iraq and Iran*. Oxford: Clarendon. Reprint New Jersey: Gorgias Press 2002.

Drower, E (1956) *Water into Wine: A Study of Ritual Idiom in the Middle East*. London: John Murray.

Drower, M (1982) The Early Years. In TGH James (ed) *Excavating in Egypt: The Egypt Exploration Society 1882–1982*. London: British Museum, 9–36.

Drower, M (1985) *Flinders Petrie: A Life in Archaeology*. London: Victor Gollancz. 2nd edn with a new introduction 2000.

Drower, M (2004) *Letters from the Desert. The Correspondence of Flinders and Hilda Petrie*. Oxford: Aris & Phillips.

DuQuesne, T (1991) *A Coptic Initiatory Invocation (PGM IV 1–25)*. Thame Oxon: Darengo.

DuQuesne, T (1995) Raising the Serpent Power. Some Parallels between Egyptian Religion and Indian Tantra. In T DuQuesne (ed) *Hermes Aegyptiacus: Egyptological Studies for BH Stricker on his 85th Birthday*. Oxford: DE Publications (Special Number 2), 53–68.

DuQuesne, T (1999) Egypt's Image in the European Enlightenment. *Seshat* 3: 32–51.

DuQuesne, T (2001a) Concealing and Revealing: The Problem of Ritual Masking in Ancient Egypt. *Discussions in Egyptology* 51: 5–31.

DuQuesne, T (2001b) The Spiritual Heritage of Egypt and Africa. *Cahiers Caribéens d'Egyptologie* 2: 87–95.

DuQuesne, T (2002a) La déification des parties du corps. In Y Koenig (ed) *La magie en Égypte: à la recherche d'une définition*. Cycle de conférences, Musée du Louvre 2000. Paris: La Documentation Française, 237–71.

DuQuesne, T (2002b) 'Effective in Heaven and on Earth': Interpreting Egyptian Religious Practice for Both Worlds. In J Assmann and M Bommas (eds) *Ägyptische Mysterien?* Munich: Wilhelm Fink, 37–46.

DuQuesne, T (2003) Ancient Egyptian Religion and its Relevance in Today's World. *Discussions in Egyptology* 56: 11–24.

Dykstra, D (1994) Pyramids, Prophets, and Progress: Ancient Egypt in the Writings of ᶜAli Mubarak. *Journal of the American Oriental Society* 114: 54–67.

Effland, A (2003) '*Es sind Männer hier gewesen, deren Berichten man Glauben schenken muß*' Karl May und die Krokodilgrotte von Maabda. In N Kloth, K Martin and E Pardey (eds) *Es werde niedergelegt als Schriftstück. Festschrift für Hartwig Altenmüller zum 65 Geburtstag*, 57–69.

Empereur, J-Y (1998) *Alexandria Rediscovered*. Translated from French by M Maehler. London: British Museum Press.

Enan, M (1969) *Miṣr Al-Islamiyah*. Cairo: Lajnat Al-Ta'lif.

Enan, M (1991) *Mu'rikhu Miṣr Al-Islamiyah wa Maṣadir Al-Tarikh Al-Miṣry*. 2nd edn. Cairo: Mukhtar.

Engelbach, R *et al* (1915) *Riqqeh and Memphis VI*. With chapters by A Murray, H Petrie and W Petrie. London: British School of Archaeology in Egypt and Bernard Quaritch.

Esbroeck, M van (1998) La légende d'Apa Jermias et Apa Johannes et les fragments Chester Beatty Copte 829. *Orientalia* 67: 1–23 and tables I–V.

Étienne, M (2000) *Heka: magie et envoûtement dans l'Égypte ancienne*. Paris: Réunion des musées nationaux.

Etman, A (1990) *Cleopatra and Antony: A Study in the Art of Plutarch, Shakespeare and Ahmed Shawky*. 2nd edn. Cairo: Aegyptus (Arabic text with English summary).

Ewais, S (1966) *Al-Khulud fi Al-Turath Al-Thaqafi Al-Miṣri*. Cairo: Al-Maᶜarif.

Ewais, S (1978) *Rasail ila Al-Imam Al-Shafᶜi*. 2nd edn. Cairo/Kuwait/Amsterdam: Alshaya Publishing House. First published Cairo 1965.

Eyre, C (2002) *The Cannibal Hymn*. Liverpool: Liverpool University Press.

Fahd, T (1971) Ibn Waḥshiyya. *Encyclopaedia of Islam*, 2nd edn 3: 963–65.

Fahd, T (1993) (ed) *L'Agriculture Nabatèenne. Ibn Waḥšiyya*. 2 vols, Damascus: Institut Français de Damas.

Fahim, H (1989) *Adab Al-Raḥalat*. Kuwait: ᶜAlim Al-Maᶜrifah No 138.

Fahmy, K (1997) *All the Pasha's Men: Mehmed Ali, his Army and the Making of Modern Egypt*. Cambridge: CUP.

Fairman, H (1943) Notes on the Alphabetic Signs Employed in the Hieroglyphic Inscriptions of the Temple of Edfu. *Annales du Service des Antiquités de l'Egypte* 43: 193–318.

Fakhry, A (1952) *An Archaeological Journey to Yemen (March–May 1947)*. Part 1. Cairo: Service des Antiquités de l'Égypte, Government Press.

Farag, F (1964) *Sociological and Moral Studies in the Field of Coptic Monasticism*. Supplement I to the Annual of Leeds University Oriental Society. Leiden: Brill.

Faris, A (1938) *The Antiquities of South Arabia*. Connecticut: Hyperion.

Faris, A (1966) *The Book of Knowledge. Translation of Kitab al-ᶜIlm of Al-Ghazzali's Iḥya' ᶜUlum al-Din*. Lahore: Sh Muhammad Ashraf.

Farmer, H (1931) *The Organ of the Ancients*. London: William Reeves.

Faulkner, R (1924) The 'Cannibal Hymn' From the Pyramid Texts. *Journal of Egyptian Archaeology* 10: 97–103.

Faulkner, R (1962) *A Concise Dictionary of Middle Egyptian*. Oxford: Griffith Institute.

Faulkner, R (1969) *The Ancient Egyptian Pyramid Texts*. Oxford: OUP.

Faulkner, R *et al* (1994) *The Egyptian Book of the Dead*. San Francisco: Chronicle Books.

Ferrand (1925) see under Al-Gharnaṭi in Arabic sources.

Ferré, A (1991) Un autuer Mystérieux Ibrahim B Wasif Šah. *Annales Islamologiques* 25: 139–51.

Ferro, M (1984) *The Use and Abuse of History, or How the Past is Taught*. London: Routledge and Kegan Paul.

Feucht, E (1995) *Das Kind im alten Ägypten*. Frankfurt: Campus.

Fiey, J (1972/3) Coptes et Syriaques. Contacts et échanges. *Studia Orientalia Christiana Collectanea* 15: 297–365.

Finneran, N (2002) *The Archaeology of Christianity in Africa*. Gloucestershire: Tempus.

Fletcher, J and D Montserrat (1998) The Human Hair in the Tomb of Tutankhamun: A Re-Evaluation. In C Eyre (ed) *Proceedings of the Seventh International Congress of Egyptologists. Cambridge, 3–9 September 1995*. Leuven: Peeters, 401–07.

Fodor, A (1970) The Origins of the Arabic Legends of the Pyramids. *Acta Orientalia* 23: 335–63.

Fodor, A (1974) The Metamorphosis of Imhotep – A Study in Islamic Syncretism. In *Akten des VII Kongresses für Arabistik und Islamwissenschaft*, 155–81.

Fodor, A and L Fóti (1976) *Haram* and Hermes: Origin of the Arabic Word *Haram* Meaning Pyramid. *Studia Aegyptiaca* 2: 157–67.

Fodor, S (1970) The Origin of the Arabic Sūrīd Legend. *Zeitschrift für Ägyptische Sprache und Altertumskunde* 96: 103–09.

Fodor, S (1992) Traces of the Isis Cult in an Arabic Love Spell from Egypt. In U Luft (ed) *The Intellectual Heritage of Egypt. Studies Presented to László Kákosy*. Budapest: University Press (*Studia Aegyptiaca* 14), 171–86.

Fontinoy, C (1989) Les noms de l'Égypte en hébreu et leur étymologie. *Chronique d'Égypte* 64: 90–97.

Fouad, H (1992) The Symbolism of the Letter *Alif* in Ibn ᶜArabi. *Alif: Journal of Comparative Poetics*, American University in Cairo, 12: 145–77.

Fowden, G (1986) *The Egyptian Hermes: A Historical Approach to the Late Pagan Mind*. Princeton: Princeton University Press.

Frantz-Murphy, G (1991) Conversion in Early Islamic Egypt: The Economic Factor. In Y Rāġib (ed) *Documents de l'Islam médiéval: nouvelles perspectives de rescherche. Actes de la table ronde, le Centre National de la Recherche Scientifique (Paris, 3–5 mars 1988)*. Cairo: Institut Français d'Archéologie Orientale du Caire (TAEI 29), 11–17.

Fraser, P (1972) *Ptolemaic Alexandria*. 3 vols, Oxford: Clarendon. Reprint 1984.

Free, J (1944) Abraham's Camels. *Journal of Near Eastern Studies* 3: 187–93.

Fück, J (1951) The Arabic Literature on Alchemy According to An-Nadim (AD 987). *Ambix: The Journal of the Society for the Study of Alchemy and Early Chemistry* 4: 81–144.

Fynes, R (1993) Isis and Pattini: The Transmition of a Religious Idea from Roman Egypt to India. *Journal of the Royal Asiatic Society of Great Britain and Ireland* 377–91.

Galen (1956) *On Anatomical Procedures*. Ed and translated Ch Singer. Oxford: OUP. Reprint 1999.

Ghalioungui, P (1985) *ᶜAbd Al-Laṭif Al-Baghdadi*. Edition of text and commentary Cairo: Al-Hay'ah Al-Miṣriyah Al-ᶜAmah li-Al-Kitab. 2nd edn.

Gardiner, A and K Sethe (1928) *Egyptian Letters to the Dead*. London: Egypt Exploration Society.

Garven, K (1993) Causal Origins of Egyptian Conceptual Thinking. *Bulletin of the Australian Centre for Egyptology* 4: 7–16.

Gascoigne, A (2003) The Medieval City of Tinnis. *Egyptian Archaeology: The Bulletin of the Egypt Exploration Society* 22: 25–27.

Gauthier, H (1906) Un précurseur de Champollion au XVIᵉ siècle. *Bulletin de l'Institut Français d'Archéologie Orientale du Caire* 5: 65–86.

Gawad, M (1947) Mu'rikh Al-Ahram wa Abi Al-Hawl, Jamal Al-Din Abu Jaᶜfar Al-Idrisi. *Majalat Al-Kutab*, Cairo (April 1947) 3: 858–68.

Geary, P (2001) Sacred Commodities: The Circulation of Medieval Relics. In A Appadurai (ed) *The Social Life of Things: Commodities in Cultural Perspective*. Cambridge: CUP. First published 1986, 169–91.

Geoffroy, E (1997) Al-Suyuṭi. *Encyclopaedia of Islam*, 2nd edn 9: 913–16.

Gerbi, A (1973) *The Dispute of the New World: The History of a Polemic, 1750–1900*. Originally published in Milano-Napoli: Riccardo Ricciardi 1955. Revised and enlarged edn translated by J Moyle. Pittsburgh: University of Pittsburgh Press.

Germer, R (1982) Nun. *Lexikon der Ägyptologie*, 7 vols, Wiesbaden 1975–87. 4: 534–35.

Gershoni, I and J Jankowski (1986) *Egypt, Islam and the Arabs: The Search for Egyptian Nationhood, 1900–1930*. Oxford: OUP.

Gese, H, M Höfner and K Rudolph (1970) *Die Religionen Altsyriens, Altarabiens und der Mandäer*. Stuttgart: Kohlhammer.

Ghali, E (1993) *Muᶜamalat ghyr Al-Moslemin fi Al-Mujtamaᶜ Al-Islami*. Cairo: Maktabat Gharib.

Gilis, Ch-A (1984) *Le coran et la fonction d'Hermès*. Paris: Les Éditions de l'Oeuvre.

Gilliot, C (2002) Yaḳut al-Rumi. *Encyclopaedia of Islam*, 2nd edn 11: 264–66.

Giorgini, M (1965) *Soleb 1*. Florence: Sausoni.

Giveon, R (1971) *Les bédouins Shosou des documents Égyptiens*. Leiden: Brill.

Al-Ghonimi, A (1993) *ᶜUrubet Miṣr qabl Al-Islam*. Cairo: Dar Al-Ishᶜaᶜ.

Godwin, J (1979) *Athanasius Kircher*. London: Thames and Hudson.

Goebs, K (1995) 'Horus der Kaufmann' als Name des Planeten Jupiter. *Enchoria* 22: 218–21.

Goedicke, H (1971) *Re-used Blocks from the Pyramid of Amenemhet I at Lisht*. New York: Metropolitan Museum of Art.

Goedicke, H (1993) The 'Seal of the Necropolis'. *Studien zur Altägyptischen Kultur* 20: 67–79.

Goedicke, H (1998) *Pi(ankh)y in Egypt. A Study of the Pi(ankh)y Stela*. Baltimore: Halgo.

Goitein, S (1963) Between Hellenism and Renaissance – Islam, the Intermediate Civilization. *Islamic Studies* 2: 215–33.

Goldwasser, O (1995) *From Icon to Metaphor. Studies in the Semiotics of the Hieroglyphs*. University Press Fribourg Switzerland: Vandenhoeck & Ruprecht Göttingen (OBO 142).

Golénischeff, W (1906) Le Papyrus No 1115 de L'Ermitage Imperial de Saint-Petersbourg. *Recueil de travaux relatifs à la philologie et à l'archéologie Égyptiennes et Assyriennes* 28: 1–40.

Goodman, L (1995) Al-Razi. *Encyclopaedia of Islam*, 2nd edn 8: 474–77.

Gottheil, R (1907) Al-Ḥasan ibn Ibrahim ibn Zulaḳ. *Journal of the American Oriental Society* 28: 254–70.

Goyon, J-C (1988) Momification et recomposition du corps divin: Anubis et les canopes. In J Kamstra, H Milde and K Wagtendonk (eds) *Funerary Symbols and Religion. Essays dedicated to Professor M Heerma van Voss*. Kampen: JH Kok, 34–44.

Graefe, E (1911) *Das Pyramidenkapitel in Al-Maqrizi's 'Ḫitat'*. Leipzig: Kreysing.

Graf, D (1997) *Rome and the Arabian Frontier, from the Nabataeans to the Saracens*. Ashgate: Variorum.

Gray, J (1949) The Canaanite God Horon. *Journal of Near Eastern Studies* 8: 27–34.

Greaves, J (1646) *Pyramidographia: A Discourse of the Pyramids in Egypt*. London: Geore Badger.

Grelot, P (1972) *Documents araméens d'Égypte*. Paris: Éditions du Cerf.

Griffith, FL (1900) *Stories of the High Priests of Memphis*. 2 vols, Oxford: OUP.

Gril, D (1978) Le personage coranique de pharaon d'après l'interprétation d'Ibn 'Arabi. *Annales Islamologiques* 14: 37–57.

Grimal, N (1981) *Études sur la propagande royale égyptienne I: La stèle triomphale de Pi('ankh)y au Musée du Caire (JE 48862 et 47086–47089)*. Cairo: Institut Français d'Archéologie Orientale du Caire. (MIFAO 105).

Grimal, N (1992) *A History of Ancient Egypt*. Translated from French by I Shaw. Oxford: Blackwell.

Grohmann, A (1938) *Arabic Papyri in the Egyptian Library*. Vol 3. Cairo: Dar Al-Kutub Al-Miṣriyah.

Grohmann, A (1952) *From the World of Arabic Papyri*. Cairo: Al-Maaref Press.

Grossmann, P (2001) On Some Lesser Known Churches and Monasteries in Egypt. In *Festschrift A Abdel Tawab Dirasat wa Buḥuth fi Al-Athar wa Al-Ḥaḍarah Al-Islamiyah*. 2 vols, Cairo: Supreme Council of Antiquities. Vol 2: 171–202.

Grube, E (1962) Studies in the Survival and Continuity of Pre-Muslim Traditions in Egyptian Islamic Art. *Journal of the American Research Center in Egypt* 1: 75–97, plus figures 1–5 and plates.

Guest, A (1902) A List of Writers, Books, and other Authorities mentioned by al-Maqrizi in his Khitat. *Journal of the Royal Asiatic Society of Great Britain and Ireland* (January 1902): 103–25.

Gundlach, R (1982) Min. In W Helck and E Otto (eds) *Lexikon der Ägyptologie* 7 vols, Wiesbaden 1975–87. 4: 136–40.

Haarmann, M (1991) *Das moderne Ägypten und seine pharaonische Vergangenheit*. Unpublished PhD thesis, University of Albert-Ludwig, Fribourg.

Haarmann, U (1978) Die Sphinx. *Saeculum* 29: 367–84.

Haarmann, U (1980) Regional Sentiment in Medieval Islamic Egypt. *Bulletin of the School of Oriental and African Studies* 43: 55–66.

Haarmann, U (1982a) Al-Idrisi. *Encyclopaedia of Islam*, 2nd edn. Supplement 1: 5/6: 407–08.

Haarmann, U (1982b) Quellen zur Geschichte des islamischen Ägypten. *Mitteilungen des Deutschen Archäologischen Instituts Abteilung Kairo* 38: 201–10.

Haarmann, U (1984) Luxor und Heliopolis: Ein Aufruf zum Denkmalschutz aus dem 13 Jahrhundert n Chr. *Mitteilungen des Deutschen Archäologischen Instituts Abteilung Kairo* 40: 153–57.

Haarmann, U (1990) Das Pharaonische Ägypten bei Islamischen Autoren des Mittelalters. In E Hornung (ed) *Zum Bild Ägyptens im Mittelalter und in der Renaissance/Comment se représente-t-on l'Égypte au moyen âge et à la renaissance?* University Press Fribourg: Vandenhoeck & Ruprecht Göttingen (OBO 95), 29–58.

Haarmann, U (1991a) *Kitab Anwar ᶜUlwiyy Al-Aǧram fi Al-Kašf ᶜan Asrar Al-Ahram*. Arabic text ed with an introduction in German by U Haarmann under the title *Das Pyramidenbuch Des Abu Ǧaᶜfar Al-Idrisi*. Beirut and Stuttgart: Steiner.

Haarmann, U (1991b) In Quest of the Spectacular: Noble and Learned Visitors to the Pyramids Around 1200 AD. In W Hallaq and D Little (eds) *Islamic Studies Presented to Charles J Adams*. Leiden: Brill, 57–67.

Haarmann, U (1996) Medieval Muslim Perceptions of Pharaonic Egypt. In A Loprieno (ed), *Ancient Egyptian Literature: History and Forms*. Leiden: Brill, 605–27.

Haarmann, U (2001) Islam and Ancient Egypt. In D Redford (ed) *Oxford Encyclopaedia of Ancient Egypt*. 3 vols, Oxford: OUP. Vol 2: 191–94.

Habachi, L (1940) The Monuments of Biyahmu. *Annales du Service des Antiquités de l'Egypte* 40: 721–32.

Habachi, L (1969) *Features of the Diefication of Ramesses II*. Glückstadt: Augustin.

Habachi, L (1984) *The Obelisks of Egypt*. Cairo: American University of Cairo Press.

Al-Hadi (1996) see Arabic sources under Ibn Al-Faqih.

Hadj-Sadok (1971) Ibn Khurradadhbih. *Encyclopaedia of Islam*, 2nd edn 3: 839–40.

El-Hagagy, M (1968) *Abou El Haggag Eloksory* [*sic*]. Cairo: Dar Al-Taḍamun.

El-Hagagy, M (1997) *Al-Uqsur fi Al-ᶜAṣr Al-Islami (Islamic Luxor)*. 3rd edn. First published 1978 Cairo: Al-Hay'ah Al-Miṣriyah Al-ᶜAmah li-Al-Kitab.

Haikal, F (1993) Demotic Documentation in the International Context. In *Acta Demotica: Actes of the Fifth International Conference for Demotists, Pisa, 4th–8th September 1993*.

Haiying, Y (1998) The Famine Stela: A Source-Critical Approach and Historical-Comparative Perspective. In C Eyre (ed) *Proceedings of the Seventh International Congress of Egyptologists*. Leuven: Peeters, 515–21.

Hajji Khalifa (1999) *Kashf Al-ẓunun ^{c}an Asami Al-Kutub wa Al-Funun*. 6 vols, Beirut: Dar Al-Fikr.

Hall, M (1971) *The Pneumatics of Hero of Alexandria*. London: Macdonald and New York: American Elsevier Inc.

Halm, H (1997) *The Fatimids and their Traditions of Learning*. London: Tauris.

Ḥamarneh, S (1971) The Ancient Monuments of Alexandria according to Accounts by Medieval Arab Authors (IX–XV Century). *Folia Orientalia* 13: 77–110.

Ḥamarneh, S (1989) see under Ibn Al-Quff.

Al-Ḥamd, M (1999) *Al-Ta'thir Al-Arami fi Al-Fikr Al-^{c}Arabi*. Damascus: Dar Al-Ṭali^{c}ah.

Hamdan, G (1995) *Shakhiṣiyat Miṣr*. 4 vols, Cairo: Dar Al-Hilal.

Hämeen-Anttila, J (2002/3) The *Nabatean Agriculture*: Authenticity, Textual History and Analysis. *Zeitschrift für Geschichte der Arabisch-Islamischen Wissenschaften* 15: 248–80.

Ḥamidov, I (2002) Al-Adab Al-Adhrabaijani fi Al-Drasat Al-^{c}Arabiyah wa Azmat Al-Adab Al-Muqarin. *Adab wa Naqd* (Cairo, December 2002) 208: 99–103.

Hammer, J (1806) *Ancient Alphabets and Hieroglyphic Characters Explained; with an Account of the Egyptian Priests, their Classes, Initiation, and Sacrifices in the Arabic Language by Ahmad Bin Abubekr Bin Wahshih*. London: Bulmer.

Hamza, M (1937) The Statue of Meneptaḥ I Found at Athar En-Nabi and the Route of Pi^{c}ankhi from Memphis. *Annales du Service des Antiquités de l'Égypte* 37: 233–42 and plates 1–5.

Hannig, R (1995) *Großes Handwörterbuch Ägyptisch-Deutsch*. Mainz am Rhein: Philipp von Zabern.

Hanson, A (1992) Egyptians, Greeks, Romans, Arabs, and *IOUDAIOI* in the First Century AD. Tax Archive from Philadelphia: P Mich Inv 880 Recto and P Princ III 152 Revised. In J Johnson (ed) *Life in a Multi-Cultural Society: Egypt from Cambyses to Constantine and Beyond*. Chicago: Oriental Institute of the University of Chicago, 133–45.

Haq, SN (1994) *Names, Natures and Things. The Alchemist Jabir ibn Hayyan and his Kitab al-Aḥjar (Book of Stones)*. Dordrecht, Boston and London: Kluwer (Boston Studies in the Philosophy of Science 158).

Haridi, A (1983–84) *Index des Ḫitat: Index analytique des ouvrages d'Ibn Duqmaq et de Maqrizi sur le Caire*. 3 vols, Cairo: Institut Français d'Archéologie Orientale du Caire.

Harle, J (1992) The 'Indian' Terracottas from Ancient Memphis: A Hitherto Unknown Deity? In C Jarrige *et al* (eds) *South Asian Archaeology 1989. Papers from the Tenth International Conference of South Asian Archaeologists in Western Europe, Musée national des Arts asiatique Guimet, Paris, France, 3–7 July 1989*. Monographs in World Archaeology No 14. Madison: Prehistory Press, 375–84.

Harvey, P (1987) Local and Regional Cartography in Medieval Europe. In J Harley and D Woodward (eds) *The History of Cartography*. Vol I: *Cartography in Prehistoric, Ancient and Medieval Europe and the Mediterranean*. Chicago and London: University of Chicago Press, 464–501.

Hassan, F (1993) Town and Village in Ancient Egypt, Ecology, Society and Urbanization. In T Shaw *et al* (eds) *The Archaeology of Africa*. London: Routledge, 551–69.

Hassan, F (1998) The Earliest Goddesses of Egypt. In L Goodison and C Morris (eds) *Ancient Goddesses: The Myth and the Evidence*. London: British Museum Press, 98–112.

Hassan, F (1999) Memorabilia: Archaeological Materiality and National Identity in Egypt. In L Meskell (ed) *Archaeology Under Fire: Nationalism, Politics and Heritage in the Eastern Mediterranean and Middle East*. London: Routledge, 200–16.

Hassan, F (2002) (ed) *Alexandria Graeco-Roman Museum*. Cairo: National Center for Documentation of Cultural and Natural Heritage and Supreme Council of Antiquities.

Hassan, F (forthcoming) *Apocalypse: Death on the Nile*. London: Thames and Hudson.

Hassan, H (1984) *Ḥaḍarat Al-^{c}Arab fi ^{c}Aṣr Al-Jahliyah*. Beirut: Al-Mu'ssasah Al-Jam^{c}iyah li-Al-Drasat wa Al-Nashar wa Al-Tawzi^{c}.

Hassan, S (1936) Al-^{c}Adat Al-Miṣryiah Al-Qadimah Al-Baqiyah ila alaan fi Miṣr Al-Ḥadithah. *Bulletin de l'Association des Amis des Églises et de l'Art Coptes* 2: 1–25.

Hassan, S (1951) *Le Sphinx: son histoire à la lumière des fouilles récentes*. Cairo: Maṭbaᶜat Miṣr.
Hawkins, G (1971–72) Preliminary Results of an Investigation of Astronomical Alignments of 'Structural Antiquities in Egypt'. *Bulletin de l'Institut Egyptien* 53: 173–76.
Hazzard, R (2000) *Imagination of a Monarchy: Studies in Ptolemaic Propaganda*. Toronto: University of Toronto Press.
Henein, N and T Bianquis (1975) *La Magie par les Psaumes*. Edition and translation of the Arabic text. Cairo: Institut Français d'Archéologie Orientale du Caire.
Hero of Alexandria: see under Hall 1971.
Herodotus, *Histories*. Translated with notes by G Rawlinson with an introduction by T Griffith. Hertfordshire: Wordsworth Editions 1996.
Hess, R (1993) *Amarna Personal Names*. Indiana: Eisenbrauns.
Hill, D (1993) *Islamic Science and Engineering*. Edinburgh: Edinburgh University Press.
Hillenbrand, R (1994) *Islamic Architecture*. Edinburgh: Edinburgh University Press.
Hinz, W (1955) *Islamische Masse und Gewichte*. Leiden: Brill.
Hitti, P (1970) *History of the Arabs*. 10th edn. London: Macmillan.
Hobson, C (1987) *Exploring the World of the Pharaohs*. London: Thames and Hudson.
Hoch, J (1994) *Semitic Words in Egyptian Texts of the New Kingdom and Third Intermediate Period*. Princeton: Princeton University Press.
Hofmann, T (2001) Majestät und Diener. Zur Dialektik des Begriffes *ḥm*. *Zeitschrift für Ägyptische Sprache und Altertumskunde* 128: 116–32.
Hölbl, G (2001) *A History of the Ptolemaic Empire*. London: Routledge.
Holmyard, E (1926) Abu Al-Qasim Al-ᶜIraqi. *Isis* 8: 405–26.
Holmyard, E (1937) Aidamir Al-Jildaki. *Iraq* 4: 47–53.
Holmyard, E (1957) *Alchemy*. Harmondsworth: Penguin. Reprinted 1968.
Holt, P (1968) Ottoman Egypt (1516–1798): An Account of Arabic Historical Sources. In P Holt (ed) *Political and Social Change in Modern Egypt*. Oxford: OUP, 3–12.
Hopfner, T (1922–25) *Fontes Historiae Religionis Aegyptiacae*. 5 parts in 2 vols, Bonn: Marcus and Weber.
Hopkins, J and N Levtzion (1981) *Corpus of Early Arabic Sources for West African History*. Cambridge: CUP.
Horapollo, *Hieroglyphica*. Translated and introduced by G Boas with a new foreword by A Grafton. New Jersey: Princeton University Press 1993.
Horn, S (1969) Foreign Gods in Ancient Egypt. In *Studies in Honor of John A Wilson*. Chicago: Oriental Institute of the University of Chicago, 37–42.
Hornung, E (1990a) *The Valley of the Kings*. Translated by D Warburton. New York: Timken.
Hornung, E (1990b) The Pharaoh. In Donadoni (ed) *The Egyptians*. Chicago: University of Chicago Press, 283–314.
Hornung, E (1992) *Idea into Image: Essays on Ancient Egyptian Thought*. Translated from German by E Bredeck. New York: Timken.
Hornung, E (1999) *The Ancient Egyptian Books of the Afterlife*. Translated from German by D Lorton. Ithaca and London: Cornell University Press.
Hornung, E (2001) *The Secret Lore of Egypt*. Translated from German by D Lorton. Ithaca and London: Cornell University Press.
Horovitz, J (1927) The Origins of 'The Arabian Nights'. *Islamic Culture* 1: 36–59.
van der Horst, P (1982) The Way of Life of the Egyptian Priests according to Chaeremon. In In M Heerma van Voss, D Hoens, G Mussies, D van der Plas and H te Velde (eds) *Studies in Egyptian Religion Dedicated to Professor J Zandee*. Leiden: Brill, 61–71.
Horovitz, J (1984) *Chaeremon. Egyptian Priest and Stoic Philosopher*. Leiden: Brill (EPRO 101).
Al-Ḥosni, ᶜA (1986) *Kitab Ḍiya' Al-Nibras fi Ḥall Mufradat Al-Anṭaki bi-Lughat Fas*. Al-Rabat: Dar Al-Turath.
Houlihan, P (1996) *The Animal World of the Pharaohs*. London: Thames and Hudson.
Hourani, G (1971) *Islamic Rationalism: The Ethics of 'Abd al-Jabar*. Oxford: Clarendon.

Hovestreydt, W (1997) Secret Doors and Hidden Treasures: Some Aspects of Egyptian Temple Treasuries from the New Kingdom. In J van Dijk (ed) *Essays on Ancient Egypt in Honour of Herman te Velde*. Groningen: Styx Publications, 187–206.

Hoyland, R (2001) *Arabia and the Arabs from the Bronze Age to the Coming of Islam*. London: Routledge.

Huff, T (1993) *The Rise of Early Modern Science: Islam, China, and the West*. Cambridge: CUP.

Hughes-Hallett, L (1990) *Cleopatra*. London: Vintage.

Hunt, L-A (1985) Christian-Muslim Relations in Paintings in Egypt of the Twelfth to Mid-Thirteenth Centuries: Sources of Wallpainting at Deir es-Suriani and the Illustration of the New Testament MS Paris Copte-Arabe 1/Cairo, Bibl 94. *Cahiers Archéologiques* 33: 111–55. Reprinted in Hunt 1998: 205–81.

Hunt, L-A (1998) Churches of Old Cairo and the Mosques of al-Qahira: A Case of Christian-Muslim Interchange. In L-A Hunt *Byzantium, Eastern Christendom and Islam: Art at the Crossroads of the Medieval Mediterranean*. Vol 1. London: Pindar, 319–42.

Ḥusayn, Ṭ (1938) *Mustaqbal Al-Thaqafah fi Miṣr*. Cairo: Reprint Dar Al-Ma^carif 1996.

Iamblichus, *On the Mysteries of the Egyptians, Chaldeans, and Assyrians. And Life of Pythagoras to which have been added Ethical and Political Fragments of Ancient Pythagorean Writers*. Translated by Thomas Taylor. Somerset: Prometheus Trust, new reprint. First published 1818–22.

Ibrahim, F (1984) *Khalid ibn Yazid*. Baghdad: Manshurat Wizarat Al-Thaqafah wa Al-Iᶜlam (Silsilat Drasat 362).

Ibrahim, M (1943) The Petrified Forest. *Bulletin de l'Institut d'Égypte*. Part 1, 25: 159–82 plus plates 1–6. Part 2, 34 (1953): 317–28.

Ikram, S and A Dodson (1998) *The Mummy in Ancient Egypt*. London: Thames and Hudson.

Irwin, R (1994) *The Arabian Nights: A Companion*. Harmondsworth: Penguin.

Isler, M (2001) *Sticks, Stones, and Shadows: Building the Egyptian Pyramids*. Oklahoma: University of Oklahoma Press.

Isma'il, ᶜA (1934) *Folk Medicine in Modern Egypt*. Translation by J Walker of parts of the original Arabic 'Ṭibb Al-Rukka' published in Arabic in two vols in Cairo 1892–94. London: Luzak & Co.

Ismail, T (1989) *Classic Arabic as the Ancestor of Indo-Europian [sic] Languages and Origin of Speech*. Cairo: Al-Ahram Press.

Ittig, A (1982) A Talismanic Bowl. *Annales Islamologiques* 18: 79–94.

Iversen, E (1993) *The Myth of Egypt and its Hieroglyphs*. Princeton: Princeton University Press. 2nd edn. First published 1961, Copenhagen: Gad.

ᶜIz Al-Din, M (1990) *Abu Al-ᶜAbas Al-Qalqashandi mu'rikha*. Beirut: ᶜAlim Al-Kutub.

Jakeman, J (1993) *Abstract Art and Communication in 'Mamluk' Architecture*. Unpublished PhD thesis, Faculty of Oriental Studies, University of Oxford.

James, TGH (1997) *Egypt Revealed*. London: Folio Society.

Janssen, J (1963) Eine Beuteliste von Amenophis II und das Problem der Sklaverei im alten Ägypten. *Jaarbericht van het Vooraziatisch-Egyptisch Genootschap 'Ex Oriente Lux'* 17: 141–47.

Jasnow, R (1997) The Greek Alexander Romance and Demotic Egyptian Literature. *Journal of Near Eastern Studies* 56: 95–103.

Jasnow, R and K Zauzich (1998) A Book of Thoth? In C Eyre (ed) *Proceedings of the Seventh International Congress of Egyptologists. Cambridge, 3–9 September 1995*. Leuven: Peeters, 607–18.

Jeffreys, D (1985) *The Survey of Memphis*. Vol 1. London: Egypt Exploration Society.

Jeffreys, D (1998) The Topography of Heliopolis and Memphis: Some Cognitive Aspects. In H Guksch and D Polz (eds) *Stationen, Beiträge zur Kulturgeschichte Ägyptens. Rainer Stadelmann gewidmet*. Mainz am Rhein: Philipp von Zabern, 63–71.

Jeffreys, D (1999) *Written and Graphic Sources for an Archaeological Survey of Memphis, Egypt: from 500 BCE to 1900 CE, with special reference to the papers of Joseph Hekekyan*. Unpublished PhD thesis, University of London.

Jeffreys, D and A Tavares (1994) The Historic Landscape of Early Dynastic Memphis. *Mitteilungen des Deutchen Archäologischen Instituts Abteilung Kairo* 50: 143–73.

Johnson, J (1999) Ethnic Considerations in Persian Period Egypt. In E Teeter and J Larson (eds) *Gold of Praise: Studies on Ancient Egypt in Honor of Edward Wente*. Chicago: Oriental Institute of the University of Chicago, 211–22.

Jolivet, J (1996) Classifications of the Sciences. In IR Rashed (ed) *Encyclopedia of the History of Arabic Science*. 3 vols, London: Routledge, 3: 1008–25.

Jones, D (2000) *An Index of Ancient Egyptian Titles, Epithets and Phrases of the Old Kingdom*. 2 vols, Oxford: Archaeopress (BAR International Series 866).

Juvenal, *The Sixteen Satires*. Translated with an introduction and notes by P Green. Harmondsworh: Penguin 1967.

Kaḥalah, ᶜU (1957–61) *Muᶜjam Al-Mu'lifin*. 7 vols, Damascus: Maṭbaᶜat Al-Taraqi (used here). New edn 15 vols Beirut: Dar Iḥya' Al-Turath Al-ᶜArabi, nd. One vol supplement Dar Al-Risalah.

Kahn, D (1995) *Hermès Trismégiste. La Table d'Émeraude et sa tradition alchimique*. Paris: Les Belles Lettres.

Kákosy, L (1981) Problems of the Thoth-Cult in Roman Egypt. In L Kákosy Selected Papers. *Studia Aegyptiaca* 7: 41–46.

Kákosy, L (1982) A Christian Interpretation of the Sun-Disk. In M Heerma van Voss, D Hoens, G Mussies, D van der Plas and H te Velde (eds) *Studies in Egyptian Religion Dedicated to Professor J Zandee*. Leiden: Brill, 69–75.

Kákosy, L (1989a) Hermetic Obelisks. In Studia in Honorem L Fóti. *Studia Aegyptiaca* 12: 235–38.

Kákosy, L (1989b) Survival of Ancient Egypt. Religion, Other Domains of Culture, Egyptian Influence on Gnosticism and Hermetism, A Brief Survey. In Studia in Honorem L Fóti. *Studia Aegyptiaca* 12: 263–87.

Kákosy, L (1990) Survival of Ancient Egyptian Gods in Coptic and Islamic Egypt. In W Godlewski (ed) *Coptic Studies: Acts of the Third International Congress of Coptic Studies, Warsaw, 20–25 August 1984*. Varsovie: PWN-Éditions Scientifiques de Pologne, 175–77.

Kákosy, L (1993) Plato and Egypt. The Egyptian Tradition. In *Gedenkschrift I Hahn Herausgegeben von György Németh*. Budapest: Annales Universitatis Scientiarum Budapestinensis de Rolando Eötvös Nominatae (Sectio Historica 26), 25–28.

Kákosy, L (1995) Ouroboros on Magical Healing Statues. In T DuQuesne (ed) *Hermes Aegyptiacus: Egyptological Studies for BH Stricker on his 85th Birthday*. Oxford: DE Publications (Special Number 2), 123–29.

Kákosy, L (1999) *Egyptian Healing Statues*. Torino: Museo Egizio.

Kamal, A (1896) *Tarwiḥ Al-Nafs fi Madinat Al-Shams (Heliopolis)*. Cairo: Al-Maṭbaᶜah Al-Kubra Al-Amiriyah.

Kamal, A (1902) Les Idoles Arabes et les Divinités Egyptiennes. *Recueil de Travaux Relatifs à la Philologie et à l'Archéologie Égyptiennes et Assyriennes* 24: 11–24.

Kamal, A (1903) Notes sur La Rectification des noms arabes des anciens rois d'Égypte. *Bulletin de l'Institut Égyptien*, ser 4 (1903–04), 89–127.

Kamal, A (1907) *Al-Dur Al-Maknuz wa Al-Sir Al-Maᶜzuz fi Al-Dalayal wa Al-Khabaya wa Al-Dafa'n wa Al-Kunuz*. Cairo: Egyptian Antiquity Service.

Kamal, A (1909) *Bughayat Al-Ṭalbin fi ᶜUlum wa ᶜAwaid wa Ṣanaiᶜ wa Aḥwal Qudma' Al-Miṣrien*. Cairo: Maṭbaᶜat Bulaq. Reprinted recently Cairo: Madbouli (nd).

Kamal, A (1917) Le procédé graphique chez les anciens Egyptiens, l'origine du mot Égypte, les noms géographiques désignant cette contrée et ses primitives. *Bulletin de l'Institut Egyptien*, ser 5: 325–38.

Kamal, A (2002) *Mu^c^jam Al-Lughah Al-Miṣryiah Al-Qadeemah*. Vol 1. Cairo: Supreme Council of Antiquities Press.

Kamal, Y (1926–51) *Monumenta cartographica Africae et Aegypti*. 5 vols in 16 books. Cairo/Leiden: Brill. (Vol 3 in 5 books deals with Arabic sources 1930–35.)

Kaufman, I (1967) New Evidence for Hieratic Numerals on Hebrew Weights. *Bulletin of the American Schools of Oriental Research* 188: 39–41.

Kent, R (1953) *Old Persian. Grammar – Texts – Lexicon*. New Haven: American Oriental Society.

Kervran, M (1972) Une statue de Darius découverte à Suse. Le contexte archéologique. *Journal Asiatique* 260: 235–39.

Khalidi, T (1974) *Islamic Historiography: The Histories of Mas^c^udi*. Albany: State University of New York Press.

Khalidi, T (1994) *Arabic Historical Thought in the Classical Period*. Cambridge: CUP.

Khashim, A (1998) *Alihat Miṣr Al-^c^Arabiya*. 2 vols, Cairo: Al-Hay'ah Al-Miṣriyah Al-^c^Amah li-Al-Kitab.

El-Kholi, S (2003) The Lost Colossus of the Mate of the Sphinx (Surriat Abu al-Holl). In Z Hawass and L Brock (eds) *Egyptology at the Dawn of the Twenty-first Century. Proceedings of the Eighth International Congress of Egyptologists, Cairo, 2000*. Cairo: American University in Cairo Press, 2: 352–61.

Kingsley, P (1995) *Ancient Philosophy, Mystery and Magic. Empedocles and Pythagorean Tradition*. Oxford: Oxford University Press.

Kircher, A (1636) *Prodomus Coptus Sive Aegyptiacus*. Rome: S Cong de propaganda fide.

Kircher, A (1643) *Lingua Ægyptiaca Restituta*. Rome: H Scheus.

Kircher, A (1652–54) *Œdipus Ægyptiacus*. 3 vols, Amsterdam.

Kircher, A (1666) *Ad Alexandrum VIII Obelisci Aegyptiaci Nuper inter Isaei Romani Effossi Interpretatio Hieroglyphica*. Rome: Varesij.

Kircher, A (1676) *Sphinx Mystagoga*. Amsterdam: Jansson-Waesberg.

Kitchen, K (1982) *Pharaoh Triumphant: The Life and Times of Ramesses II*. Cairo: American University in Cairo Press.

Kitchen, K (1986) *The Third Intermediate Period in Egypt (1100–650 BC)*. 2nd edn with supplement. Warminster: Aris & Phillips.

Kitchen, K (1994) *Documentation for Ancient Arabia. Part I: Chronological Framework and Historical Sources*. Liverpool: Liverpool University Press.

Kitchen, K (2000) *Documentation for Ancient Arabia. Part II: Bibliographical Catalogue of Texts*. Liverpool: Liverpool University Press.

Kramers, J (1954) Al-Ushmunain in den arabischen Quellen des Mittelalters. *Analecta Orientalia: Posthumous Writings and Selected Minor Works*. Leiden: Brill. Vol 1, 166–71.

Kraus, P (1986) *Jabir Ibn Ḥayyan*. Reprint Paris: Les Belles Lettres.

Krause, M (1980) Koptische Sprache. In W Helck and E Otto (eds) *Lexikon der Ägyptologie*. 7 vols, Wiesbaden 1975–87, 3: 731–38.

Krachkovski, I (1957) *Istoria Arabskoi Geograficheskoi Literatury*. Moscow. Translated from Russian into Arabic by S Hashim. Cairo: Lajnat Al-Talif wa Al-Trajamah wa Al-Nashr. 2 vols, 1963–65. 2nd rev edn Beirut: Dar Al-Gharb Al-Islami in one vol 1987 (used here).

Kruj, R (1996) Ibn Ṭufayl: A Medieval Scholar's Views on Nature. In L Conrad (ed) *The World of Ibn Ṭufayl*. Leiden: Brill, 69–89.

Kruchten, J-M (1981) *Le décret d'Horemheb: traduction, commentaire épigraphique, philologique et institutionnel*. Brussells: Université libre de Bruxelles, Faculté de Philosophie et Lettres.

Kubaissi, M (2000) *Malamiḥ Fiqh Al-Lahajat Al-^c^Arabiyat*. Damscus: Dar Shimal.

Kuhlmann, K (1983) *Materialien zur Archäologie und Geschichte des Raumes von Achmim*. Mainz am Rhein: Philipp von Zabern.

Kuhrt, A (1999) The Exploitation of the Camel in the Neo-Assyrian Empire. In A Leahy and J Tait (eds) *Studies on Ancient Egypt in Honour of HS Smith*. London: Egypt Exploration Society, 179–84.

Kurz, O (1977) Mamluk Heraldry and *Interpretatio Christiana*. In M Rosen-Ayalon (ed) *Studies in Memory of Gaston Wiet*. Jerusalem: Institute of Asian and African Studies, Hebrew University of Jerusalem, 297–307.

Labib, P and S Abu Talib (1972) *Tashrīᶜ Ḥoremḥeb*. Cairo: Al-Hay'ah Al-Miṣriyah Al-ᶜAmah li-Al-Kitab.

Lacau, P (1913) Suppressions et modifications de signes dans les texts funéraires. *Zeitschrift für Ägyptische Sprache und Altertumskunde* 51: 1–64.

Lacau, P and H Chevrier (1977) *Une chapelle d'Hatshepsout à Karnak*. 2 vols, Cairo: Service des antiquités de l'Égypte and Institut Français d'Archéologie Orientale du Caire.

La'da, C (1993) Ethnicity, Occupation and Tax-Status in Ptolemaic Egypt. In *Acta Demotica: Actes of the Fifth International Conference for Demotists, Pisa. 4–8 September 1993*, 183–89.

La'da, C (2002) *Foreign Ethnics in Hellenistic Egypt*. Leuven: Peeters.

Lambert, J (1988) Hermopolis, Memphis, Latopolis et les Dogan. *Revue de l'Histoire des Religions* 205: 133–49.

Lameer, J (1997) From Alexandria to Baghdad: Reflections on the Genesis of a Problematical Tradition. In G Endress and R Kruk (eds), *The Ancient Tradition in Christian and Islamic Hellenism: Studies on the Transmission of Greek Philosophy and Sciences dedicated to HJ Drossaart Lulofs on his 90th Birthday*. Leiden: Research School CNWS, 181–91.

Layton, B (2000) *A Coptic Grammar*. Wiesbaden: Harrassowitz.

Leahy, A (1984) Death by Fire in Ancient Egypt. *Journal of the Economic and Social History of the Orient* 27: 199–206.

Legrain, G (1945) *Un Famille Copte de Haute-Égypte*. Brussells: Édition de la Fondation Égyptologique Reine Élisabeth.

Lehner, M (1997) *The Complete Pyramids*. London: Thames and Hudson.

Levey, M (1966) *Medieval Arabic Toxicology. The Book on Poisons of Ibn Waḥshīya and its Relation to Early Indian and Greek Texts*. Philadelphia: American Philosophical Society.

Levtzion, N (1979) The Twelfth-Century Anonymous Kitab Al-Istibṣar: A History of a Text. *Journal of Semitic Studies* 24: 201–17.

Lewicki, T (1978) Al-Ḳazwini. *Encyclopaedia of Islam*, 2nd edn 4: 865–67.

Lewis, G (1974) *The Book of Dede Korkut*. New York: Penguin.

Lexa, F (1925) *La magie dans l'Egypte antique*. 3 vols, Paris: Librairie Orientaliste Paul Geuthner.

Lichtheim, M (1980) *Ancient Egyptian Literature. Vol III The Late Period*. Berkeley: University of California Press.

von Lieven, A (1999) Divination in Ägypten. *Altorientalische Forschungen* 26: 77–126.

Lloyd, Lord (1933) *Egypt since Cromer*. London: Macmillan.

Loret, V (1894) Études de droguerie égyptienne. *Recueil de travaux rélatifs à la philologie et à l'archéologie Égyptiennes et Assyriennes* 16: 134–62.

Loret, V (1900) Les livres III et IV (animaux et végétaux) de la scala magna de Schams-ar-riasah. *Annales du Service des Antiquités de l'Égypte* 1: 48–63, 215–29.

Loret, V (1903) Horus-le-faucon. *Bulletin de l'Institut Français d'Archéologie Orientale du Caire* 3: 1–24.

Loukianoff, G (1936) Une statue parlante ou oracle du dieu Re-Harmakhis. *Annales du Service des Antiquités de l'Égypte* 36: 188–93 and plate 1.

Louth, A (1996) A Christian Theologian at the Court of the Caliph: Some Cross-cultural Reflections. *Dialogos: Hellenic Studies Review* 3: 4–19.

Luck, G (1985) *Arcana Mundi: Magic and the Occult in the Greek and Roman World*. Baltimore and London: Johns Hopkins University Press.

Lunde, P and C Stone (1989) *The Meadows of Gold: The Abbasids*. London and New York: Kegan Paul International.

Lutfi, H (1998) Coptic Festivals of the Nile: Aberrations of the Past. In T Philipp and U Haarmann (eds) *The Mamluks in Egyptian Politics and Society*. Cambridge: CUP, 254–82.

Lyall, C (1903) The Words 'Ḥanif' and 'Muslim'. *Journal of the Royal Asiatic Society of Great Britain and Ireland* 771–84.

Lyons, M (1995) *The Arabian Epic: Heroic and Oral Story-telling*. 3 vols, Cambridge: CUP.

MacCoull, L (1991) Duke University MS C25: Dreams, Visions, and Incubation in Coptic Egypt. *Orientalia Lovaniensia Periodica* 22: 123–32.

MacCoull, L (1993) Coptic Alchemy and Craft Technology in Islamic Egypt: The Papyrological Evidence. In *Coptic Perspectives on Late Alchemy*. Hampshire, Variorum (Ch XV), 101–04.

McCleary, R (1992) Ancestor Cults at Terenouthis in Lower Egypt: A Case for Greco-Egyptian Oecumenism. In J Johnson (ed) *Life in a Multi-Cultural Society: Egypt from Cambyses to Constantine and Beyond*. Chicago: Oriental Institute of the University of Chicago, 221–31.

McCullough, W (1967) *Jewish and Mandaean Incantation Bowls in the Royal Ontario Museum*. Toronto: University of Toronto Press.

McDowell, A (1990) *Jurisdiction in the Workmen's Community in Deir El-Medina*. Leiden: Nederlands Instituut voor het Nabije Oosten (Egyptologische uitgaven 5).

McGing, B (2002) Illegal Salt in the Lycopolite Nome. *Archiv für Papyrusforschung* 48: 42–66 and pl IV.

Mackay, E, L Harding and F Petrie (1929) *Bahrein and Hemamieh*. London: British School of Archaeology in Egypt.

Mahdi, M (1994) Religious Belief and Scientific Belief. *American Journal of Islamic Social Sciences* 11: 2: 245–59.

de Maigret, A (1996) *Arabia Felix*. London: Stacey International.

Majino, G (1975) *The Healing Hand: Man and Wound in the Ancient World*. Cambridge, MA: Harvard University Press. Paper print 1991.

Makdisi, G (1981) *The Rise of Colleges: Institutions of Learning in Islam and the West*. Edinburgh: Edinburgh University Press.

Al-Ma^{c}luf, ^{c}I (1923) A Lecture in the Commemoration Ceremony for Ahmad Kamal Pasha held by Members of the Arab Academy of Damascus. *Revue de l'académie arabe (Majalat Al-Majma^{c} Al-^{c}Ilmi Al-^{c}Arabi)* 3: 294–307.

Malek, J (1993) *The Cat in Ancient Egypt*. London: British Museum Press.

Malek, J (2000) Old-Kingdom Rulers as 'Local Saints' in the Memphite Area during the Middle Kingdom. In In M Bárta and J Krejčí (eds) *Abusir and Saqqara in the year 2000*. Praha: Archiv orientální, Academy of Science of the Czech Republic, Oriental Institute, 241–58.

Al-Manawi, M (1966) *Nahr El-Nil fi Al-Maktabah Al-^{c}Arabiyah*. Cairo: Al-Dar Al-Qawmiyah.

Manetho. Translated by W Waddell. Cambridge, MA: Harvard University Press, Loeb Classical Library 1936.

Manniche, L (1987) *Sexual Life in Ancient Egypt*. London and New York: Kegan Paul International.

Margoliouth, G (1896) The Liturgy of the Nile. *Journal of the Royal Asiatic Society of Great Britain and Ireland* 677--731.

Marlowe, J (1970) *Cromer in Egypt*. London: Elek.

Martin, G (1981) *The Sacred Animal Necropolis at North Saqqara*. London: Egypt Exploration Society.

Martin, G (1994) A Relief of Nectanebo I and Other Reused Blocks in Apa Jeremias Monastery, Saqqara. In C Eyre, A Leahy and L Leahy (eds) *The Unbroken Reed. Studies in the Culture and Heritage of Ancient Egypt in Honour of AF Shore*. London: Egypt Exploration Society, 205–15.

Martinez, F (1990) The King of Rūm and the King of Ethiopia in Medieval Apocalyptic Texts from Egypt. In W Godlewski (ed) *Coptic Studies. Acts of the Third International Congress of Coptic Studies, Warsaw, 20–25 August 1984*. Varsovie: PWN-Éditions Scientifiques de Pologne, 247–59.

Marzuq, M (1974) *Al-Funun Al-Zukhrifiyah Al-Islamiyah fi Miṣr qabl Al-Faṭimien*. Cairo: Anglo-Egyptian Bookshop.

Maspero, G (1899) Review of Carra de Vaux 'L'Abrégé des Merveilles'. *Journal des Savants*, 69–86, 154–72, 277–78.

Maspero, G (1902) Review of K Sethe 'Imhotep oder Asklepios der Ägypter'. *Journal des Savants*, 573–85.

Maghawri, S (1996) *Al-Pardiyat Al-ᶜArabiya fi Miṣr Al-Islamia*. Cairo: Al-Hai'a Al-ᶜAma li-Qusur Al-Thaqafa.

Massé, H (1971) Ibn Al-Faḳih. *Encyclopaedia of Islam*, 2nd edn 3: 761–62.

Massignon, L (1981) Inventaire de la littérature hermétique arabe. An appendix to AJ Festugière, *La Révélation d'Hermès Trismégiste*. 2nd edn. Paris: Les Belles Letres. Vol 1: 385–400.

Matthews, R (2003) *The Archaeology of Mesopotamia: Theories and Approaches*. London: Routledge.

Mayer, L (1933) *Saracenic Heraldry*. Oxford: OUP. Reprinted Sandpiper Books 1999.

Mazzaoui, M (1991) Alexander the Great and the Arab Historians. *Graeco-Arabica* 4: 33–43.

Meeks, D (2002) Coptos et les chemins de Pount. *Topoi*, Suppl 3: 267–335.

Meeks, D (2003) Locating Punt. In D O'Connor and S Quirke (eds) *Mysterious Lands*. London: UCL Press, 53–80.

Meinardus, O (1965) *Christian Egypt: Ancient and Modern*. Cairo: Institut Français d'Archéologie Orientale du Caire.

Meinecke-Berg, V (1985) Spolien in der mittelalterlichen Architektur von Kairo. In *Ägypten, Dauer und Wandel: Symposium anlässlich des 75 jährigen Bestehens des Deutschen Archäologischen Instituts Kairo, am 10 und 11 Oktober 1982*. Deutsches Archäologisches Institut, Abteilung Kairo. Mainz am Rhein: Philipp von Zabern, 131–42.

Memon, M (1976) *Ibn Taimīya's Struggle against Popular Religion*. The Hague and Paris: Mouton.

Ménant, J (1887) La Stéle de Chalouf. *Recueil de travaux rélatifs à la philologie et à l'archéologie Égyptiennes et Assyriennes* 9: 131–57.

Mertens, M (1995) *Zosime de Panopolis*. In the series 'Les Alchimistes Grecs', Vol 4 Part 1. Paris: Les Belles Lettres.

Mertens, M (2002) Alchemy, Hermetism and Gnosticism at Panopolis c 300 AD: The Evidence of Zosimus. In A Egberts *et al* (eds) *Perspectives on Panopolis*. Leiden: Brill, 165–75.

De Meulenaere, H and P MacKay (1976) *Mendes*. Vol 2. Warminster: Aris & Phillips.

Meyer, M and R Smith (1994) *Ancient Christian Magic*. San Francisco: Harper.

Meyerhof, M (1930) Von Alexandrien nach Baghdad. In *Sitzungsberichte der Preüßischen Akademie der Wissenschaften* 23: 389–429.

Miquel, A (1978) Al-Istakhari. *Encyclopaedia of Islam*, 2nd edn 4: 222–23.

Mokhtar, G (1965) Ahmed Kamal. *Egyptian Historical Review* 12: 43–57.

Monnot, G (1997) Al-Shahrastani. *Encyclopaedia of Islam*, 2nd edn 9: 214–16.

Morenz, L (1996) *Beiträge zur Schriftlichkeitskultur im Mittleren Reich und in der 2. Zwischenzeit*. Wiesbaden: Harrassowitz.

Morkot, R (2000) *The Black Pharaohs: Egypt's Nubian Rulers*. London: Rubicon Press.

Morsy, A (1986) *Studies on Priests and Oracles in Graeco-Roman Egypt*. Unpublished PhD thesis, University College London.

Moyer, I (2002) Herodotus and an Egyptian Mirage: The Genealogies of the Theban Priests. *Journal of Hellenic Studies* 122: 70–90.

Muhammad, M (1979) Al-ᶜIlaqat Al-Miṣriyah Al-ᶜArabiyah fi Al-ᶜUṣur Al-Qadeemah: Maṣadir wa Drasat. In A Abdalla, S Al-Sakkar and R Mortel (eds) *Studies in the History of Arabia: Proceedings of the First International Symposium on Studies in the History of Arabia, 23–28 April 1977*. Riyadh: University of Riyadh. Vol 1: 13–38 of the Arabic section.

Müller, W and G Vittmann (1993) Zu den Personennamen der aus Ägypten stammenden Frauen in den sogenannten 'Hierodulenlisten' von Maᶜin. *Orientalia* 62: 1–10.

Muntaṣer, ᶜA (1973) *Tarikh Al-ᶜIlm wa Dor Al-ᶜUlma' Al-ᶜArab fi Taqadumihi*. 3rd edn. Cairo: Dar Al-Maᶜarif.

Murad, M (1996) Al-Arḍ wa Al-Sulṭah fi ᶜUhud Al-Khilafah Al-ᶜArabiyah Al-Islamiyah. *Al-Ijtihad* (Beirut) 8/33: 19–70.

Murnane, W (1995) The History of Ancient Egypt: An Overview. In J Sasson *et al* (eds) *Civilizations of the Ancient Near East* I & II. Massachusetts: Hendrickson, 691–717.

Murnane, W (2000) Imperial Egypt and the Limits of Power. In R Cohen and R Westbrook (eds) *Amarna Diplomacy*. Baltimore and London: Johns Hopkins University Press, 101–11.

Murnane, W and C Van Siclen III (1993) *The Boundary Stelae of Akhenaten*. London: Kegan Paul International.

Murphy, E (1990) *The Antiquities of Egypt*. New Brunswick and London: Transaction.

Mussies, G (1982) The Interpretatio Judaica of Thoth-Hermes. In M Heerma van Voss, D Hoens, G Mussies, D van der Plas and H te Velde (eds) *Studies in Egyptian Religion dedicated to Professor Jan Zandee*. Leiden: Brill, 90–120.

Muṣṭafa, H (2002) *Al-Islam wa Al-Gharb: min Al-Taᶜaeush ila Al-Taṣadum*. Cairo: Al-Hay'ah Al-Miṣriyah Al-ᶜAmah li-Al-Kitab.

Myśliwiec, K (2000) *The Twilight of Ancient Egypt. First Millennium BCE*. Ithaca and London: Cornell University Press.

Nagel, T (1986) Ḳiṣaṣ Al-Anbiya'. *Encyclopaedia of Islam*, 2nd edn 5: 180–81.

Najib, A (1893–94) Kunuz Dahshour. *Al-Muqtaṭaf* 18: 466–69.

Najib, A (1895) *Al-Athar Al-Jalil li-Qudma' Wadi Al-Nil*. Cairo: Al-Matbaᶜah Al-Amiryah. Reprinted Cairo: Madbouli 1991.

Nasr, S (1968) *Science and Civilization in Islam*. Cambridge, MA: Harvard University Press.

Nasr, S (1978) *An Introduction to Islamic Cosmological Doctrines*. 2nd rev edn. London: Thames and Hudson. First published 1964.

Nasr, S (1987) *Islamic Art and Spirituality*. New York: State University of New York Press.

Naville, É (1917) Some Geographical Names. *Journal of Egyptian Archaeology* 4: 228–33.

Naẓeer, W (1967) *Al-ᶜAdat Al-Miṣriyah bayn Al-Ams wa Al-Yawm*. Cairo: Dar Al-Katib Al-ᶜArabi.

Needham, J, Ho Ping-Yü, Lu Gwei-Djen and N Sivin (1980) *Science and Civilisation in China*. Vol 5 part 4. Cambridge: CUP.

Nemoy, L (1939) The Treatise on the Egyptian Pyramids (*Tuḥfat al-kiram fi khabar al-ahram*) by Jalal al-Din Al-Suyuṭi. Edited with introduction, translation and notes. *Isis* 30: 17–37.

Netton, I (1991) *Muslim Neoplatonists*. Edinburgh: Edinburgh University Press.

Neugebauer, O (1962) 'Years' in Royal Canons. In *A Locust's Leg: Studies in Honour of SH Taqizadeh*. London: Percy Lund & Humpheries, 209–12.

Nibbi, A (1979) Some Remarks on Ass and Horse in Ancient Egypt and the Absence of the Mule. *Zeitschrift für Ägyptische Sprache und Altertumskunde* 106: 148–68.

Nock, A (1944) Later Egyptian Piety. In *Coptic Egypt*. New York: Brooklyn Museum, 21–29.

Nothdurft, W and J Smith (2002) *The Lost Dinosaurs of Egypt*. New York: Random House.

Nunn, J (1996) *Ancient Egyptian Medicine*. London: British Museum Press.

Nurbakhsh, J (1999) *Dhun-Nun Mesri*. London: Khaniqahi-Nimatullahi.

Nureldin, MA (1998) *Al-Lughah Al-Miṣriyah Al-Qadeemah*. Cairo: Dar Al-Taᶜawin.

O'Connor, D and S Quirke (eds) (2003) *Mysterious Lands*. London: UCL Press.

O'Leary, de L (1937) *The Saints of Egypt*. London. Reprint Amsterdam: Philo Press 1974.

O'Leary, de L (1957) *How the Greek Science Passed to the Arabs*. London: Routledge and Kegan Paul. Third impression. First published 1949.

Osing, J (1998) *Hieratische Papyri aus Tebtunis I*. Copenhagen: Museum Tusculanum Press (CNI publication 17).

Otto, E (1975) Ägypten im Selbstbewußtsein des Ägypters. In W Helck and E Otto (eds) *Lexikon der Ägyptologie*. 7 vols, Wiesbaden 1975–87, 1: 76–78.

Paré, A (1951) *The Apologie and Treatise of Ambroie Paré*. Ed with introduction by Geoffrey Keynes. London: Falcon Educational Books.

Parkinson, R (1997) *The Tale of Sinuhe and Other Ancient Egyptian Poems*. Oxford: OUP.

Parkinson, R (1999) *Cracking Codes: The Rosetta Stone*. London: British Museum Press.

Al-Pasha, H (1989) *Al-Alqab Al-Islamiyah fi Al-Tarikh wa Al-Watha'q wa Al-Athar*. Cairo: Al-Dar Al-Fanniyah.

Patai, R (1964) Indulco and Mumia. *Journal of American Folklore* 77 (January–March) 3–11.

Patai, R (1994) *The Jewish Alchemists*. Princeton: Princeton University Press.

Peden, A (2001) *The Graffiti of Pharaonic Egypt: Scope and Roles of Informal Writings (c 3100–332 BC)*. Leiden: Brill.

Pellat, C (1991) Al-Masᶜudi. *Encyclopaedia of Islam*, 2nd edn 6: 784–89.

Penelas, M (2001) *Kitāb Hurūšiyūš. Traducción Árabe de las Historiae Adversus Paganos de Orosio*. Madrid: Consejo Superior de Investigaciones Científicas.

Perry, B (1966) The Egyptian Legend of Nectanebus. *Transactions and Proceedings of the American Philological Association* 97: 327–33.

Pestman, P *et al* (1981) *A Guide to the Zenon Archive*. Leiden: Brill.

Petrie, WMF (1906) *Hyksos and Israelite Cities*. London: British School of Archaeology in Egypt.

Petrie, WMF (1907) *Gizeh and Rifeh*. London: University College and Bernard Quaritch.

Petrie, WMF (1909a) *Memphis*. Vol 1. London: University College and Bernard Quaritch.

Petrie, WMF (1909b) *Memphis*. Vol 2. London: University College and Bernard Quaritch.

Petrie, WMF (1911) *Egypt and Israel*. London: Society for the Promotion of Christian Knowledge.

Petrie, WMF (1914) *Amulets*. London: Constable & Company Ltd.

Petrie, WMF (1926) *Glass Stamps and Weights*. London: British School of Archaeology in Egypt.

Petrie, WMF (1934) *Palestine and Israel*. London: Society for the Promotion of Christian Knowledge.

Petrie, H (nd) *Side Notes on the Bible from Flinders Petrie's Discoveries*. London: Search Publishing Company.

Petry, C (1991) Copts in Late Medieval Egypt. *Coptic Encyclopaedia* 2: 618–35.

Pettigrew, T (1834) *A History of Egyptian Mummies*. London. Reprint Los Angeles 1983.

Pezin, M (1978) Les Etiquettes de Momies du Musée de Picardie à Amiens. *Enchoria* 8/2: 9–12 and plates 3–4.

Piankoff, A and N Rambova (1957) *Mythological Papyri*. 2 vols, New York: Pantheon Books.

Piccione, P (1990) Mehen, Mysteries, and Resurrection from the Coiled Serpent. *Journal of the American Research Center in Egypt* 27: 43–52.

Pielow, D (1995) *Die Quellen der Weisheit: die arabische Magie im Spiegel des Uṣul al-Ḥikma von Ahmad Ibn ᶜAli al-Buni*. Hildesheim, Zurich and New York: Georg Olms.

Pinch, G (1993) *Votive Offerings to Hathor*. Oxford: Griffith Institute.

Pines, S (1971) *An Arabic Version of the Testimonium Flavianum and its Implications*. Jerusalem: Israel Academy of Sciences and Humanties.

Pingree, D (1968) *The Thousands of Abu Maᶜshar*. London: Warburg Institute, University of London.

Plessner, M (1954) Hermes Trismegistus and Arab Science. *Studia Islamica* 2: 45–59.

Plessner, M (1960) Aghathudhimun. *Encyclopaedia of Islam*, 2nd edn 1: 247.

Plotinus, *The Enneads*. Translated by S MacKenna and abridged with introduction and notes by J Dillon. Penguin Classics 1991.

Plutarch, *Moralia*. Vol 5 translated F Babbitt. Cambridge, MA: Harvard University Press, Loeb Classical Library 1936.

Pope, M (1999) *The Story of Decipherment*. First published 1975. London: Thames and Hudson.

Porter, B and R Moss (1974) *Topographical Bibliography of Ancient Egyptian Hieroglyphic Texts, Reliefs, and Paintings*. Vol 3 part 1. 2nd rev edn. Oxford: Clarendon.

Posener, G (1936) *La première domination perse en Égypte. Recueil d'inscriptions hiéroglyphiques*. Cairo: Institut Français d'Archéologie Orientale.

Posener, G (1957) Les Asiatiques en Egypte sous les XIIe et XIIIe Dynasties. *Syria* 34: 145–63.

Al-Qaddumi, G (1996) *Book of Gifts and Rarities. Kitab al-Hadaya wa Al-Tuḥaf*. Harvard: Harvard University Press.

Al-Qaradawi, Y (1999) *The Lawful and the Prohibited in Islam*. Translated from Arabic by K El-Helbawy *et al*. Indiana: American Trust Publications. Reprint from 1994 edn.

Qiladah, WS (1993) *Al-Masihiyah wa Al-Islam fi Miṣr*. Cairo: Sina Press.

Quack, J (1993) Ägyptisches und Südarabisches Alphabet. *Revue d'Égyptologie* 44: 141–51. With a correction note (1994) 45: 197.

Quirke, S (1998) (ed) *Lahun Studies*. Surrey: Sia Publishing.

Quirke, S (2001) *The Cult of Ra: Sun-worship in Ancient Egypt*. London: Thames and Hudson.

Rabi^{c}, A (2001) *Al-Israeliyat fi Tafsir Al-Ṭabari: Drasah fi Al-Lughah wa Al-Maṣadir Al-^{c}Ibriyah*. Cairo: Al-Majlis Al-A^{c}la li Al-Sh'un Al-Islamiyah.

Rabie, H (1972) *The Financial System of Egypt*. Oxford: OUP.

Rabinowitz, I (1956) Aramaic Inscriptions of the Fifth Century BCE from a North-Arab Shrine in Egypt. *Journal of Near Eastern Studies* 15: 1–9.

Radtke, B (1992) *Weltgeschichte und Weltbeschreibung im mittelalterlichen Islam*. Beirut and Stuttgart: Franz Steiner (Beiruter texte und Studien 51).

Ranke, H (1935) *Die ägyptischen Personennamen*. Glückstadt. Vol 1.

Rashid, R (2002) Al-^{c}Ulum Al-^{c}Arabiyah bayn Naẓaraiyat Al-Ma^{c}rifah wa Al-Tarikh. In *Essays in Honour of Salah al-Din al-Munajjid* (no editor). London: Al-Furqan Islamic Heritage Foundation Publication, 297–315.

Ray, J (1986) Psammuthis and Hakoris. *Journal of Egyptian Archaeology* 72: 149–58.

Ray, J (1992) Are Egyptian and Hittite Related? In A Lloyd (ed) *Studies in Pharaonic Religion and Society in Honour of J Gwyn Griffiths*. London: Egypt Exploration Society, 124–36.

Ray, J (1994) Osiris in Medieval Egypt. In C Eyre, A Leahy and L Montagno Leahy (eds), *The Unbroken Reed. Studies in the Cultural and Heritage of Ancient Egypt in Honour of AF Shore*. London: Egypt Exploration Society, 273–80.

Razmjou, S (2002) Assessing the Damage: Notes on the Life and Demise of the Statue of Darius from Susa. *Ars Orientalis* 32: 81–104.

Redford, D (1986) *Pharaonic King-Lists, Annals and Day-Books*. Mississauga: Benben Publications.

Redford, D (2003) The Writing of History of Ancient Egypt. In Z Hawass and L Brock (eds) *Egyptology at the Dawn of the Twenty-first Century. Proceedings of the Eighth International Congress of Egyptologists, Cairo, 2000*. Cairo: American University in Cairo Press, 2: 1–11.

Reeves, N and R Wilkinson (1996) *The Complete Valley of the Kings*. London: Thames and Hudson.

Reichman, E (1997) The Impact of Medieval Medicine on Medical *Halachah*: *Mummia*. In F Rosner (ed) *Pioneers in Jewish Medical Ethics*. New Jersey: Jason Aronson, 27–52.

Reid, D (1985) Indigenous Egyptology: The Decolonization of a Profession? *Journal of the American Oriental Society* 105: 233–46.

Reid, D (1990) *Cairo University and the Making of Modern Egypt*. Cambridge: CUP.

Reid, D (2002) *Whose Pharaohs? Archaeology, Museums, and Egyptian National Identity from Napoleon to World War I*. Berkeley and London: University of California Press.

Reitemeyer, E (1903) *Beschreibung Ägyptens im Mittelalter aus den geographischen Werken der Araber*. Leipzig: Seele.

Reynolds, D (1995) *Heroic Poets, Poetic Heroes. The Ethnography of Performance in an Arabic Oral Epic Tradition*. Ithaca and London: Cornell University Press.

Rhodokanakis, N (1924) Die Sarkophaginschrift von Gizeh. *Zeitschrift für Semitistik und verwandte Gebiete* 2: 113–33.

Ritner, R (1992) Egyptian Magic: Questions of Legitimacy, Religious Orthodoxy and Social Deviance. In A Lloyd (ed) *Studies in Pharaonic Religion and Society in Honour of J Gwyn Griffiths*. London: Egypt Exploration Society, 189–200.

Ritner, R (1993) *The Mechanics of Ancient Egyptian Magical Practice*. Chicago: Oriental Institute of the University of Chicago. 2nd edn with minor corrections (used here) 1995 (SAOC 54).

Rizkana, I (1964) Al-Athar Al-Miṣriyah ᶜind Muwafaq Al-Din ᶜAbd Al-Laṭif Al-Baghdadi. In D Ṣadiq (ed) *Muwafaq Al-Din ᶜAbd Al-Laṭif Al-Baghdadi fi Al-Dhikra Al-Mu'awiyah Al-Thaminah li-Miladih*. Cairo: Al-Dar Al-Qawmiyah, 63–72.

Rizkana, I (1971) Al-Qabail Al-ᶜArabiyah fi Miṣr ᶜind Al-Maqrizi. In *Drasat ᶜan Al-Maqrizi*. Cairo: Al-Hay'ah Al-Miṣriyah Al-ᶜAmah li-Al-Ta'lif wa Al-Nashr, 81–93.

Roaf, M (1974) The Subject Peoples on the Base of the Statue of Darius. *Cahiers de la Délégation Archéologique Française en Iran* 4: 73–160.

Roberts, A (2000) *My Heart My Mother: Death and Rebirth in Ancient Egypt*. East Sussex: Northgate.

Robin, C (1994) L'Égypte dans les inscriptions de l'arabie méridionale préislamique. *Hommages à Jean Leclant*, Vol 4. Cairo: Institut Français d'Archéologie Orientale du Caire, Bibliothèque d'Étude, 106/4: 285–301.

Robinson, J (ed) (1996) *The Nag Hammadi Library in English*. 4th edn. Leiden: Brill.

Roccati, A (1992) Writing Egyptian: Scripts and Speeches at the End of Pharaonic Civilization. In J Johnson (ed) *Life in a Multi-Cultural Society: Egypt from Cambyses to Constantine and Beyond*. Chicago: Oriental Institute of the University of Chicago, 291–94.

Roemer, H (1985) Der Islam und das Erbe der Pharaonen. In *Ägypten, Dauer und Wandel: Symposium anlässlich des 75 jährigen Bestehens des Deutschen Archäologischen Instituts Kairo, am 10 und 11 Oktober 1982*. Deutsches Archäologisches Institut, Abteilung Kairo. Mainz am Rhein: Philipp von Zabern, 123–30.

van Rompay, L and A Schmidt (2001) Takritans in the Egyptian Desert: The Monastery of the Syrians in the Ninth Century. *Journal of the Canadian Society for Syriac Studies* 1: 41–56.

Ronca , I (1995) 'Senior de Chemia': A Reassessment of the Medieval Latin Translation of Ibn Umayl's Al-ma al-waraqi wa l-ard al-najimiyya. *Bulletin de Philosophie Médiévale* 37: 9–31.

Rosenthal, F (1958) *Ibn Khaldun: The Muqaddimah: An Introduction to History*. 3 vols, London: Routledge and Kegan Paul. 2nd edn Princeton: Princeton University Press 1967.

Rosenthal, F (1962) The Prophecies of Bâbâ the Ḥarrânian. In *A Locust's Leg: Studies in Honour of SH Taqizadeh*. London: Percy Lund & Humpheries, 220–32.

Rosenthal, F (1966) Muslim Definition of Knowledge. In C Leiden (ed) *The Conflict of Traditionalism and Modernism in the Muslim Middle East*. Austin: University of Texas Press, 117–33.

Rosenthal, F (1971) Ibn ᶜAbd Al-Ḥakam. *Encyclopaedia of Islam*, 2nd edn 3: 674–75.

Rosenthal, F (1975) *The Classical Heritage in Islam*. Reprint London: Routledge 1992.

Rosenthal, F (1991) Al-Maḳrizi. *Encyclopaedia of Islam*, 2nd edn 6: 193–94.

Rosner, F (1994) *Biblical and Talmudic Medicine*. 2nd edn. New Jersey: Jason Aronson.

Rosner, F (1995) *Moses Maimonides' Glossary of Drug Names*. Haifa: Maimonides Research Institute.

Rowlandson, J (1998) (ed) *Women & Society in Greek & Roman Egypt*. Cambridge: CUP.

Rufailah, Y (1898) *Tarikh Al-Umah Al-Qibiṭiyah*. Cairo. 2nd edn 2000.

Ruska, J (1935) Studien zu Muhammad Ibn Umail al-Tamimi's Kitab al-Ma'a al-Waraqi wa 'l-Ard an-Najmiyah. *Isis* 24: 310–42.

Ryding, K (1997) The Heritage of Arabic Alchemy: The Multiculture Matrix. In A Hasnawi, A Elamrani-Jamal and M Aouad (eds) *Perspectives arabes et médiévales sur la tradition scientifique et philosophique grecque* (OLA 79). Leuven and Paris: Peeters and Institut du monde arabe, 235–48.

Ryholt, K (1998) A Parallel to the Inaros Story of P Krall (P Carlsberg 456 and P CtYBR 4513): Demotic Narratives from the Trbtuns Temple Library (I). *Journal of Egyptian Archaeology* 84: 151–69.

El-Saaddy, H (1999) Various Concepts Concerning Regal Authority and its Relationship to Creed in Pharaonic Egypt. *Arab Journal for the Humanities: Kuwait University* 66: 119–42 (in Arabic with an English title).

Al-Ṣabagh, cI (1998) *Al-Aḥnaf*. Damascus: Dar Al-Ḥaṣad.

Sabanu, A (1982) *Hermes Al-Ḥakeem bayn Al-Uluhiyah wa Al-Nibuah*. Damascus: Dar Qutaibah.

Sabanu, A (1983) *Kitab Al-Ifadah wa Al-Ictibar*. Damascus: Dar Qutaibah.

Sachau, E (1888) *Al-Biruni's India*. 2 vols, London: Trübner & Co.

Al-Sacdi, cA (1992) *Yaqut Al-Ḥamawi*. Beirut: Dar Al-Ṭalicah.

Sadek, A (1987) *Popular Religion in Egypt during the New Kingdom*. Hildesheim: Gerstenberg (HÄB 27).

Ṣadiq, D (1964) Jughrafiyat Miṣr fi Kutub Muwafaq Al-Din cAbd Al-Laṭif Al-Baghdadi. In D Ṣadiq (ed) *Muwafaq Al-Din cAbd Al-Laṭif Al-Baghdadi fi Al-Dhikra Al-Mu'awiyah Al-Thaminah li-Miladih*. Cairo: Al-Dar Al-Qawmiyah, 31–45.

Said, E (1995) *Orientalism* (with new introduction). Harmondsworth: Penguin. First published London: Routledge and Kegan Paul 1978.

Said, R (1950) Geology in the Tenth Century Arabic Literature. *American Journal of Science* 248: 63–66.

Said, R (1990) (ed) *The Geology of Egypt*. Rotterdam: Balkema.

Said, R (2003) *Riḥlat cUmr*. Cairo: Al-Hay'ah Al-Miṣriyah Al-cAmah li-Al-Kitab.

Saidan, A (1988) *Muqaddimah li-Tarikh Al-Fikr Al-cImi fi Al-Islam*. Kuwait: cAlim Al-Macrifah No 131.

Saied, L (1999) cIlm Al-Miṣriyat: mata yuṣbiḥ Miṣriyan? In *Aḥwal Miṣriya*. Cairo. 5: 170–76.

Saied, L (2002) *Kamal wa Yussef. Atharyan min Al-Zamn Al-Jamil*. Cairo: Supreme Council of Antiquities Press.

Salamah, G (1966) *Athar Al-Iḥtilal Al-Birṭani fi Al-Taclim Al-Qawmi fi Miṣr 1882–1922*. Cairo.

Saleh, cA (1962) *Hadarat Miṣr Al-Qadeemah wa Athariha*. Vol 1. Cairo: Anglo Bookshop. Reprinted 1992.

Saleh, cA (1966) *Al-Tarbiyah wa Al-Taclim fi Miṣr Al-Qadeemah*. Cairo: Al-Dar Al-Qawmiyah.

Saleh, cA (1970) Some Monuments of North-Western Arabia in Ancient Egyptian Style. *Bulletin of the Faculty of Arts, Cairo University* 28: 1–31.

Saleh, cA (1972) The Gnbtyw of Thutmosis III's Annals and the South Arabian Gebbanitea of the Classical Writers. *Bulletin de l'Institut Français d'Archéologie Orientale du Caire* 72: 245–62.

Saleh, cA (1978) Arabia and the Northern Arabs in Ancient Egyptian Records. *Journal of the Faculty of Archaeology, Cairo University*, 2: 3: 69–77.

Saleh, cA (1980) *Al-Sharq Al-Adna Al-Qadeem. Vol I Miṣr wa Al-cIraq*. 3rd edn. Cairo: Anglo Bookshop.

Saleh, ᶜA (1981) Notes on the Ancient Egyptian *T3 Nṯr*. 'God's Land'. *Bulletin de l'Institut Français d'Archéologie Orientale du Caire*: 81 Suppl, 107–17.

Saleh, ᶜA (1992) *Tarikh Shebh Al-Jazirah Al- ᶜArabia fi ᶜUsuriha Al-Qadeemah*. Cairo: Anglo Bookshop.

Salem, S and A Kumar (1991) *Science in the Medieval World 'Book of the Categories of Nations'*. Austin: University of Texas Press.

Sallam, H (1998) Ahmad Kamal Pasha (1851–1923): A Family of Egyptologists. In C Eyre (ed) *Proceedings of the Seventh International Congress of Egyptologists. Cambridge, 3–9 September 1995*. Leuven: Peeters, 1015–19.

Salomon, R (1991) Epigraphic Remains of Indian Traders in Egypt. *Journal of the American Oriental Society* 111: 731–36.

Salmon, G (1902) *Études sur la topographie du Caire – La kalᶜat al-kabch et la birkat al-fil*. Cairo: Institut Français d'Archéologie Orientale du Caire (MIFAO 7).

Sandison, A (1975) Balsamierung. In W Helck and E Otto (eds) *Lexikon der Ägyptologie*. 7 vols, Wiesbaden 1975–87. 1: 610–14.

Sarton, G (1954) *Galen of Pergamon*. Kansas: University of Kansas Press.

Satzinger, H (1994) An Old Coptic Text Reconsidered: PGM 94 ff. In S Giversen, M Krause and P Nagel (eds) *Coptology: Past, Present, and Future*. Leuven: Peeters, 213–24.

Sauneron, S (1950) Deux mentions d'Houroun. *Revue d'Égyptologie* 7: 121–26.

Sauneron, S (1952) Le Temple d'Akhmim décrit par Ibn Jobair. *Bulletin de l'Institut Français d'Archéologie Orientale du Caire* 51: 123–35.

Sauneron, S and J Yoyotte (1950) Traces d'établissements asiatiques en Moyenne-Égypte sous Ramsés II. *Revue d'Égyptologie* 7: 67–70.

Al-Sayyar, N (1995) Qudma' Al-Miṣreen Awal Al-Muaḥdeen. Cairo.

Sayyid, A (1988) *Waṣf Madinat Al-Qahirah wa Qalᶜat Al-Jabal*. An Arabic translation and study of Jomard, Description de la ville et de la citadelle du Caire, in *Description de l'Égypte*. Paris: Panckoucke, 26 vols and plates 1821, 1829. Vol 18: 113–535.

Sayyid, A (1992) *Al-Dawlah Al-Faṭimiyah fi Miṣr: tafisir jadid*. Cairo: Al-Dar Al-Masriah Al-Lubnaniah.

Sayyid, A (1995) *Le Manuscrit autographe d'al-Mawaᶜiẓ wa-al-Iᶜtibar fi Dhikr al-Khiṭaṭ wa-al-Athar de Taqi al-Din Aḥmad b ᶜAli n ᶜAbd al-Qadir al-Maqrizi*. London: Al-Furqan Islamic Heritage Foundation.

Sayyid, F (1985) (ed) *Tabaqat Al-Aṭibba' wa Al-Ḥukama' of Ibn Juljul*. Followed by *Tarikh Al-Aṭibba' wa Al-Falasifa of Ibn Ḥunain*. 2nd edn. Beirut: Al-Risalah.

Schenke, H-M (1999) Das Berliner 'Koptische Buch' (P 20915) und seine Geheimnisse. *Zeitschrift für Ägyptische Sprache und Altertumskunde* 126: 61–70.

Schenkel, W (1965) *Memphis, Herakleopolis, Theben. Die epigraphischen Zeugnisse der 7–11 Dynastie Ägyptens*. Wiesbaden: Harrassowitz (ÄA 12).

Schmitz, M (1978) Kaᶜb Al-Aḥbār. *Encyclopaedia of Islam*, 2nd edn 4: 316.

Schneider, T (1992) *Asiatische Personennamen in ägyptischen Quellen des Neuen Reiches*. University Press Fribourg Switzerland: Vandenhoeck & Ruprecht Göttingen (OBO 114).

Schneider, T (1993) Asiatic Personal Names from the New Kingdom. An Outline with Supplements. In *Sesto Congresso Internazionale di Egittologia*. Torino: International Association of Egyptologists. Vol 2: 453–70.

Schoff, W (2001) *The Periplus of the Erythrean Sea*. New Delhi: Munshiram Manhoharlal. First published New York 1912.

Scholz, P (1993) Die Kontinuität des Altägyptischen in der Ikonizität und Theologie des orientalischen Christentums. In *Sesto Congresso Internazionale di Egittologia*. Vol 2: 471–77.

Scott, W (1985) *Hermetica*. 4 vols. Reprinted Boston: Shambhala.

Sezgin, F (1967–) *Geschichte des arabischen Schrifttums* [GAS]. 9 vols, Leiden: Brill.

Sezgin, U (1988) *Light on the Voluminous Bodies to Reveal the Secrets of the Pyramids*. Frankfurt am Main: Institute for the History of Arabic-Islamic Science, Johann Wolfgang Goethe University.

Sezgin, U. Pharaonische Wunderwerke bei Ibn Waṣif as-Ṣabi' und al-Masᶜudi. Einige Reminiszenzen an Ägyptens vergangene Grösse und an Meisterwerke der alexandrinischen Gelehrten in arabischen Texten des 10. Jahrhunderts. Chr. Four parts in *Zeitschrift für Geschichte der Arabisch-Islamischen Wissenschaften*: (1994) Part I, 9: 229–91; (1997) Part II, 11: 189–249; (2001) Part III, 14: 217–56; (2002/3) Part IV, 15: 281–312.

Sezgin, U (2002) Al-Waṣifi. *Encyclopaedia of Islam*, 2nd edn 11: 163–64.

Serpico, M and R White (2000) Resins, Amber and Bitumen. In P Nicholson and I Shaw (eds) *Ancient Egyptian Materials and Technology*. Cambridge: CUP, 430–44.

Al-Shaᶜrawi, M (1995) *Magic and Envy in the Light of Qur'an and Sunna*. London: Dar Al Taqwa.

Al-Shami, ᶜA (1981) *Mudun Miṣr wa Quraha ᶜind Yaqut Al-Ḥamawi*. Kuwait: University of Kuwait.

Shawqi, G (1990) *Al-ᶜUlum Al-ᶜAqliyah fi Al-Manẓumat Al-ᶜArabiyah*. Kuwait: Mu'sasat Al-Kuwait li-Al-Taqadum Al-ᶜIlmi.

El-Shayyal, G (1962) *A History of Egyptian Historiography in the Nineteenth Century*. Alexandria, Faculty of Arts, Publication no 15. This is the full text (used here), part of which was published as 'Historiography in Egypt in the Nineteenth Century' in B Lewis and P Holt (eds) *Historians of the Middle East*. Oxford: OUP 1962, 403–21.

Shboul, A (1979) *Al-Masᶜudi and His World*. London: Ithaca.

Shisha-Halevy, A (1978) An Early North-West Semitic Text in the Egyptian Hieratic Script. *Orientalia* 47: 145–62.

Al-Shishtawi, M (1999) *Mutanazhat Al-Qahirah fi Al-ᶜAṣrayn Al-Mamluki wa Al-ᶜUthmani*. Cairo: Dar Al-Afaq Al-ᶜArabiyah.

Shore, A (1971) Christian and Coptic Egypt. In JR Harris (ed), *The Legacy of Egypt*. Oxford: OUP, 390–433.

Al-Shurbagi, A (1994) *Ru'yat Al-Raḥalah Al-Moslemin li-Aḥwal Miṣr Al-Iqtiṣadyah fi Al-ᶜAṣr Al-Faṭimi*. Cairo: Al-Hay'ah Al-Miṣriyah Al-ᶜAmah li-Al-Kitab, Series Tarikh Al-Miṣreen 73.

Sidarus, A (2002) La tradition sahidique de philologie gréco-copto-arabe (manuscrits des XIIIᵉ–XVᵉ siècles). *Études Coptes* 7: 265–304.

Siggel, A von (1937) Das Sendschreiben. Das Licht über das Verfahren des Hermes der Hermesse dem, der es begehrt. *Der Islam* 24: 287–306.

Simons, E and D Tab Rasmussen (1990) Vertebrate Paleontology of Fayum: History of Reseach, Faunal Review and Future Prospects. In R Said (ed) *The Geology of Egypt*. Rotterdam: Balkema, 627–38.

Skeat, T and E Turner (1968) An Oracle of Hermes Trismegistos at Saqqara. *Journal of Egyptian Archaeology* 54: 199–208.

Slane, Baron de (1883–95) *Bibliothèque Nationale: Catalogue des Manuscrits Arabes*. Paris: Imprimerie Nationale.

Smelik, K and E Hemelrijk (1984) 'Who knows not what monsters demented Egypt worships?' Opinions on Egyptian Animal Worship in Antiquity as part of the Ancient Conception of Egypt. *Aufstieg und Niedergang der römischen Welt. Geschichte und Kultur Roms im Spiegel der neueren Forschung* [ANRW] II. 17. 4: 1852–2000 and indices 2337–57.

Smith, H (1974) *A Visit to Ancient Egypt. Life at Memphis & Saqqara (c 500–30 BC)*. Warminster: Aris & Phillips.

Smith, H (1992) Foreigners in the Documents from the Sacred Animal Necropolis, Saqqara. In J Johnson (ed) *Life in a Multi-Cultural Society: Egypt from Cambyses to Constantine and Beyond*. Chicago: Oriental Institute of the University of Chicago, 295–301.

Smith, M (1965) D̲h̲u 'l-Nun. *Encyclopaedia of Islam*, 2nd edn 2: 242.

Smith, S and C Gadd (1925) A Cuneiform Vocabulary of Egyptian Words. *Journal of Egyptian Archaeology* 11: 230–39. With additional note by E Peet 239–40.

Sobhy, G (1950) *Common Words in the Spoken Arabic of Egypt of Greek or Coptic Origin*. Cairo: Société d'Archaéologie Copte.

El Sokkary, A (1973) *Arabs and Geology*. Alexandria: Al-Maᶜarif Establishment.

Solé, R and D Valbelle (2001) *The Rosetta Stone: The Story of the Decoding of Hieroglyphics*. London: Profile. Translated by S Rendall from the French *La pierre de Rosette*. Paris: Seuil 1999.

Soliman, AM (1985) *Scientific Trends in the Quran*. London: Taha.

Sommerfeld, W (1995) The Kassites of Ancient Mesopotamia: Origins, Politics, and Culture. In J Sasson (ed) *The Civilisations of the Near East*. Vols 1–2. Massachusetts: Hendrickson, 917–30.

Sonbol, A (2000) *The New Mamluks: Egyptian Society and Modern Feudalism*. Syracuse: Syracuse University Press.

Sorman, G (2003) *Les enfants de Rifaa: musulmans et modernes*. Paris: Fayard.

Sourdel-Thomine, J (1971) Al-Harawi. *Encyclopaedia of Islam*, 2nd edn 3: 178.

Spence, K (2000) Ancient Egyptian Chronology and the Astronomical Orientation of the Pyramids. *Nature* 408 (16 November): 320.

Spencer, J (1982) The Delta. In TGH James (ed) *Excavating in Egypt: The Egypt Exploration Society 1882–1982*. London: British Museum, 37–50.

Spencer, P (1984) *The Egyptian Temple: Lexicographical Study*. London: Kegan Paul International.

Staffa, S (1974) The Culture of Medieval Cairo as Reflected in Folk Literature. *Middle Eastern Studies* 10: 333–47.

Stanton, C (1990) *Higher Learning in Islam: The Classical Period AD 700–1300*. Maryland: Rowman & Littlefield.

Stapleton, H, M Husain and T 'Ali (1933) Three Arabic Treatises on Alchemy by Muhammad Bin Umail (10th century AD). *Memoirs of the Asiatic Society of Bengal* 12: 1–213.

Stavenhagen, L (1974) *A Testament of Alchemy*. New Hampshire: Brandies University Press.

Stern, S (1960) ᶜAbd Al-Laṭif Al-Baghdadi. *Encyclopaedia of Islam*, 2nd edn 1: 74.

Sternberg, H (1982) Mumie, Mumienhülle. In W Helck and E Otto (eds) *Lexikon der Ägyptologie*. 7 vols, Wiesbaden 1975–87. 4: 214–16.

Stetkevych, J (1996) *Muhammad and the Golden Bough: Reconstructing Arabian Myth*. Bloomington and Indianapolis: Indiana University Press.

Stevenson, J (1996) The Holy Sinner: The Life of Mary of Egypt. In E Pope and B Ross (eds) *The Legend of Mary of Egypt in Medieval Insular Hagiography*. Dublin: Four Courts Press, 19–98.

Stillman, Y (1997) Textiles and Patterns Come to Life through the Cairo Geniza. In M ᶜAbbas *et al* (eds) *Islamische Textilkunst des Mittelalters: Aktuelle Probleme*. Riggisberg: Abegg-Stiftung, 35–64.

Stolzenberg, D (1999) Unpropitious Tinctures. Alchemy, Astrology & Gnosis according to Zosimos of Panopolis. *Archives Internationales d'Histoire des Sciences* 49: 3–31.

Strabo. *The Geography of Strabo*. 8 vols translated by H Jones. Loeb Classical Library. First published 1932, rev edns 1935, 1949. Reprinted 1982.

Streck, M (1900) *Die alte landshaft Babylonien nach den Arabischen geographen*. Leiden: Brill.

Stricker, B (1939) Le naos vert de Memphis. *Annales du Service des Antiquités de l'Egypte* 39: 215–20 and plates 31–32.

Stricker, B (1942) La prison de Joseph. *Acta Orientalia* 19: 100–37.

Stricker, B (1997) Tantrism. *Discussions in Egyptology* 39: 5–62.

Strohmaier, G (1971) Ibn Umayl. *Encyclopaedia of Islam*, 2nd edn 3: 961–62.

Stronach, D (1972) Description and Comment. *Journal Asiatique* 260: 241–46.

Stroumsa, S (1999) *Freethinkers of the Medieval Islam*. Leiden: Brill.

Swiggers, P (1995) A Minaean Sarcophagus Inscription from Egypt. In K van Lerberghe and A Schoors (eds) *Immigration and Emigration within the Ancient Near East, Festschrift E Lipiński*. Leuven: Uitgeverij Peeters (OLA 65), 335–43.

Al-Ṭaba[c], E (2003) *Manhaj Taḥqiq Al-Makhṭuṭat wa ma[c]ahu Kitab Shauq Al-Mustaham fi Ma[c]rifat Rumuz Al-Aqlam*. Damascus: Dar El-Fikr.

Al-Ṭaba[c], [c]U and [c]A Al-Hashimi (1993) *Abu Al-Riḥan Al-Biruni Mauso[c]at Al-[c]Arab*. Beirut: Al-Ma[c]arif.

Tait, J (1994) Egyptian Fiction in Demotic and Greek. In J Morgan and R Stoneman (eds) *Greek Fiction: The Greek Novel in Context*. London: Routledge, 203–22.

Tait, J (1996) Demotic Literature: Forms and Genres. In A Loprieno (ed) *Ancient Egyptian Literature: History and Forms*. Leiden: Brill, 175–87.

Takács, G (1999) *Etymological Dictionary of Egyptian*. Vol 1: *A Phonological Introduction*. Leiden: Brill.

Tarn, W (1929) Ptolemy II and Arabia. *Journal of Egyptian Archaeology* 15: 9–25.

Al-Ṭayb, A (2002) Dhu Al-Nun Al-Miṣri. *Al-Hilal* (Cairo, November) 111: 62–69.

Taylor, J (2001) *Death and the Afterlife in Ancient Egypt*. London: British Museum Press.

Taylor, JG (1993) *Yahweh and the Sun. Biblical and Archaeological Evidence for Sun Worship in Ancient Israel*. Sheffield: Sheffield Academic Press.

Taylor, S (1949) *The Alchemists*. New York: Henry Schuman.

Temple, R (2000) *The Crystal Sun: Rediscovering a Lost Technology of the Ancient World*. London: Century.

Thissen, H-J (1994) Horapollinis Hieroglyphika Prolegomena. In M Minas and J Zeidler (eds) *Aspekte spätägyptischer Kultur, Festschrift für Erich Winter*. Mainz am Rhein: Philipp von Zabern, 255–63.

Thompson, D (1988) *Memphis under the Ptolemies*. Princeton: Princeton University Press.

Thorndike, L (1958) *A History of Magic and Experimental Science*. New York: Columbia University Press, Vol VIII.

Tibawi, A (1979) *Second Critique of English-Speaking Orientalists and their Approach to Islam and the Arabs*. London: Islamic Cultural Centre.

Torrey, C (1921) *The History of the Conquest of Egypt, North Africa and Spain*. New Haven: Yale Oriental Research Series III.

Toussoun, O (1922–23) *Mémoire sur les anciennes branches du Nil*. Cairo: Institut Français d'Archéologie Orientale du Caire.

Toussoun, O (1931) *Kitab Maliyat Miṣr min [c]Ahd Al-Fara[c]inah ila al-an*. Reprinted Cairo: Madbouli 2000.

Toussoun, O (1936) Description du phare d'Alexandrie d'après un auteur arabe du XIIe siècle. *Bulletin de la Société d'Archéologiqe d'Alexandrie* 30/1: 49–53.

Trigger, B (1989) *A History of Archaeological Thought*. Cambridge: CUP.

Troy, L (1986) *Patterns of Queenship in Ancient Egyptian Myth and History*. Uppsala: Acta Universitatis Upsaliensis (BOREAS 14).

Tuplin, Chr (1991) Darius' Suez Canal and Persian Imperialism. In H Sancisi and A Kuhrt (eds) *Achaemenid History VI: Asia Minor and Egypt: Old Cultures in a New Empire. Proceedings of the Groningen 1988 Achaemenid History Workshop*. Leiden: Nederland Institut voor het Nabije Oosten, 237–83.

Ullmann, M (1972a) Kleopatra in einer arabischen alchemistischen Disputation. *Wiener Zeitschrift für die Kunde des Morgenlandes* 63/4: 158–75.

Ullmann, M (1972b) *Die Natur und Geheimwissenschaften im Islam*. Leiden: Brill.

Ullmann, M (1997) *Islamic Medicine*. Edinburgh: Edinburgh University Press. Reprinted from 1st edn 1978.

Vachala, B and F Ondráš (2000) An Arabic Inscription on the Pyramid of Neferfra. In M Bárta and J Krejčí (eds) *Abusir and Saqqara in the Year 2000*. Prague: Academy of Science of the Czech Republic, Oriental Institute, 73–76.

Valbelle, D (1994) *L'égyptologie*. Reprint from 1st edn 1991. Paris: Presses Universitaires de France.

Vandier, J (1936) *La Famine dans l'Égypte Ancienne*. Cairo: Institut Français d'Archéologie Orientale.

Vandier, J (1937) A propos d'un depôt de provenance asiatique trouvé a Tôd. *Syria* 18: 174–82.

Vandier, J (1950) *Mo'alla: La tombe d'Ankhtifi et la la tombe de Sébekhotep*. Cairo: Institut Français d'Archéologie Orientale.

Vantini, G (1975) *Oriental Sources Concerning Nubia*. Heidelberg and Warsaw: Society for Nubian Studies.

Vasunia, P (2001) *The Gift of the Nile: Hellenising Egypt from Aeschylus to Alexander*. Berkeley: University of California Press.

Vatikiotis, P (1980) *The History of Egypt from Muhammad Ali to Sadat*. 2nd edn. London: Weidenfeld and Nicholson.

Vattier, P (1666) *L'Egypte de Murtadi, fils du Gaphiphe*. Paris: Reprinted with a study by G Wiet. Paris: L'École des langues orientales 1953.

te Velde, H (2003) The History of the Study of Ancient Egyptian Religion and its Future. In Z Hawass and L Brock (eds) *Egyptology at the Dawn of the Twenty-first Century. Proceedings of the Eighth International Congress of Egyptologists, Cairo, 2000*, Cairo: American University in Cairo Press. 2: 42–47.

Vercoutter, J (1992) Le déchiffrement des hiéroglyphes égyptiens 1680–1840. In U Luft (ed) *The Intellectual Heritage of Egypt, Studies Presented to L Kákosy*. Budapest University, *Studia Aegyptiaca* 14: 579–86.

Vereno, I (1992) *Studien zum ältesten alchemistischen Schrifttum: auf der Grundlage zweier erstmals edierter arabischer Hermetica*. Berlin: Klaus Schwarz.

Vergote, J (1964) L'Etymologie de ég *r3-pr* copte *rpe* ar *birba*. *Zeitschrift für Ägyptische Sprache und Altertumskunde* 91: 135–37.

Verner, M (2000) Who was Shepseskara, and When did he Reign? In M Bárta and J Krejčí (eds) *Abusir and Saqqara in the year 2000*. Prague: Oriental Institute, 581–602.

Vernet, J (1971) Ibn Al-Bayṭar. *Encyclopaedia of Islam*, 2nd edn 3: 739.

Viaud, P (1978) *Magie et coutumes populaires chez les Coptes d'Egypte*. Paris: Editions Présence.

Vittmann, G (1998) Beobachtungen und Überlegungen zu fremden und hellenisierten Ägypten im Dienste einheimischer Kulte. In W Clarysse *et al* (eds) *Egyptian Religion: The Last Thousand Years*. Leuven: Peeters (OLA 85) 2: 1231–50.

Vittmann, G (2003) *Ägypten und die Fremden im ersten vorchristlichen Jahrtausend*. Mainz am Rhein: Philipp von Zabern.

Vycichl, W (1990) *La vocalisation de la langue égyptienne*. Vol 1. Cairo: Institut Français d'Archéologie Orientale du Caire.

Vycichl, W (1991) Sullam. In A Atiya (ed in chief) *Coptic Encyclopedia*. New York: Macmillan. 8: 204–07.

Wagner, G (1976) Une dédicace à Isis et à Héra de la part d'un négociant d'Aden. *Bulletin de l'Institut Français d'Archéologie Orientale du Caire* 76: 277–81 plus plates L–LI.

Wagtendonk, K (1976) The Stories of David in al-Thaᶜalabi's Qiṣaṣ al-anbiya'. In *Actes du 8me Congress de l'Union Europeenne des Arabisants et Islamisants*, Aix-en-Provence, 343–53.

Wainwright, G (1931) The Search for Hidden Treasure in Egypt. *Man* 190: 196–98.

Wallin, P (2002) *Celestial Cycles: Astronomical Concepts of Regeneration in the Ancient Egyptian Coffin Texts*. Uppsala: Uppsala University (Uppsala Studies in Egyptology 1).

Walsem, R van (1997) The Struggle Against Chaos as a 'Strange Attractor' in Ancient Egyptian Culture. A Descriptive Model for the 'Chaotic' Development of Cultural Systems. In J van Dijk (ed) *Essays on Ancient Egypt in Honour of Herman te Velde*. Groningen: Styx, 317–42.

Ward, W (1994) Foreigners Living in the Village. In L Lesko (ed) *Pharaoh' s Workers*. Ithaca and London: Cornell University Press, 61–85.

Wassef, C (1971) *Pratiques rituelles et alimentaires des Coptes*. Cairo: Institut Français d'Archéologie Orientale du Caire.

Weeks, K (1996) Toward the Establishment of a Pre-Islamic Egyptian Archaeological Database. In P Der Manuelian (ed) *Studies in Honor of William Kelly Simpson*. 2 vols, Boston: Musem of Fine Arts. 2: 843–54.

Wensinck, A (1965) Fir^c^awn. *Encyclopaedia of Islam*, 2nd edn 2: 917–18 (article revised by G Vajda).

Wente, E (1990) *Letters from Ancient Egypt*. Atlanta: Scholars Press.

Westendorf, W (1977) *Koptisches Handwörterbuch*. Heidelberg: Carl Winter.

Wheeler, B (1998) Moses or Alexander? Early Islamic Exegesis of Qur'an 18: 60–65. *Journal of Near Eastern Studies* 57: 191–215.

Wiedemann, A (1906) Mumie als Heilmittel. *Zeitschrift des Vereins für rheinische und westfälische Volkskunde* 3: 29–38.

Wiet, G (1953) *L'Égypte de Murtadi, fils du Gaphiphe*. Paris: L'École des langues orientales.

Wildung, D (1969) *Die Rolle ägyptischer Könige im Bewußtsein ihrer Nachwelt. Vol 1, Posthume Quellen über die Könige der ersten vier Dynastien*. Berlin: Bruno Heßling (MÄS 36).

Wildung, D (1977a) *Egyptian Saints: Deification in Ancient Egypt*. New York: New York University Press.

Wildung, D (1977b) *Imhotep und Amenhotep*. München and Berlin: Deutscher Kunstverlag.

Wilkinson, R (1994) *Symbol & Magic in Egyptian Art*. London: Thames and Hudson.

Wilkinson, T (1999) *Early Dynastic Egypt*. London: Routledge.

Wilson, J (1954) Islamic Culture and Archaeology. *The Middle East Journal* 8: 1: 1–9.

Wilson, P (1997) *A Ptolemaic Lexikon*. Leuven: Peeters (OLA 78).

Winkler, D (1997) *Koptische Kirche und Reichskirche: Altes Schisma und neuer Dialog*. Innsbruck: Tyrolia (Innsbrucker Theologische Studien 48).

Witt, R (1997) *Isis in the Ancient World*. Baltimore: Johns Hopkins University Press (originally published London: Thames and Hudson 1971).

Witteveen, H (1997) *Universal Sufism*. Dorset: Element.

Wood, M (1998) The Use of the Pharaonic Past in Modern Egyptian Nationalism. *Journal of the American Research Center in Egypt* 35: 179–96.

Wortham, J (1971) *British Egyptology 1549–1906*. Newton Abbot: David and Charles.

Wüstenfeld, F von (1879) see under Al-Qalqashandi *Ṣubḥ*.

Wüstenfeld, F von (1979) *Macrizi's Geschichte der Copten*. Hildesheim.

Yahuda, A (1944) The Osiris Cult and the Designation of Osiris Idols in the Bible. *Journal of Near Eastern Studies* 3: 194–200.

Yakan, F (1994) *Ḥukm Al-Islam fi Al-Siḥr wa Mushtaqatih*. Beirut.

Yamani, S (2001) Roman Monumental Tombs in Ezbet Bashendi. *Bulletin de l'Institut Français d'Archéologie Orientale du Caire* 101: 393–414.

Yaqṭin, S (1994) *Dhakhirat Al-^c^Ajaib Al-^c^Arabiyah: Saif Ibn Dhi Yazan*. Beirut: Al-Markaz Al-Thaqafi Al-^c^Arabi.

Yasin, N (1950) Al-Itjar bi Ghanaim Al-Ḥarab fi ^c^Aṣr Al-Rashidin wa Bani Omiyah. Majalat Al-Majma^c^ Al-^c^Ilmi Al-^c^Iraqi (*Journal of the Academy of Science*), Baghdad. 44: 2: 217–50.

Yates, F (2002) *Giordano Bruno and the Hermetic Tradition*. Reprinted London: Routledge. First published 1964.

Yeiven, S (1969) An Ostracon from Tel Arad Exhibiting a Combination of Two Scripts. *Journal of Egyptian Archaeology* 55: 98–102.

Yihya, L (1979) *Al-ᶜArab fi Al-ᶜUṣur Al-Qadeemah*. Beirut: Dar Al-Nahḍah Al-ᶜArabiyah.

Young, D (1981) A Monastic Invective Against Egyptian Hieroglyphs. In D Young (ed) *Studies Presented to HJ Polotsky*. Massachusetts: Pirtle and Polson, 348–60.

Yousef, F (2002) Review of ᶜA Al-Khaṭib, Al-Thaluth Al-Kawkabi Al-Muqadas. *Adumatu* 6: 75–78.

Youssef, A (1991) *Miṣr fi Al-Qur'an wa Al-Sunnah*. Cairo: Dar Al-Maᶜarif. 3rd rev edn (used here). First published Cairo 1973.

Youssef, A (2000) *From Pharaoh's Lips: Ancient Egyptian Language in the Arabic of Today*. Cairo: American University in Cairo Press.

Youssef, A (1998) *La fascination de l'Égypte: du rêve au projet*. Paris: L'Harmattan.

Yoyotte, J (1972) Une statue de Darius découverte à Suse. Les inscriptions hiéroglyphiques: Darius et l'Égypte. *Journal Asiatique* 260: 253–66.

Žába, Z (1953) *L'orientation astronomique dans l'ancient Égypte, et la précession de l'axe du monde*. Prague: Éditions de l'Académie Tchécoslovaque des Sciences.

Zaman, M (2002) Al-Yaᶜḳubi. *Encyclopaedia of Islam*, 2nd edn 11: 257–58.

Zarins, J (1989) Ancient Egypt and the Red Sea Trade: The Case for Obsidian in the Predynastic and Archaic Periods. In A Leonard Jr and B Williams (eds) *Essays in Ancient Civilization Presented to Helen J Kantor*. Chicago: Oriental Institute of the University of Chicago, 339–68.

Zauzich, K-T (1991) Einleitung. In P Frandsen (ed) *Demotic Texts from the Collection: The Carlsberg Papyri 1*. University of Copenhagen, 1–11.

Al-Zerekly, K (1999) *Al-Aᶜlam*. 14th edn. Beirut: Dar El-ᶜIlm li-Al-Malayin.

Zimmels, H (1952) *Magicians, Theologians and Doctors: Studies in Folk-medicine and Folk-lore as Reflected in the Rabbinical Responsa, 12th–19th Centuries*. London: Goldston.

Zimmermann, F (1915) Koptisches Christentum und altaegyptische Religion. *Theologische Quartalschrift* 94: 592–604.

Zivie-Coche, C (2002) Sphinx: History of a Monument. Translated from French by D Lorton. Ithaca and London: Cornell University Press.

Zotenberg, H (1883) *Chronique de Jean, évêque de Nikiou*. Paris: Imprimerie Nationale.

INDEX